SOUTH:
MODERN SOUTHERN LITERATURE
IN ITS CULTURAL SETTING

SOUTH:

MODERN SOUTHERN LITERATURE
IN ITS CULTURAL SETTING

EDITED BY

LOUIS D. RUBIN, JR., and ROBERT D. JACOBS

GREENWOOD PRESS, PUBLISHERS
WESTPORT, CONNECTICUT

Library of Congress Cataloging in Publication Data

Rubin, Louis Decimus, 1923-   ed.
    South: modern Southern literature in its cultural
setting.

    Reprint of the ed. published by Doubleday, Garden
City, N. Y., which was issued as no. C316 of Dolphin
books.
    Bibliography: p.
    1. American literature--Southern States--Addresses,
essays, lectures. I. Jacobs, Robert D., 1918-   joint
ed. II. Title.
[PS261.R65   1974]   810'.9'975   73-16744
ISBN 0-8371-7224-1

Originally published in 1961 by Doubleday & Company, Inc.,
Garden City, New York

Reprinted with the permission of Doubleday & Company, Inc.

Reprinted from an original copy in the collections of
The University of Illinois Library

Reprinted in 1974 by Greenwood Press,
a division of Williamhouse-Regency Inc.

Library of Congress Catalog Card Number 73-16744

ISBN 0-8371-7224-1

Printed in the United States of America

Special acknowledgment is made to the following, who have granted permission for the reprinting of copyrighted material from the books and periodicals listed below:

"Experience in the West," from *Collected Poems of John Peale Bishop*. Reprinted by permission of Mrs. Margaret G. H. Bronson.

"Let Me Lie," "Beyond Life," and "Straws And Prayer-Books," by James Branch Cabell. Reprinted by permission of Margaret Freeman Cabell.

"Lines Written for Allen Tate on His Sixtieth Anniversary" appeared in *The Sewanee Review* (Autumn 1959). Copyright © 1959 by The University of the South. Copyright © 1959 by Donald Davidson. Reprinted by permission of the author.

"Gradual of the Northern Summer," from the forthcoming volume, *The Ninth Part of Speech and Other Poems,* by Donald Davidson. Reprinted by permission of the author.

"Plowshares from Heaven," from *Man with a Bull-Tongue Plow,* by Jesse Stuart. First edition, copyright 1934 by E. P. Dutton & Company, Inc. New revised edition, copyright © 1959 by Jesse Stuart. Dutton Everyman Paperback. Reprinted by permission of the publisher.

The Family Reunion, by T. S. Eliot. Copyright 1939 by T. S. Eliot. Reprinted by permission of Harcourt, Brace & World, Inc., and Faber & Faber, Ltd.

The Web and the Rock and *You Can't Go Home Again,* by Thomas Wolfe. Reprinted by permission of Harper & Brothers and William Heinemann, Ltd.

"Irradiations," from *Selected Poems,* by John Gould Fletcher, published by Holt, Rinehart & Winston, Inc. Copyright 1938 by John Gould Fletcher. Reprinted by permission of the publisher.

The Ballad of the Sad Café, by Carson McCullers, originally published in *Harper's Bazaar,* copyright 1943, and also published by Houghton, Mifflin Company as part of an anthology by Carson McCullers under the title of *The Ballad of the Sad Café,* copyright 1951. Reprinted by special permission of Carson McCullers.

"Captain Carpenter," "Persistent Explorer," and "Conrad in Twilight," from *Selected Poems by John Crowe Ransom;* "Plowing on Sunday," from *Harmonium,* by Wallace Stevens. Reprinted by permission of Alfred A. Knopf, Inc.

"Ave Maria" (from "The Bridge"), from *Collected Poems of Hart Crane.* Copyright © R-1961, Liveright Publishing Corporation. Reprinted by permission of Liveright Publishers, N.Y.

"Why the South Has a Great Literature," from *Still Rebels, Still Yankees,* by Donald Davidson. Reprinted by permission of Louisiana State University Press.

Collected Poems of W. B. Yeats, definitive edition, copyright © 1956 by The Macmillan Company. Reprinted by permission of Mrs. W. B. Yeats, Macmillan & Company, Ltd., and The Macmillan Company.

"At the Hour of the Breaking of the Rocks," from *Selected Poems 1923–1943,* by Robert Penn Warren. Copyright 1944 by Robert Penn Warren. Reprinted by permission of the William Morris Agency.

Poems, by Gerard Manley Hopkins. Reprinted by permission of Oxford University Press, Inc.

Brother to Dragons, by Robert Penn Warren. Copyright 1953 by Robert Penn Warren. Reprinted by permission of Random House, Inc.

Intruder in the Dust, by William Faulkner. Copyright 1948 by William Faulkner. *Absalom, Absalom!*, by William Faulkner. Copyright 1936 by William Faulkner. *Requiem for a Nun*, by William Faulkner. Copyright 1950, 1951 by William Faulkner. *The Sound and the Fury*, by William Faulkner. Copyright 1929 and renewed 1956 by William Faulkner. *Light in August*, by William Faulkner. Copyright 1932 and renewed 1959 by William Faulkner. All reprinted by permission of Random House, Inc.

"The Brilliant Leaves" and "Old Red," from *The Forest of the South*, by Caroline Gordon. *The Women on the Porch*, by Caroline Gordon. "Epithalamion," from *Now with His Love*, by John Peale Bishop. Copyright 1933 by Charles Scribner's Sons. All reprinted by permission of Charles Scribner's Sons.

"Lee in the Mountains" (copyright 1934 by Donald Davidson), "The Running of Streight," "The Deserter: A Christmas Eclogue" (copyright 1938 by Donald Davidson), "The Tall Men," "Epilogue: Fire on Belmont Street," "The Breaking Mould," "The Sod of Battle-Fields" (copyright 1927 and renewed 1955 by Donald Davidson), from *Lee in the Mountains and Other Poems Including The Tall Men*, by Donald Davidson. Reprinted by permission of Charles Scribner's Sons.

"The Last Days of Alice" (copyright 1931 by New Republic, Inc.), "The Mediterranean" (copyright 1933 by Yale University), "Sonnets at Christmas I" (copyright 1934 by New Republic, Inc.), "Aeneas at Washington" (copyright 1936 by Allen Tate), "Ode to the Confederate Dead" (copyright 1937 by Charles Scribner's Sons), "The Seasons of the Soul" (copyright 1945 by Allen Tate), "The Buried Lake" (copyright 1953 by Allen Tate), "The Swimmers" (copyright 1952 by Allen Tate), from *Poems 1960*, by Allen Tate. Reprinted by permission of Charles Scribner's Sons and Eyre & Spottiswoode, Ltd.

The Story of a Novel, by Thomas Wolfe. Copyright 1936 by Charles Scribner's Sons. *Of Time and the River*, by Thomas Wolfe. Copyright 1935 by Charles Scribner's Sons. Reprinted by permission of Charles Scribner's Sons and William Heinemann, Ltd.

Letters of Thomas Wolfe, edited by Elizabeth Nowell. *Thomas Wolfe's Letters to His Mother*, edited by John Terry. Reprinted by permission of Charles Scribner's Sons.

ACKNOWLEDGMENTS

Four of the essays in this book, and portions of four others, appeared originally in *Southern Renascence: The Literature of the Modern South*, published by the Johns Hopkins Press in 1953, and the editors wish to thank Mr. Harold Ingle and the Johns Hopkins Press for permission to reprint them. The essay on Carson McCullers, by Oliver Evans, appeared first in *New World Writing I*, and the editors wish to thank New American Library, Inc., and Mr. Evans for permission to reprint it in slightly revised form. In its original form the essay entitled "Southern Literature: the Historical Image" appeared in the *Journal of Southern History* for May 1956, and the editors are grateful for permission to reprint it. Much of the material contained in the essay entitled "Two in Richmond: Ellen Glasgow and James Branch Cabell" was originally published in Louis D. Rubin, Jr., *No Place on Earth: Ellen Glasgow, James Branch Cabell, and Richmond-in-Virginia*, Austin, Texas: University of Texas Press, 1959, and the author wishes to thank President Harry H. Ransom, Mr. Frank Wardlaw, and the University of Texas Press for permission to use it in this volume.

Again, for Elliott Coleman

CONTENTS

SOUTHERN WRITING AND THE CHANGING SOUTH

This is a book of essays about the literature of the modern
South, the men and women who have created it, and the
social, cultural, and historical setting out of which their books
have come. It consists of twenty-one essays by various hands,
together with a bibliographical checklist. Most of the major
figures in what has been called the Southern Literary Renascence are subjected to critical analysis and an effort made to
understand something of the complex relationship between the
individual work of art and the region. The accent is at least as
much on the works of art as on the South—which is surely
appropriate when one considers that, among other things, the
modern South has produced a distinguished body of literary
criticism based squarely on the premise of the entire autonomy
of the individual story and poem. Yet that attitude itself possesses cultural implications. It is no accident that it has been
an aesthetic criticism, and not a social, that was developed
by the poet-critics of Vanderbilt University who have provided most of the body of theoretical work that has accompanied the stories and poems of the Southern Renascence.

It is not merely the obvious presence of so many accomplished writers, come as it were almost precipitously into
existence at a particular time and place, when before them
there was very little writing of more than historical significance, that accounts for the Southern Renascence. One cannot look at the phenomenon without a conviction that whatever it was that made the work possible, the region from which
the writers sprung was deeply involved. H. L. Mencken's
famous comment about the Sahara of the Bozart was, by and
large, true when he said it in 1920, yet within five years after,

it was true no longer, and it has not been true ever since. Without subscribing to an environmentalist interpretation of origins, we must still recognize that *something* about the place and especially the time must have caused all those writers to appear and to flourish, when before them there was almost nothing of a Southern literary tradition to draw on.

Furthermore, if we are to make a case for a *Southern* Renascence instead of merely a renascence in the South, we have more than the collective presence of many books and authors upon which to base our argument. We find, upon reading the novels and poems, that there are shared characteristics, shared attitudes toward certain important matters, the more profound for the very fact that they are in large measure implicit. The Southern writers seem unusually concerned with the sensuous properties of language and its imaginative use. They have tended to depict man's nature as being religious, to view the individual very much as a creature of time and history, to assume the individual's commitment to society and his determining role within it.

At first glance, for example, we may perceive little similarity in the fiction of two such Southern authors as Thomas Wolfe and Erskine Caldwell. Yet if we contrast the work of either with, say, that of John Dos Passos, we recognize that whatever the differences in the work of the two Southerners, the fictional characters of both share at least one trait largely absent in Dos Passos' people: a kind of cantankerous individualism that manifests itself, regardless of all social pressures. In Caldwell this attitude shows through even in the face of his ideological predilection toward collectivism. Jeeter Lester, in *Tobacco Road*, supposedly is what he is because of his victimization by a grasping capitalistic society. Yet Jeeter's individuality keeps thrusting itself into the characterization, and the reader cannot avoid feeling that, for all the iniquities of the sharecropper system and the avarice of landlords, Jeeter is the kind of man he is because of Jeeter, not economics. Whatever Caldwell's ideological convictions, he could not make himself envision Jeeter as anything other than a human being ultimately responsible for his own actions.

However, in the Southern novel man as an individual does not exist apart from a social framework. If we compare the work of either Wolfe or Caldwell with that of Ernest Hemingway, we observe at once that the Hemingway character can set up his own private code and exist within it, outside of and in personal isolation from society, while Wolfe's and Caldwell's characters won't and can't. For better or for worse they are individuals dwelling within the social framework; however much Eugene Gant in *Look Homeward, Angel* conceives of himself as alone and lonely, he must always define himself in terms of the community in which he lives. This conflict—the individual within society, product of it and often as not its victim, yet at the same time a free agent with the responsibility for his actions—is present in every one of the Southern writers. In the novels of the greatest of them, William Faulkner, it frequently takes on tragic proportions.

Let it be said at once that the characteristics we have described as typical of Southern writing are by no means exclusively or peculiarly so. Robert B. Heilman remarks this in his essay when, after singling out certain attributes of the Southern literary temper, he asserts that "no one of these endowments is unshared; but their concurrency is not frequent." Not the exclusive existence of any of these characteristics in modern Southern fiction and poetry, but the collective presence of all of them together, typifies the work of the writers of the Southern Renascence. Granted the great differences between writer and writer, the variety in the constellation that is modern Southern literature, still, we keep returning again and again to common themes, common attitudes, common preoccupations. No attempt has been made in this book to provide a uniformity of approach, much less of critical judgment, among the individual essayists. Yet one is struck by the persistent recurrence of themes, values, standards of judgment in the analyses of individual works. For not only the writers under observation, but most of the contributing essayists too, are Southerners.

The present volume appears at a time when recent political and social developments have fixed worldwide attention upon the region south of the Potomac and the Ohio rivers. Readers all over the world have naturally enough looked to the novelists and poets of the modern South for clues to the sometimes baffling behavior of its inhabitants. There can be little doubt that much of the attraction that books by Southern writers have had for the contemporary reader is that he needs to know the human implications of the social drama going on within the South, and it is from the writings of the novelists and poets that he derives this knowledge. For the literary image is always human, and takes for its elements the behavior of people living in a particular place and time, caught, as they often are, between conflicting loyalties and beliefs, between what they want to be and what they must be. From Ellen Glasgow to William Styron, the writers of the twentieth-century South have addressed themselves to the milieu in which they and their fellow Southerners have their being. Though as artists their primary impulse is not to write social history but to depict the fullness of experience, it is hardly surprising that the image they have provided of the region they knew best gives aid if not always comfort to those who would understand that region's actions.

Consider, for example, three Southern novels published within a period of forty years: Ellen Glasgow's *One Man in His Time*, Robert Penn Warren's *All the King's Men*, and George Garrett's *The Finished Man*. Each of these novels concerns itself with a man of the people who seeks to exercise political leadership. Yet in the efforts of the authors to portray the nature of political man in the South, each has also succeeded in transcending the immediate subject matter by illuminating the problems and attitudes of the people at large, so that the student of social as well as political behavior has as much to learn from these novels as from historical accounts, economic registers, and statistical analyses; and what he gets is the experienced knowledge of a work of art, not the abstract formulations of the social sciences. Immersed as the authors of these novels were in the life of their region, the image in which they have revealed their characters is a Southern image, an image that interprets flesh-and-blood Southerners. As one distinguished historian has declared, "The Southern novelist is more concerned with the meaning of events than with the technical accuracy of their recording. He heeds the legends, the undying superstitions and prejudices of the people. His willingness and ability to use these in his tales is where his genius lies" (Francis B. Simkins, "Tolerating the South's Past," *Journal of Southern History*, XXI [1955], 15).

To speak of the South today is to speak of the Negro. During the past decade there took place the decision of the United States Supreme Court, in *Brown* vs. *Board of Education*, whereby segregation by race was outlawed in the public schools. Agitation over the Negro's status in Southern society has of course been going on for more than a century, but the impact of the Court's decision has served to highlight in dramatic fashion the issues that have concerned the people of the South—and the North—since before the Civil War. And though it is not with Supreme Court edicts and school referendums that writers are primarily concerned when they create their poems and novels, still, it can hardly be gainsaid that so momentous an issue is bound to have its impact upon the artistic image that writers will create out of Southern life. It is too early, perhaps, to say what it will mean, and yet, as previously remarked, the problem of the roles of Negro and white is not a new one for the South, and the 1954 decision of the Court only gave a kind of ultimate dimension to an issue that is almost as old as the region itself.

To the editors—and it must be emphasized that here as throughout this introduction they speak for themselves only, and by no means for the individual contributors of the various essays—it would seem that the Negro's role in Southern life will continue to be for its writers what it has always been: a symbol of change, of the way in which human beings are confronted with change, of the process by which the customs and attitudes of what had been a settled and contained society must be adjusted to the demands of a modern, eclectic world that increasingly makes its presence felt upon fixed habits and beliefs. In attempting to hold onto its traditional modes of thought and behavior so far as the Negro is concerned, the South seeks to retain a social structure doomed in and by time. In so doing, it fights a losing battle, in which racial segregation is but the immediate issue—for with the passing of segregation there must also pass important features of a pattern of life based upon a fixed, closely knit rural and small-town society. Whether or not the essential characteristics of such a society are actually dependent upon racial segregation is a matter for dispute; but it cannot be denied that many of the particular lineaments of life as lived in the Southern states before the coming of the modern era were based upon the presence of a supposedly inferior race, hewers of wood and drawers of water, to till the fields and wait upon table and otherwise perform the role of a peasantry.

Whatever the attractions of such a society for the participants, the peasantry has now declined to continue performing its function, and wherever the society has been dependent upon the presence and the co-operation of that peasantry, it will have to make new, arrangements. The former peasantry now demands full rights and privileges of membership, in the status not of fixed inferiority but of equal participation insofar as its individual members are equal to the opportunity. In so demanding, the former peasantry is not only encouraged but indeed impelled by the breaking up of that old, closed agrarian society, and its replacement by a cosmopolitan, fluid industrial society in which social status and economic stratification are constantly changing. The Negro insists that institutions be made to conform to the conditions of such an open society, and specifically that the same educational opportunities be available to his children as to the children of his white neighbors. To use a literary illustration, Du Bose Heyward's *Mamba's Daughters* ends with a scene in which a young Negro woman leaves the city of Charleston, South Carolina, to secure vocal training and become famous as an opera singer in the North, while her grandmother remains contentedly in her place, the South, where she will watch her granddaughter's success from afar. Everyone concerned thus lives happily ever after. *Mamba's Daughters* was published in 1929. For a novelist today to provide a similar ending for his story would be utterly to ignore the realities of present-day Southern life. The implied compromise that Heyward's novel suggested is no longer accepted.

To live in a period of drastic social adjustment is both a fascinating and a painful thing—fascinating and painful for all concerned—and none have explored this condition, in terms of the human problems it presents, more thoroughly than the novelists and poets of the South, whose task, we have noted, is to write about what being human means at such times. A Negro novelist, Ralph Ellison, has expressed his awe at the way that William Faulkner has gone about exploring each and every facet of the Negro's role in the South, both as it involves the Negro and the white man.

This is precisely what Faulkner has done, and yet never with the primary intent of analyzing and describing a social condition. His interest has been in individuals—Lucas Beauchamp, Gavin Stevens, Chick Mallison, Quentin Compson, Joe Christmas, Nancy Mannigoe—and it was because he created these characters in the image of men and women as he had known them all his life, which is to say, Southern men and women, that his writings deal with what politicians would term "the civil-rights issue." The process was beautifully illustrated by Faulkner himself in a student interview. Asked how he came up with the idea for *Intruder in the Dust,* he replied:

> "Well, it began with the notion—there was a tremendous flux of detective stories going about at that time and my children were always buying them and bringing them home. I'd stumble over them everywhere I went. And I thought of an idea for one would be a man in jail just about to be hung would have to be his own detective, he couldn't get anybody to help him. Then the next thought was, the man for that would be a Negro. Then the character of Lucius—Lucas Beauchamp came along. And the book came out of that" (*Faulkner in the University,* ed. Frederick L. Gwynn and Joseph L. Blotner, 1959, 141–42).

The book that "came out of that" involved a Negro whose near lynching was foiled by a young white boy who believed in his innocence when to adult whites it was clear that the Negro was guilty. In the course of the book the boy's uncle moralized at great length about the Negro and his place, and the need for the South to give "Sambo," as he called him, his full rights without interference from the North. But it was the boy, not the uncle, who, cutting through the elaborate rhetoric and rationalization of his elders, simply listened to the Negro and believed in his innocence.

The topical relevance of *Intruder in the Dust* was obvious, and Edmund Wilson even went so far as to review the novel in *The New Yorker* as "William Faulkner's Reply to the Civil-Rights Program." Wilson, of course, ignored the fact that the uncle who philosophized about "Sambo" and noninterference in the South's problems was not William Faulkner but a created character, and that the boy's simple, direct human response to a Negro friend in trouble gave the lie to all his uncle's rationalizations.

The point is, however, that for all the topical relevance, Faulkner did not set out to write a novel "about" civil rights. He wanted to show a doomed man without friends, and because Faulkner was a Southerner, "the man for that would be a Negro." To the Southern writer, the question of the Negro's role in Southern life presents itself in human rather than theoretical terms: the image is of Man, not Southern Negro. Yet so omnipresent is the Negro "problem" that the Southern writer naturally finds himself seeing human beings in ways that illustrate and comment on the current race issue. And since all signs indicate that segregation and integration will be an important issue in the South for years to come, we may expect that Southern writers will frequently be dealing with it in their novels and poems.

What of the Southern writer who is a Negro? What does the question of the Negro's role in the South mean for him?

The fact is that, until very recently, literary work by Southern Negroes has been of very little *literary* importance, though of considerably more *social* importance. There have been Southern Negro authors ever since George Moses Horton's *Hope of Liberty* was published in Raleigh, North Carolina, in 1829, but only in our own day have Southern Negroes produced literary work that has made its appeal on aesthetic grounds, rather than because it was written by a Negro or because of its particular subject matter. The success of such writings as the poems of Countée Cullen and even of James Weldon Johnson was due, one feels, in large part to the circumstances of their composition and the racial identity of its authors. Johnson's novel, *Autobiography of an Ex-Colored Man*, published anonymously at first, attracted considerable attention, but, like the poems of his *God's Trombones,* the appeal was essentially one of subject matter. In the novel Johnson wrote daringly of a Negro whose light skin enabled him to pass for a white man. The fine sermons in verse of *God's Trombones* were avowedly an attempt to preserve some of the fervor of the old-time Negro revivalist preacher before his kind vanished. So accurately did Johnson succeed in his task that recently the conclusion of one of the poems was quoted in prose form in the London *Times Literary Supplement* as an actual Negro prayer!

Richard Wright's *Native Son* was a tremendous sensation when it appeared in 1940. Like Faulkner's *Intruder in the Dust* of a decade later, it too was reviewed and discussed widely and almost without exception for what it had to say about the mistreatment of Negroes in Wright's native Mississippi and in Northern slums, and the consequences of such oppression. Unlike Faulkner's novel, however, Wright's purpose was precisely that of social protest. And it is the purpose that has impeded the Negro novelist. So passionate were Wright's views on the civil-rights issue that artistic objectivity, by which is meant the subordination of the "message" to the literary demands of the material, was impossible for him. Faulkner has stated the dilemma wisely. Referring to the need for the Negro writer to "have equality in terms that he can get used to it and forget that he is a Negro while he's writing," he commented that, "You can't write sympathetically about a condition when it's constant outrage to you, you see" (*Faulkner in the University,* 53–54). The reader of Wright's autobiographical *Black Boy* can understand why he wrote as he did in *Native Son,* but the fact remains that the novel is seldom read nowadays.

It was with the publication of Ralph Ellison's *The Invisible Man* in 1951 that a Southern Negro novelist became a novelist who was a Southerner and a Negro. Strictly speaking, Ralph Ellison is not from the Solid South, having been born in Oklahoma; but he studied at Tuskegee Institute in Alabama, and his work shares most of the characteristics of the writers of the Southern Renascence. *The Invisible Man* draws heavily upon the Southern scene, but unlike Wright's novel it does so without distorting the scene beyond artistic credibility. Like

Wright, Ellison went through a Marxist period in which his work was heavily naturalistic; unlike him, he emerged from it convinced that, in his own words, "To see America with an awareness of its rich diversity and its almost magical fluidity and freedom, I was forced to conceive of a novel unburdened by the narrow naturalism which has led after so many triumphs to the final and unrelieved despair which marks so much of our current fiction" ("Light on Invisible Man," *Crisis* LX [1953], 157–58, quoted in Robert A. Bone, *The Negro Novel in America*, 1958, 198).

The Invisible Man describes a Negro, first as a child and at a Southern college, then as a factory worker, then as a member of the Brotherhood, an organization much like the Communist Party, and finally as he lives an entirely solitary existence in a room underneath the basement of an apartment building, lighted by no less than 1369 electric bulbs with current supplied from a tapped power line.

The protagonist comes to realize that his color has been a shield whereby nobody, black or white, can see him for the individual human being he is. In the eyes of the world he is invisible.

Ellison's novel obviously does not look sideways at the Negro's difficulties, but his protagonist's story transcends the immediate social and political implications and becomes a parable of the human quest for identity. Robert Bone rightly likens it to Dostoievsky's *Notes from the Underground,* for both novels illumine the individual who exists outside of society, unable to define himself as a man by the conventional rules, and in his solitary contemplation existing as a criticism of society. "The evil now stares out of the bright sunlight," Ellison has written on another occasion ("Society, Morality, and the Novel," *The Living Novel,* ed. Granville Hicks, 1957, 90) —and his triumph is that he has been able to work his way through the social mask that his society has tried to force upon him as a Negro and to confront reality on individual terms. Ellison is a notable admirer of Faulkner, and his fiction displays the same richness of language and syntax, the concatenation of sentences and flow of rhetoric that Faulkner has made his trade-mark. Ellison has also made extensive use of folk motifs, and particularly of jazz music, but, unlike James

Weldon Johnson, the effect is never one of self-conscious arti-
ficiality.

The Invisible Man suffers toward the close from a too-
chaotic effort at surrealism; perhaps the finest scenes are those
in the beginning, when the protagonist is a student at a Negro
college in the South, while later the symbolism sometimes tends
to be expressed at the expense of the narrative. Even so, The
Invisible Man richly deserved the National Book Award for
fiction that it received in 1952. Since then Ellison has published no new novels; one waits to see whether he can go on
from there.

It is very possible that, if The Invisible Man is any augury,
Southern writing may be considerably enriched in the future
by the work of Negro authors. Meanwhile the question presents itself: Is the present Southern Literary Renascence over?
Has the flow of distinguished writing from the Southern states
begun to subside? This is a question, of course, that can be
answered only by novelists and poets, not by critics. Yet in the
work produced by several of the younger Southern novelists
one can detect some signs that may point to an answer.

In addition to Ellison, the two Southern novelists whose fiction attracted the greatest critical attention during the past
decade have been William Styron and James Agee. Styron's
first novel, Lie Down in Darkness, earned him an enviable reputation, and in 1960 he published a second full-length novel,
Set This House on Fire, which received mixed reviews. Agee
died in 1955, at the age of forty-five, and his novel A Death
in the Family was released posthumously. Along with Flannery
O'Connor, whose novels have not been as impressive as her
short stories, these are the younger writers whose work has
been thought most worthy of continuing the novelistic tradition set by Faulkner, Warren, Wolfe, and the others of the
pre-World War II literary generation.

Styron's two novels are set squarely in contemporary times.
Both feature protagonists who are isolated from the life around
them. Peyton Loftis of Lie Down in Darkness becomes quite
schizophrenic toward the end, and finally commits suicide after
failing to find a rationale for life in New York City. Cass
Kinsolving of Set This House on Fire lives in Europe and

learns to face up to his talents as a painter and a man in solitude. Thus in both novels the protagonists are unlike those of the earlier novelists, very much set apart from the society of their origins.

Agee's *A Death in the Family* differs greatly from the Styron novels, in that the manner of its relating is both too immediate and too distant for any attempt at tragedy. The novel describes the death of a man in an automobile accident, and the impact on his wife and small son. The account is detailed, and much of it seen through the child's eyes. The child knows that something terrible has happened, but he is not sufficiently aware of the implications to give it its meaning, while the mother is so caught up in shock and grief that she too can only begin to grasp the implications. What is most unusual about this novel, however, is the perspective from which the story is told. The narrator, one comes to realize very soon, is the child Rufus, but Rufus as he remembers and pieces together the episode many years later. The death of his father was the culminating event in Rufus's growing awareness of himself as a separate, individual, lonely person. It is the order in which the events occur to the perceiver, and his apparently objective but actually quite personal description of them, that give the novel its form.

Yet, though the Styron and Agee novels are greatly different in form and attitude, they have several striking similarities to each other, and differences from the novels of the earlier writers. Both are built squarely upon the growing and finally complete isolation of the protagonists from their society. Also, in neither is there a vital historical sense—that is, measurement of the present by the standards of the past, or depiction of the present as being importantly determined by the past.

In Styron's *Lie Down in Darkness,* for example, the protagonist, Peyton Loftis, even as a child is so far removed from the community of Port Warwick that there is no question of her possible participation in it. The tragedy derives not from this isolation but from her inability to live with herself. She is isolated from the human race, not merely from Port Warwick. If we compare her plight with that of Quentin Compson in Faulkner's *The Sound and the Fury,* on which Styron admittedly modeled his book, we notice the difference. For though

Quentin, like Peyton, is living far away from his Southern home when he takes his own life, he is nonetheless still a citizen of Yoknapatawpha County, even in Harvard, and his death comes not from his separation but from his inability to escape his impossible Compson heritage in a world in which that heritage and the role it prescribes for him are no longer possible. Peyton, on the other hand, is no longer a citizen of Port Warwick. Her parents' failings may have caused her to be what she is, but they fail as parents, not as degenerate representatives of an outdated dynastic concept of family. It is an interesting distinction, for the actual family situation is supposedly similar in both novels. Peyton's father even has a garrulous, moralizing father of his own, who talks much like Quentin Compson's father does. Dramatically, however, we seldom think of the Loftises as embodying the decline and fall of a once-vigorous aristocracy. Quentin's trouble in *The Sound and the Fury* was that he loved "some concept of Compson honor" that no longer bore any relationship to real life; Peyton Loftis's family's past does not even exist, so far as her motivations and characterization are concerned. Both novels portray crass times; but whereas in *The Sound and the Fury* the Compsons have decayed with the times, in *Lie Down in Darkness* disintegration is complete, the society no longer exists, and Peyton is on her own. We accept the reality of her being cut off; the tragedy lies not in that but in her personal failure. With Quentin it is quite the reverse; his tragedy comes *because*, being a Compson, he is cut off from his society.

If we labor the distinction, it is because it is essential: what is at stake is a whole conception of society and of history. Faulkner sees isolation from a community as tragedy; Styron sees it as a fact. Faulkner sees the isolation as the result of an historical process; Styron gives it no such dramatic roots in the past.

As for the protagonist of James Agee's *A Death in the Family*, his identity is already so far removed from the community, from his past, that the novel becomes an act of redeeming some of the personal meaning of what has long since been lost in time. In this sense Agee's book is reminiscent not of Faulkner but of Thomas Wolfe, who, despite his protagonist's strong sense of community, could not envision his separation from it as tragic. With both Agee and Wolfe the aesthetic process was that of recapturing moments in time, but with Agee the detachment was far greater than with Wolfe. Eugene Gant of *Look Homeward, Angel* may have hated his community, but he was strongly bound to it, and he pitted himself consciously in opposition to it; the narrator of *A Death in the Family* sees Knoxville, Summer 1915, only as a dream, a hazy, faraway time and place which may once have helped to mold him into what he is but is now irrevocably vanished in time. A key passage will illustrate this. Early in the novel Rufus is asleep, and his father sets out in the family car on the trip back to the mountains from which he will never return alive. As the narrator tells us:

> by the time he heard the creaking and departure of the Ford, he was already so deeply asleep that it seemed only a part of a dream, and by next morning, when his mother explained to them why his father was not at breakfast, he had so forgotten the words and the noises that years later, when he remembered them, he could never be sure that he was not making them up.

At first glance that seems a violation of the point of view; but only at first glance, for it confirms what we have suspected all along: that the perspective from which the entire story is being related is that of Rufus as he remembers what happened many years later. It all took place long ago, way off in another land.

What all this means, or seems to mean, is that to the extent that the Southern novel has always presupposed a strong identification with a place, a participation in its life, a sense of intense involvement in a fixed, defined society, the best work of the leading younger Southern writers is not in these respects "Southern." Just as the South itself has changed until it has lost much of its old, closely knit, small-town and rural character, so its most recent novelists have lost their sense of community, of involvement within a limited, bounded universe. The kind of community that was Yoknapatawpha County, created by a known and felt history, marked off into distinct, recognizable parts, each with its proper function and in its proper relationship to the others, is gone. Towns have become cities, cities have become huge metropolises. The landed dynasties have almost all fallen, or have changed over from feudal to commercial operations. The tradition of aristocratic leadership, and the sense of betrayal at its failure, are of less imaginative importance. The closeness and solidarity of the older Southern concept of family has been breached. The Negro is no longer the faithful, childlike peasant he once seemed to be. And so on. It was the very process of disintegration that helped to make possible *The Sound and the Fury*, *Absalom, Absalom!*, *All the King's Men*, *The Golden Apples*, *Look Homeward, Angel*. Now the fixed center is gone, and the younger Southern writers, as Walter Sullivan declares, must look for something else to take its place.

The novels of William Styron, James Agee, George Garrett, Flannery O'Connor, of Walter Sullivan himself, remain "Southern" by virtue of their attitude toward language, their conception of man as a limited, dependent being. Only the memory, fading, distant, of the old community remains. That, and an attitude. The historical sense, the idea of community-as-all, are nearly gone, and the protagonists of the recent Southern novel are moderns who live in a fluid, changing world.

LOUIS D. RUBIN, JR.
Hollins College, Virginia
ROBERT D. JACOBS
University of Kentucky

SOUTH:
MODERN SOUTHERN LITERATURE
IN ITS CULTURAL SETTING

SOUTHERN LITERATURE: THE HISTORICAL IMAGE

BY LOUIS D. RUBIN, JR.

Toward the end of his long life, the Confederate General
James Longstreet is supposed to have visited the town of Oxford, Mississippi, where his sister lived and where his uncle,
the Judge Longstreet of the *Georgia Scenes,* had once resided.
It was after Longstreet's extended dispute with other former
Confederate leaders over the responsibility for the Southern defeat at Gettysburg, and so when a small boy came up to the
old man and asked him, "General, what happened to you at
Gettysburg?" Longstreet almost suffered a stroke then and
there. The name of the small boy, the story goes, was William
Faulkner.

The episode almost certainly never took place. Longstreet's
biographer places it in 1898, when Faulkner was one year old,
and not even William Faulkner would have displayed such
precocity as that. It probably happened in Chicago, not Oxford, and if anyone asked such a question of Longstreet, it was
Faulkner's long-time friend Phil Stone.

The point is, however, that it does not *seem* an implausible
story. It *might* have happened; indeed, one could even maintain that it *should* have happened. For given Faulkner, given
the South, given the fact of Southern history, what would
seem more normal than that story?

The anecdote recalls a passage from Faulkner's *Intruder in
the Dust.* Lawyer Gavin Stevens is talking to his young
nephew, Chick Mallison:

> "It's all *now* you see. Yesterday wont be over until to-
> morrow and tomorrow began ten thousand years ago. For
> every Southern boy fourteen years old, not once but
> whenever he wants it, there is the instant when it's still

not yet two o'clock on that July afternoon in 1863, the brigades are in position behind the rail fence, the guns are laid and ready in the woods and the furled flags are already loosened to break out and Pickett himself with his long oiled ringlets and his hat in one hand probably and his sword in the other looking up the hill waiting for Longstreet to give the word and it's all in the balance, it hasn't happened yet, it hasn't even begun yet, it not only hasn't begun yet but there is still time for it not to begin against that position and those circumstances which made more men than Garnett and Kemper and Armstead and Wilcox look grave yet it's going to begin, we all know that, we have come too far with too much at stake and that moment doesn't even need a fourteen-year-old boy to think *This time. Maybe this time* with all this much to lose and all this much to gain: Pennsylvania, Maryland, the world, the golden dome of Washington itself to crown with desperate and unbelievable victory the desperate gamble, the cast made two years ago; or to anyone who ever sailed even a skiff under a quilt sail, the moment in 1492 when somebody thought *This is it*: the absolute edge of no return, to turn back now and make home or sail irrevocably on and either find land or plunge over the world's roaring rim."

As Chick Mallison recalls those words of his uncle, he faces the decision of what to do about Lucas Beauchamp, the Negro who faces a lynch mob. At this critical juncture, he thinks instinctively in historical terms of the problem that confronts him. That Faulkner has him do this is of far more importance than whether, when a boy, he actually went up to General Longstreet and asked about Gettysburg; it was of this historical moment of transcendent Southern ambition and destiny that Faulkner thought when he set about to describe a young Mississippi boy at the point of decision.

When in the course of twenty-five or thirty years a distinct geographical and historical region, noted for its artistic barrenness, produces a veritable galaxy of important novelists and poets, then naturally we look at the time and the place in order to see what might have caused so spectacular a literary explosion. And when that sudden outburst of distinguished literature is filled with historical images, crowded with the events and the attitudes of the region's history, we think at once to examine that history to determine what its relation to the literature might be.

Most of the Southern writers whose stories and poems attained prominence during the 1920s were born in the two decades immediately preceding and following the close of the nineteenth century. William Faulkner was born in 1897. John Crowe Ransom was born in 1888, Donald Davidson and Erskine Caldwell in 1893. Katherine Anne Porter was born in 1894, Caroline Gordon in 1895, Allen Tate in 1899, Thomas Wolfe in 1900, and Robert Penn Warren in 1905.

All of these writers, whose literary excellence has caused their time to be known as the period of the Southern Literary Renascence, grew up in a period when the Southern states were just emerging from a condition of shock. The South had engaged in a war. It had been beaten, and for fifteen years occupied by its conqueror. When, by the 1870s, the occupation forces were withdrawn and the carpetbag governments ousted, what remained was an exhausted land. For the succeeding generations, poverty was the rule. Southerners saw the American Union growing stronger and greater all around them. The great railroad trunk lines drew the West and the Pacific Coast toward the industrial East, and the nation became richer—while they remained where they were, sweating to gain a living from the soil, without capital goods, with little power in the national government, a colonial people. The New South of Henry W. Grady came, without making very many inroads upon the region's precarious farming economy. The Gradys, Walter Hines Pages, John Spencer Bassetts, and Francis Warrington Dawsons might preach the gospel of industrialization. Maurice Thompson might compose poems like the following:

> *The South whose gaze is cast*
> *No more upon the past*
> *But whose bright eyes the skies of promise sweep*
> *Whose feet in paths of progress swiftly leap*
> *And whose fresh thoughts like cheerful rivers run*
> *Through odorous ways to meet the morning sun.*

Yet the facts were otherwise. The chief occupation was still the land. The prosperity of the semicolonial South depended upon farm prices. The farmer was the backbone of the South —and a mighty droopy one much of the time. The new century was well under way before the South really began to come back into the American Union, to regain its place in the sun. Not until after 1900 did industrialization become much more than a slogan for most of the South.

For many years after Appomattox, then, the South struggled to make a bare living. It was left to itself, to think about the past, to brood over the price of union. Almost every Southern family had felt the war, shared in the defeat. The specter of the Lost Cause was there to contemplate. The war, memories of the war, results of the war, dominated life in the South for four decades or more. Walter Hines Page declared that he

> sometimes thought that many of the men who survived that unnatural war unwittingly did us a greater hurt than the war itself. It gave every one of them the intensest experience of his life and ever afterward he referred every other experience to this. Thus it stopped the thought of most of them as an earthquake stops a clock. The fierce blows of battle paralyzed the mind. Their speech was a vocabulary of war, their loyalties were loyalties, not to living ideas or duties, but to old commanders and to distorted traditions. They were dead men, most of them, moving among the living as ghosts; and yet, as ghosts in a play, they held the stage (Burton J. Hendrick, *The Life and Letters of Walter Hines Page*, 1922–1925, I, 90–91).

Richard M. Weaver has remarked that "for thirty years the atmosphere was so suffused with the sense of tragedy and frustration that it was almost impossible for a Southern man to take a 'normal' view of anything" ("Agrarianism in Exile," *Sewanee Review*, LVIII [1950], 587). On every street corner Confederate veterans were to be found. Not to have served in the war was almost to be disqualified from a political career. In most Southern houses gilded frames enclosed lithographs of Lee and Jackson. As Douglas Freeman expressed it, "The Confederate tradition was for fifty years the strongest influ-

ence, political and social, in the South" (*Lee's Lieutenants,*
1942–1944, III, 587).

History—defeat, the war, the past; in the South these were
not abstractions. To a child growing up in the South, they
were very real. Southerners knew that history was not merely
something in books. In his *Origins of the New South*, C. Vann
Woodward quotes a passage from Arnold Toynbee:

> I remember watching the Diamond Jubilee procession
> myself as a small boy. I remember the atmosphere. It
> was: Well, here we are on the top of the world, and we
> have arrived at this peak to stay there—forever! There
> is, of course, a thing called history, but history is some-
> thing unpleasant that happens to other people. We are
> comfortably outside all that. I am sure, if I had been a
> small boy in New York in 1897, I should have felt the
> same. Of course, if I had been a small boy in 1897 in the
> Southern part of the United States, I should not have felt
> the same; I should then have known from my parents
> that history had happened to my people in my part of the
> world (Woodward, *Origins of the New South, 1877–
> 1913,* 1951, viii).

It was this kind of atmosphere, charged with the image of
the war and the past, into which most of the writers of the
Southern Renascence were born.

Then, as the twentieth century got under way, the South
gradually began to change. The old veterans were dying off;
the old loyalties were adjusted to conform to new conditions.
"By far the greater portion of the generation which had listened with awe while the guns boomed in Virginia and the
ships of war steamed on the Mississippi," the historian Paul H.
Buck has written of the South after 1900, "slept in silent graves
in which the issues for which they had contended were buried
with them. The old had given way to the new. Around the
lingering survivors pressed eager youth. Slowly the bent figures
of the past took their leave" (*The Road to Reunion, 1865–
1900,* 1937, 304–5). In the "formative years" of Faulkner,
Wolfe, Tate, Davidson, Ransom, and the others, the industrial
New South which had been so much talked about and, save

in some few cities such as Richmond, Birmingham, and Atlanta, so little evident, finally began to make its impact on the region. Various writers have described the expanding development of the business and commercial South in the new century. "Looms and furnaces, factories and stores, railroads and water power," Edwin Mims remarked of the twentieth-century South, "have led to the prosperity of the few and the wellbeing of the many" (*The Advancing South*, 1926, 112). Such journals as John Spencer Bassett's *South Atlantic Quarterly* and the older *Sewanee Review,* which William Peterfield Trent had founded in 1892, spoke the new note for literature and culture no less than the *'Manufacturers' Record* of Baltimore proclaimed it for business and industry.

With the First World War, the South was back in the Union again. Thousands of young Southerners went into training camps all over the North and West. Many more thousands of persons from other parts of the Union came to live in the South. Even before that, the South had been getting set for the change. Chambers of commerce made their appearance. Upon a basically agrarian, ingrown, easygoing, impecunious society, industrial America moved in.

Change—this was the keynote of Southern life during the years when the writers of the Southern Renascence were growing to manhood. Here is how Thomas Wolfe chose to describe life in Libya Hill just before young George Webber was born:

> The railroad was then being built and would soon be finished. And only a year or two before, George Willetts, the great Northern millionaire, had purchased thousands of acres of the mountain wilderness and had come down with his architects to project the creation of a great country estate that would have no equal in America. New people were coming to town all the time, new faces were being seen upon the streets. There was quite a general feeling in the air that great events were just around the corner, and that a bright destiny was in store for Libya Hill.
>
> It was the time when they were just hatching from the shell, when the place was changing from a little isolated mountain village, lost to the world, with its few thousand

native population, to a briskly-moving modern town, with railway connections to all parts, and with a growing population of wealthy people who had heard about the beauties of the setting and were coming there to live (*The Web and the Rock*).

In Asheville, in Nashville, in cities and towns all over the South, things were going on. What the parents of the future writers of the Southern Literary Renascence had known as certainty seemed to their children to be less and less sure. New ways, new beliefs, new interests were making themselves felt. The three specters of Walter Page's South—"the Ghost of the Confederate dead, the Ghost of religious orthodoxy, the Ghost of Negro domination"—began to relinquish their hold over the Southern mind.

"Progress" came increasingly to be the favorite slogan. Every Southern town and city had its booster club, its chamber of commerce. As Donald Davidson remembered it:

In those years industrial commercialism was rampant. In no section were its activities more blatant than in the South, where old and historic communities were crawling on their bellies to persuade some petty manufacturer of pants or socks to take up his tax-exempt residence in their midst. This industrial invasion was the more disturbing because it was proceeding with an entire lack of consideration for its results on Southern life. The rural population, which included at least two-thirds of the total Southern population, was being allowed to drift into poverty and was being viewed with social disdain. Southern opinion, so far as it was articulate, paid little serious attention to such matters. The older liberals of the Walter Hines Page school still believed in the easy humanitarianism of pre-World-War days. The younger liberals were damning the Fundamentalists, and rejoicing in the efforts of the sociological missionaries who were arriving almost daily from the slum-laboratories of Chicago and New York. The business interests were taking full advantage of the general dallying with superficial issues ("'I'll Take My Stand': A History," *American Review*, V [1935], 304–5).

There was the moral impact of the First World War itself, with its sudden and awful impression of death, bestiality, waste. Donald Davidson and John Ransom served as army officers overseas; William Faulkner trained in the Royal Air Corps. And for all the others, as well, there was the sudden letdown of idealism, the swift transition from Woodrow Wilson to Teapot Dome. Thomas Wolfe describes it vividly in the opening pages of *Of Time and the River*. Marcus Cunliffe, in his history of American literature, has remarked that the young Americans were in the World War for only a comparatively short time and yet, paradoxically, the war's impact upon their idealism seems to have been extraordinarily strongly pronounced. Donald Mahon, in Faulkner's *Soldiers' Pay*, comes home, the mutilated hulk of what once was a young man. Young Bayard Sartoris, his brother dead in France, arrives home, in the novel *Sartoris*, to race his automobile along country roads and finally to die in a plane wreck, deliberately courting death to avoid the everyday tedium. The army veteran of Donald Davidson's *The Tall Men* applies for a job:

> *'Well, what are your*
> *Qualifications?' I said 'Qualifications?*
> *In the army I learned the Impossibles.'*
> *He said, 'We'll file your application.' I said,*
> *'Thank you, sir,' and walked out buttoning tarnished*
> *Buttons and swinging O.D. sleeves with a yellow V,*
> *Meaning fodder for moths and spider-webs.*

The Southern Literary Renascence occurred in a period of transition for the South. Certain young writers, reared in one kind of world, saw that world changing into another kind. They were themselves *of* that new, changed world, and yet apart from it and conscious of the difference. In Allen Tate's words: "After the war the South again knew the world, but it had a memory of another war; with us, entering the world once more meant not the obliteration of the past but a heightened consciousness of it; so that we had, at any rate in Nashville, a double focus, a looking two ways, which gave a special dimension to the writings of our school—not necessarily a superior quality—which American writing as a whole seemed to lack" ("The Fugitive, 1922–1925," *Princeton University Li-*

brary Chronicle, III [1942], 83). Tate sensed that the unique quality which seemed to give force and range to the work of himself and his contemporaries was a kind of historical vision. "With the war of 1914–1918," he has elsewhere written, "the South re-entered the world—but gave a backward glance as it stepped over the border: that backward glance gave us the Southern renascence, a literature conscious of the past in the present" ("The New Provincialism," *On the Limits of Poetry*, 1948, 292).

The writers of the Southern Renascence were able to re-create the life around them, about which they were writing, not simply because they were blessed with somewhat superior powers of description, but as if they had been gifted with a kind of historical perspective, which translated what they saw in terms of what *had been* as well as what now *was*. They were able to observe the South and its people *in time*, as they were in the present and as they used to be in the past. They could understand the older South as well as their own South. They could see a Thomas Sutpen, a Bayard Sartoris, a George Posey, a Percy Munn, not only as moderns saw figures remote in time, but as these men were seen in their own right, by their own contemporaries. The present was focused into perspective by the image of the past lying behind it.

The two-way vision was possible to the Southern writers of Tate's generation not only because of their ability to believe in the value and meaningfulness of their people's past but also *because they could disbelieve.* Being of that first twentieth-century generation of Southerners, they had been strongly reared in the ways of an older South, vividly taught the beliefs and loyalties of the nineteenth century as the South knew them. But they were of the twentieth century, not the nineteenth. They understood equally well the attraction of the new ways, as the writers of the previous generation could not have done. A mutation was demanded of them: a qualitative change in values and outlook. And being artists, gifted with the perception of artists, they sensed only too clearly the meaning of what was happening. They could believe in the old Army of Northern Virginia kind of belief, and yet share the self-consciousness and skepticism of postwar America and the world.

In *The Web and the Rock,* Thomas Wolfe uses the figure of an old house set back from the highway to illustrate what happened to the South. After the war and the troops, he says, an old man went back into the house and did not emerge again. The grass and weeds grew, obliterating the path to the house, and the house stayed on.

It shone faintly through that tangled growth like its own ruined spectre, its doors and windows black as eyeless sockets. That was the South. That was the South for thirty years or more.

That was the South, not of George Webber's life, nor of the lives of his contemporaries—that was the South they did not know but that all of them somehow remembered. It came to them from God knows where, upon the rustling of a leaf at night, in quiet voices on a Southern porch, in a screen door slam and sudden silence, a whistle wailing down the midnight valleys to the East and the enchanted cities of the North, and Aunt Maw's droning voice and the memory of unheard voices, in the memory of the dark, ruined Helen in their blood, in something stricken, lost, and far, and long ago. They did not see it, the people of George's age and time, but they remembered it.

They had come out—another image now—into a kind of sunlight of another century. They had come out upon the road again. The road was being paved. More people came now. They cut a pathway to the door again. Some of the weeds were clear. Another house was built. They heard wheels coming and the world was *in,* yet they were not yet wholly of that world.

Of the New South, and yet not of it, seeing the life of the 1920s against the image of an earlier period, the young Southerners began to write their novels and stories and poems and plays and essays. In Nashville, they started a magazine, *The Fugitive.* In the first number it was announced that the contributing poets were fleeing most of all from "the high-caste Brahmins of the Old South." By that they meant the sentimentalists, the mint julep South of Thomas Nelson Page and a host of lesser local colorists. They wanted no truck with local color, with the pleasant provinciality of iron grillwork, magnolia, and the resident poetry society. Instead they proposed a hard, meaningful, disciplined art of full engagement and intellectual judgment. They were poets, they believed in poetry, and they were not going to stand for any nonsense from ladies' clubs and poetesses laureate of the United Daughters of the Confederacy.

At this time, in the early 1920s, the Fugitives rather thought of themselves as representatives, on the literary plane, of the idea of the new, modern, progressive South. It was in this light too that exponents of the New South saw *The Fugitive*, welcoming it as evidence that Southern literature was, along with Southern culture, Southern education, and Southern business, throwing off the blinders of the South's past. As the Nashville *Tennessean* remarked: "For one thing, *The Fugitive* is an advertising instrument for this city and this state, which reaches a public that could be reached in no other way and by no other means. There are a good many people in different parts of the world, who, a year ago, if the word 'Nashville' had been mentioned would have had a vague idea of a city somewhere or other in the South, but who, today, at the mention of the name would say, 'Oh, yes; Nashville. That's the city in Tennessee where *The Fugitive* is published'" (May 27, 1923).

In *The Advancing South* (198–201), Edwin Mims saw the work of his younger literary colleagues and students at Vanderbilt as representing "a critical intelligence, a sense of literary values, and a reaction against sentimentalism and romance which has not been hitherto regarded as characteristic of Southern writing." Of one of the Vanderbilt poets, John Crowe Ransom, Mims declared that "He, like the other poets of the group, has little or no local colour, and is not consciously Southern except in an indirect protest against a sentimentalized South and commercialized South."

Yet before long it began to be evident to the leading Fugitive poets—Tate, Ransom, Davidson, Warren—that the chief opposition would not come from sentimentalists about the Old South. Even when presented in so polished a form as the romances of Du Bose Heyward and other local-color novelists and poets, Southern ancestor worship did not constitute much of a threat. Instead the menace was something quite different.

Soon the leading Fugitives were taking their stand as Agrarians and were pounding away at it.

What was wrong was just what Maurice Thompson had hailed some decades before: "The South whose gaze is cast/ No more upon the past." All around them the young Southern writers saw a country doing its best to become "modern," "progressive," "up-to-date," and, as they viewed it, achieving only faddishness, unbelief, and a tawdry commercialism. In the South's eager race to emulate the rest of the country, all the things that they had been taught were good were being cast aside. Business was in the saddle; the chamber of commerce reigned. Intellectually, culturally, economically, the South was courting modernity. What was most frothy, most rootless, most amoral about the 1920s, they felt, was being held up to the South as the model it should follow. In its eagerness to become progressive, to throw off the taint of provincialism, to "belong" to the age, the South was callously throwing off cherished ways of faith and life.

Others, not so socially and politically articulate as the Nashville group, nevertheless shared the basic artistic impulses that underlay the attitudes in *I'll Take My Stand*. Like the young men of letters who produced the Agrarian symposium, Faulkner, Wolfe, and the other Southern novelists and poets felt the spiritual unrest, the dissatisfaction with the modern mode, the distrust of conventional standards and values that characterized American and European literature during the years between the two world wars. It was not, for example, in the poetasters of the pre-World War I South that the Fugitives found their poetic confreres; rather, they looked toward Eliot, Pound, Yeats, Mann, Hart Crane, Robert Graves, Wallace Stevens. It was not Southern local color that Wolfe and Faulkner studied; it was Sherwood Anderson, Sinclair Lewis, Dreiser —above all, Joyce. They were part of a world literary movement, a worldwide artistic questioning of their time and place.

Yet they were Southern, and their modernity was spoken with the Southern accent. The artistic achievement of their response, the quality and quantity of their novels, stories, and poems inevitably directs our attention to their time, their region, their particular history and tradition. It was not an abstract "tradition" that confronted them, both as it hung on and as it gave way before the new. It was the Southern tradition, a particular set of attitudes and values produced by a particular history in a specific and bounded American region.

Again and again, throughout the work of the writers of the Southern Renascence, we find pictured the debasement of Southern tradition. In all of Thomas Wolfe's fiction, there is no more moving episode than that in which Eliza Gant rents out her home as a boardinghouse and begins speculating in real estate. To her family, it constitutes a betrayal of her femininity. Donald Davidson's epic poem *The Tall Men* is about many things, and especially it is a lament for the vanishing image of the Tennessee frontiersman and his old virtues, before the cheap lures of modernity.

> *The Fire! What fire? Why God has come alive*
> *To damn you all, or else the smoke and soot*
> *Have turned back to live coals again for shame*
> *On this gray city, blinded, spoiled, and kicked*
> *By fat blind fools. The city's burning up?*
> *Why, good! Then let her burn!*

What is Temple Drake's own particular corruption in Faulkner's *Sanctuary* but Southern womanhood defiled and mocked, the flower of her tradition who goes to school mostly to extend her sexual range and who, imprisoned in a Memphis bawdyhouse, neither seeks to flee nor complains, because it is what she really wants? Equally ineffective if only somewhat less corrupted is Gowan Stevens, young Southern gentleman, University of Virginia graduate, who can neither hold his liquor nor protect his lady.

From this judgment of the present by standards of an impossible past, Faulkner's whole Yoknapatawpha saga takes much of its theme and tone. Sartorises and Compsons, sons of the older families, lose their strength and their belief. As they become increasingly incapable of handling the modern world, up from the South's thickets and gully lands rise the swarming hordes of Snopeses, lacking principle or code, rapacious, sterile, evil, to take over the ravaged land. "I've seed de first en de last," the Negro cook Dilsey says in *The Sound and the Fury*. "I seed de beginnin, en now I sees de endin." Of all the members of the once-proud Compson family that she had served, only the gelded idiot Benjy and the sordid Jason survive, and Jason has ceased to be a Compson and has become a Snopes in all but the name.

The image of the heroic past renders the distraught present doubly distasteful, just as it is the guilt and falseness of this same heroic past that has caused the present. This they saw too. This is the burden of the South: the impossible load of the past that kills Quentin Compson in *The Sound and the Fury*, the heroic and immense figures of Sutpens and Compsons, the terrifying impact of their characters, against whose history a Quentin Compson cannot hope to measure himself with pride. In their rooms at a New England college, Quentin tells the Canadian Shreve McCannon the tragic history of Thomas Sutpen that constitutes the story of *Absalom, Absalom!* Mirrored in it is the story of the South, and the nation as well. To the Canadian it is a fascinating tale.

"Jesus, if I was going to have to spend nine months in this climate, I would sure hate to have come from the South. Maybe I wouldn't come from the South anyway, even if I could stay there. Wait. Listen. I'm not trying to be funny, smart. I just want to understand it if I can and I don't know how to say it better. Because it's something my people haven't got. Or if we have got it, it all happened long ago across the water and so now there aint anything to look at every day to remind us of it. We dont live among defeated grandfathers and freed slaves (or have I got it backward and was it your folks that are free and the niggers that lost?) and bullets in the dining room and such, to be always reminding us to never forget. What is it? something you live and breathe in like air? a kind of vacuum filled with wraithlike and indomitable anger and pride anger and pride and glory at and in happenings that occurred and ceased fifty years ago? a kind of entailed birthright father and son and father and son of never forgiving General Sherman, so that forevermore as long as your children's children produce children you wont be anything but a descendant of a long line of colonels killed in Pickett's charge at Manassas?"

"Gettysburg," Quentin said. "You cant understand it.
You would have to be born there."

Quentin tells his story in 1910, at Harvard, but though the
events he describes occurred for the most part many years ago,
they are not over. The entire time structure of *Absalom, Absalom!* is interwoven, working back on itself. Thomas Sutpen's
past causes his present and future, and the lives of all with
whom he comes into contact are changed because of that past.
Gavin Stevens' remark in *Requiem for a Nun* that "the past
is never dead, it's not even past," is descriptive of *Absalom,
Absalom!*—for in the consciousness of Quentin Compson as he
pieces out the events in Sutpen's saga, yesterday and today are
inextricably intertwined. "The South," Shreve McCannon says
after the story is concluded, "the South. Jesus. No wonder you
folks all outlive yourselves by years and years and years."
Surely this is so for Quentin. "I am older at twenty than a lot
of people who have died," he tells Shreve. And in *The Sound
and the Fury* he finds time so inescapable, so remorseless in
its progress, that he smashes his watch and drowns himself to
get outside of his time.

The interplay of past and present, of the historical and
the contemporaneous, causes all the modern Southern writers
to be unusually sensitive to the nature and workings of time.
Allen Tate's *Ode to the Confederate Dead* closes with one certainty—the omnipresence of time:

> *Leave now*
> *The shut gate and the decomposing wall:*
> *The gentle serpent, green in the mulberry bush,*
> *Riots with his tongue through the hush—*
> *Sentinel of the grave who counts us all!*

The ancient symbol of time, the serpent, stays on, while the
modern watcher at the gate no more than the buried Rebels
may live and die.

Thomas Wolfe's time consciousness is not merely sensitivity,
but close to preoccupation. Everything in the Wolfe novel is
cast against a backdrop of time. At all points along the way,
one is forcibly reminded of that added dimension. Allen Tate
has written that it is the awareness of time that marks the

difference between the true regional writer and the provincial local-color artist. Regionalism, he says, is "that consciousness or that habit of men in a given locality which influences them to certain patterns of thought and conduct handed to them by their ancestors. Regionalism is thus limited in space but not in time." Upon the historical sense to which he falls heir, the regional artist draws in order to see persons historically and to make them think and act along lines of history. In contrast to this, Mr. Tate continues, is the provincial attitude, which

> is limited in time but not in space. When the regional man, in his ignorance, often as extensive and creative ignorance, of the world, extends his own immediate necessities into the world, and assumes that the present moment is unique, he becomes the provincial man. He cuts himself off from the past, and without benefit of the fund of traditional wisdom approaches the simplest problems of life as if nobody had ever heard of them before ("The New Provincialism," 286).

Thus a Howard Fast, let us say, or a Joseph Hergesheimer or a Kathleen Winsor, can read up on the events of the history of a previous era, concoct a plot or a message, decorate it with the historical paraphernalia, in order to give it "color" and "atmosphere," and produce a best seller. Yet an historical sense of time and place and region is hardly involved. To decorate one's own thoughts and problems in antique garb is not to understand the past. Howard Fast's characters live in bygone times, but they are not people of bygone times; they are purely and markedly modern, created to pursue modern goals and make contemporary political points, and only in their artificial historical trappings do they bear any resemblance to the people of the age in which their author has placed them. The genuine historical consciousness, rather, is to be seen in *Absalom, Absalom!*, in *World Enough and Time*, in *The Long Night*. In such novels as these the true and deepest understanding of an earlier time and earlier men is possessed by the author and transmitted to the reader, not on modern terms alone, but independently and for the sake of the historical moment itself. It is then that the universal ele-

ments of time and character, present both then and now, are
best revealed, because it is in the particulars, the day-by-day
issues and habits and beliefs, that the true universals are embodied—not in the false draping of moderns in historical clothes
to provide "atmosphere." Living in his time, Thomas Sutpen
is a nineteenth-century Southerner. His concerns are of the
day, and his values, passions, and actions are directly attuned
to the events of his time. Faulkner makes no point, tells no
story that would not be true and suitable for Sutpen's time.
Yet in the very particularity, in the fidelity to historical time,
the universal pity and terror and love and honor stand out.
Sutpen, riding into the town of Jefferson, is not merely a particular individual coming into a Mississippi town to seek his
fortune. He is the Man on Horseback, the stranger, coming
from nowhere into somewhere. He is the Myth, cast up against
a background of past, present, and future, assuming his depth
in perspective. We see him *then,* not as a mere reflection of
now, but *then* in his own right; and he looms large, for Faulkner saw him that way.

The historical perspective works both ways. We remember
that the image of the Confederates facing the unknown at
Gettysburg illuminates Chick Mallison's hour in *Intruder in
the Dust.* Thomas Wolfe expresses the same notion in *The
Web and the Rock.* George Webber and his friends from North
Carolina visit Richmond for a football game, and walk in the
streets of the former capital of the Confederacy:

> They felt in touch with wonder and with life, they
> felt in touch with magic and with history. They saw the
> state house and they heard the guns. They knew that
> Grant was pounding at the gates of Richmond. They
> knew that Lee was digging in some twenty miles away at
> Petersburg. They knew that Lincoln had come down from
> Washington and was waiting for the news at City Point.
> They knew that Jubal Early was swinging in his saddle at
> the suburbs of Washington. They felt, they knew, they
> had their living hands and hearts upon the living presence
> of these things, and upon a thousand other things as well.
> They knew that they were at the very gateways of the
> fabulous and unknown North, that great trains were here

to do their bidding, that they could rocket in an hour or two into the citadels of gigantic cities. They felt the pulse of sleep, the heartbeats of the sleeping men, the drowsy somnolence and the silken stir of luxury and wealth of lovely women. They felt the power, the presence, and the immanence of all holy and enchanted things, of all joy, all loveliness, and all the beauty and the wonder that the world could offer. They knew, somehow, they had their hands upon it. The triumph of some impending and glorious fulfillment, some impossible possession, some incredible achievement was thrillingly imminent. They knew that it was going to happen—soon. And yet they could not say how or why they knew it.

Not only do George Webber and Thomas Wolfe remember the historical past; they identify themselves with it. It is their past. They are part of the history. Now is then, and then is now; they walk the streets of the capital of the Confederacy in the 1900s, and in the year 1864. They are in Richmond, they face northward, and the enemy is there.

But they *did* go north; that is the point. Almost all the young Southern writers at one time or another packed their suitcases and headed for the cities of the Northeast, toward the center of modernity, toward the new. Some turned around and came back to stay; others remained. No matter; the North, the new, the modern world had come to the South too, and come to stay. All their lives they had been feeling its impact. The trunk-line railroads daily brought a steady stream of newcomers into the South, and an equally steady stream of young Southerners northward to the schools and commercial opportunities in the metropolitan centers of the Northeast. Freight trains rumbled into town with the mass-produced goods of industrial America, the mail cars laden with bundles of the magazines and newspapers published in New York and Philadelphia. Along the right of way the telegraph lines hummed with news. In Richmond, in Charleston, Atlanta, New Orleans, Memphis, Savannah, Nashville, the modern world was received and transmitted to the rural South.

Desirable or undesirable, what happened to the South in the twentieth century now seems inevitable. And the very inevitability has been instrumental in producing the tensions, the dramatic contrasts that helped nourish the amazing outburst of Southern writing in our own times. The history of the twentieth-century South is one of continuity and change, with all the cross-purposes involved therein. It was this interaction that provided the images that so vividly figure in the work of the modern Southern writers. One cannot pick up a novel by a modern Southern writer, or a volume of poetry, without constantly encountering the image of change. Southern literature is dominated by time, the awareness of it, its consequences. Molded by the past, tempered by the present, the literature of the modern South is truly an historical literature. The attitude of the writers who created it was historical, and both the way they saw their task and the way they approached it are deeply grounded in Southern history.

"Real historical understanding," Herbert Butterfield has written, "is not achieved by the subordination of the past to the present, but rather by our making the past our present and attempting to see life with the eyes of another century than our own" (*The Whig Interpretation of History,* 1951, 16). Born as they were into one kind of world, and growing up as that world was swiftly changing into another, the Southern writers of the twentieth century were gifted with the perspective to achieve just such an understanding. What they did with it is a matter of record. That the history of the South gave it to them seems clear.

THE SOUTHERN TEMPER

BY ROBERT B. HEILMAN

The Southern temper is marked by the coincidence of a sense of the concrete, a sense of the elemental, a sense of the ornamental, a sense of the representative, and a sense of totality. No one of these endowments is unshared; but their concurrency is not frequent. This concurrency is *a* condition of major art and mature thought. The endowments, like most endowments, are not possessed in entire freedom, without price. If you buy an endowment, you don't buy something else. To live with an endowment runs risks, and even the concurrency of several endowments does not guarantee a funding of the counter-deficiency which may accompany the possession of any single one.

The Southern temper is not the temper of all Southerners, who, despite the predeterminations of Northerners from Portland, Maine, to Portland, Oregon, are as various as dwellers in other regions. The South generally—the politico-economic-social South, the problem South, the South in need of precept and reprimand—is not my business. It is after all so much like so much of the rest of the country that there is not much to say. The temper I will try to describe is that of certain novelists, poets, and critics who have now, for some twenty or twenty-five years, been at least in the corner of the literate public's eye.

The sense of the concrete, as an attribute of the fiction writer, is so emphatically apparent in Faulkner, Warren, and Wolfe, so subtly and variously apparent in Porter, Welty, and Gordon, and so flamboyantly so in someone like Capote (who hardly belongs here at all) that everybody knows it's there. It is there, too, in the poetry of Ransom, Tate, and Warren. In fact, the lesson that fiction and poetry must be grounded in the sensory world, in the dramatic situation, has been learned very thoroughly in our day; everybody—even the students in writing courses whose goal is an abstraction, the omnipurchasing formula—knows how to go out and record the broken eggshells on the pavement, the smell of armpits and violets, the feel of chewing gum, the sound and fury, the synesthetic shocks. Too many experts in sensography do not know what to do with their bursting haul, for they have not inherited or been provided with an adequate way of thinking about it or with it, and hence are likely to stop short with a record as lush as a seed catalogue, as miscellaneously hard as hoofs on concrete, and as variously pungent as a city market toward the end of the day. In using but not being buried in audio-visual aids, as we shall see, the Southerners are better off.

In criticism, the Southern sense of the concrete takes the form of a preoccupation with the individual work and the precise means by which its author goes about his business. Eliot, Richards, and Empson were predecessors in this critical mode; in America, Burke has long been working in it; and many successors have learned it, even to providing, at times, an embarrassment of explicatory riches. But in neither country is there any other group which, whatever its differences in opinion, can, because of its common background and its shared allegiances, be thought of as a group and which has so much sheer talent in all its parts as Ransom, Tate, Brooks, and Warren. Instinctively they move always to the individual poem; in answering challenges they incline not to linger in the realm of theory as such but to hurry on to the exemplary case. The concretist method extends over into their textbooks and is perhaps more conspicuous there than anywhere else. In the vast influence of these textbooks, imitated almost as widely as they are used (an influence gloomily and often suspiciously complained of), we see the spontaneous welcome of a method of literary study which has put adequate substance where not enough of it had been before. The critical analysis of concrete works by first-rate minds has been the chief influence in getting literary study out of the doldrums of the first three decades of the century, in giving it intellectual respectability, and in making it as attractive to gifted students as physics, mathematics, and medicine. The older schools of literary study gravely lacked intellectual distinction; the neo-humanists, while at least they did offer the excitement of ideas and therefore some maturity of appeal, were deficient in the reading of the concrete work; but the literary historians, interested neither in ideas nor in the concrete work, lavished an essentially clerical perseverance and ingenuity upon matters in the main external to literature. As students of literature, they too often chose the realm of the "pseudo concrete."

In one direction the more recent type of literary study, to which the chief impetus in this country has been given by Southerners, has tended to create a new order of teacher-critics; in another direction it has tended to create—a fact not yet noted, I believe—a more competent general reader. In this respect these critics, sometimes called "reactionary," have done a considerable service to democracy. The older historical mode of study had little to offer the general reader except occasional dashes of extracurricular enthusiasm but of its nature was concerned largely with training a rather narrow professional class —a technocracy of the humanities. Often the literature was forgotten entirely, with serious loss to the community.

The extraordinary competence in dealing with the concrete work is not matched at the level of theory; on the whole I suspect—and this may seem disputable—that Southern critics have not found the most effective theoretical formulations for their insights. Perhaps I should say "have not *yet* found"; or perhaps they have a deep suspiciousness of abstraction which inhibits the formulatory aspect of thought. In contrast with their enormous influence in focusing attention upon the individual work and its organic relations and in gaining adherents for the single theoretical position implied in their practice— namely, that the individual work and its structure are the ultimate concern of literary study—the Southerners have had relatively little influence in other matters of theory: concepts of genre, stylistic and structural modes, etc. This is perhaps less true of Tate, though his intellectual impact is more marked in nonliterary matters. The Southerners have broken trail for Wellek and Warren, and for some very effective generalizations by Wimsatt. But in the specifications of literary form and function, in the extension of theory into new domains and problems, they have been much less influential, say, than Burke. Yet the true counterpoint to the Southerners is not Burke but the Chicagoans, elaborating dogmatic theory, providing a valuable center of speculation but living predeterminedly, monastically, away from the concrete work, remaining therefore almost without influence, seeming content to issue caveats and Everlasting No's and to ambush those who are affirming the living literature and enlarging its status. If their peculiarly arid rationalist plateau could be irrigated by a fresh flow of the literary works themselves, freely submitted to and spontaneously experienced, they might find a more fruitful role than that of erecting such inexorable proofs and securing so little conviction. In their high abstractionism they are at the opposite extreme from the "pseudo concretism" of the old-line scholars.

In their social criticism the Southerners are led, by their sense of the concrete, to suspect the fashionable abstraction, the clichés and slogans, which to the unperceiving may seem the very embodiment of truth but which on inspection are found to ignore many realities of the actual human being. Progress? The concrete evidence of the human being is that he does not change much, that he may actually be harmed by the material phenomena usually implied by *progress,* and that in any case his liability to moral difficulty remains constant. The mechanized life? The concrete evidence is that man is up to it only within limits, that its exactions are more damaging than those of a slower and more laborious mode of life, that he needs regular work in an individualized context, and that few human beings are capable of making leisure fruitful rather than destructive. Political utopias? Man is perfectly capable of making certain improvements in social and political order, but to assume that the millennium is here or will ever come is to ignore the concrete facts of the nature of man. In such realizations the Southerners are by no means alone. Yet it is worth while rehearsing such points, though they are neither unique nor unfamiliar, to suggest the relationship between the creative writing, the criticism, and the social thought, and to call attention to the extreme concreteness of the regionalist and agrarian aspects of Southern thought, which have been felt to be very unfashionable and "unpractical." What about the American ideal of the "practical"? May not practicality itself be, paradoxically, an abstraction from reality—that is, another instance of the "pseudo concrete"? This is certainly what is implied in Warren's persistent concern, from his own fiction to his essay on Conrad, with the problem of the "idea" (or even the "illusion")—the ideal or meaning or value which establishes the quality of the deed or "redeems" it. In terms of man's need for spiritual grounding we have "the idea as concrete." This rejection of a moral positivism implies a similar objection to philosophical positivism as another mode of addiction to the "pseudo concrete." But that attitude, which is expressed recurrently by Tate, carries us into another aspect of the Southern temper, with which we must deal later.

The sense of the elemental and the sense of the ornamental are roughly complementary phases of the Southern temper—complementary at least to the extent that in our historical context an awareness of the elements is likely to lead to a rejection of ornament, and a devotion to ornament may make the elements seem unacknowledgeable. Fifty years ago, of course, ornament was in the lead, whereas now—not always without self-deception—we tender greater devotion to the elements. In architecture the shift from Victorian Gothic to "modern," with its utilitarian aesthetics, is one symbol of the change in emphasis. But despite our almost professionally anti-Victorian pursuit of the elemental, we are likely to be caused considerable discomfort by the amount of violence in Faulkner and Warren, by their sense of the furious drives that contort and distort men, by the crazy transformations of personality in people under stress, by the unornamented varieties of sex, by all the passions unamenable to sentimentalizing diminuendo. And equally, we should add, by the juxtaposing of life and death in Porter, the insistent awareness of death in Porter and Gordon, and by a certain mystery that accompanies the closest factuality in Elizabeth Madox Roberts and Welty. These are only for the mature. For the others, there will be satisfaction with Wolfe, with whom the elemental is not very much more than an orchestral wind soughing through the pines with a kind of calculated unhappiness (there are occasional such accents in Randall Jarrell, too)—an enchanting tune for young men, who thus, with little imaginative commitment or risk, are permitted to enjoy the sensation of being torn by force and sorrow. For the others, also, there is Caldwell, who does not disturb but reassures by selecting materials which elevate almost any reader to an Olympian eminence. But his appropriate marriage of the libidinous and the farcical reduces the elemental to the elementary. Another way of saying this is that he is not sufficiently concrete; just as one may be concrete without being elemental—as in the standard "realistic" novel, or in the work of a satirist like Mary McCarthy—so one may strive for the elements and end in an abstraction: with Caldwell, lust is almost a paradigm or an idea, withdrawn from a concrete human complexness. For these others, who like the elements easy, there will be difficulty in the conception of man as linked to nature, in Ransom's idea that man must make peace with nature. This kind of elementalism is hardly welcome to an age given to two other forms of naturalism—the literary sort, in which man is a victim of nature and nature-like forces and can feel sorry for himself; and the scientific sort, in which man is a victor over nature and can feel proud of himself. The man of the age who may be puzzled by Ransom may find it easier going with Hemingway, who is inclined to view nature as conquerable, and who, furthermore, for all of his feeling for death and deathliness, is hampered—and not quite willingly—by a fastidiousness that constricts his presentation of the elemental.

As a society we oscillate uneasily between bareness and overstuffed elegance; Hollywood plays it stark one minute, lush the next. Either extreme is hostile to true grace, social or spiritual. If we are uncomfortable with the elemental, we also shy at the true ornament, that of manner and mind (though we are rather tolerant of the spurious kinds). For that reason, the Southern sense of both is distinctive. To speak of the Southern sense of the ornamental is in one way rather startling, for the literary criticism of Southerners has been marked by the severity of its functionalism (with some exceptions, perhaps, for Ransom); yet I am by no means sure that the formal perfection which is the implied standard of judgment in many of Southerners' literary analyses is not itself the essence of ornament. For by ornament I do not mean superfluous or distracting embellishment; rather I mean non-utilitarian values; whatever comes from the feeling for rhythm, the sense of the incantatory, the awareness of style as integral in all kinds of communication; the intangible goods that lie beyond necessity; grace. A political reflection of the sense of the ornamental is "Southern oratory"—in most of its present manifestations debased, parodistic, really pseudo-ornamental. A social reflection is "Southern manners," a reality which has virtually been blotted out by promotional facsimiles—the unhappy fate of any virtue that is popularized and made the object of public self-congratulation. Something more than a social reflection appears in contemporary Southerners' assertions of the grace of ante-bellum life; the very assertion attests to the sense of which I speak. These assertions, which are a way of affirming a value, raise an important issue, for hostile critics charge that the social cost of the achievement was prohibitive. Though we may acknowledge that the cost was too high, we must also face the counter-problem of the cost of doing without the value—a problem of which the Southerners at least serve to remind us. To return to literature: the critical manner of the Southerners, even in vigorous controversy, is on the whole urbane—indeed, strikingly so, compared with such others as the scholarly cumbersome style, the *Partisan* truculent, and the Chicago opaque. The sense of nuance, refinement, the special communication by tone and color, are conspicuously acute. Finally, the sense of ornament appears in the rhetorical bent of Warren and Faulkner—not that with either of them style itself is a subject, amenable to decorative arrangement on the surface of another subject (characters, ideas, etc.), but that there is a special awareness of the verbal medium, a disposition to elaborate and amplify as a fundamental mode of communication, a willingness to utilize the rich and the rhythmical, an instinctive exploration of the stylistic instrument to the ultimate point at which one senses something of the supererogatory but not yet the excessive or obtrusive. At least in its application to Faulkner, this statement will run into objections. But even in most cases where Faulkner apparently lays himself open to the charge of mannerism or sheer lack of control I believe it demonstrable that his main devices—length of sentence and frequency of parenthesis—are meaningful as formal equivalents of a central imaginative impulse: to view experience as inclusively as possible, to mold-together-into-one, to secure a godlike view of present and past as one. But this brings us to a point for which we are not yet ready: the Southern sense of totality.

If the sense of the ornamental and the sense of the elemental at least in part complement each other, so the sense of the concrete and the sense of the representative may interact fruitfully. To have, as a writer, a sense of the concrete but not a sense of the representative is to exemplify in one way the modern dilemma—to have the concrete world, apparently controlled, more or less at one's finger tips, and not to know what it means. To have a sense of the representative alone is to be in danger of falling into hollow allegory. The Southerners, we have seen, always cling to the concrete—in fiction and poetry, in literary and social criticism—but they are not chained to the concrete. The best fictional characters are always individuals, but something more than individuals too: Willie Stark is Willie Stark, but his career adumbrates a philosophical issue; the Snopeses are so representative as to have become a byword; in Welty's work we see Everyman as salesman, in Gordon's as sportsman, in Porter's as a soul lost in the currents of time. Warren and Faulkner both dig into the past, not for the past's sake, but because of a sense of the immanence of past in present, and for the sake of finding or creating tales of mythic value. It is presumably for some success in this endeavor that the Southerners have won a substantial audience. They certainly cannot appeal either to hunters of the trivial exotic or to the devotees of the stereotype or "pseudo representative"— that product of an imagination weak at the general or universal (and, for that matter, at the concrete too). Under sense of the representative we can include Warren's preoccupation with the "idea"—a significant reaction against American anti-Platonism. Again, if Southern criticism is marked by its devotion to the concrete work and to the concrete structural elements, it is equally marked by a sensitivity to the symbolic, to the work as symbolic of the writer, or, more particularly, to the meanings and values symbolically present. It boldly assumes as axiomatic the symbolic quality of all works, and finds in the explication of the symbolic content a basic means of distinguishing the trivial and the important. And to give one final instance of the sense of the representative, this one from the social criticism: if regionalism is on the one hand marked by a sense of the concrete necessities of immediate living and has emphasized the specificities of local place and manner, it is also true that regionalism has been said to provide a sound base for internationalism. From this point of view regionalism has not been a vain separatism or a sterile cult of uniqueness, but at once a rejection of the abstract "differentness" implied by nationalism and a search for a mode of embodying the representative human values on which both individual life and a sound internationalism must rest.

Finally, the sense of totality: it is a sense of time, of the extent of human need and possibility, of world and of spirit. It appears in Faulkner's style; in the critical focusing on the organic whole; in the anti-nominalism which has been most explicitly formulated by Richard Weaver; in Tate's emphasis on mythic or non-scientific values; in the conjunction, in numerous pieces of fiction, of violence and spiritual awareness (a conjunction disturbing to readers who are used to taking one part of the whole at a time); in the penumbra of mystery —a mystery to be accepted, not solved—always bordering the clean light of Welty's characters and scenes; in the nostalgia, so frequent in Porter, for the reality felt behind the stage of action; in the questioning of nostrum and panaceas which can exist only by treating a part of human truth as if it were the whole; in suspecting our inclination to separate the present from all the rest of time, to exhaust all devotion in the religion of humanity, and to consider scientific inquiry as the only avenue to truth.

Whereas Hemingway's most reliable talent is that for seizing upon the lyric moment, Warren's enveloping mind can hardly go in short stories but needs all the room to be found in the novel (or the long poem); Faulkner is impelled to invent whole sagas; Gordon's stories expand into the myth of a recurrent character. In their instinct for inclusiveness, these and others, in both fiction and social criticism, dig into and rely upon the past. For the past is in the present; we do not live alone in time, thrust into eminence, and into finality, by what went before, servile and unentangling. With their sense of the whole, the Southerners keep reminding us that we are not altogether free agents in the here and now, and that the past is part master. The past also provides allegiance and perspective—not as an object of sentimental devotion but as a storehouse of values which may be seen in perspective and at the same time may permit an entirely necessary perspective on our own times. Through a sense of the past we may escape provincialism in time, which is one mark of the failure of a sense of totality.

With a comparable unwillingness to be uncritically content inside fashionable limits, the Southerners apparently find the religion of humanity inadequate. Not that any of them do not value the human; the question is whether the obligation to be humane can be secured by a secular religion, and whether humanity alone can adequately engage the religious imagination. Inclined to question whether suffering is totally eliminatable or univocally evil, the Southerners are most aware that, as Tate has put it, man is incurably religious and that the critical problem is not one of skeptically analyzing the religious impulse or of thinking as if religion did not exist for a mature individual and culture, but of distinguishing the real thing and the surrogates. They have a large enough sense of reality not to exclude all enlightenment that is not laboratory-tested. For them, totality is more than the sum of the sensory and the rational. The invention of gods is a mark, not of a passion for unreality, but of a high sense of reality; is not a regrettable flight from science, but perhaps a closer approach to the problem of being. The Southerners utilize and invoke reason no less than, let us say, any follower of John Dewey; but also they suspect an excessive rationalism which mistakes the ailerons for the power plant and fosters the illusion that all non-rationalities have been, or can be, discarded.

This kind of evidence of the sense of totality is plain enough in Southern criticism and fiction (though the latter, as yet, has difficulty in finding a dramatic form for the sense). I am inclined to add that the whole man is really not very fashionable right now, and that the sense of totality is likely to get one into disrepute as a kind of willful and fanciful archaist, for we are supposed to have got man properly trimmed down to a true, i.e., naturalistic, dimension. Aside from this intellec-

tual majority pressure, there is another difficulty in that institutions that historically stand for the sense of totality have
suffered from loss of belief in their role and from an addiction
to organizational politics, so that to be believed to be unre-
servedly *en rapport* with them may lead to misconceptions of
one's role. But the Southerners have been content to take their
chances, with very little effort at self-protection by evasive
movement.

The Southerners, indeed, have a surprisingly "liberal" com-
plexion; they are in the classical American tradition of "protest." Their agrarianism could be read as a protest against
both capitalist giantism and Marxism, their regionalism as a
protest against abstract nationalism and uniformitarianism,
their essential critical habits as a protest against the relativist
antiquarianism of literary study (their fondness for "paradox"
a protest against an exaggerated view of the straightforward-
ness of literature; for symbolism, a protest against the hamper-
ing limitations of realism, which had assumed a normative
role). And their sense of totality, we have seen, leads to overt
or implied protests against the restrictions of secular rationalism. There is, of course, protest and protest. In its most familiar manifestations, protest is topical; a social or political injustice brings it forth, often in a historical context that may
require great bravery and sacrifice of the protestant—and is
alleviated. Yet this context may so mold the style of the
liberal protestantism that it may go on like a habit, the old
slogans becoming platitudes, the old courage replaced by flu-
ency and complacency, the old vitality declining into sheer
forgetfulness of the calendar. Then there is another protest,
the protest exemplified by the Southerners—what I should call
a radical protestantism, because it is rooted in the sense of
totality. It is a philosophical protest against lack of wholeness,
against exclusions that restrict human potentiality, against the
naturalist closure of other avenues to wisdom. Though it is
nowadays a minority operation, we may perhaps risk calling
it, according to its actual nature, catholic. I suspect—if I may
be forgiven the word play—that the Southerner who becomes
Catholic will remain protestant in temper, just as Southern
protestantism will be catholic in tone.

I want to re-emphasize my earlier statement that it is the

strength and the *combination* of the qualities enumerated that make the Southern temper distinctive. No trait is distinctively Southern, of course, and all of them may be found to some extent in other American literature and thought, i.e., in the American temper. As a people we doubtless have a considerable sense for the concrete, yet we often take up with abstractions that will not bear much critical inspection—e.g., freedom as an absolute. We like to be at once "down to earth" and up to the amenities, but we are perhaps too Victorian to feel at ease with the elemental, and too anti-Victorian to trust the ornamental. As for a sense of the representative: we have produced Hawthorne and Melville and James, though it is only lately that we have begun to estimate them seriously; and we are inclined to take a rather particularistic view of ourselves. We have enjoyed special immunities, and they tend to seem an inalienable grace. And though we like the phrase "the whole man," it is perhaps the sense of totality which is least widely possessed among us. On the philosophical side, it is our bent to take the naturalist part for the whole; and since those who would argue for a larger view seem contrary, out of line, unwilling to "advance" with the rest, and even prone to the last sin against the times—invoking the past—we are honestly ready to regard them as in headlong retreat. This view must often have tried the Southern temper, and have seemed to invite a reply in the words of Agatha in *Family Reunion:*

> *In a world of fugitives*
> *The person taking the opposite direction*
> *Will appear to run away.*

THE SENSE OF PLACE

BY FREDERICK J. HOFFMAN

I

There is some justice in the suggestion that much modern literature is a literature without place, one that does not identify itself with a specific source. Partly this is a result of much exploration of universals, or of the fragments of universals. Human tensions are not necessarily associated with points on the map; in fact, they are often a consequence of the deprivation of place. Many crucial scenes in modern literature depend for their importance upon stereotype; details are not specifically related to geography but rather deny its function. The tendency is away from specificity, in the direction of archetypical resemblance. The value of a personality diminishes as the virtues of his identity blur; he moves toward anonymity. A scene also suffers loss of identity, as its spatial values become more and more isolated from cultural associations. Much of the psychic imbalance described in modern literature occurs in an abstracted setting; it is not identified with a place, a culture, or a family. There are objects, and they are spatially situated, but they do not suggest either a place or a history.*

The values of place in literature (as distinguished from *scene*, which is merely unindividualized space) come from its being fixed but also associated with neighboring spaces that share a history, some communicable tradition and idiom, according to which a personality can be identified. The interrelationship of personal and cultural history provides for a balance in human events that enhances meaning and locates

* The most incisive literary portrayal of this failure occurs in Allen Tate's *Ode to the Confederate Dead,* discussed elsewhere in this volume.

it. Place is indispensable to scene in any literature that is more than merely abstract. Narrowly defined, a scene is merely a location in which certain things happen. The nature of objects arranged in a scene tells something about the quality of the acts; they depend indispensably upon their relation to place for any values that may exist beyond their distribution in space. The imagination is privileged to function in terms of scene, but in this role its opportunities are limited. It is only when a scene is identified with place that the full powers of the literary imagination can be challenged and used.

Eudora Welty has shrewdly defined the role of place in literature; its function is primarily to attach precise local values to feeling.

Place in fiction is the named, identified, concrete, exact and exacting, and therefore credible, gathering-spot of all that has been felt, is about to be experienced, in the novel's progress. Location pertains to feeling; feeling profoundly pertains to place; place in history partakes of feeling, as feeling about history partakes of place (*South Atlantic Quarterly*, LV [1956], 62).

These values are what precisely distinguish place from scene. It is really a question of types of knowledge and kinds of emotional commitment. In any truly successful literary experience, a place is endowed both with specificity of detail and a finely drawn line of association with time. The quality of a place inevitably derives from its existence in time; and as persons inhabit a place, they provide meaningful elaborations upon its intrinsic nature. Place may therefore be defined as the present condition of a scene that is modified through its having been inhabited in time. The "eccentricities" of a scene are given it by such habituation; they are also the particulars of a scene, and when they suggest a shared experience, they move into patterns of history.

The great hazards of the literary evocations of place are the risks taken in overstressing emotional values, of distorting their intrinsic qualities, or of isolating them from the geographical or historical patterns that help to contain them. An orderly progress from scene to place in literature involves a steady accretion of associative meanings; the particulars enlarge into generalities while retaining their identity as particulars. Thus a place metaphor is essentially a space image enlarged. Such a metaphor may be used—as Miss Welty uses it in *A Still Moment*—to suggest many implicit variants of meaning; it becomes a localized "morality image" in this case. The most successful developments of place in literature occur when the rhythms of time and generation are shrewdly and acutely used, to give a pattern or design to a place that its merely static detail scarcely suggests.

Places are redefined as *regions* when the characteristics of their geography and history maintain a surviving consistency of manner, despite local dissimilarities. This consistency is partly a matter of the weather; or, to put it another way, the weather helps to define a pattern of behavior, makes a manner of behaving possible or necessary. The rhythms of seasonal change, the relative persistence of degrees of heat or cold, the effect of long periods of either upon the density or thinness of the landscape—these are all determinants of a regional quality, to set off a place qualitatively from neighboring regions.

In *The Comedian As the Letter C* and elsewhere, Wallace Stevens has defined the extremes of North and South as excesses of order and excesses of natural abundance. In the one case, nature is sparse and intellectual mastery of it seems speciously easy; in the other, there is so great a profusion of natural objects that one is tempted to surrender to them, to give up trying to impose restraints. The implications for a social or regional way of life are obvious enough: where there are few natural objects, the mind moves quickly to impose an abstracting order; one is more likely, in a Southern landscape, to measure life close to the natural quality and pace of objects' growth. Thus order is more important in one kind of world, and natural lines of growth and being dominate in the other. One must account for objects where there are so many, and adjust to their peculiarities of growth and manner. One may generalize further, to suggest that a Southern landscape will perhaps have a more intimate history—that is, that it will account for many more particulars of being; and that, once a reasonable order of living is found, it will be valued more highly for its accommodation to life than for its demonstration of abstract principle.

The South as a region has these important distinguishing features: it is rich in natural detail; its pace is slow and close to the rhythms of natural sequences; it tends to develop historically in a slow accession of patterns which accommodate to the atmospheric and biological qualities of setting; it generates loyalties to place that are much more highly emotionally charged than is any dedication to ideas; finally, its rhythm of social motion is passive rather than active. All these characteristics tend to encourage a conviction, one that gradually changes into a belief, that human processes and natural rhythms are closely associated and that the passing of time has in itself the generative function of shaping and solidifying tradition. Southern tradition tends therefore to remain static, to be self-protective, and to encourage fierce loyalties to its condition of being.

II

This is perhaps the major reason why history plays so large a role in Southern literature. Even when there is no explicit reference to its history, the Southern character is assumed in terms of a sectional history. The Civil War is of course crucial, but it is significant as a *defeat,* as a war—followed by a bitter thirty-year struggle against change—that forever fixed the value of a *status quo ante* and heightened the desirability of maintaining a devotion to what was imagined to be precious and inviolable. On one level, the Civil War enforced the Southerner's love of place by strengthening—perhaps even, in a sense, creating—platitudes of loyalty to it. Vicissitudes of regional difference became fixed emotional habits. Southern literature has frequently analyzed these cultural platitudes, chiefly in the description of mob violations of human proprieties. Beyond these, there is an abundance of place metaphors which, mainly in consequence of the psychological impact of defeat, emphasize the virtues of scene, atmosphere, climate, and landscape. The Southern scene is heavily charged with the task of communicating a special quality of atmosphere.

Far more important than any of these is the literary analysis of the South's psychological and symbolic inheritance. We may describe this as the "burden of the past." In large part, the errors and enormities of Reconstruction years are responsible for the overemphasis upon the Southerner's unique, independent, special fate and responsibility. As W. J. Cash put it, the postwar Yankee failed dismally in his effort to change the Southerner's view of himself.

And so far from having reconstructed the Southern mind in the large and in its essential character, it was this Yankee's fate to have strengthened it almost beyond reckoning, and to have made it one of the most solidly established, one of the least *reconstructible* ever developed (*The Mind of the South,* 1941, 107).

Instead of forcing an awareness of a universal moral guilt, the Reconstructionist encouraged the Southerner to consider the moral "burden" of his past as a special problem, quite independent of a priori considerations of morality, a unique and a serious responsibility. The Southerner has therefore reminded himself of his past, of its imagined glory and its inherited obligation. There is a great moral intensity in much of modern Southern literature, but it is neither the complex inner analysis that one sees in the New England literature of the nineteenth century nor the post-Calvinist rebelliousness of modern Midwestern writing. In many respects it suggests an attempt to purify the individual's sense of moral guilt by forcing an intolerable regional burden upon a single representative character.

It is perhaps unnecessary to say that this moral quality is not literary nostalgia. In Faulkner's analysis of the Southern mind, for example, he condemns as the worst of sins that of cultural stasis, symbolized in those "stubborn back-looking ghosts" that Quentin Compson imagines as he listens to Rosa Coldfield's recital of a hateful past (*Absalom, Absalom!*). Faulkner's brilliant analyses of the burden of the past emphasize again and again the risks of hardening any emotion with respect to history. They are at once a criticism of Southern truculence and of superficial Northern pieties.

III

It is impossible to speak of the South as place without discussing it as a region possessing a uniquely clear and responsible memory of its past. A scene becomes a vividly identifiable place when it is shown to have a culture that has experienced time. The psychological consequences of the Southern endurance in time have led to the use of the South as a pattern, an economy that has become a "way of life." Much is made in Southern literature of the ceremony of living and of the fact that living acquires certain habitudes if it persists evenly in time. A crucial theme in modern Southern literature is the contrast between the formal and the formless life. The man of boundless but empty energy, the directionless sensibility, seems to be either a Northerner or a "modern" phenomenon. The forms are derived from habits of family living through predictable generations, and from the symbolic values implicit in inherited and inheritable particulars. It is difficult at times to determine if the novelist wants us to believe in any one cause of breakdown; often, as in the figure of George Posey in Allen Tate's *The Fathers*, it seems almost as though the collapse of forms were a matter of history itself, as though no traditional strength could have withstood the drive toward "modernity" and the loss of formal values consequent upon its arrival. Perhaps the interpretation suggested in Faulkner's works most adequately explains this. The untraditional man here forces a practical result outside time and tradition and thus violates all formal means of human containment. But Faulkner is remarkably *unhistorical* in his analysis of the past; his indictment of the moral evil in man is essentially an attack upon moral errors that occurred at the beginning of white Southern history.

Often in modern Southern literature the change from the "Old South" to modern times is dramatized in terms of a character who is unemotional, unattached, and amoral. The range of characterization is great, from Margaret Mitchell's Rhett Butler to Faulkner's Flem Snopes. *Gone With the Wind* is, in fact, the simplest and most superficial of historical equations; Butler, Scarlett O'Hara, and Ashley Wilkes provide the most obvious of speculations upon the weakness of the Southern historical metaphor. In each case—Faulkner, Tate, Miss Mitchell, Caroline Gordon—inner weakness conspires with external forces to threaten the center of the metaphor. Nevertheless, the place metaphor persists as a symbol of a value regionally preserved. It is always a place in which—as a consequence of nature's bounty, human strength and persistence, and a strong sense of loyalty to tradition—humanity is a concern, and its formal, even ceremonial, values are treasured. Implicitly at least, often quite openly, this metaphor is threatened by an inhuman, impersonal agent which exploits and destroys nature without love of it or respect for the ceremonies of man's living with it. Faulkner speaks powerfully against these forces, nowhere more vehemently than in *The Bear*, where he describes the "doomed wilderness whose edges were being constantly and punily gnawed at by men with plows and axes who feared it because it was wilderness . . ." (*Go Down, Moses*).

IV

Substantially, the moral implications of these several fictions have to do with the problem of using space. Once again it is a question of the difference between Northern sparseness and Southern abundance of natural imagery. Those Southern novels which speak historically of the move westward (Caroline Gordon's *Green Centuries* and Elizabeth Madox Roberts' *The Great Meadow*, among them) describe the lure of rich lands, unexploited and ready for human habitation. But the moral relationship of man to nature is also closely emphasized here. The figure of Daniel Boone serves both Miss Gordon's and Miss Roberts' novels as a symbol of human discretion and an unspoken code of manners. Part One of *Green Centuries* has as its epigraph this statement of Boone's: "I think it time to remove when I can no longer fall a tree for fuel so that its top will lie within a few yards of my cabin." Miss Gordon's historical novels define the progress of a fine balance of man and nature—the gradual and natural evolution of families, houses, estates, and communities. In this case, the place has achieved its status as metaphor in the literature of the South by a finely balanced movement into and through nature, which is not a "temple" so much as a dwelling place.

This metaphor—of the land as a place on which one may respectfully and sensibly live—is linked to the power of the human mind, an outward expression of self-identity. This metaphor strongly informs the writings of Elizabeth Madox Roberts. For the heroine of *The Great Meadow* the acts of life and the rhythms of nature had instinctively sought out and achieved a rapport, which is central to her conception of place.

> The curing of the meat filled the late autumn, work going forward all day in the frosty air, and the wind washed over their bodies in a fine subtle spray. For many weeks none had come from the outside. The dusk would fall and the nights were long. There were long evenings by the fireside in the new house.

History is here seen as a manner in which men contain themselves, within a necessary, functional architecture and routine. Similarly, Ellen Chesser in the fine novel, *The Time of Man*, endures all human vicissitudes in the confidence that she is situated in space and that there is a place for her uniquely in it:

> There a deep sense of eternal and changeless well-being suffused the dark, a great quiet structure reported of itself, and sometimes out of this wide edifice, harmonious and many-winged, floating back into blessed vapors, released from all need or obligation to visible form, a sweet quiet voice would arise, leisured and backward-floating, saying with all finality, "Here I am."

The history of the Southern place is essentially one of human agreements made with nature. Miss Roberts' heroines are often too awkwardly and too easily moved by a backwoods idealism, though she atones for these excesses by her careful and precise portrayal of folk identities. Throughout the Southern literary evocations of the Southern past, this metaphor of a place inhabited, worked, and loved, dominates. Its opposite is the place destroyed, ignored, or despised. The evil of man's acts is most frequently described in terms of the destruction of place images—or, as in Faulkner's *Intruder in the Dust*, the construction of places not worthy of their setting. Sometimes the decline of the human world is shown in terms of the reduction of the space itself. The very complex space metaphor of Faulkner's *The Sound and the Fury* describes for us a steady diminishing of the Compson world during the thirty years of the novel, until in Part Four one really sees only the kitchen of the house where the only fully living person, Dilsey, works. This very intense moral judgment is seen at work in other Southern novels as well. The disastrous collapse of human dignity is described in William Styron's *Lie Down in Darkness*, in a series of images in which space values have been all but eliminated. Peyton Loftis, whose suicide reminds us in some ways of Quentin Compson's, is first inadvertently buried in Potter's Field off Manhattan; then her body is rescued and shipped to her father's home in Virginia, the survivors suffering one agony after another on the funeral journey. The ignominy of death repeats the indignity of her life. While this novel cannot be called "Southern" in its use of setting, its central concern is the loss of that rapport that has been celebrated or defended in other novels of its place and time.

V

The importance of place in Southern literature begins with the image, the particular of the Southern scene, a quality of atmosphere or a simple human detail. Its specific Southern quality may be simply an eccentricity of genre; it may be and frequently is a detail of idiom or manner which used to be labeled "local color." Place builds out from it; it is made up of a cluster, or a mosaic, or an integrated succession, of images. The significance of place argues some accepted history or co-ordinated memory which is attacked, defended, or maligned (it is never ignored, or merely set aside). History within an established set of spatial circumstances moves easily into local culture, or tradition. Relationships of class or race or peoples have their own ways of modifying memory or adjusting to historical change.

The most eloquent of Southern "place" fictions are quite clearly fixed in "pure" images of setting. They begin there, but they don't remain there. How they begin, and with what precision of meaning they will ultimately be used, is a matter of the knowledge and love of place. As Miss Welty has said, the quality of a described place is an index of the precision of feeling. Her work is a remarkable testimony of the literary significance of place. Much more than Miss Mitchell's Georgia (which never stands still) or Mrs. Rawlings' Florida (which rarely moves), her delta country clearly establishes its meaning in the rich detail which is its substance. The detail affronts the senses from the very beginning; in *Delta Wedding*, as Laura approaches the community of Fairchilds, Miss Welty says, "The land was perfectly flat and level but it shimmered like the wing of a lighted dragonfly. It seemed strummed, as though it were an instrument and something had touched it." The landscape quickly assumes a particular quality; it "fills in." There is a succession of images, with or without personal reference, each of them adding some minor poetic quality to the scene. Before the day has concluded, the scene has become a place, the place has acquired a character, the character, an implicit history. It is a remarkably unified place; everybody "was kin." Both the strength and weakness of Fairchilds rest upon that fact, and the conflict that builds the narration is a commentary upon it.

Delta Wedding is a superb illustration of literary sensibility informing place, and being informed by it. The progress is in terms of discrete entities, which yield slowly to formal orders and ultimately give way to a major commentary upon certain universal human qualities. Miss Welty has fully realized her "place"—as, in quite a different sense, Faulkner "realizes" the area not too far to the north of it; as, indeed, Thomas Wolfe vividly represents the Asheville of his youth, at least in *Look Homeward, Angel*. Certain special qualities of place are sometimes developed thematically, to some advantage. The mountains that "rimmed" Altamont acquire a special value in the economy of Eugene Gant's romantic disposition; they come eventually to symbolize the containment of what Wolfe calls "the core and desire of dark romanticism." They do not contain so much as frustrate, and the degree of frustration is marked by the excesses of what Eugene's parents do to adjust to their separate conditions.

More specifically, the heat is made an atmospheric quality of the Southern place. It is always present, even if momentarily it may not exist. It is to be endured, but it also often takes over, to dominate the meaning of a place. The atmosphere of Faulkner's "long summer" (*The Hamlet*) mingles with the sound of the cotton gin, to create but one melancholy effect.

> The dry, dust-laden air vibrated steadily to the rapid beat of the engine, though so close were the steam and the air in temperature that no exhaust was visible but merely a thin feverish shimmer of mirage.

In this heat-laden world Faulkner plays out the mock idyll of Ike Snopes and the Houston cow. Frequently the heat atmospherically deceives, as in Lena Grove's slow progress along the road to Jefferson in the beginning of *Light in August*, until suddenly one realizes that it has hung over a setting of violence.

These particulars are not in themselves especially significant of place; it is what they ultimately do, by providing either an incidental *décor* or a thematic substance, that is important. In the end, it is not the heat or the color or the lines of terrain in *Delta Wedding* that are significant, but what they cumulatively and ultimately make of the images of the two houses at Fairchilds: Shellmound, where life flourishes, and Marmion, where it has scarcely entered. Such details—odors, colors, temperatures—play the imagistic supplementary role in Faulkner's *Absalom, Absalom!* They define the moral economy according to which Quentin is finally to appraise the story of Thomas Sutpen and to determine what his attitude toward it will be. Throughout this novel, as well as in Part Two of *The Sound and the Fury*, the nature of his self-judgment is given in terms of atmospheric clashes: the iron, cold New England room clashes with the hot, pine-winy, heavily scented Yoknapatawpha world, bringing him closer to his own act of violent resolution.

There are many Southern novels which offer an abundance of scenic detail, but do not, for all that, use the scene to any great purpose, and often the knowledge of region has to stand almost by and for itself. Marjorie Kinnan Rawlings' Florida "scrub country," for example, is fully evoked in *Cross Creek*,

and in such novels as *South Moon Under, Golden Apples,* and
The Yearling. The last, a great popular success, is an excellent
example of a literature which is full of atmospheric detail,
much of it convincing and instructive, but which tells a story
that is painfully slight and trivial. There is no question of Mrs.
Rawlings' success in communicating the surface of the place:
the difficult, all-but-primitive wilderness, the impact of the
weather (calamities of both drouth and rain), the struggle
to make a livelihood in the face of extraordinary obstacles and
misadventures. All of this convinces the reader that he "has
been there," but he is also asked to accept a narrative line
which—except when it pauses within the scene itself—is childish and superficial.

Du Bose Heyward's fiction is of a quite different quality;
two of his novels, *Porgy* and *Mamba's Daughters,* make the
most of "local color" by portraying Negro life, habit, manner, and speech. However, this raises the risk of allowing the
"quaintness" of dialect and behavior to dominate and put the
reader in the uncomfortable position of condescending to the
novels almost from the start. There is no doubt from the evidence of his books that Heyward knows his characters in the
idiomatic sense; they are "folk" whose rhythms and mannerisms he had experienced at firsthand. The Charleston Negro
life in *Porgy* testifies again and again to a surface accuracy
and honesty. Nevertheless, there is reason for feeling that the
tragedy of the crippled Porgy is a "play-acting" event; one
almost feels that the novel deliberately anticipated the play
Heyward and his wife adapted from it, perhaps even Gershwin's opera, *Porgy and Bess.*

As a novelist, Heyward is too much the white-man master
of ceremonies. The tone of his introductions is slick and artificial; as a result, the specifics of character and dialogue come
almost as a surprise; the reader is scarcely ever more than a
man in an audience, having the particulars of a scene pointed
out to him by a man who has learned his lines and the appropriate folk accents. "In those days," he says by way of
introducing Porgy, the profession of beggary "was one with a
tradition. A man begged, presumably, because he was hungry,
much as a man of more energetic temperament became a
stevedore from the same cause." The same quality shows in

the passages of dialogue, which in itself has a richly phonetic flavor:

". . . Yao; my belly fair ache wid dis Noo Yo'k talk. De fus t'ing dat dem nigger fuhgit is dat dem is nigger. Den deh comes tuh dese decent country mens and fills um full ob talk wut put money in de funeral ondehtakuh pocket." Breathless, she closed her arraignment by bringing a fist the size of a ham down upon the table with such force that her victim leapt from his chair and extended an ingratiating hand toward her.

Hamilton Basso's chronicling of Southern manners bears some resemblance to J. P. Marquand's portrayal of the New England social manner. Frequently the Basso hero is an "intellectual"—a scientist, a professional man, a journalist—who is handicapped by inherited prejudice, economic circumstance, or other difficulties in his effort to achieve self-knowledge or a proper situation in life.

The View from Pompey's Head is Basso's most typical use of the Southern theme; it is at once his most popular and his best book. He "gets at" his subject in a fairly conventional way: an "exiled" Southerner, who had gone to New York for his career, returns on assignment from his law office to the home of his youth and his past. Basso has him work not only for the completion of his mission but, more important, for the clues to his love of the South and the undercurrent of attachment he has always had for the region. Basso neither entirely attacks nor altogether defends the South; he is primarily concerned with setting its virtues against its weaknesses, and the latter are primarily associated with a false pride of ancestry (Southern Shintoism, as the hero had once labeled it).

The novel maneuvers easily through its details of place, heritage, and mannerism. It is "liberal-ethical" in its moral position with respect to the South, and combines a critical with a nostalgic sentiment toward the South Atlantic town of Pompey's Head as a symbol of the South. In his position as rational analyst of Southern view, the hero, Anson Page, describes its "trouble" as the sentimental image of a landscape: "It's a kind of never-never land, everything, everything about it—the moss in the trees, the way the sun sets, the haze on the river and those fogs we get just before dawn . . . it's not real, only there it's real, and so the true reality is somehow lost and nothing seems improbable but the world as it actually is."

This book and, in another way, its successor, though not its sequel, *The Light Infantry Ball,* gives a panoramic view of both space and time; it muses editorially over human passions in a Southern setting. It is slick and rather agreeably obvious in its narrative line (one can easily imagine its having been "run" as a serial publication); but there is little beyond this surface impression. Neither the characters nor the scene gives more than a two-dimensional effect.

The Yearling, Porgy, and *The View from Pompey's Head* illustrate the popular exploitation of the Southern scene. As impressions of that scene, they do not conspicuously succeed: the Negro dialect (painstakingly ever-present) of Heyward's *Porgy;* the rather thin line of narrative concern with juvenile brooding over the maturing of animals in Mrs. Rawlings' *The Yearling;* the rather arbitrary plot strategies of Hamilton Basso's *The View from Pompey's Head.* While they are "South," they scarcely communicate except to a touristic interest in regional differences. When the images of place convincingly group, to suggest ideas and moral substance, when they exist both on the level of independent objects and in terms of a history or a tradition or even a memory of men related to a quality of place in generations of time, they contribute to a literature of place. The intensity of the moral vision that informs them, in terms of a succession of significant human disasters, makes them valuable. Above all, the *sense* of place, which is associated with a reading of the human destiny, defines precisely the meaning, at both the beginning and the conclusion of moral reflection.

Allen Tate, speaking of Emily Dickinson's poetry, finds in it "a tension between abstraction and sensation, in which the two elements may be, of course, distinguished logically, but not really" ("Emily Dickinson," *On the Limits of Poetry,* 1948, 204). He is, of course, applauding her sense of personal involvement with "ideas," but it is above all the specificity of image that charms and not the awesome importance of the idea. In literature, ideas help to define and direct emotions, which have the specific value and quality of their situational and historical conditions. They are thus transmuted into images large and small, varied and simple, which endure, to which loyalties, responsibilities, "burdens" are attached. These literary growths become the cultural history of place.

The "lesson" Katherine Anne Porter's Miranda learns in *Pale Horse, Pale Rider* points up the readjustments to place necessary from generation to generation. She at first acknowledges place and tradition in terms of souvenirs treasured by her grandmother. The past is threatened by evidences of its decay; Miranda is disabused of the past's value by the presence of near-ghosts. Yet, in a revised context, tradition is resumed in her. The keepsakes of her grandmother's world are revivified (even though, *as objects*, they are destroyed) as they pass through time. The ceaseless struggle of a place against the threat of its being contained and made absolutely static by an obsessive memory is an important part of the dynamics of place literature. Time fixations are an influential aspect of both Northern and Southern literature; one need only remember the several frightening objects of the past which destroy the present in O'Neill's *Mourning Becomes Electra* to realize that this is so. No more devastating Southern counterparts need be indicated than Faulkner's *A Rose for Emily* and Warren's *The Circus in the Attic*. The most vividly concrete particular can become the worst kind of abstraction if it is allowed to work erosively upon the present. That is why the most successful of place literature is that which presents its details as freshly and intimately renewable. In the finest work of Eudora Welty—notably, *Delta Wedding* and the superb book, *The Golden Apples*—the minutiae of place are vividly clear and precise, even at the moment of their dying, because of the promise of and the provision for their imaginative renewal. But one must remember that truly evocative place literature, like Miss Welty's, gives us more than a reiterative idiom or mere "local color"; these last are more of antiquarian than literary interest.

The literature of Southern place belongs in three major classes: that which defines, describes, and preserves the tradition, without abstracting it (Miss Roberts, Caroline Gordon, Ellen Glasgow); that which reveals the genuinely native particulars of a scene, while at the same time communicating their existence in time and commenting on it (Miss Welty, Shirley Ann Grau, Carson McCullers, Flannery O'Connor); and that which explores the complex inward influence of place as moral "fable," directing or at the least influencing the rhetoric and the pace, and ultimately serving a decisive role in the novel's substantial meaning (Faulkner, Wolfe, Warren). The values of all three of these classes ultimately depend upon their having successfully fused ideas and particulars in a manner that adds to the comprehension of each.

NOTES ON THE DECLINE OF OUTRAGE

BY JAMES DICKEY

I

To be a white Southerner in the mid-twentieth century is to realize the full bafflement and complexity of the human condition. It is not only to see parts of one's world fall irrevocably away, but to feel some of them, tenaciously remaining, take on an accusing cast that one would not have thought possible, and long-familiar situations assume a fathomless, symbolic, and threatening weight. It is also to feel the resentment, the old sense of outrage rise up again toward all those who are not Southerners—against those who would change the world which one's people have made, insisting that it conform to a number of principles with which no one could possibly argue, but which the social situation as it exists must be radically altered to fit. To the "average" Southerner, who, like the average person anywhere, does not think much about issues in the abstract—though abstractions are everywhere implicit in his conduct—the continuing and increasing pressure being brought upon the white South to "do something" about the Negro is felt simply as a return of the indignation that attended Reconstruction—a resolve that the white Southerner shall continue to exercise autonomy in his own affairs and shall resist conforming to the dictates (for that is how he conceives them) of others living in other parts of the country.

This resolve is indicated by any number of private and public rationalizations, but these in themselves are not as important as what they connote: the Southerner's belief that his self-determination is being sapped and bled away by forces that have neither his interests in mind nor an adequate knowledge of his basic situation in its day-to-day reality. Negroes, who heretofore had seemed to occupy a place in the social structure which was, as far as many white Southerners were concerned, as good as ordained by God, have now taken on an entirely new dimension, and it is especially troubling that this new dimension is simply that of their ordinary humanity, long deferred by a series of historical circumstances reaching back for hundreds of years and rooted in the greed and callousness of men long dead. It is also beginning to be shockingly apparent that, in the simplest, easiest, and most obvious way in the world, generations of men later than the slave traders and plantation owners have kept human beings essentially like themselves in a state of economic and social bondage scarcely to be believed, and have done so with absolutely no qualms or even any notice of what was in fact taking place, lulled within a kind of suspended judgment with respect to the Negro's humanity, which allowed him to exist only in a special way, limiting his experience and even his being to areas where they conformed, not only to the ideas about Negroes most congenial to the white Southerner's preconceptions about race, but to the white man's opinion of himself.

It is an even more terrible paradox that the very quality that has been obscured all this time—the Negro's ordinary, everyday humanness—is obscured even more thoroughly, now that he has become a symbol which concretizes the historical uneasiness of an entire people, pointing up, as nothing else in this country has ever done before, the fearful consequences of systematic and heedless oppression for both the oppressed and the oppressor, who cannot continue to bear such a burden without becoming himself diminished, and in the end debased, by such secret and cruel ways that he is never really sure of what is happening. No act of redress is possible for the thousands who have been spiritually maimed, to say nothing of the countless lives wasted on the hardest and most unrewarding kind of labor, amidst the most degrading and soul-breaking life situations that have ever existed in America.

All these things are now in the minds of Southerners; they are charged with hidden significance whose true import comes from history's inadvertent and almost poetic power of revelation; and they in turn charge innumerable personal relations—thousands of them each day—with the chagrin, the helplessness, and the indwelling terror that come from centuries of wrongdoing that those who began and fostered them never, incredibly, conceived as wrong, or at least not wrong enough to do anything about. This is absurd, one thinks. How could anyone fail to see the Southern Negro's situation as wrong, as completely, blindingly, hauntingly wrong? The point is that Southerners did not, or that they refused to see the life the Negro has been given for what it actually is, pleading historical causes, jackleg theories of race, economic considerations, and a good many other things—none of which, not even the cotton empire or the age-old power of money to purchase labor, has any permanent meaning before the fact that millions of people have served in utter hopelessness through no fault but that of their birth, and for no reason but that others, differently born, should benefit.

It is a problem which, to many, admits of no solution, but toward a solution of either a merely painful or a starkly terrible kind it appears to be moving. It is not too much to say that in the "Negro problem" lies the problem of the South itself. Because of it, people are wondering now, as never since the 1860s, "What does it mean to be a Southerner? What does the social and economic and cultural history of this part of the country mean to *me*, to my life?" Above all they ask, "What will happen now, and *how* will it happen?" Rather than deal in generalities, it is better to go back to the individual as he exists in a predicament in which these questions come implicitly into play, and to attempt to understand the manner in which he asks them, not of others, but of himself.

II

On a downtown corner of a Southern city in midsummer, a man, a youngish though not quite young man, is waiting for a bus. He is not used to riding on buses, as he has his own car: in truth, he dislikes buses now more than ever, for he is aware that they have recently become a great deal more than the groaning, clumsy vehicles they have always seemed to be. They have been transformed into small, uncomfortable rolling arenas wherein the forces hidden for a hundred years in the structure of his society threaten to break loose and play themselves out each time a bus pulls away from a corner. Here, a city injunction has just been passed permitting Negroes to occupy any empty seat they prefer. The bus that appears, however, is not tossing with conflict or running blood from the windows. As usual, the Negroes are sitting well toward the back, and, as usual, our man prepares to pick a seat toward the front, as much toward the front as possible, perhaps next to a thin man in a flowered sports shirt and steel-rimmed glasses.

But suddenly he realizes that quite another thing is now possible. Seized by a desperate logic and a daring he cannot and does not want to account for, he walks past this man and on into the section occupied by Negroes. As he passes the last of the whites he has a powerful sense of pure transgression which gives way immediately to a kind of guilty, clandestine joy even more powerful. It is the sense of crossing a boundary beyond which there will be no going back, and it has all the exhilaration and fear, all the intimations of possibility and danger that might be occasioned by passing a real frontier into a strange land, perhaps even into the country of an enemy.

But *what* enemy? And why an enemy? He sees only two immense Negro women, a man in overalls and a painter's cap, a mulatto girl in a white uniform, ten or twelve others of both sexes, so familiar as to be indistinguishable from each other, and a plump, tea-colored young man who holds a small, even lighter-colored boy on his lap. None of these people seems to wish him ill, or to hold anything against him; yet he is more conscious of his own color at this moment than he ever remembers being, for he recognizes it in the light in which he is told the rest of the world regards it: the color of the unjust man, more damning than the whiteness of the leper. In spite of this, or more likely because of it, he takes a firm grip on the rail of the lurching bus and slides into the seat beside the plump man and his son. After all, has not the city edict, has not the Emancipation Proclamation, freed *him* as well as the Negro? He realizes only too well his intense self-consciousness about the meaning of his gesture; for it is purely that. At the same time, through an awesome silence, he hears his mind repeat every cliché about Negroes he has ever heard: "Would you want one living next door to you?" Or, coming not so much from himself as out of the very air he breathes, out of the tremendous sunlight itself: "Would you want your sister to marry one?"

Though he has heard these questions asked rhetorically all his life, he has never before entertained them at any real depth of interest. His sister has not married "one," and it is highly unlikely that a Negro will move in next door to him, for thus far zoning laws in his neighborhood have been rigidly maintained. Yet over and above the information asked for and the responses demanded by these questions, he is aware of a far more significant thing: the spirit of outrage that surrounds the words, the assumption that even to *ask* the questions is outrageous, and that such a transgression is to be set right only with the collaboration of the questioned, whose most violent denial is needed to place things in their customary perspective again. He cannot imagine answering such questions in the affirmative; or, if he can barely imagine it, he is at the same time conscious of the withering climate of indignation that would attend the answers, an indignation more killing than any other he can think of, because it would include, in addition to that of his contemporaries, the infinitely more terrible condemnation of his own past.

At this moment he is very much aware of himself as a Southerner, and that he is in some way betraying someone or something, even though the impulse which brought him to his present seat on the bus may have been completely laudable, *sub specie aeternitatis.* Oddly enough, he cannot help feeling also a sharp upswing of defiant joy at remembering that he *is* a Southerner, a joy that in no way wishes to distinguish approval from disapproval, right from wrong, good from evil. He is of the people from whom the Army of the Confederacy was drawn, and this is and has always been a source of intimate personal strength to him. The lives of both his grandfathers are with him, he believes, whenever they need to be, and help him understand what men may mean to each other in a common cause, regardless of whether or not history labels the cause worthy of their effort. Yet nothing like Pickett's Charge, nothing like the Shenandoah campaigns of Stonewall Jackson exists, any longer, to give Southernness an atmosphere of accomplishment, destiny, and glory. Of the spirit that

caught up the Confederate Army and made Jackson, Lee, and
Jeb Stuart the demigods of his people, almost none remains,
and what of it does still exist has no adequate channel through
which to flow. Southern autonomy, qua Southern, now tends
instead to come out in petty, vindictive acts of ill will toward
the Negro, and he wants no part of that.

All this he knows, but at the same time he recognizes the
fact that the South still stands for . . . for something. He has
read W. J. Cash, and so has been told the "truth" about the
much-advertised codes of Southern honor, the cult of Southern womanhood, the Southerner's characteristic extroversion
and his "habit of command," the cultural shallowness of the
nineteenth-century South, and so on. He knows the verdict of
history on his people. He knows one more thing about history
too: that it has trapped the Southern white just as securely in
his complex of racial attitudes as it has trapped the Southern
Negro in his deplorable social, physical, and psychological
environment. And he knows that with the increase of industry
and "business," with their attendant influx of thousands of
people each month from other parts of the country, the "solidarity" of the South, in manners as well as in attitudes about
race, is breaking down more and more rapidly, and that when
the older patterns of behavior are gone, there will be nothing
to put in their place save the empty money-grubbing and
soul-killing competitive drives of the Northern industrial concerns. He knows that, as a Southerner, he has only a few things
left to him: the intonation of his voice, an appetite for certain
kinds of cooking, a vague familiarity with a few quaint folkways far off in the mountains, and his received attitude toward the Negro; and that of these the only one important as
a rallying point for his Southernness, as an effective factor in
producing sectional assent, as a motivating force in political
action, is the last.

It is abundantly apparent that his people do not want their
sense of being Southerners to die. This may be the reason that
there is, all around him, a tremendous, futile yearning back
toward the time of the Civil War, when something concrete
could be done, when a man could pick up a gun and *shoot*
at something, in a setting of purpose and meaning. In the light
of the Supreme Court ruling on segregation, the Civil War has

come to seem no longer a defense of slavery and of states' rights, as Southerners had reluctantly begun to admit, but of the South against the encroachment of Others, and so heroic —the battle for one's home and one's mind against the invaders. Perhaps because of this his own brother is obsessed by the Civil War in a particularly curious way. He is a collector of relics. Accompanying his brother to the battlefield sites that surround the city, as well as to some others farther off in the country, he has walked slowly through farms, climbed over breastworks, waded through stream beds in the fraught, stammering heat of August, swinging the flat metal plate of his brother's mine detector over acres of weeds and brush in search of the war buried here for a hundred years a few inches beneath the pine straw. He has heard the lifeless and desperate cry of rusted metal, and dug with a totally inexplicable en-thusiasm and dread, perhaps unearthing a piece of a parrot shell, a Minié ball, part of a canister container, a belt buckle, a branding iron, a corroded mess tin, and once even a sword transformed by the earth and time into a long, warped shape like a huge burned matchstick, whose brass handle, under polishing, later took on its soft, fiery, original sheen. But look-ing at the decrepit guns on the walls of his brother's house, at the golden, breadlike patina of rust on the thousand frag-mentary metals of destruction, and pondering on the un-earthly, leper-white Minié balls and canister shot, he knows that the continuing power of the Civil War is not in these things but in its ability to dramatize and perpetuate a feeling about a way of life. It is actually a symbol of his people's defense of their right to be Southerners, and as such is more effective now than it has been at any other time during his own life.

As he sits at the present moment, however, he is not a Con-federate soldier in whose hands these weapons are new and bright. He is merely a man moving slowly in a public convey-ance through a heat-shimmering city built on land where such swords and bayonets have lain underground for a century. May he not take this fact itself as a new beginning place for self-definition? Why may he not simply be a man, like and unlike others, living from day to day as best he can? Yet as he asks this question he is struck by a peculiarly terrifying thought. Can the past so easily be denied? Whether the past has been right or wrong, intelligent or mindless, good or evil, it is still the past, the only one, and it cannot change. Because of it, he is who he is; of the subjects occasioned by his reverie, every one wells up out of history—the history of his people as Southerners. Yet may there not be feelings, states of being which underlie and do not depend exclusively upon the past?

On the pretext of looking out the window, he glances at his companions. The young Negro father has got over his initial self-consciousness, which, to tell the truth, was not even in the beginning very pronounced. He has set his light porkpie hat on the back of his head and is playing with his tiny son, who, to the other man in the seat, looks exactly like every other small Negro boy he has ever seen, except for being dressed in a white shirt and short, dark blue wool pants with halters and very bright black shoes. The man is now sticking out his wide pink tongue at his son, who swipes at it. They are both laughing. Well, what does one do next, if one is obviously looking, not out the window at all, but at another person no more than a foot away? "That's a fine boy you've got there," the young man does in fact say, and for the first time the Negro looks at him, a little shyly but squarely. In his gaze there is, thank God, no real mistrust, though he ends his reply with "sir." And there the conversation ends.

But something has happened, and it brings with it a new flood of questions more demanding than any others the young man has asked himself. What, actually, *is* his attitude toward Negroes, over and above gestures, over and above received opinions? And how does he really feel about the South—the actual South he lives in, that is, stand as it may in the shadow of that other, dead, undead, imagined, magnificent, and tragic South? And how are these questions related? For it is certain that they *are* related in some profound and fundamental way. He must admit immediately that he has always concurred, or as good as concurred, in the assumptions about Negroes that his forebears and contemporaries have had, and have. The unspoken rationale underlying these assumptions is that, inexplicably but in perfect keeping with the natural order of things, Negroes have been endowed with human shape and certain rudimentary approximations of human attitudes, but that they possess these only in a kind of secondary or inferior way, and, to the end of having this be readily recognizable, have also been given a skin pigmentation and a facial bone structure which make their entire status apparent at a glance, and even from a very great distance. Spoken or unspoken, these are the beliefs that have assigned every Negro, from the lowest hod carrier up through the ministry and the medical profession, his place in the Southern scheme of things.

The notion that the Negro must be "acclimated" slowly to the Caucasian world, now advanced among some Southerners as a genteel refinement on the above idea, is in reality not nearly so honest an appraisal of an actual state of mind as the more fundamental assumption from which it proceeds. As a result of the practices rather than the "theories" concerning the Negro, the worst possibility, the most fearful dream the white Southerner can have—or at least that the young man can imagine himself as having—is to have been born a Southern Negro. As he is, as he has existed among the circumstances of his life, he has always rather liked Negroes, in an offhand, noncommittal way, though it is certain that he has never formed a deep man-to-man (or, for that matter, man-to-woman) relation with one. Yet he realizes that he has just as surely always participated in the popular belief that the Negro is more or less a child, happy and easily diverted, or, more properly, somewhere between a child, a pet, and a beast of burden, but prone to flare up, especially among his own kind, into a terrible jungle violence. The Negro is also commonly thought to be the victim of a lust so powerful that before it all laws, all social codes and restrictions are as nothing, and during these seizures may leap from a sheltering fringe of bushes, like a wild shadow cast from Africa, and attack a solitary white woman working in a field, a girl on her way home from high school. He knows that there is enough misconstruction placed upon certain aspects of the Negro's life in his past and present environment to give these assumptions the outward cast or appearance of an entire truth, and that any isolated instance of Negro-white rape, for example, is enough to corroborate and intensify this feeling, and the others which attend it, all over the South, and to bring halfway to the surface disturbing dreams of all-out racial conflict and an intolerable sense of impending anarchy which must at all costs be put down.

But where does he, the questioner, stand in these matters? What *does* he believe? Does he believe that Negroes are essentially children? No; he does not. He believes that the Negro is a man like any other, woefully stunted and crippled by his circumstances but with amazing reserves of tolerance and humor, and a resilience that should eventually take its place among the most remarkable shows of human adaptability in history. Does he then believe in denying the Negro the social and economic concomitants of his humanity? No; he does not. There is no possible justification of such a denial. Yet why then does he *act* as if he believed, exactly to the extent that the veriest redneck or country politician rabble-rouser believes, *all* these admittedly indefensible ideas? Well, because . . . because he is a Southerner, and these attitudes are part of his past, of his "heritage" as a Southerner, and he suspects that if he relinquishes them, he also gives up his ancestry, to say nothing of severing an essential bond between himself and his contemporaries, all of whom are struggling in various ways to preserve segregation.

At present, with an impersonal materialism visiting its final ravages on the only place on earth he has ever really belonged, he does not want the *sense* of this place, the continuity of time as it has been lived, the capacity of the past to influence and if possible to assist him in thought and action, to disappear entirely. With others of his generation, he has wandered a great deal, and now, staring forward into the comfortable abyss of middle age, he wants, *really* wants, to regrow his roots, if such a thing is yet possible, in the soil from which he sprang. He does not believe the South to be merely a matter of climate and fried chicken; he understands it as a place where certain modes of thought are mutually held without the necessity of constant analysis and definition. One of these, and increasingly the main one, is the white Southerner's attitude toward the Negro, as the Negro exists in *his* "place." What that place is, however, he does not yet want to examine. Setting aside momentarily the "Negro question," what of the South itself, the South that he remembers? In what ways has it made him what he is?

Of the world in which he grew up, he can honestly recall only a very few things which he would identify as characteristically Southern, but these are powerfully centered in his consciousness. He has lived elsewhere in the United States, for example, and he can think of no other region where the family, on out through distant cousins, nephews, great-uncles and aunts, has such actual solidity and warmth as it does in the South. It is not that members of Northern and Midwestern families care for each other any the less, so much as it is that there seems to be in the South (or seemed in those years to be) a more vivid and significant belief that blood ties underlie and bolster the human affections in a way not to be explained by either logic or environment. There seemed, there still seems to him, something indisputably right about this. Though he has many relatives for whom he does not greatly care, he has always valued even those as part of the family association, the great chain of being that attached him truly, by ties surpassing in power anything the mere mind of man can invent, to other human beings in a group.

Something of this feeling extends outside the circle of kinship, also. A good deal of snobbery notwithstanding, it is hard for a Southerner to feel anything but a sense of basic comradeship with other Southerners, regardless of their relative social status. And this too seems valuable. To be told, with all the authority of the United States Supreme Court, that some of the beliefs proceeding from this community are wrong, and have been wrong from the beginning, for all the time the community has been alive, seems not only monstrous but preposterous as well, and appears to have more than a tinge of the *hubris* of man trying to set himself up against the existing nature of things, and to dictate by abstractions rather than by the realities in which people live. The sense of community and belonging is probably the most important single good that a society can bestow; it has been strong in the South, though including, as it manifestly does, a number of grievous injustices; it has been strong, and now it is fast disappearing; and he is dismayed and even frightened to see it go. He remembers something, long since thought forgotten, he once read in a book in France, laboriously puzzling out the sentences with the aid of a glossary. Perhaps it was in one of the *Journals* of Julian

Green, himself of American Southern parentage: "The South did not really lose the Civil War until around 1920, when it consented to follow the lead of the North." With this statement he heartily concurs. That is, he concurs emotionally. As soon as he examines what might have happened, and probably would have happened, if the South had *not* consented to follow the lead of the North, he sees that the present trend of industrialism and business was not only more or less inevitable, but probably even for the best, dreadful as some of its results have been.

Could the South, in fact, have remained a farming region? With machines doing more and more of the farm labor and consequently decreasing the number of agrarian jobs, how could a population consisting entirely of farmers have been supported? Or should the South deliberately have turned its back on the machine, and insisted upon using the modes of labor, transportation, and distribution of a hundred, of a hundred and fifty years ago? Can one forget that a machine, the cotton gin, helped to create and maintain the infinitely rich cotton empire of the Old South? How then have the machine and not have it? How change and not change? How in all conscientiousness deny advances in medicine, public health, education, to say nothing of agriculture? Should the South have willfully turned itself into an enclave of clannish, half-educated farmers, hopelessly outmoded in every phase of contemporary life, even in the one profession which they knew and lived by?

Obviously not. To insist upon such artificial means to preserve a few admittedly desirable features of family and community life is to ignore everything in the human make-up that moves and wants to improve itself and the conditions among which it exists. There is no compromise between the old modes of Southern life and "progress," a word which no one likes, but which one must inevitably use. With the machine, and the shifting and mixing of populations it encourages, the sense of place is attenuated, and with it the sense of belonging by right to a given segment of the earth, held in common with other human beings to whom one is tied by the immense force of the past, by the lives of forebears who knew and in their time lived on the same part of the earth, who fought for it, who are buried in it, and who, somehow, seem still to be brooding over and watching the ground which they possessed in a profundity now become unattainable to their heirs.

Nowhere else in this country, not even in New England, is the ancestor held in so much real reverence as he is in the South—his opinions, his acts, his idiosyncrasies, his *being*. Consequently, nowhere else is his spirit, his ghost, so powerful, disturbing, and influential. "Why, your grandfather Tom would turn over in his grave if he thought . . ." or, "What would your dead mother think, if she could see you now?" Questions like this, perhaps more than any the living could ask, require answers. Well, what *would* his dead mother—or, worse still—what would his grandfather Swift think if he *could* see him now, sitting in the same seat in a bus with a Negro? His grandfather's first reaction would be, he is sure, incredulity, and then . . . and then . . . outrage. "What in the world has happened to you, boy?" he would no doubt ask, in a rising, irresistible, and particularly terrible tide of resentment, and a bewilderment even more terrible. He feels a quick, deep flush of shame thinking of this; he has loved and honored his grandfather; he loves and honors him still.

Of the old man he retains several images of tremendous depth and authority. The most important of these is simply a recollection of sitting on the porch of a house in the country, listening to his grandfather tell of his experiences in the troop of General John B. Gordon. For a moment, in speaking of a battle, he had rested his steady and very old hand on the child's shoulder and said, "I wish you could have been there with me." He can still feel the touch of his grandfather's hand. And he has always liked to think that in some way he *was* with his grandfather that day, and that he did not falter, but acted with the unhesitating courage and authority he is sure his grandfather must have displayed, not because the situation required it, but because his life did. Never has he had so much reverence for anyone else as for his grandfather Swift, the kindest, gravest old man he can remember, or would ever want to remember, whose manners proceeded from the most scrupulous consideration for others with whom he came in contact, but even more from a kind of climate of courtesy which belonged to the world that had created him. He remembers also his grandfather's behavior with Negroes: considerate, but admitting of no argument and no redress. So far as he had been able to tell, the Negroes accepted and even welcomed these conditions, and he recalls the uncontrollable grief of many of them as they stood by his grandfather's coffin.

These memories are now intolerably confused. He asks himself if the good of his grandfather's life, and of the kind of life which produced his grandfather's character, were not inextricably entangled with attitudes which, rightly seen, are and have always been indefensible, inhuman, corrupt, and corrupting. It hardly matters that such attitudes have been implicit in human affairs ever since the first primitive man realized that it would be more profitable and considerably easier for him if he could get another to perform certain tasks instead of having to do them himself; he is occupied at the moment mainly with the knowledge that his grandfather's indignation, his *outrage,* could he see his grandson now (and in this land of powerful and eternal ghosts, does he not see?), would be limitless, and would include a betrayed, bewildered, and unbearable sadness. The young man understands himself as the victim of a cruel and fathomless paradox, a dilemma between the horns of which only a god could survive and still retain his identity. But perhaps he has led himself into an absurd train of logic. Is it in fact true that he cannot really be the grandson he wishes to be without seeing Negroes as his grandfather saw them? Can he truly be his grandfather's kinsman, torn as he is by a thousand doubts that never would have troubled those of his grandfather's generation?

To state the issues in this way is undoubtedly to insist upon their extremes, but he knows that sooner or later the public fruit of what is now opinion must ripen, and that in the end he will have to go on record as being of a certain mind, having taken a stand. After the Supreme Court decision on segregation, and with the admission of Negroes to buses and streetcars on an equal footing with whites, with their entry into white residential areas and private clubs and eating places, and, above all, into the public schools, he knows he will have to assert himself one way or the other on the Question. He needs no one to remind him of the consequences of the position he may take; if he sides with Negroes instead of against them, he will have helped as effectively as he could ever hope to do to kill the South and lay it in its grave.

Yet he is, after all, not his grandfather. He recognizes only too well the distance of his fall, the gulf between his grandfather's character and his own. Still, he does not in all honesty believe that he can by an effort of will, even for the sake of retaining his identity as a "Southerner," take opinions and attitudes for his own which are not his, and against which his whole nature as a sentient and rational man rebels. He cannot, either, regard himself as a "neutral," to be which is an ultimate impossibility. Then where, exactly, *does* he belong?

As nearly as he can tell, he sees his position, and the South's, more in terms of an image, a vision or daydream, than in a logical formulation. It is a banal image, but for him at least it is endowed with the capacity to define the situation in just such a set of clear-cut and dramatic opposites as a subtler, more considered approach might fail to furnish. It is the image of a wall, an old, high, crumbling but still massive wall along the top of which are set sharp, rusty spikes and broken bottles. He has actually seen such a wall, not in the Southern United States, but somewhere in Europe. However, in his mind he sees himself, his family, and his ancestors living on one side of the wall. He lives on the side he does because his forebears have lived there, because he has been joined to them by the divine accident of birth, and because they built the wall. On the other side, there because they were once brought and purchased like beasts, in indescribable poverty and humiliation which they have learned by their own means to turn into a kind of virtue accessible to none but them, live Negroes. This is the Negro's "place," the place in which he must stay to be allowed his identity by those who determine the forms and limits which that identity may take.

Through the closely guarded door in the wall come certain Negroes, under all-but-constant surveillance of whites. Through it, in point of fact, and under this constant scrutiny, come very nearly all Negroes at one time or another, and most of them every day—the men to work at menial, badly paid jobs, tearing up and laying down railroad track, driving trucks, lifting heavy weights, running elevators, digging, piling, sweating, grunting, and heaving, with amazing musculature and unquestioning patience; the women to wash clothes, to look after white children, to serve the tables and clean the houses of the whites. At night they return through the wall, and the door is closed. Behind the wall, what happens, when the Negro is once again inside the one poor world he can call his, when he is "in his place"? The young man has never had more than a fragmentary and inadequate notion of what lay behind the wall, in the easily violated world of the American Southern Negro, but he feels continually the human force trapped and maimed there. He knows that the Negro's place is squalid, dark, and huddled, and he suspects it is filled with an undercurrent of violence scarcely to be borne. When in high school, and drawn there by some obscure, compulsive reason, he spent part of a Saturday night in the emergency ward of a city hospital, and watched the attendants bring in the victims of that violence, shot in the belly at close range with shotguns, slashed with razors, gored and spitted and gouged with ice picks and pocketknives, beaten with pokers, bleeding, unconscious, or moaning slowly and hopelessly, accompanied by women, relatives, and even children. Somewhere among this background, among the locked-together, filthy shacks and the unseen menace of Saturday night and its duels with straight razors and bread knives, the man sitting next to him is attempting to raise a family in decency, and, yes, in love.

Upon what tremendous power does this man draw, to be able to play with his child here in perfect unself-consciousness, with no apparent resentment toward anyone, content in his own being and in the small fact of his son? Or is the Negro, in this light, simply the victim of another's self-abasing sentimentality? Is there and has there been at the very heart of the South, all these years, such a source of unused intelligence, unwanted friendship, thwarted and never-defeated affection as would make one catch one's breath even to think of? Yes; and nothing has thwarted these possibilities so much as the zealous guardianship of Southern uniqueness and identity, admittedly in some ways a good, but not *the* good. The South, once crippled beyond humiliation and now clinging to its prejudices as the last vestige of its autonomy, its irreplaceable sense of destiny and glory, is a South he does not believe should be preserved at all costs—that is, at the cost of condemning millions more like the man beside him to lives of the most brutal and hopeless degradation.

For all these reflections, he himself is not any the less a Southerner than he has always been. He is by no means sure that traces of what he has been raised to look upon as his "natural" advantages over Negroes will not remain with him for the rest of his life, do what he will to get rid of them. Not for a moment does he entertain the notion that these prejudices are just, fitting, or reasonable. But neither can he deny that they belong to him by inheritance, as they belong to other Southerners. Yet this does not mean that they cannot be seen for what they are, that they cannot be appraised and understood. The greatest danger, he believes, resides in the assumption that there is no reason to struggle against such prejudices, since they have been closely woven into the very fabric of Southern reality for at least a hundred and seventy-five years. Again, where does this leave him? He is quite convinced that it is just as wrong to love a man solely because he is black as it is to hate him solely because he is black. If there is a solution to the South's dilemma it must come from the individual, or rather from a number of personal relationships, each composed of a Negro and a white who have discovered (the Negro as well as the white, for he has much to learn of the white in any role other than that of master) the common basis for their lives as men, a thing more fundamental than any environment or set of social customs could supply.

With the practical means by which this kind of relationship might be fostered he is as yet unconcerned. It may begin with as simple a thing as a conversation on a bus. In order for this to come about, of course, it is first necessary that it be made possible for the Negro and white in question to sit together on a bus. The basis for such legislation as would bring this about, it is to be hoped, is that by such means both Negro and white can begin to comprehend their likenesses as men more readily, and that their differences may begin to lose the importance that they have had. Yet legislation is completely self-defeating if such is not the outcome, and if "civil rights" simply set the Negro up as an out-and-out enemy, to be despised, flouted, and openly disdained, where hitherto he had been tolerated, so long as he remained "in his place." Legislation is undoubtedly involved in the answer, but legislation is of no value whatever without good will and the part that must be played by the real and not the advertised heart.

He is glad that he is not amazed by his own feelings at this moment, and that the thought of his grandfather's outrage is not so saddening and terrible as it had seemed at first. He is glad that he has communicated on a human level, though briefly and as though across an immense gulf, with the young Negro man and his son. To extend his private emotions into a social panacea is not within his strength, and he has no wish to do so, especially since such an attempt might well destroy the personal and so the only value of those emotions. He believes, however, that if such feelings are possible to him, they are to others also. He laughs a little ruefully as he discovers that all the time he has been thinking he has been murmuring to himself, as a semi-unconscious accompaniment, "The past is dead, the past is dead."

But even as he realizes what he is saying, he knows that it is not true. The past is never entirely dead, nor should it be disowned or forgotten. His powerful and perhaps foolish pride in the military effort of the Confederacy is not dead, nor is the memory of his grandfather. The human insufficiency of the Southern "cause" in no way diminishes the steady courage and devotion to each other of his forebears, nor do the racial beliefs of his grandfather destroy his kindness, his seriousness, his quaint and marvelous honesty, courtesy, and directness. Perhaps his grandfather would have been an even better man had he gone among the Negro slaves like Christ, preaching the gospel of freedom, but as it is, he has been good enough; he has been a far better man than his grandson in every way but this. And is the grandson's behavior, even here, superior? If so, how? It is probably true that he will retain at least to some degree some of the attitudes he has inherited with his way of life. But he can now separate them and attain a partial objectivity, and so a partial mastery over them, which his grandfather had never seen any reason to do. If he cannot quite envision a cocktail party composed of Southern Negroes and whites, all enjoying each other's company as if they were all white, or all Negro, and if he still flinches at the idea of Negro-white intermarriage, he can at least begin to recognize the common humanity of himself and the young man sitting beside him, though their differences, both as to racial heritage and countenance, may still appear, and be, enormous.

When the Negro and his son get up to leave the bus, the young man, no more self-consciously than might be expected, raises his hand in good-by, and the Negro smiles, no more self-consciously than might be expected. A few blocks farther on, the young man gets off and enters his office building, harboring a bargain with himself that he knows he cannot possibly keep in all its implications. But the core of what he has come to believe is not an illusion, he suspects. He tells no one about it, for he correctly assumes that such things must be entirely personal and freely arrived at to be valuable. He goes in to work for a firm almost all of whom are Northerners, the products of forces other than those which have shaped him and brought about his reverie. He knows in a way they do not even suspect that most of the uniquely Southern traditions and characteristics he loves (and that they, occasionally, joke with him about in a vague, uninvolved fashion) cannot continue to exist without the social milieu, the entire complex of attitudes and mutually held opinions that nourished them, since social customs are not subject to the tampering of sociologists in their efforts to promote the desirable aspect of mores and eliminate the undesirable. The best he can do, he reflects, is to go outward toward persons whom he respects, admires, and likes, "regardless of race, color, or creed."

In his case, given his time, his background, and the temper of unrest that exists in the South, this may well be as destructive a thing as he could do, for whatever Negroes he may wish to know as well as for himself. But he must believe that in the end it will not be destructive, and so he must take the consequences, also, of believing that in this place where he was born and where he will probably die, where the Negro must become either a permanent enemy or an equal, where in one form, one body, unsteadily balanced, live the ex-slave, the possible foe, and the unknown brother, it can be a greater thing than the South has ever done to see that the last of these does not die without showing his face.

THE *PIETAS* OF SOUTHERN POETRY

BY LOUISE COWAN

Poetry in the South today is active, accomplished, and all but indistinguishable from poetry in the rest of the nation. Despite its locale, it is no longer Southern poetry. What should be considered Southern poetry, if the term is to have any real meaning, is a particular corpus containing the poems of John Crowe Ransom, Allen Tate, Donald Davidson, the early Robert Penn Warren, some of John Peale Bishop, perhaps the late John Gould Fletcher, and the sporadic work of a host of minor poets in the 1920s and 30s. But, though most of this work appeared in the same two decades, the classification is not merely historical. Something besides the accidental accolade of history designates a poem as Southern, something so marked as to be unmistakable and yet so fused with the work as to be almost unidentifiable. Such a differentiating principle cannot be located in externals of meter, language, tone, or subject; the obvious traits of Ransom are not those of Tate, and Tate's are not Davidson's. Nor is it a sense of place that sets a poem off as Southern, the work of Randall Jarrell, William Jay Smith, James Dickey, and other writers of the current South being almost as alien to Southern poetry as is the work of Karl Shapiro, John Ciardi, or Richard Eberhart. What, then, distinguishes a Southern poem?

It is safer, certainly, to turn to an example than to fashion a prescription. An ode recently published in *The Sewanee Review*, written by Donald Davidson to Allen Tate for the occasion of Tate's sixtieth birthday, comes like a straggler to challenge the contention that Southern poetry is virtually a completed body of work. Intimately personal yet nonetheless formal, it is a brilliantly Southern poem. Let us see if an examination of it will not disclose its generic essence:

The sound of guns from beleaguered Donelson
Up river flowed again to Benfolly's hearth.
Year to familiar year we had heard it run
World-round and back, till Lytle cried out: "Earth
Is good, but better is land, and best
A land still fought for, even in retreat;
For how else can Aeneas find his rest
And the child hearken and dream at his grandsire's feet?"

You said: "Not Troy is falling now. Time falls
And the victor locks himself in his victory
Deeming by that conceit he cancels walls
To step with Descartes or Comte beyond history.
But that kildee's cry is more than phylon or image
For us, deliberate exiles, whose dry rod
Blossoms athwart the Long Street's servile rage
And tells what pilgrimage greens the Tennessee sod."

So, Allen, you have kindled many an evening
When the creed of memory summoned us to your fire.
I remember that blazon, remember firelight blessing
Owsley's uplifted head, Ransom's gray eye,
The Kentucky voice of Warren, until that household's
Oaken being spoke like a plucked lyre
And we turned as men who see where a battle unfolds;

And as now, once more, I see young faces turn
Where the battle is and a lonelier kildee's cry,
Exultant with your verses to unlearn
The bondage of their dead time's sophistry;
They know, by Mississippi, Thames, or Seine,
What city we build, what land we dream to save,
What art and wisdom are the part of men
And are your music, gallant and grave.

Among these—if with shortened breath—I come
Bearing an old friend's garland in these lines,
Scarred but surviving the Telchins' lance and bomb,
To join the long procession where it winds
Up to a Mountain home—
No marshals but the Muses for this day
Who in other years did not veil their sacred glance

Or from you look askance
And will not cast you off when you are gray.

Among contemporary verses, this poem is remarkable on several counts: it has classical form and a clear rational framework; it possesses dignity and elevation of style, yet it is at the same time simple and familiar. And, far from exhibiting the brooding loneliness and isolation of most modern poems, it manifests loyalty and affection. As conditions for its composition, it required not only an author and an addressee of some nobility but, further, a bond between the two based on something outside themselves to which they acknowledged allegiance. Quite clearly this binding entity is the whole life of a people, still possessed of enough coherence to unite men in a common cause and to enable them to respect and trust each other. In the twentieth century the presence of these special qualities marks a poem in English as being almost certainly of the American South, a section whose very backwardness in industrial progress has allowed it to retain many of the traditional virtues. We could note other qualities that seem peculiarly Southern—the classical references, particularly to *The Aeneid*, the Civil War memories, the sense of a speaker behind the language, the sacramental view of the physical world (the conception of it as a reality in itself and at the same time a sign of something beyond itself)—but we can hardly avoid the conclusion that the chief distinguishing feature of Davidson's ode is the shared cultural commitment on which it rests.

In an earlier essay in this volume the idea is developed that the primary distinction of modern Southern literature is a sense of history. And, one must agree, it is history that forms the immediate basis for the mutual devotion demonstrated in Davidson's poem. It is the history flowing upriver from "beleaguered Donelson" that gives the men in Tate's home (Benfolly) their awareness of themselves as Southerners, though defeated:

"Earth
Is good, but better is land, and best
A land still fought for, even in retreat;
For how else can Aeneas find his rest
And the child hearken and dream at his grandsire's feet?"

Davidson here has one of his assembled friends (Andrew Lytle) find in *The Aeneid* a correlative for the Southern situation. Just as Aeneas and his men thought of themselves as Trojans all the more as they were forced to leave their burning homes, so the Southerners identified themselves in the instance of defeat. But, as Aeneas's concern was more with continuity than with the ashes of the old Troy, similarly, the impelling quest of which Davidson speaks is the joint enterprise of "building a city." In this phrase is strong indication that something more fundamental than a shared history lies behind the unity of the South—something that has made Southerners remember their history and preserve their customs and traditions. If we explore the indicated parallel further, we shall recall that Aeneas's mission was not only to found a city but to introduce his gods into Latium. At the base of the Trojan—and Southern —attitude toward history, we see, was a sense of sacredness connected with their cultural traditions, those local and familiar manifestations of the universal and mysterious.

The regional origin of these lares and penates of a community has been described by John Crowe Ransom in an essay entitled "The Aesthetic of Regionalism":

> As the community slowly adapts its life to the geography of the region, a thing happens which is almost miraculous; being no necessity of the economic system, but a work of grace perhaps. . . . As the economic patterns become perfect and easy, they cease to be merely economic and become gradually aesthetic. They were meant for efficiency, but they survive for enjoyment, and men who were only prosperous become also happy . . . and the fine arts arise, superficially pure or non-useful, yet faithful to the regional nature and to the economic and moral patterns to which the community is committed (*American Review*, II [1934], 296–97).

One could go further than Ransom and say with Christopher Dawson that as a community adapts itself to a way of life a conciliation of the divine and the human orders may be effected within it. In such a society, economic, moral, and aesthetic patterns, transformed by a kind of grace, lose their exclusively secular character and begin to assume a sacredness within the community; and loyalty between members of the community rests on this essentially metaphysical basis. Men do not bow to each other but to the divine as it manifests itself in their communal life. Such an attitude is what the Romans called *pietas*, reverence before the gods and before one's ancestors. It is not a conception very likely to be understood today. Nevertheless, one might conceivably argue that any genuine culture possesses this *pietas*, and possesses it with good reason: it represents a people's awareness of the twofold nature of human society.

The consciousness of a numinous invasion of human history is clear in the Vergilian epic; this divine element manifests itself by signs, prophecy, oracles; it points to a destiny which is not solely the will of the gods, but of God. The South had some such concept of itself, debased as this concept was to become in its popular "Old South" forms. But the spuriousness of the false image should not be allowed to militate against the real one; and Davidson's identification of the Southerners with the Trojans is a guide to the true way in which the South has thought of itself. Aeneas's followers honored and loved their vanquished heroes instead of forgetting their names and dishonoring their memories; so, too, Southerners remembered and honored such men as Robert E. Lee, Nathan Bedford Forrest, and Stonewall Jackson, not merely because they had fought bravely, but because they had fought for a cause that was, in some sense, sacred. The South did not tend to view defeat as a divine judgment—at least not until the twentieth century, when many Southerners began to imitate the national worship of success. Before this, like the Trojans, most Southerners conceived of their loss as something neither good nor evil, but merely incomprehensible, like the "wrath of Juno," bringing upon them hardship and tribulations. But Venus, they thought, was on their side; and, from a much higher view of things, they believed their ultimate destiny, according to the will of high Jupiter himself, would be to prevail.

This *pietas* is the direct antithesis of the pietism by which a given society equates itself with the kingdom of God. We might take as an example of false piety a society that has had an abiding influence on our modern world, that established by the Puritans of seventeenth-century England. In their conscious effort to behave with obvious rectitude, they were, in general, destructive of culture. Since they conceived that God had chosen them to their high estate and, as Milton put it, had sealed His choice by their victory in the Rebellion, they felt it incumbent upon them to show forth His glory. This Puritan attitude, based essentially on the exaltation of a people rather than on their submission to divine mystery, continues to be with us today in the automatic assumption of national superiority by many Americans. On a different level, it is this attitude to which Waldo Frank refers in his Foreword to *The Complete Poems of Hart Crane* when he writes:

> There is a tradition in our land as old as Roger Williams and the Pilgrims. It takes the term New World with literal seriousness. America, it declares, shall be the New Jerusalem, the kingdom of Heaven brought down from within each man to earth, and expressed in the forms of our American society. . . . And of course Walt Whitman is its major prophet, not only in his apocalyptic poems but in the fierce social and cultural criticism of *Democratic Vistas*. . . . Hart Crane is the poet of our recent time who most consciously inherits this tradition, and most superbly carries it on (1958, xi).

To see the vast difference between this New World mysticism of which Frank speaks and the *pietas* of the Southerner, we might compare two poems with approximately the same theme: Crane's *Ave Maria* and Allen Tate's *The Mediterranean*. Both poems make use of the motif of westward progress as it is expressed by the search for a new land; both are concerned, ultimately, with man's extension of borders, physical and mental, with his breaking the barriers of space and spirit. Crane's poem is the second piece in his sequence called *The Bridge;* it represents the transition not only from Old to New World, but also from past to future, from immaturity to wisdom. A dramatic monologue spoken by Columbus, *Ave Maria* shows the Spanish explorer on his return journey, after the discovery of America, when he can cry triumphantly, "I bring you back Cathay!" He recalls his first sight of the new land, when "faith, not fear/ Nigh surged [him] witless." He prays to the Virgin for a safe return, "For here between two worlds, another, harsh,/ This third, of water, tests the word." It is in this transitional world, the ocean, that Columbus is caught up in an ecstatic vision of that great spirit that broods over all:

> *O Thou who sleepest on Thyself, apart*
> *Like ocean athwart lanes of death and birth,*
> *And all the eddying breath between dost search*
> *Cruelly with love thy paradigm of man—*
> *Inquisitor! incognizable Word*
> *Of Eden and the enchained Sepulchre . . .*

It is the immanent God that Columbus encounters, whose "teeming span" reaches "From Moon to Saturn in one sapphire wheel" and who elicits from him the rhapsodic cry:

> *—round thy brows unhooded now*
> *—The kindled Crown! acceded of the poles*
> *And biassed by full sails, meridians reel*
> *Thy purpose—still one shore beyond desire!*
> *The sea's green crying towers a-sway, Beyond*
>
> *And kingdoms*
>   *naked in the*
>   *trembling heart—*
> Te deum laudamus
>   *O Thou Hand of Fire*

In contrast, Tate's *The Mediterranean* is spoken by a modern man who sees western progress in terms of the journey westward of Aeneas. Several journeys are merged in this complex and subtle poem: the journey of Aeneas, the journey of the American colonists, the journey of the exiled modern in search of tradition:

> *Where we went in the boat was a long bay*
> *A slingshot wide, walled in by towering stone—*
> *Peaked margin of antiquity's delay,*
> *And we went there out of time's monotone;*
>
> *Where we went in the black hull no light moved*
> *But a gull white-winged along the feckless wave,*
> *The breeze, unseen but fierce as a body loved,*
> *That boat drove onward like a willing slave . . .*

As in Crane's *Ave Maria,* the protagonist here too has a vision that inspires him to passionate desire, though in Tate's poem it is the promised land that he contemplates, not the vast ocean:

> *Where derelict you see through the low twilight*
> *The green coast that you, thunder-tossed, would win,*
> *Drop sail and hastening to drink all night*
> *Eat dish and bowl to take that sweet land in!*

In comparison with this human hunger, this eagerness for the attainment of a goal long pursued and now glimpsed in actuality, Crane's vision of the new land reveals itself as the product of what Tate in another context has called "the angelic imagination." In its etherealization of matter, it is bodiless and inhuman. The apocalyptic utterance "still one shore beyond desire! . . . Beyond/ And kingdoms naked in the trembling heart" stands in marked contrast to Tate's concrete and graphic "Eat dish and bowl to take that sweet land in!"

Crane's vision of the New World turns out in the end to be personal and not communal, based on a private mythology rather than on an inherited and traditional world view. Though he uses the "local color" of Spanish Catholicism for flavor, the god whom he encounters in the "Hand of Fire" is a pantheistic God, to be worshiped for his vastness and power. Crane's poem contains no wit, no antidote to its strained seriousness; its language is romantic and inflated, as befits the utterance of one who has seen in the mighty new ocean and the new continent "the heel of Elohim," much as the American tourist continues to be awestruck by the Grand Canyon or Niagara Falls. Tate's vision of the new land, on the other hand, is of one where

> *Fat beans, grapes sweeter than muscadine*
> *Rot on the vine . . .*

Though we have "cracked the hemispheres with careless hand" in the course of our westward progress, we may still come back to our source, Tate shows, in keeping with the prophecy: "in that land were we born." The land Hesperia was the origin of the Trojans' earliest ancestor; and in finding one's source, Tate implies, one comes to nothing new or strange, but to the self, long covered over and hidden by grandiose deceptions. And though the land is man's kingdom, not God's, it possesses a sweet sacredness because of having been sought by means of divine prophecy. Implicit within Tate's poem is the assumption that we do not save ourselves alone, but together.

This *pietas* that is the Southerner's instinctive feeling toward society and toward history is clearly expressed in another Southern poem, John Peale Bishop's *Experience of the West*. Again the reference is to *The Aeneid*. As Aeneas carried on his shoulders the old Anchises, his father, Bishop shows, the American colonists carried with them the European past:

They followed the course of heaven, as before
Trojan in smoky armor westward fled
Disastrous walls and on his shoulders bore
A dotard recollection had made mad,

Depraved by years, Anchises: on the strong
Tall bronze upborne, small sack of impotence;
Yet still he wore that look of one who young
Had closed with Love in cloudy radiance.

So the discoverers when they wading came
From shallow ships and climbed the wooded shores;
They saw the west; a sky of falling flame
And by the streams savage ambassadors.

O happy, brave and vast adventure! Where
Each day the sun beat rivers of new gold;
The wild grape ripened; springs reflected fear;
The wild deer fled; the bright snake danger coiled.

They too, the stalwart conquerors of space,
Each on his shoulders wore a wise delirium
Of memory and age; ghostly embrace
Of fathers slanting toward a western tomb.

A hundred and a hundred years they stayed
Aloft, until they were as light as autumn
Shells of locusts. Where then were they laid?
And in what wilderness oblivion?

The aspect of Aeneas's piety that Bishop emphasized in this poem is less his dutifulness in founding a new city than the reverence in his treatment of his father. By this emphasis he illuminates the nature of the tradition brought by the colonists, the ideals and pieties that restrained them and prevented complete ruthlessness, even in a raw, new land. The Americans stood in relation to the European traditions, Bishop makes clear, as a son stands to a father, one who is old and impotent, useless and burdensome, but who in the past has known love and had at least transient contact with divinity. This poem is not *about* the South, certainly, any more than it is about New England or New Amsterdam. But in presenting the ties with Europe as a precious burden rather than a mere encumbrance, its attitude is Southern.

What the recurrence of the allusions to *The Aeneid* in these and other modern Southern poems reveals is the very source of the South's reverence for tradition: like the Rome that was finally established—the new Troy—America was (to Southerners) a transplanted shoot from a loved and valued parent vine. And it shows further the Southerner's feeling about what the relationship between men should be.

When modern poetry first began to make its appearance in the South of the 1920s, it gave no evidence of this sort of cultural commitment. In between Mencken's cynical pronouncement that "Down there a poet is as rare as an oboe player, a dry-point etcher, or a metaphysician" ("The Sahara of the Bozart," *A Mencken Chrestomathy*, 1949, 184) and the acknowledged triumph of the Fugitives in poetry, there was the general burgeoning, all over the section, of the poetic impulse. Besides *The Fugitive, The Double Dealer, The Reviewer, The Lyric,* and the Poetry Society of South Carolina, many other groups and publications were testimony to the fact that the South had become "a nest of singing birds." Yet the lyrical and regional voices were not very hardy, and the experimental "free verse" movement took little root in the section. The members of the most serious group—the Fugitives —insisted that they were not writing as Southerners and went to some pains to make known their disapproval of poetry that limited itself to local color, regional subjects, or any sort of supposed Southern literary tradition.

Indeed, as Ransom, Tate, Davidson, and Warren knew, there was no Southern literary tradition. Their own work represents a complete break with, not only the sentimental verse being written in the early twentieth-century South, but the earlier, more serious poetry in the section as well. From a purely literary point of view, their poetry seems to be *sui generis*, the verse written by Southerners with a classical education, a spoken Southern language, and an interest in philosophic speculation (in the old sense of inquiring into the nature of things)—Southerners who had recently come in contact with the European mode of living, with serious English poetry, and with the new experimentalism in vers libre and imagism. To find the tradition that modern Southern poetry embodies, we look in vain through the earlier appearances of poetry in the South. There may be some trace of it in the oral tradition of songs, ballads, and rough frontier rhymes, but not in the consciously literary pieces.

To be sure, we find a few similar attitudes that hindsight renders significant. Knowing, as modern readers, of the Southern critical tenet concerning "anonymity," the necessity of suppressing the private, introspective element in a poem, we note in eighteenth- and early nineteenth-century Southern poetry its distance from the reader, its consciousness of being a patterned work of "art," its formality—a survival of the seventeenth-century lyric tradition; and, continuing, we are aware of the Southern idealism, the purity, the gentle courtesy to ladies, and the delicate treatment of the theme of love. But Romantic elements, imported from England and the continent, blur any further similarities; and we are justified in saying that there is no actual connection between earlier Southern poetry and the poetry that in the 1920s began expressing the view of the world that had long been held by Southerners.

Whatever the poetry of their own region may have been like, the Fugitives had available to them the sort of purely literary tradition outlined for the modern in T. S. Eliot's "Tradition and the Individual Talent." This is a heritage of great works from many cultures, the only tradition available to the poet in a world lacking order, coherence, and an agreed-upon structure of belief. And, for a few years of serious work, this literary tradition was sufficient. Exploring their intellectual inheritance and expressing themselves in its forms, the Fugitives established their position in the continuity of letters. They were less deliberate in their experimentalism than their contemporaries, Tate alone studying the French Symbolists seriously, but they were nonetheless conscious of the individual's responsibility to develop his own poetic medium in a proper expression of his time. What became apparent to them with their increased mastery of poetic craft, however, was their habitation within a universe of traditional feeling and instinctive belief, as well as a growing ability to realize this universe in poetic form.

Why was this cultural gift available to a group of poets writing at a given time and not to earlier ones? In "Why the Modern South Has a Great Literature," Donald Davidson gives the most satisfactory answer to this question when he describes the recent South as "a traditional society which had arrived at a moment of self-consciousness favorable to the production of great literary works":

> Greece in the fifth century, B.C., Rome of the late Republic, Italy in Dante's time, England in the sixteenth century all give us examples of traditional societies invaded by changes that threw them slightly out of balance without at first achieving cultural destruction. The invasion seems always to force certain individuals into an examination of their total inheritance that perhaps they would not otherwise have undertaken. They begin to compose literary works in which the whole metaphysic of the society suddenly takes dramatic or poetic or fictional form. Their glance is always retrospective, but their point of view is always thoroughly contemporary. Thus Sophocles, in his *Oedipus Tyrannos*, looks back at an ancient Greek myth, but he dramatizes it from the point of view of a fifth-century Athenian who may conceivably distrust the leadership of Pericles. This is what I mean by the moment of self-consciousness. It is the moment when a writer awakes to realize what he and his people truly are in comparison with what they are being urged to become (*Still Rebels, Still Yankees*, 1957, 172–73).

There have been three such "moments" within the last century in Western civilization—in Russia, Ireland, and the American South—when even these few last outposts of traditional culture have been shaken by the technology and thoroughly secular social ideology arising from the cultural revolution of seventeenth-century Europe. Each of these three societies has been the scene of a literary quickening in which the same themes and attitudes run through the work of a group of writers. And in each instance the "renascence" has begun with poetry.

Certainly the foundations for the whole movement known as the Southern Literary Renascence were laid first in poetry. A body of attitudes and themes, as well as the technique and the language for expressing them, was established in the poetry of the Fugitives some time before a distinctively Southern fiction or criticism appeared.

The South became "modern" in the twentieth century. England had taken the step earlier, in the mid-seventeenth century. Because in many ways the South was a continuation of English life, deeply conservative, the poets who began expressing its culture bore more than a superficial resemblance to the diverse seventeenth-century English poets. What Milton, Donne, and Herrick had in common is a set of common assumptions about man and his place in the universe, assumptions which had little, perhaps nothing, to do with their own conscious, analytical, learned thinking. As a man and as a prose writer, Milton, for instance, was a Puritan; yet in his poetry he created a world based on those vast conceptions of the great medieval synthesis, embodied earlier by St. Augustine and continued unbroken until the Lutheran and Calvinistic theologies destroyed them, in parts of Europe, at any rate, including England. John Donne, too, inhabited this large and orderly universe, at least in his creative imagination, despite his speculative and tormented mind. Herrick and Marvell, Herbert and Vaughan, all had access to this rational and coherent structure, the objective reality and the unity of which they never doubted. Hence, each could explore an aspect of that world without having to elevate the aspect to the position of totality. It was a universe based on a principle of plenitude, one in which all creatures reflected the Creator, without, of course, ever adding up to Him.

In the same way, the modern South has produced different kinds of poets who, though they hold different beliefs and write with different techniques about different subjects, have behind them a common view of man, his place in nature, and the place of nature in the Chain of Being. Behind them, in short, they have the world view that was lost to the rest of the English-speaking world in the mid-seventeenth century. The elements constituting this world view govern the attitudes and provide the substance of Southern poetry; hence a detailing of them would be important in its own right. But what is important to the present consideration is the fact of agreement: that such a shared structure of belief was part of the cultural heritage of the South.

As we have seen earlier, the determining mark of the Southern poetry is a certain *pietas* indicating that the poet accepts rather than rejects his people. This attitude is the more remarkable when we consider that it made its appearance in an era in which, as Tate has written, "everybody acts his part . . . in the plotless drama of withdrawal" ("The Man of Letters in the Modern World," *The Forlorn Demon,* 1953, 9). The kind of life the Southern poets came to accept early, "before they had minds of their own" (to borrow a phrase from John Peale Bishop), was a good-natured and mannerly life, in which family custom, dress, decoration, food, and courtesy were important. Ransom has written in his poem *Old Mansion* that Southerners expressed themselves in "grave rites and funerals," even if "their peacock *was* a pigeon." The South had a brief existence before the Civil War, to be sure. But, as Bishop has stated in his essay "The South and Tradition," manners do not require a long genealogy. Actually, as he points out, "a grandfather will do" (*Collected Essays,* ed. Edmund Wilson, 1948, 8).

Proper manners are more than externals; they structuralize and convey the natural virtues of courage and honor and the supernatural virtue of charity. Just as the medieval gentilesse of deportment could express both the chivalric code of a Sir Gawain and the genuine spirituality of a St. Francis, so the courtesy of the Southern people was an expression of both inner heroism and piety. Davidson has spoken of John Gould Fletcher's gallantry as being "so rare that it must seem archaic and quixotic to the present generation" ("In Memory of John Gould Fletcher," *Still Rebels, Still Yankees,* 39) and as an example of Fletcher's chivalry he quotes an early poem of which the following stanza is the conclusion:

> *God willing, we shall this day meet that old enemy*
> *Who has given us so many a good beating.*
> *Thank God we have a cause worth fighting for,*
> *And a cause worth losing and a good song to sing.*

Fletcher's poem has essentially the same theme as Ransom's *Captain Carpenter,* which depicts a constantly defeated but nonetheless bellicose warrior. Left with only tongue and heart of all his anatomy, the captain is finally dispatched by

> *a sleek upstart*
> *That got the Captain finally on his back*
> *And took the red red vitals of his heart*
> *And made the kites to whet their beaks clack clack.*

That Ransom views his subject with irony, that "ultimate mode of great minds," does not negate the essentially gallant and tender attitude; it merely seasons it by an acknowledgment that the universe—or perhaps even the man next door—may not regard the captain's bravery in the same light that the poet does.

Ransom's individual fantasy in seeing as a lost lady a bird who "eyed her image dolefully as death" calls upon a communal consciousness in its query:

> *"Who has lost a delicate brown-eyed lady*
> *In the West End section? Or has anybody*
> *Injured some fine woman in some dark way*
> *Last night, or yesterday?"*

The classical motif of metamorphosis, the Southern politeness, and Ransom's own gentle irony combine to produce a poem that is unmistakably Southern. Ironic courtliness is one of the distinguishing marks of Ransom's poetry, so that one has only to call to mind such poems as *Janet Waking, Here*

Lies a Lady, Old Mansion, Antique Harvesters, or *Blue Girls* to be made aware of their tone of fond tribute. A gallant attitude toward ladies, reflected so well in Ransom's poetry, is to be found also in the work of the other Fugitives, though less obviously, and in the poetry of John Gould Fletcher and William Alexander Percy. This courtesy closely resembles the courtly attitudes encountered in the literature of the European Middle Ages and continued, though diluted, through the seventeenth century. Add to it other medieval qualities—a love of faërie, a pungent earthiness, and a sophisticated wit—and one has the complex blend of human qualities to be encountered in the Southern social tradition and in the Southern poetry of the 1920s.

From a purely literary point of view, the greatest gift a traditional culture imparts to a poet is a sense of form—the ability to see how to make a poem of a subject at the same time that he sees the subject itself. The Southern poet does not tend to confuse poetry with life, morality, social propaganda, or autobiography. A poem to him is no vehicle for exploring his private disillusionments, sensuous delights, dreams, sexual experience. To Ransom, Tate, Davidson, the early Warren, the late Fletcher, Bishop, to Percy, Alec B. Stevenson, and the other poets of the early-twentieth-century South, a poem is something made, something artificial, a "concrete universal" constructed out of language which has been given order, pattern, and a certain anonymity. Where there is no real creative intuition, the result is verse instead of poetry, as in much of Stevenson's, Percy's, and the minor Fugitives' work. Where creative insight is present, the discipline of formal pattern, of impersonality and detachment, imparts to the poem a parabolic, or mythic, or allegorical life that raises it above the level of verse into the realm of poetry, as in Ransom's *The Equilibrists, Bells for John Whiteside's Daughter,* and *Here Lies a Lady;* Tate's *Ode to the Confederate Dead, The Mediterranean,* and *Mr. Pope;* Warren's *Original Sin* and *Revelation;* and Davidson's *Lee in the Mountains, Sanctuary,* and *The Nervous Man.* Even such prolific and unstudied poets as Merrill Moore and Jesse Stuart, who have lacked a conscious aesthetic, are provided by the South with an instinctive sense of form, so that their poetry is never rhapsodic, merely diffuse, or embarrassingly introspective.

A comparison of two fairly undistinguished poems may clarify what I mean by this sense of form permeating the Southerner's work. One of Jesse Stuart's sonnets from his *Man with a Bull-Tongue Plow* goes as follows:

Fields will be furrowed time and time again.
They will be furrowed by tall men unborn
As they were furrowed by men now forlorn
In dust—And fences will be built again
By men like me and fields be cleaned of brush
By men like me only to grow again.
Other poets will plow and cut the brush
And earn their bread by hot sweat from their brows
Behind their steady mules and turning-plows!
I wonder if new plow boys will take time
To sit down by their plows and spin their rhymes
Then common folks will read in future times!
What man was this that trailed a cutter plow
And wrote a rhyme about sweat on his brow!

The other poem is by an Easterner, Wallace Stevens.

The white cock's tail
Tosses in the wind.
The turkey-cock's tail
Glitters in the sun.

Water in the fields,
The wind pours down.
The feathers flare
And bluster in the wind.

Remus, blow your horn!
I'm ploughing on Sunday,
Ploughing North America,
Blow your horn!

Tum-ti-tum,
Ti-tum-tum-tum!
The turkey-cock's tail
Spreads to the sun.

The white cock's tail
Streams to the moon.
Water in the fields,
The wind pours down.

Stuart's poem exhibits a completed idea embodied in a con-crete situation and a specific instance. It is based on an ac-ceptance of and a respect for the finite order. His theme is, roughly, the great theme of the Renaissance lyricists: the sur-vival of art far beyond the survival of the artist or of the sub-ject he celebrates. Where his poem fails is in the strict disci-pline of art; in Stuart the tradition has become stagnant, unrefreshed by any real effort of his own. The other poem, by Stevens, is an attempt at "pure" poetry; it seeks to convey some sort of symbolic value vaguely derived from outdoor ex-ercise, the concept of a great continent, and nature in general. But it shows no reverence for the existing order of things. And in its mere presentation of images, its imitation of sounds, its intended diffusion rather than coherence, it has substituted the effect of a childishly pure sensory apparatus for the mature and reflective mind of the poet. I confess that I think we should be hard put to it to choose between the two: a per-fectly ordinary sonnet leaning too heavily on group sentiment and an extraordinary but meaningless effusion relying too heavily on individual fantasy. But Stuart's poem has a kind of form (in the sense of intelligibility and unity) that Stevens' poem lacks completely.

A more successful Southern poem concerned with a similar subject is Warren's *At the Hour of the Breaking of the Rocks,* from his *Kentucky Mountain Farm* sequence:

Beyond the wrack and eucharist of snow
The tortured and reluctant rock again
Receives the sunlight and the tarnished rain.
Such is the hour of sundering we know,
Who on the hills have seen to stand and pass
Stubbornly the taciturn
Lean men that of all things alone
Were, not as water or the febrile grass,
Figured in kinship to the savage stone.
The hills are weary, the lean men have passed;

The rocks are stricken, and the frost has torn
Away their ridged fundaments at last,
So that the fractured atoms now are borne
Down shifting waters to the tall, profound
Shadow of the absolute deeps,
Wherein the spirit moves and never sleeps
That held the foot among the rocks, that bound
The tired hand upon the stubborn plow
Knotted the flesh unto the hungry bone,
The redbud to the charred and broken bough,
And strung the bitter tendons of the stone.

Gravely, solemnly the present scene finds its meaning in eschatology. All that is actual and dear, all that the heart demands to endure will pass, Warren says, but not to an endlessly fructifying process, not to a Whitmanian incessantly rocking cradle, but to that final Being Whose will was done and Who was the source of our piety. No less than the Davidson ode quoted at the beginning of this essay, this poem is distinctly Southern; and if it is history that marks it, it is history in this sense: the land and the men who fought for it, with rifle or with plow, are sacred and, though they disintegrate, will prevail.

To return briefly to the Aeneas figure—surely this choice of hero by the Southern poets reveals a conviction of cultural crisis. Heroic sacrifice was required of Aeneas by his *pietas;* could we not say that the act of giving form to a poetic insight, based as it is on faith, reverence, and integrity of personality, requires in a measure the same heroism? When such an act of faith seems no longer possible—possibly because the moment of self-consciousness of which Davidson spoke has been prolonged into a moment of hesitation and doubt—it is still within the symbolism of the Aeneas story that a Southern poet describes the cultural loss. In *Persistent Explorer* Ransom ruefully laments the absence of any pious connection with a particular land. He hears the sound of a waterfall, and, though he knows he should hear oracular voices, "as those that rang around a man/ Walking by the Mediterranean," he hears only the simple naturalism of water:

> *Its cloud of froth was whiter than the cloud*
>
> *That clothed the goddess sliding down the air*
> *Unto a mountain shepherd, white as she*
> *That issued from the smoke refulgently.*
> *The cloud was, but the goddess was not there.*

Nothing supernatural at all is to be heard; no message either good or bad reaches him from the gods:

> *So be it. And no unreasonable outcry*
> *The pilgrim made; only a rueful grin*
> *Spread over his lips until he drew them in;*
> *He did not sit upon a rock and die.*

> *There were many ways of dying; witness, if he*
> *Commit himself to the water, and descend*
> *Wrapped in the water, turn water at the end*
> *And flow with a great water out to sea.*

> *But there were many ways of living too,*
> *And let his enemies gibe, but let them say*
> *That he would throw this continent away*
> *And seek another country,—as he would do.*

The shared journey of a people, sacred in its divine urgency, has become the lonely "journey to Byzantium," that private moving to higher ground which, however admirable, leaves one's people behind. *Persistent Explorer* is still Southern in form and attitude; but its subject is the decline of that cultural faith, that *pietas,* that has made possible the very existence of the poem. Warren's piece, too, for all its Southern attitude, is a kind of valediction to the South. For Warren a stoic acceptance of disintegration was possible, though his stoicism was colored by traditional pieties in his early poetry. His latest verse is not Southern. Tate and Davidson, in their infrequent appearances, still write Southern poetry. Ransom writes no poetry at all. We can say with safety, I think, that in its poetic form the Southern Literary Renascence is effectively over. But it has left us a precious legacy.

TWO IN RICHMOND:
ELLEN GLASGOW AND JAMES BRANCH CABELL

BY LOUIS D. RUBIN, JR.

Ellen Glasgow and I are the contemporaneous products of as nearly the same environment as was ever accorded to any two writers. From out of our impressions as to exactly the same Richmond-in-Virginia, she has builded her Queenborough, and I my Lichfield; yet no towns have civic regulations more widely various.

James Branch Cabell

I

Richmond, Virginia, in the decades before the turn of the twentieth century, was a city with a past—the four years when it had been the besieged capital of the Confederate States of America. Lost Cause though it was, the Confederate tradition was of sustaining importance in Richmond. Most of the old and middle-aged men in the city had worn the gray; almost all, men and women alike, had shared in the ambitions of the new nation and had suffered in the common defeat. The hopeless bravery of the doomed Confederate cause had left memories that would shape Richmond life for decades afterward.

As the war years receded into the past, the heritage became a legend. All Confederate leaders became stainless and true, all engagements had been fought against overwhelming odds. Flesh-and-blood soldiery which had battled profanely and unwashed in the hot, savage summer campaigns became now, in retrospect, heroic, dauntless knights. Throughout the latter decades of the century the Confederate legend was industriously cultivated. Confederate memorial days, the numerous reunions of the old Army, the periodic dedication of statuary along Monument Avenue and elsewhere in Richmond, the storytelling of veterans who had fought through the war and of women who had waited at home—all combined to raise the halo of myth about the graying veterans who frequented the parlors of Richmond homes. "They spoke," James Branch Cabell remembered, "of womanhood, and of the brightness of hope's rainbow, and of the tomb, and of right upon the scaffold, and of the scroll of fame, and of stars, and of the verdict of posterity. But above all did they speak of a thin line of heroes who had warred for righteousness' sake in vain, and of four years' intrepid battling. . . ." General Lee, their leader, became "a god, or at any rate a demigod," and, "there was no flaw in it when, upon tall iron-gray Traveller, he had ridden among them, like King Arthur returned from out of Avalon, attended by the resplendent Launcelots and Tristrams and Gareths and Galahads, who, once upon a time, had been the other Confederate generals."

"To a child, who could not understand that for the health of human ideals every national myth needs to be edited and fostered with an unfailing purpose, the discrepancy was puzzling," Mr. Cabell remembered. For discrepancy there was; the Richmond that Mr. Cabell and Miss Glasgow knew as children was not a legendary city at all. Public and commercial life in Virginia during the 1870s, 1880s, and 1890s was not conducted upon a noticeably mythological plane. Richmond was a busy commercial and industrial center, with a tremendous tobacco-manufacturing trade, an extensive iron-and-metal industry (Miss Glasgow's father was manager of the Tredegar Iron Works), and distribution facilities that supplied goods to the entire Southeast. Within three decades after the war had ended, the city population and area had more than doubled; though never a boom town, Richmond recovered considerably more quickly and soundly than most Southern cities from the destruction of the war.

Nor were the former Confederates who dominated the city's business and political life mythological figures. They were men, with all the usual vices, habits, and compromises of men. Some did not hesitate to use the legend of the Lost Cause for political and financial profit, to talk of duty while seeking emolument. Richmonders were certainly no better, and no worse, than other Americans of the time.

The Richmond of the seventies, eighties, and nineties, then, was a contrasting mixture of the old and the new. The Confederate tradition was still very much alive; the days "before de Wah" were not forgotten, were indeed cloaked in an aura of romance more fabled and lovely than earth.

Even that witty old humorist George W. Bagby, known otherwise for his realistic portraits of Virginia life, dispensed with both irony and objectivity when he looked back on the good old days before the Union armies came. "Sorrows and cares were there—where do they not penetrate? but oh! dear God, one day in these sweet, tranquil homes outweighed a lifetime in the gayest cities of the globe."

And yet there was the everyday life of postwar Richmond, the mortal and gaslit city with the smoking factories, grain mills, warehouses, trolley cars, hotels, department stores, breweries, schools and hospitals—no tranquil paradise, no Valhalla for martial heroes, but a busy American city.

As for the literature written by Virginians of the period, whatever its virtues and defects, it reflected little of the latter element of Virginia life. It was a romantic literature, set for the most part in the prewar period and the war years. By far the dominant author of the day was Thomas Nelson Page, with his heartwarming tales of noble aristocrats, pristine belles, and faithful darkies. One of James Branch Cabell's characters pridefully extols a literature on the Page model: "I love to prattle of 'ole Marster' and 'ole Miss,' and throw in a sprinkling of 'mockin'buds' and 'hants' and 'horg-killing time,' and of sweeping animadversions as to all 'free niggers'; and to narrate how 'de quality use ter cum'—you spell it c-u-m because that looks so convincingly like dialect—'ter de gret hous.' Those are the main ingredients. . . ." To his last day Thomas Nelson Page never faltered in his appointed task of glorifying the old ways. He earned thereby an international reputation. When he died in 1923, after a distinguished career as novelist and diplomatist, the flag over the capitol in Richmond flew at half-mast, schools and colleges adjourned, and kings, premiers, and presidents telegraphed their messages of sympathy.

This was the time and place then, into which Ellen Glasgow and James Branch Cabell were born, and this was the literary milieu which they were soon to enter, and do so much to change.

II

Conventionally romantic though Ellen Glasgow's first two novels, *The Descendant* and *Phases of an Inferior Planet*, may seem to a modern audience, they were not considered so in their own day. For when Miss Glasgow published her first novel, anonymously, in 1897, young Virginia ladies were not supposed to know about most of the considerations that motivated her protagonist as he strove to make his way in New York journalistic circles. The bleak pessimism that marked both that book and its successor drew hardly at all on Virginia literary models; as Rosewell Page declared several years later in a sketch of Miss Glasgow for the *Library of Southern Literature,* Miss Glasgow was nearer to Ibsen than to George Eliot. So she was, and nearer perhaps to Stephen Crane and Frank Norris than to either of them. She had read much of the deterministic, naturalistic writing of the day; she was always vastly interested in ideas, and "kept up" with intellectual affairs to the end of her life. Though properly loyal to his fellow Virginian author, Rosewell Page tempered his encomium with certain reservations: her second novel, he wrote, "is in many respects real; but the keynote is one of pessimism." Pessimism, of course, was not an accepted literary attitude in early-twentieth-century Virginia.

It was not until her third novel, *The Voice of the People* (1900), that Ellen Glasgow turned to the Virginia scene in her fiction. Once she did, she continued with it until the end of her life. For the better part of forty years she devoted her literary talents to an intensive scrutiny of society in Virginia, exploring as many facets of it as she knew existed. Though it is doubtful that she was consciously compiling a "social history" of Virginia from the start, as she later claimed, there is no question that this was what she was in effect accomplishing. She peopled her novels with aging gentlemen and ladies of the "first families," young blue bloods coming to grips with the modern world, serene Episcopal communicants, gospel-ridden Fundamentalists, freethinkers, heroines of high birth and of low estate, good country folk, politicians, bankers, lawyers, Confederate generals, clerks, factory hands, industrial tycoons, ministers, farmers of tobacco, peanuts, and wheat, dairymen, ladies of the old school and women of the market place, emancipated modern girls and tradition-bound ladies of high degree, Negroes and whites, recent immigrants and old settlers, mountain and valley folk and Tidewater aristocrats. "I intended to treat the static customs of the country, as well as the changing provincial patterns of the small towns and cities," she wrote. "Moreover, I planned to portray the different social orders, and especially, for this would constitute the major theme of my chronicle, the rise of the middle class as the dominant force in Southern democracy."

The Voice of the People is the story of a poor farm boy's rise to political power, and is intended to typify the coming of the rural middle class into control of the state, a control it still retains today. Certainly in the year 1900 much of its contents must have appeared quite "realistic," even downright vulgar, to many readers. Not merely the lynching scene at the close, but such other matters as adultery, illegitimacy, a hint or two of loose sexual goings-on, conniving politicians—some of whom bore honored names—a no-holds-barred description of a state political convention, a less-than-idyllic description of the monotony and brutality of dirt farming were unusual fare, especially in novels by young Southern ladies. In the 1920s Stuart P. Sherman declared that with *The Voice of the People,* "realism crossed the Potomac twenty-five years ago going North." Miss Glasgow herself thought it probably "the first work of genuine realism to appear in Southern fiction."

For all that, however, *The Voice of the People* does not seem a very realistic novel today. The protagonist, Nick Burr, is nobody's realistic man of the world. As a boy he seems romantic and idealized; as a man, hollow and lifeless. The meaning of the novel depends on his being a martyr to truth, progress, and democratic ideals, and he is too unreal to be a martyr to anything. For the fact is that beyond the level of the pat abstraction, Miss Glasgow had no real knowledge of what the new democracy meant, and could give him no meaning. Once she had Nick elected governor and was forced to make good on his idealism, the only solution she could find for his career was to have him killed while attempting to save a Negro from being lynched.

It is with this novel that the modern reader first encounters an essential aspect of Miss Glasgow's "social history"—often enough the true social history lies not in what Miss Glasgow writes about it but in the fact that it is Miss Glasgow who is writing it. The rise of the common man to dominance in Virginia *ought* to be heroic and meaningful, she felt; but though she tried twice to achieve this meaning in her fiction, she never managed to succeed. In *One Man in His Time* (1922), her technique was more subtle, and by focusing, not directly upon the poor boy rising to power this time, but upon an aristocratic young Richmonder who comes to admire him, she managed several chapters of excellent social portraiture. Yet this novel too foundered on the same rock that had done in *The Voice of the People*. The most effective parts in the novel come when Stephen Culpeper, aristocratic young Queenborough resident, ceases to meditate about high political ideals and ponders instead the mores and manners of Queenborough society. In what is otherwise a poor novel we are treated to a little of what later became the focus of Miss Glasgow's best work: the aristocracy faced with defining its own shrinking function in the face of increasing middle-class infiltration. For that, as we shall see, was something Miss Glasgow *knew*, in a way that she could never know the ideological virtues of the new democracy.

In both these novels, what Miss Glasgow excelled in was the occasional moment in which a member of the first families of Virginia confronts someone of lower status in a situation that has social implications. At such times Miss Glasgow senses the problems of definition that are involved, and presents them with real understanding. It is this theme that provides the best portions of all of Ellen Glasgow's novels. It is one part of the "social history" that is convincingly genuine.

Perhaps the most successful of all her early novels, *The Miller of Old Church* (1911), is based squarely upon this theme of the function of class. Jonathan Gay, high-born young dilettante, comes home to southside Virginia but cannot adapt himself to the non-aristocratic rural community. His closest attachment is to Molly Merryweather, a girl born out of wed-

lock to a mother from a country family and a father with social status. But Abel Revercomb, the plain, virtuous miller of
Old Church, loves Molly, and Molly eventually comes to realize that the good Abel is her true desire, thus electing a clean
life of honest toil with the humble miller rather than one of
aristocratic frivolity with her own class.

It is fascinating to watch Miss Glasgow at work, trying to
bring this off. By all Miss Glasgow's theories, and by her intentions, the task should have been one of making Molly
worthy of Abel—he is the sturdy one, the man of the people,
the embodiment of the solid virtues of the new man. But instead we find the author bending every effort at making the
plain, upright miller worthy of the tempestuous, complex,
aristocratic Molly.

It is a good thing that Jonathan Gay, Molly's far-from-
disinterested cousin, is shot to death before the novel ends, as
if to eliminate any possibility of Molly's backsliding. We feel
somewhat better, too, for knowing that, after all, Molly is
only *partly* aristocratic in birth, and she *was* born out of wed-
lock. Even so, the final union is not quite convincing; for all
of Miss Glasgow's valiant attempts at preparing for the result,
one never quite feels that Molly is ready permanently to wed
and bed with Abel.

When a Glasgow heroine contemplates marriage, particularly in the earlier novels, the problem is usually one of
whether to marry beneath her social station or not to wed at
all. It is interesting to speculate upon this. For Ellen Glasgow
was a young woman of intellect, interested in literature, in all
the latest ideas. She declined the usual coming-out party in
Richmond society, concerned herself instead with such matters as Henry George's *Progress and Poverty* and Fabian so-
cialism, joined the City Mission, visited the inmates of charity
hospitals. Yet as James Branch Cabell has noted, Miss Glasgow was never remotely a social egalitarian. Certainly she
seems never to have found in Richmond society any eligible
male with whom she might be temperamentally and intellectually congenial.

The novel that followed *The Miller of Old Church* was
Virginia (1913), which Miss Glasgow called "the first book
of my maturity." One can agree wholeheartedly. The protago-

nist, Virginia Pendleton Treadwell, is a girl raised according to the old standards. "The chief object of her upbringing, which differed in no essential particular from that of every other well-bred and well-born Southern woman of her day, was to paralyze her reasoning faculties so completely that all danger of mental unsettling, or even movement, was eliminated from her future." Virginia falls in love with and marries a young playwright, who tries for a time to fit into the prevailing business life, then forsakes his earlier dramatic ideals, becomes a writer of comedies, and after becoming successful soon tires of his wife and deserts her for more sophisticated company.

Virginia is very much a creature of limitation, and Miss Glasgow's original intention was to satirize her inadequacies. But as Miss Glasgow tells us, during the writing of the book her irony grew fainter and "yielded at last to sympathetic compassion." Virginia does indeed grow in attractiveness and the reader's sympathy as the novel develops. At the last, one has the conviction that perhaps it is not Virginia's old-fashioned values that are at fault, but those of the crass new times.

Ellen Glasgow pictured Virginia Pendleton Treadwell as being everything that she, Ellen Glasgow, was not. She herself was not sentimental and old-fashioned; she was a realistic, intellectually alert modern. Yet when one reads the self-portrait of Miss Glasgow that constitutes her posthumously published autobiography, *The Woman Within*, one wonders. For the author of that memoir is more than a little sentimental, and despite her intellectual accomplishments very much an idealist of the old school. One feels that there is much more of Ellen Glasgow in Virginia Pendleton Treadwell's make-up than her creator was willing to admit.

Because Miss Glasgow was able to conceive of Virginia as a limited, bounded person, she achieved a convincing and harmonious characterization. That part of Ellen Glasgow that was Virginia—the idealistic, old-fashioned, warmhearted Southern girl—she knew and understood very well, though she did not recognize it in herself. The other side of Miss Glasgow's character, the rebellious, intellectually alive, firm-minded modernist, she did not understand nearly so well, did not perceive the limitations. And when she put that kind of person into her novels, her troubles began.

Miss Glasgow's masterpiece, in her own estimation and in
that of many readers, is *Barren Ground* (1925). "What I saw,
as my novel unfolded," she wrote later, "was a complete reversal of a classic situation. For once, in Southern fiction, the
betrayed woman would become the victor instead of the
victim." Dorinda Oakley, the central figure of the novel, is a
farm girl who is betrayed in her love for Jason Greylock, a
young man of high caste but weak will. Dorinda proceeds to
rise above it. She flees to New York, earns a living there for
a while, then comes back home and converts her father's run-
down dirt farm into a prosperous commercial-dairy operation,
achieving what is presented as a satisfying life. Her chief virtues, as we are frequently informed by the author, are her integrity and courage. Dorinda, says Miss Glasgow, was "universal. She exists wherever a human being has learned to live
without joy, wherever the spirit of fortitude has triumphed
over the sense of futility."

But where exactly does Dorinda's vaunted courage reside?
Supposedly in her decision to turn her back on those things
which as a girl she had most desired—love, affection, sexual
fulfillment, a husband and family. She learns "to live without
joy." She makes up her mind to become as hard, as unromantic,
as business-minded as any man. Her triumph is one of super-
human self-sufficiency over human dependence and love.

It is a triumph, most of all, of sterility. For *Barren Ground*
is an aptly named novel. Dorinda's life is a progressive espousal
of barrenness. As a woman, she abhors, fears, sexual love. As a
farmer, she converts the land from agriculture to pasture for
commercial dairying. As a character, too, Dorinda is lifeless,
impersonal, once the brief romance at the beginning of the
novel is done. Her choice of the joyless existence is unconvincing: supposedly a passionate decision, it seems peculiarly cold-
blooded, inhuman. In writing *Barren Ground*, Miss Glasgow
declared, she felt she had "found a code of living that was
sufficient for life or for death." One agrees, ironically, for as a
living, feeling, believable human being, Dorinda ceases to exist once her romantic moment is done.

Now there is no doubt that Miss Glasgow thought of herself in the same way she thought of Dorinda. She had "per-
severed in the face of an immense disadvantage," and no less

than Dorinda had "faced the future without romantic glamour, but . . . faced it with integrity of vision." She had rejected the sentimental, the romantic, she felt, just as Dorinda did. But the truth is that Ellen Glasgow only *thought* she was like Dorinda; in actuality she was much more. Persevere she did, and surely she possessed more than her fair share of "integrity of vision," of firm Presbyterian resolve to hold to her course in spite of all obstacles. But as a person—we have *The Woman Within* for witness, and the testimony of her friends, and we have the novels—she retained much of what she had Dorinda deny: the craving for affection, for acclaim, for admiration. There was no more gracious hostess in Richmond; she maintained many stanch friendships in the literary world. For fame, and acclaim, she was always most zealous. The lady who wrote *The Woman Within,* who wrote the *Selected Letters,* was no Spartan, like her Dorinda Oakley; she was much too human, much too warm a person for that.

If it was spiritual self-portrait, then, that Ellen Glasgow meditated in *Barren Ground,* as it so clearly seems, her effort was hardly complete. It leaves out too much; and I suggest that if we are to look for what is left out, the place to look is not in *Barren Ground* at all. It is Virginia Pendleton Treadwell, the heroine of *Virginia,* feminine, eager for affection, in no way reconciled to a joyless, passionless, stoical life. Virginia Pendleton Treadwell, Miss Glasgow believed, was all that she herself was not; *she* was Dorinda, the firm-minded, the woman who would do without joy. She would deny the needs of Virginia; she would be strong, spurning the feminine weakness that required love, affection. She would be emancipated, "modern," unromantic, intellectual. She would be like Dorinda Oakley. But she was both of them. And, realizing this, we understand what Mr. Cabell meant when he remarked that the true theme of the "social history" was "the Tragedy of Everywoman, As It Was Lately Enacted in the Commonwealth of Virginia."

In *Barren Ground,* Miss Glasgow had written a novel about a woman who was defiantly superior to all need for joy. Now she proceeded joyfully to write three novels about people who were not so fortunate. In *The Romantic Comedians* (1926), *They Stooped to Folly* (1929), and *The Sheltered Life* (1932), she dealt directly and humorously with the ironies of love, marriage, procreation. Her heroes and heroines are all members of upper-level Richmond society, and the situations are drawn out of what is Miss Glasgow's most consistently successful medium—social satire, the aging aristocracy in a world turning steadily more bourgeois. Because she saw her people as limited creatures, she wrote stories with believable, reasonably complete characterizations. The dominant tone is ironical, accompanied by much compassion.

The central character of *The Romantic Comedians*, Judge Gamaliel Bland Honeywell, has missed romance all his life, and attempts at the age of sixty-five to capture it, only to realize dimly at the close that one cannot turn back the clock. Had he been a younger man, it would have mattered more, but as it is, the element of passion is so little in the picture that there is no feeling that the judge is being too cruelly punished for his sins. So deft is the characterization that we accept the judge for what he is.

They Stooped to Folly is also built around an aging male protagonist, Virginius Curle Littlepage. He is a middle-aged lawyer, fallible and human, and in proportion to these traits, we like him. He is married to a high-minded and virtuous lady, and he has a high-minded and virtuous daughter. He dreams of romantic passion, and is attracted to a neighbor, Mrs. Dalrymple, a comely and not-so-high-minded woman. We wish he would gather up enough nerve to have the affair he desires, and once he almost does, but we understand it when he cannot finally do so, because Virginius is a contained, bounded creature, and Miss Glasgow intended him to be. The sensibilities of the protagonist are admirably fitted to the requirements of the story.

Miss Glasgow's next book was her triumph. *The Sheltered Life* (1932) is, more than any of her other books, a formal success, with characterization, plot development, and, above all, the tone of the prose working in near-flawless harmony to produce a little masterpiece of sensibility. The theme is that of a young girl's progression from innocence to human involvement. Jenny Blair Archbald's sensibilities are effectively shaped to the requirements of the adolescent characterization. Her drive toward passionate engagement in human desire represents something of a fated, explosive action in which she seems almost helpless in the bonds of her mortal sensuality. Similarly, her grandfather, old General Archbald, is sympathetically and beautifully done, and provides an effective thematic and dramatic counterpoint for Jenny Blair. She is too young to know what she is doing; he is too old to be able to act.

Surely this is one of the most significant perceptions of the "social history"; for what Jenny Blair Archbald basically represents is a well-born young woman, raised "traditionally" and with all the old romantic illusions carefully nurtured in her, suddenly come face to face with reality. Nothing she has been told or taught is of any real use to her in coping with it. The general's wisdom, that of the past, cannot serve as guide or model. She will have to discover her own way. Miss Glasgow manages this insight without being either sentimental or smug.

With *The Sheltered Life* Miss Glasgow ended her period of social satire. She turned back to her earlier high seriousness, and while in certain matters of technique her last two novels are superior to the earlier novels of this kind, they are distinctly less successful fiction than the satirical novels immediately preceding them. When Miss Glasgow abandoned comedy, I think, she abandoned her true forte. Only in satire could she maintain the kind of objectivity about her people that made them believable and credible in their own right.

In *Vein of Iron* (1935) she returned for good to those who suffer and live without joy. She returned, too, to the plain folk, seeking to show, as the title of the novel indicates, the human will to endure. Ada Fincastle, the heroine, lives a blighted existence, as does everyone else in *Vein of Iron*. As in *Barren Ground* what is striking is the passivity of the characters. They merely endure. The next impact is not sympathy and admiration for Ada's rock-bound qualities, but something more akin to weariness. Ada never seems a thinking, hoping, acting person, with whom the reader can feel any real rapport.

As nearly always in Miss Glasgow's novels, sex is portrayed as something ugly and ruinous for all concerned. Ada goes off into the woods with Ralph, and the result is an illegitimate child. In *Barren Ground*, Dorinda's liaison was equally blighted. In *The Sheltered Life* there is suffering aplenty because of the promiscuity of George Birdsong. When Abel Revercomb embraces Molly Merryweather early in *The Miller*

of Old Church, Molly is repelled. "I suppose most girls like
that sort of thing, but I don't, and I shan't, if I live to be a
hundred." Virginius Littlepage almost misbehaves with Mrs.
Dalrymple in *They Stooped to Folly,* then returns home to
find, almost as cause and effect, that his wife has died. Milly
Burden of that novel conceives an illegitimate child. Annabel
feels physical revulsion for the old judge in *The Romantic
Comedians.* As early as *Phases of an Inferior Planet,* marriage
for the hero and heroine is quickly followed by desperate
poverty and the death of their child, whereupon their union
disintegrates.

Miss Glasgow describes, in *The Woman Within,* a visit she
made early in her career to a professional literary adviser, who
made improper advances. " 'If you kiss me I will let you go,' he
said presently; but at last I struggled free without kissing. His
mouth, beneath his grey moustache, was red and juicy, and it
gave me forever afterwards a loathing for red and juicy lips."
The tremendous physical revulsion and fear explicit in that description is surely paralleled in her fiction.

In Miss Glasgow's last novel, *In This Our Life* (1941), there
is no true happiness or pleasure to be found for anyone. Written while its author was ill and often unable for months at a
time to continue work, it is the story of impoverished towns-
folk, vaguely members of the old aristocracy, but for whom
such identification has ceased to have any real meaning. Once
again everything is a tired, bloodless novel. The "social history"
of Virginia ends on a note of exhaustion.

When we examine the "social history" to see the accomplishment of Miss Glasgow's panorama of novels about Virginia life, from the pre-Civil War (*The Battle-Ground,* 1902)
to the 1930s, we are impressed with the unevenness of her
chronicle. The more successful novels—*Virginia, The Romantic
Comedians, They Stooped to Folly, The Sheltered Life*—stand
out brightly. What is notable is that, in each of these, Miss
Glasgow is dealing primarily with protagonists of the upper
classes, the old families. In each one we see the breakdown
of the old aristocratic tradition before the onslaught of modern life. They are all novels of *loss*—and what is lost in them
all is the aristocratic possibility. The Southern woman of the
old school in *Virginia* loses because her old-fashioned virtues,

those of Southern Womanhood, cannot cope with the demands of the twentieth century. The old judge in *The Romantic Comedians* feels that his life has been loveless and futile, but when he attempts to recapture his youth, he becomes not only further saddened but is made ridiculous as well. Virginius Curle Littlepage in *They Stooped to Folly* is rather futile from the start, and what he discovers is the impossibility of doing anything positive for himself or his friends and family. In *The Sheltered Life* Jenny Blair Archbald, nurtured an old-fashioned romance, runs right into disaster in the real world, while old General Archbald, his day long since done, cannot do anything to prevent it. Each time there is failure. And each time, too, the reader's sympathies are actively engaged, and the characterizations shine forth convincingly. Miss Glasgow understood these people; they were her own kind. What she knew, what she could portray perceptively and fully, was the collapse of the old order. Given that theme, she seldom faltered.

But when that was not her theme, her novels failed. *The Miller of Old Church* failed because the thematic intention ran counter to the characterization. Molly Merryweather should, by the dictates of all that is modern and democratic, find strength and happiness in the plain but good miller—yet Miss Glasgow wound up straining to make the miller temperamentally worthy of Molly, instead of the other way around. Both *The Voice of the People* and *One Man in His Time* failed because the man of the people who was supposed to bring honesty and progress to Virginia life could not be imbued with a dramatic characterization to fit the thematic meaning. In *The Battle-Ground,* her Civil War romance, she attempted to show the planter aristocracy in full heroism and glory; what she produced was a thinly sentimental pastiche, without firmness or conviction. In *Barren Ground* and *Vein of Iron* she turned to the common folk for her protagonists, but the heroines of both novels could only suffer lifelessly, and the rock-bound fortitude with which she sought to endow them is not strength of will so much as stolid passivity. They are not interesting people; they are tiresomely heavy. Oddly enough, she attempted in each of these novels to provide, at the close, a hopeful ending; in every case it seems unreal, forced.

What the social history in fiction succeeds in recording

vividly is the breakdown of the old families, their failure to find meaning and function in the new middle-class democracy. When the attempt is to portray the virtues of the way of life that displaced them, and of the people who succeeded them in command, the novels are unconvincing. The true social history, then, is observable not only in what Miss Glasgow succeeded in doing, but in what she could not do. She could not give a meaning to twentieth-century democracy in Virginia. As a novelist, all she knew—and she knew that so well—was the failure of the old order. Her best work is rooted in its collapse.

III

Ellen Glasgow thought of herself as a realist. "What the South needs is blood and irony," her pronouncement went—and she felt that as a novelist she was chiefly engaged in providing both these elements. By contrast, James Branch Cabell insisted that he was a romantic. For realism in literature he had considerable scorn. "Veracity," he remarked, "is the one unpardonable sin, not merely against art, but against human welfare." And again: "If 'realism' be a form of art, the morning newspaper is a permanent contribution to literature." He composed most of his fiction about an imaginary, faraway land he called Poictesme, and the time he most often selected for his work was not the twentieth century but the hazy medieval. He was in no way concerned with what a social historian would seize upon. Politics, class conflicts, economic transition, the impact of modernity upon the Virginia aristocracy—what have these to do with Mr. Cabell's fiction, whether set in Poictesme or, as sometimes happened, in Lichfield, his own version of Richmond? His people find satisfaction only in dreams; his protagonists are preoccupied with escape.

It is not surprising, then, that the term "escapist" has been applied to his work. Poictesme, the critics declared in the socially conscious decade that followed Mr. Cabell's heyday of the 1920s, was a cloud-cuckoo land, having no purpose other than to divert and to amuse. His swift decline in popularity during the 1930s has been ascribed directly to his failure to come to grips with the problems of his time. "Cabell and Hitler," declared Alfred Kazin, "did not inhabit the same universe" (*On Native Grounds*, 1941, 231).

Similarly, his relationship to the South, and to Southern literature, has been put down as one of flight. A thorough aristocrat, he is supposed to have looked out on twentieth-century Richmond-in-Virginia, frowned upon what he saw, and conjured up instead a better never-never world of imaginary heroes, noble deeds, and grand passions, all of which were notably lacking in the modern South. "Because he disliked the world he saw outside his Virginia home," Marshall Fishwick has written, "James Branch Cabell invented one inside his Virginia mind" ("Cabell and Glasgow: Tradition in Search of Meaning," *Shenandoah*, VII [1957], 24).

Perhaps. Yet before accepting so simple a solution, it might be wise to examine a few of those novels, and see just what sort of satisfyingly heroic and aristocratic life Mr. Cabell purportedly sets up in protest against the mundane present. Let us take a closer look at those romantic novels of escape which were so popular during the twenties and are so little read today. For if the Cabell canon is so everlastingly far removed from reality, we might wonder why it is that so engaged, so serious-minded a critic as Edmund Wilson learned to become such a vigorous champion of Mr. Cabell's work, to the extent of declaring that the Cabell cult of the twenties was unfortunate because its effect "was eventually to leave the impression that its object was second-rate, and this is unjust to Mr. Cabell, whose distinction is real and of an uncommon kind" ("The James Branch Cabell Case Reopened," *The New Yorker* [April 21, 1956], 29). Surely Mr. Wilson is not noted for his advocacy of escapism. Let us look, then, at a few of the novels.

Figures of Earth (1921), the seminal work in the multi-volumed *Biography of Manuel* that probably constitutes Mr. Cabell's major achievement, has to do with a swineherd who likes to sculpt figures out of clay. Manuel soon postpones sculpting, however, and departs to seek adventure. He wins in turn the love of the queenly Alianora and the divine Freydis, but leaves them both, more than mortal though they are, to win back from death one Naifer, an ordinarily attractive woman of no special charm. With her he subsequently lives and rears children in the Duchy of Poictesme, whose sover-

eignty he gains after considerable maneuvering and adventur-
ing. His life at home with Naifer is not especially blissful or
romantic, but he prefers it, even so. At the end, as he departs
for Valhalla, he sees one of his earthen statues. "What is that
thing?" he is asked. "It is the figure of a man," he replies,
"which I have modeled and remodeled, and cannot get exactly
to my liking. So it is necessary that I keep laboring at it, until
the figure is to my liking and my desire."

It would be hard to say just how Manuel's life represents
an escape from the crass present and into satisfying romance.
His heroic deeds have produced a dukedom, true; but what is
it ultimately worth to him? He has not given life to the statue
he sought to sculpt. There is still the third window of the pal-
ace, through which he cannot bear to look, and which represents all the things he had hoped to be, all he had meant to
achieve and did not because he was mortal and had grown
old without getting around to them.

It is most clear that Manuel's life was *not* one of satisfyingly
heroic achievement. His own inescapably mortal nature, his
preference for comfort and compromise, for the familiar, left
him at the last not a whit more "successful," in his own eyes,
than might have been the case had he lived in mundane
Richmond-in-Virginia in the twentieth century, instead of in
medieval Poictesme, where the heroic possibility was supposedly so abundant. The net effect is a denial of all possibility
for mortal achievement in deeds—not because of crass times,
not because of the absence of the aristocratic possibility, but
because of the nature of man. Only the earthen figures, unsatisfactory, unfinished, remain after Manuel has gone.

So in transferring his fictional world from the present to the
faraway past, Mr. Cabell has not exactly "escaped." Quite the
contrary: the past has turned out to be very much like the
present, and that seems to have been Mr. Cabell's point. Not
only in *Manuel*, but in others of his Poictesme novels, the same
discovery is made: the romantic, glorious past is found by its
inhabitants to contain no more satisfaction than the present.

Gerald Musgrave, in *Something about Eve*, continually
searches after beautiful women who will not cloy, as his mortal
mistress cloys; but each new daughter of Eve turns out to be
but a replica of Evelyn Townsend. The protagonist of *Jurgen*,

visiting eternity, turns away from fair Helen's bed, because he knows at last that only by so doing will he be able to preserve the illusion that she, unlike all other women, is something special. Florian de Puysange, not so wise, seeks out the lovely Melior of his dreams in *The High Place,* and she soon proves to be no different from his earthly wives and mistresses. Again and again the Cabellian hero manages to controvert the laws of chronology and to escape into a never-never land; his findings are always the same. He is still human; he is still subject to the usual limitations of mortality.

Mr. Cabell, H. L. Mencken has written, is "really the most acidulous of all the anti-romantics." His "gaudy heroes," he notes, "in the last analysis, chase dragons precisely as stockbrokers play golf. . . . Art, argues Cabell, is an escape from life: a doctrine quite beyond challenge. The artist seeks surcease from reality by creating an ideal world. *Soit!* But once he has moved into it he finds to his dismay that it is made of the same silicon, carbon, aluminum, oxygen, hydrogen and calcium that make the real one" (*James Branch Cabell,* 1928, 22). What the Cabell hero always finds beyond time and space is still more mortality.

It should be obvious, then, that there is something of the social history of Virginia in the Cabell novels too. Like Miss Glasgow's they too were composed by a modern descendant of the old aristocracy, a member of one of the first families of Virginia. They too were written in a time of progress, of great material advancement, of developing political democracy, when the old aristocracy lost the remnants of what control over state destinies remained to it after the Civil War had ended its hegemony. Yet what we have in the Cabell novels is hardly a hymn to progress and democracy; it is a skepticism that goes far beyond the usual lament for the "Good Old Days before de Wah," and into a wryly comic denial of the efficacy of works, a scouting of the possibilities of lasting, satisfying, heroic existence at any time.

It is odd that Mr. Cabell's novel *The Silver Stallion* (1926) has not been more thoroughly investigated for the commentary it embodies on the author's own times, in particular the last decades of the nineteenth century in the South, when the old Confederates were being so assiduously mythologized and the

Lost Cause was being transformed into a legendary struggle of heroes. This novel, which seems to me one of the best of Mr. Cabell's many works of fiction, chronicles the growth of the legend of Manuel the Redeemer after his death. We follow each of Manuel's former cronies as they attempt unsuccessfully to reconcile the growing deification of Manuel and the fictionalizing of their joint exploits with their actual memories of the leader and the times they once knew. Each must come to terms with the legend. One after another they struggle against it, protest against its unreality, then make their adjustments. Some accept it, bow to the counterfeit legend, falsify their own roles. Others retire from the scene, pursuing their private realities and forbearing to challenge the public myth-making. Finally even Donander, the Christian God that Manuel believed in, winds up in a pagan heaven by mistake and passes his days by making his little creations of worlds, obeying the customary rituals.

At the last Jurgen the pawnbroker, son of one of Manuel's old warriors, talks with Dame Naifer, Manuel's widow, and decides that the growth of the legend may be all for the best. Everything has fitted into the myth, which is palpably false and humbug—and *he* knows, for he helped to invent a story that set the myth-making off. Yet the legend has become more real than the truth.

Is this not precisely what happened with the myth of the Confederacy in Mr. Cabell's own day? In Richmond, too, certain first-class fighting men were made into stainless heroes, often in spite of themselves. In Richmond, too, the legend of the Lost Cause was made to replace the actual events themselves. As a child, Mr. Cabell had seen it happen, and the discrepancy had been puzzling: "It was confusing, the way in which your elders talked about things which no great while before you were born had happened in Richmond. . . . Richmond was not at all like Camelot or Caerlon upon Usk; and so you found it kind of curious that the way in which your elders talked, upon platforms, reminded you of your *Stories of the Days of King Arthur,* by Charles Henry Hanson, with illustrations by Gustave Doré."

This process of myth-making, set forth so quaintly by Mr. Cabell in *Let Me Lie,* is precisely the subject of *The Silver*

Stallion. The deceased Manuel's wife, Naifer, and her spiritual adviser, Holmendis, were, with the help of the population of Poictesme, busily creating a national saint out of a mortal and unsaintly man and turning his deeds and those of his followers into a legend that was only in few respects similar to the truth. In the end the myth, the legend of Manuel the Redeemer, triumphed. When Jurgen the pawnbroker ascends the statue of Manuel that his widow has caused to be erected, he finds that the jewels that adorned it were "one and all, and had been from the first, bright bits of variously colored glass." Naifer had sent Jurgen up the statue to assay the value of the jewels, for she, who had herself built the statue, had so forgotten what the reality was, as to come to believe, too, that the glasswork was jewelry!

Yet as Jurgen ponders the matter, he decides that the statue of Manuel the Redeemer was no mere fraud. Made though it was of counterfeit jewelry, nevertheless, "you knew the shining thing to have been, also, the begetter of so much charity, and of forbearance, and of bravery, and of self-denial—and of its devotees' so strange, so troublingly incomprehensible, contentment . . . ." Clearly the effect of the Manuel legend upon the succeeding generations of Poictesme had been entirely beneficent. It had civilized, ennobled, made more virtuous those who believed in it.

Of what importance, Mr. Cabell has asked, is the myth, whether for Poictesme or Richmond-in-Virginia? He answers by declaring that myth-making is the single most important fact of all human activity. He includes in this category not only Manuel the Redeemer, or the Confederate legend, but all mortal beliefs, including religion itself. "Men have, out of so many thousand years of speculation," he has written, "contrived no surer creed than . . . that 'in matters of faith it is necessary to believe blindly.' Men have discovered no firmer hope than that, in defiance of all logic and of all human experience, something very pleasant may still be impending, in —need I say?—bright lands which are in nothing familiar."

For Cabell, the dream was the myth, and the only important literary activity. He could discover nothing else sufficiently real and deserving of attention. The conviction he held about the everyday activities of humans, whether in Richmond or

Poictesme, had to do with the briefness and evanescence of men and what they did in time. To be alive was to be doomed in time: "We live *in Articulo Mortis;* our doings here, when unaffectedly regarded, are but the restlessness of a prolonged demise; and the birth-cry of every infant announces the beginning of the death-agony."

In creating and articulating myth, therefore, he was far from trying to avoid reality; rather, it was on precisely such terms that reality presented itself to him. So-called realism in art, he felt, was merely the art of paying attention to the mileposts along the way, instead of to the journey itself. "To spin romances is, indeed, man's proper and peculiar function in a world wherein he only of created beings can make no profitable use of the truth about himself. For man alone of animals plays the ape to his dreams."

Whether or not Mr. Cabell's deductions are sound is one thing; what is important is that he held the conviction, and based his art upon it. And that, it seems to me, is a telling observation about his time and place, and his relationship to them. This was what modern-day reality in Richmond meant for one discerning artist. His faraway Poictesme became for him the stage upon which all that mattered most about men was the direct and unsheltered subject of scrutiny. The meditations to which the statue of Manuel the Redeemer inspired Jurgen are no less serious because they were occasioned by events in legendary Poictesme, rather than by a contemplation of the statue of George Washington in Capitol Park in Richmond.

I have, I fear, made Mr. Cabell out to be a rather serious and somber writer. This is a mistake; the Cabell novels are ordinarily anything but grim. He is essentially a comic writer, and those who have placed him in the lineage of Boccaccio, Rabelais, Petronius Arbiter, Laurence Sterne are generally correct. Mr. Cabell is amused by the world; his novels are constructed upon that amusement. If the laughter seems sardonic sometimes, when the absurdities of his people seem only too recognizable to us, then we must remember that Mr. Cabell considers *that* rather amusing too.

The Cream of the Jest (1917), for example, contains some hilarious situations. A novelist named Felix Bulmer Kennaston gets hold of the Sigil of Scoteia, which, if he will clutch it as he goes to bed, will transport him into a dream world of timeless adventure. He becomes Horvendile, the master storyteller, and roams through time in space with a lovely and immortal maid named Ettare, while during his waking hours he writes a novel that has a career very much like Mr. Cabell's *Jurgen* of several years later. Finally Felix Kennaston finds the other half of the Sigil of Scoteia in his wife's boudoir. She was Ettare all along, he decided, and neither could tell the other, for neither was aware of the other's role. But his wife, puzzled by the significance Kennaston attaches to the Sigil, suggests he discuss it with his friend Harrowby, a student of the occult. Harrowby may be able to interpret the strange hieroglyphics on the Sigil.

His wife's suggestion, however, as we learn from Harrowby, is not prompted by any belief in the occult. It is simply that the Sigil is nothing more than the lid of a cosmetics jar, manufactured by a company of which Harrowby is an owner. Harrowby does not tell Kennaston, of course; he does not wish to shatter the poor fellow's illusions.

The scene in which Harrowby "deciphers" the mystery of the Sigil is absurdly comic. All of Kennaston's fanciful theorizing is built on something as mundane and insubstantial as the seal from a jar of cold cream! The description of the deadly serious Kennaston puzzling vainly over the secret message imprinted by the cosmetics manufacturer, finding in the tin disk the inspiration for wild and sublimely soaring flights into unreality, is almost wickedly ironic. Kennaston seems in the direct line of "my father" in *Tristram Shandy*, of Don Quixote.

But, as with all great comic artists, there is pathos behind the absurdity. At the last, is Felix Kennaston actually the absurd, impractical, ludicrous dreamer that Harrowby and his other Lichfield neighbors think him? Has he really wasted his days, as even his wife Kathleen believes? After all, Kennaston's pursuit of the radiant Ettare produced, in his waking hours, some very Cabellian novels, and brought him impressively close—much closer than his down-to-earth neighbors will ever come—to what any man hopes to achieve: beauty, immortality, art. Does it matter ultimately that the Sigil is only a cosmetic tin? For that matter, *was* that all it was? After all, Kennaston's valuation of the Sigil made possible so imposing a superstructure of dreams. Eventually what will remain of Kennaston will be the novels that grew out of the dreaming, and which in their imperfect way manage to retain a little of the wondrous vision. This alone is far more than his neighbors will leave behind. Which interpretation of the Sigil is real, then—the mundane world's, or Kennaston's? Who was at last the "practical" man—Kennaston the dreamer or Harrowby the responsible citizen? Mr. Cabell asks us this riddle, and the answer would seem to be a rather formidable commentary on the efficacy and value of that everyday life from which he was supposedly escaping so capriciously.

The famous *Jurgen* (1919) is likewise a comic book, including some episodes of rather low comedy at that. Tired of his wife, Jurgen the pawnbroker is granted the Faustian privilege of journeying through time and space. He regains his youth, by which is meant above all his aptitude for romantic love. In succession he visits and tarries for a while with Guenever, who is all chivalrous and highborn beauty (and also a little slut); Anaïtis, the incarnation of pagan, carnal delight; the Hamadryad Chloris, innocence, rustic bliss incomparable; and Florimel the vampire, all that a *femme fatale* can hope to be. There is, furthermore, the chance for Jurgen to make love to Helen herself, who is also his childhood sweetheart Dorothy la Desirée, all perfect, imagined, personally desired loveliness, the dream of one's youth, the embodiment of idealized, romantic passion.

In cavorting with these various maids and matrons, Jurgen proves "a monstrous clever fellow," and Mr. Cabell's sense of pornographic symbolism is hard at work. Yet once again the final impression is one of considerable irony. Jurgen decides, having had his choice, to go back to his unglamorous, middle-aged wife, Dame Lisa, who is what he had learned to become accustomed to. For all her faults, all her shrewishness and her failure to "understand" Jurgen, she is the known quantity, the compromise men make with ideals. Jurgen might indeed attain immortality, the stars, the heights of romance and art; being man, he prefers marriage instead. Here again the legendary trappings of Poictesme do not produce an escapist romance;

they only heighten the irony. The incorrigible humanness of the characters triumphs.

But if the quest for unattainable beauty, for perfect art, never succeeds, it is nonetheless a continual quest. The Cabell hero is a prisoner in time; he is mortal and must die, and as a mortal he cannot know fulfillment. For the artist, as a man, life represents a continual diminution of his urge to create, a hopeless and failing quest for the impossible act of pure creativity. Still, of all man's activities, only art can offer any hope of survival. It alone endures beyond death—capriciously and erratically, to be sure, but it endures.

One conviction runs through Mr. Cabell's work: the indomitable nature of man. Man knows neither why nor how he exists, but he *is*. Limited, fallible, he is a creature of courage and endurance, the central image of creation. For man has his dreams, and though he cannot for one moment prove or demonstrate their truth, they afford him his only and supreme hope. "We are being made into something quite unpredictable, I imagine: and we are sustained, through the purging and the smelting, by an instinctive knowledge that we are being made into something better. For this we know, quite incommunicably, and yet as surely as we know that we will to have it thus."

At bottom, all Mr. Cabell's cynicism, and his fond and fastidious mockery of human pretense and conceit, is based upon a kind of visceral and rock-bound humanism, a conviction that in the very absurdity of his dreams and his playing man is demonstrating that he can and will survive. The myth-maker is supreme, because it is he who, by dreaming, confutes the very nature of mortality. "And it is this will that stirs in us to have the creatures of earth and the affairs of earth, not as they are, but 'as they ought to be,' which we call romance. But when we note how visibly it sways all life we perceive that we are talking about God."

Thus did his meditations lead one Richmond novelist to decide, in the early decades of this century. His books were written in the years when the kingdom of works seemed more important than ever to his fellow citizens, whether in Richmond or elsewhere, and it is difficult to see them as anything less than a critique, wry, comic, penetrating, of his times. Art did not, for Mr. Cabell, finally lead nearly so far 'away from the social scene as has been generally thought. And remembering Felix Bulmer Kennaston and the Sigil of Scoteia, one wonders just how unrealistic Mr. Cabell's viewpoint will finally turn out to be.

IV

They were the first of the modern Southern writers. Decades before the Fugitives began assembling at Vanderbilt, before William Faulkner in New Orleans started work on a novel, before Thomas Wolfe decided to leave North Carolina for Harvard and a career as playwright, these two residents of Richmond were writing fiction. When Ellen Glasgow published *The Descendant* in 1897, James Joyce had not yet enrolled at the University in Dublin. Marcel Proust had published only one slight volume of occasional pieces. T. S. Eliot was a child in St. Louis. John Crowe Ransom was nine years old.

During their early years, the South was still mostly a conquered province; the predominantly agricultural economy of a relatively static, threadbare region had not yet been seriously changed by the industrial and commercial expansion that was transforming the Northeast and the Midwest. Only in a few Southern communities were the factories more important than the market places.

But one of these was Richmond. For Richmond was closer to the industrial cities of the North. The manufacturing interests that the Civil War had created to provide for the armies fighting just beyond the suburbs, the railroad network that had kept the city provisioned and supplied with commodities from the lower South, hung on after the war and made Richmond one of the cities in which the industrial ethic of the New South first took hold. Earlier than Tennessee, earlier than the whole lower South, Richmond espoused the new ways. And if, as seems likely, much of the impetus behind the Southern literary outburst of the twentieth century arose from the tensions resulting from the clash of the old ways and the new, then it is not surprising that Richmond should be the place where the first major authors of the Southern Literary Renascence arose.

Miss Glasgow died in 1945, Mr. Cabell in 1958. What their eventual places in the literature will be, it is difficult to say. So much of Ellen Glasgow's work seems dated now; only a few of her novels stand up in their own right, rather than as specimens in the transition from romanticism to realism in Southern literature. In any event, her place in Southern literary history would seem to be secure; it was she who led the way into the twentieth century, and the writers who came afterward, many of whom now seem more important than she, followed in her footsteps, and explored the new country that she had first visited. If from Thomas Nelson Page to William Faulkner there has been a tremendous transformation, then it is hardly too much to say that it was Ellen Glasgow who made the transformation possible.

Mr. Cabell is another matter. Today he is seldom read. His novels are almost all out of print. As a writer he was always something of an exotic; he has had few disciples, Southern or Northern. By contrast with Miss Glasgow, his role in the twentieth-century development of Southern literature was not crucial. As far as American writing as a whole goes, it is true that *Jurgen* played a part in the modern emancipation from puritanism in literature, but that aspect of his work seems least important now. Today he has only a few readers. Yet for those few he is unique, inimitable, providing something that no other modern writer offers. His work does not "date," does not seem limited to a period; it is perennially fresh, wise, and witty. There are other writers like him in the English language—writers who will never be widely popular, but will never be forgotten, who will continue to amuse and delight some few readers possessed of the taste and sophistication for the proper appreciation. That is the way Mr. Cabell would have liked it; in literature as in life, he was an aristocrat all the way.

Literary fashions come and go; nothing is more transient, more precarious than popular acclaim. But for Ellen Glasgow and James Branch Cabell at their best, some lines from a poem by Mr. Cabell in *Chivalry* will suffice for an epitaph.

*For I have got such recompense
Of that high-hearted excellence
Which the contented craftsman knows,
Alone, that to loved labor goes,
And daily does the work he chose,
And counts all else impertinence!*

WILLIAM FAULKNER: THE PASSION AND THE PENANCE

BY ROBERT D. JACOBS

Thirty years ago a certain region in north Mississippi, if not forgotten by God, was at least neglected by man. It was a land of eroded hillsides; of yellow or red earth dotted with meager cotton or corn patches (they were actually called *patches—fields* would be an overstatement); of mud-choked streams, twisting through the forests and undergrowth of the bottomland down toward the Delta and the great river. Only in this bottomland was the soil fertile; on the parched hillsides, corn stood no higher than a child, and the cotton reached only to a man's knee. When the rains came in the late fall, another layer of soil was washed from the hillside patches; the gullies bit deeper into the land; and the streams carried another load of earth to the Mississippi. Sometimes there were floods, drowning the thin cattle that wintered in the bottomland, ripping out the rickety bridges over the Tallahatchie, Coldwater, and Yocona rivers.

The towns—Sardis, Holly Springs, Coldwater, Senatobia, Grenada, New Albany (where William Faulkner was born in 1897), and Oxford—were actually mere trading posts for the hill farmers. There was no industry, little wealth, much poverty. There were no public libraries worth mentioning, no art galleries or concert halls.

If there are places which ought to produce writers, and places which ought not, then it must be considered a cause for wonder that the town of Oxford, county seat of Lafayette County, where Faulkner grew up, should have proved to be the nourishing place for a major literary talent. It has a university, to be sure, but in the second decade of the 1900s the University of Mississippi was a little provincial school with more of a reputation for its social life than its academic vitality. It had had one noted writer on its faculty, true; but that was Judge Augustus Baldwin Longstreet, author of *Georgia Scenes* (1835), and he had presided over the college's destinies before the Civil War. Stark Young had gone there and had been a member of the English faculty (1904–7), but too early to have been of any help to William Faulkner (Young did know Faulkner, through a mutual friend, Phil Stone, and invited him to New York in 1920). In fact, Faulkner did not get along too well at the university; he failed Freshman Composition and withdrew after only two semesters. Other than the university, there was nothing much to Oxford, a run-of-the-mill Mississippi town, with its Confederate monument in the town square and a population hardly distinguished for cultural activities.

Yet whatever the shortcomings of Oxford, Mississippi, then and now, it managed to do one thing that should cause it to be honored and remembered when many another town of greater cultural repute has been forgotten: it provided the model for the place and the people of a fictional universe whose dimensions are worldwide and whose implications seem to hold true for humanity at large. For out of Oxford, Lafayette County, and those years at home, Faulkner evolved the artistic image known to the literary world as Jefferson, county seat of Yoknapatawpha—an image likely to endure for more years than we care to predict.

The saga of Yoknapatawpha had to wait for Faulkner to find his medium. His first attempt was in poetry. The poems in his first book (*The Marble Faun*, 1924), published through the efforts of his friend Phil Stone, were only the muted echoes of a romantic mode. Faulkner had been reading Swinburne, Dowson, Wilde, and Housman, and the voice in the early poems was world-weary and sad, a jaded young man musing over pale lost dancers against a moon-blanched garden. Nor was either of his first two novels, *Soldiers' Pay* (1926) and *Mosquitoes* (1927), a precise augury of things to come. It was not until his third novel, *Sartoris* (1929), that Faulkner found his subject and authentic voice, if not yet his most characteristic technique. The efflorescence of his talent in the two years following the publication of *Mosquitoes* was startling, but Faulkner himself would not have us believe that, the discovery of the Yoknapatawpha material was sudden or unpremeditated. In his latest novel, *The Mansion* (1959), his prefatory note declares, "This book is the final chapter of, and the summation of, a work conceived and begun in 1925." If this is so, then the flowering between 1928 and 1930 was not as sudden as it has seemed; the seed had had time to grow.

Faulkner's statement is probably literal truth, or *Sartoris* would not serve so well as the introductory work to the Yoknapatawpha series. Many of the situations and characters that receive full development later originate in this novel. The Sartoris family itself, drawn at least in part from Faulkner's own, appears at the point of its virtual disappearance, just as in the next novel, *The Sound and the Fury*, the Compsons are limned in the swift years of their destruction. *Sartoris* is heavy with the history of the family; the past broods over the present, and John Sartoris, the Civil War colonel, long since dead, figures in the tale as if he were still alive. This is the beginning of one of Faulkner's recurrent themes, the envelopment of the present by the past, until the living merely act out roles ordained for them by the still-vital ghosts of their ancestors. The Sartoris past was not to receive extended treatment until nearly a decade later in *The Unvanquished*, but readers of *Sartoris* already know the history. In the later work Faulkner had simply to bring history to life; the outline was already there.

Though other families and characters appear in *Sartoris* (notably the Snopeses, later to be the subject of a trilogy, and the Benbows, who figure in *Sanctuary*), the focus of the novel is on young Bayard Sartoris, who is depicted with insufficient irony as the last of a doomed but gallant clan. (Bayard does leave a son, Benbow Sartoris, but this son has no role in the later novels.) *Sartoris* has been less favored by the critics than most of the Yoknapatawpha stories to date. Nearly thirty years ago Willard Thorp found it a romantic potboiler, reminiscent of Wren's *Beau Geste;* and indeed there is a superficial resemblance between the recklessness and devotion of John and Bayard Sartoris and the qualities of those British cavaliers Beau and Digby Geste.

Young Bayard (there is an old Bayard, the grandfather,

and yet a third, the "Carolina" Bayard) is one of Faulkner's returned soldiers, and though there are subplots that momentarily distract attention from his violent courtship of death, it is upon his representation of the Sartoris idea that the novel depends for its substance. Yet it is the Sartoris idea that gives Faulkner his greatest trouble, that is responsible for the most florid rhetoric of the novel—the passage ending, "there is death in the sound of it [Sartoris],and a glamorous fatality, like silver pennons down-rushing at sunset, or a dying fall of horns along the road to Roncevaux."

The tough realism of Miss Jenny, Bayard's aunt, though even she is something of a romancer, is not enough to counterbalance the book's uneasy allegiance to the Sartoris idea. Faulkner has not yet achieved aesthetic distance by centering this allegiance in a character whose own nature qualifies his attitudes, as he did three years later in Gail Hightower (*Light in August*); and *Sartoris* remains more of a tribute to the Sartoris glamour than a judgment.

Bayard remains a character whose despair is so far in excess of its motivation that he must be judged a neurotic or a sentimentalist, and apparently he is intended to be neither. In Hemingway's *A Farewell to Arms* we understand Lieutenant Henry's disillusion, because we see how it was engendered; but to Bayard Sartoris the war was a lark until his brother John sought and found death as foolishly as did the "Carolina" Bayard, Jenny's brother, who was shot in the back by a cook in his one-man raid to take anchovies from a Yankee general's supply tent. On the face of it, young Bayard's despair springs from John's death, which he did not cause, despite his self-accusation, and which he was powerless to prevent.

The trouble lies not only in the origin of the despair, which is not made convincing, but also in the nature of its manifestation. Bayard drives a sports car madly over the dirt roads of Yoknapatawpha County, frightening Negroes almost to imbecility. He drinks moonshine in incredible amounts, then rides a dangerous stallion bareback. Finally he flees home and wife to find death in an unflyable plane put together by a crackpot inventor. Only in the last of the book does the action seem appropriate to the attitude. In his brief sojourn with the Macollums, and his Christmas in the Negro cabin, Bayard's despair becomes convincing, primarily because Faulkner shifts back and forth from outer to inner action with consummate skill, and the revelation of the young man's anguish prepares us for the final episode. But until he leaves his home he seems more like a rural swashbuckler, a Yoknapatawpha "wild one," than a tragic figure. Hyatt Howe Waggoner expresses it accurately when he says, "He seems too sick a man to be a tragic hero. We are likely to think of him as a case of war nerves" (*William Faulkner*, 1959, 24).

Yet there are many good things in *Sartoris*. The passages of purely decorative description that abounded in his two earlier novels are rare in this one, and Faulkner's uncanny ability to reproduce the language and customs of his region is amply demonstrated. Only a Mississippian could recognize the absolute verity of Faulkner's account of the folkways of moonshine drinking in dry Mississippi, the lore of the "possum hunt," the habits of the rural swashbuckler (later to reappear in Dalton Ames, of *The Sound and the Fury*, Hoake McCarron, of *The Hamlet*, and Manfred de Spain, of *The Town*). The fantasy of the tall tale remains just beneath the surface: Old Man Falls, himself a splendidly drawn character, prepares a salve that removes a cancerous growth from old Bayard's cheek, to the consternation and confusion of a surgery-minded M.D.; the Macollums breed a female fox to a hound, hoping to produce a hybrid with the cunning of the fox and the stamina and nose of the hound. When all is considered, *Sartoris* would probably rank as one of Faulkner's better novels if it had not been for the overt romanticism of the Sartoris idea, inadequately qualified by the ironic vision of Aunt Jenny, who even aided and abetted the legend by her own account of Jeb Stuart and the "Carolina" Bayard's anchovy raid.

Sartoris ends the apprenticeship. *The Sound and the Fury*, published less than ten months later, is Faulkner at full strength, showing a mastery that some critics claim he has never surpassed. No other novel of Faulkner's has attracted so much attention from the critics, perhaps because few novels, past or present, have demanded such strenuous participation from the reader. Faulkner has relinquished the mode of the traditional novel along with the stylistic mannerisms of the *fin-de-siècle* aesthetes and moved directly into the modern world, the world of Proust, Joyce, Pound, and Eliot. The order of the book, as in Joyce, is not the order of time but the order of consciousness; and the experience of the past is unleashed on the present, as in Proust, by sensory stimuli. No longer is Faulkner's description functionless: odors, colors, forms have both psychological and symbolic dimensions, and through them the past is recaptured.

Yet to its first readers the structure of the book was disorderly, even perverse. Joseph Frank once said of Joyce, that he "cannot be read—he can only be reread"; and the remark is applicable to *The Sound and the Fury* as well. For years able criticism has been devoted to its rereading, sometimes even going so far as to provide elaborate chronological tables and charts. Most of such efforts seem ill advised, however, for some of them seek merely to transform the novel into what it is not, a chronological narrative. Lawrence Bowling's pioneer structural analysis (*The Kenyon Review*, Autumn 1948), which wrenches the pattern scarcely at all, is sufficient for the reader who finds it difficult to surrender himself to Faulkner's method. Of course the chronology is there for those who wish to indulge their interest in puzzles, but for others, what Conrad Aiken called the process of "immersion," a surrendering to Faulkner's method of "deliberately withheld meaning, of progressive and partial and delayed disclosure," is enough. Unlike the earlier novels, in which Faulkner moved from the outside in, *The Sound and the Fury* moves from the inside out, and it is the logic of the method that the book begins with the stream of association of the least articulate character, the idiot Benjy, and moves progressively outward until the final section, told by the omniscient author, at last lets us see what the characters —those that survive at least—actually look like. The story withholds its meaning until the end is reached, and the first two sections yield their full richness only upon a rereading, with the end in mind.

The Sound and the Fury records the decline of the Compson family. The action begins in the 1890s, when the four Compson children are small, and ends on Easter Sunday, April 8, 1928, when Benjy, the youngest, is thirty-three. It is focused on three events: Caddy's wedding (April 25, 1910), Quentin's suicide (June 2, 1910), and Caddy's daughter's flight with Jason's money (April 6, 1928). The Compson family had once been great in the land, boasting a governor and a Confederate brigadier, but it had progressively deteriorated in wealth and prestige. Jason III ("Father") had been trained as a lawyer but lived as an amateur classicist and drunkard, selling off bits of his patrimony until nothing is left except the house and grounds. Mother (a Bascomb) is a whining hypochondriac, helplessly dependent on Dilsey, her Negro cook and maid of all work. The four children are Quentin, Candace (Caddy), Jason IV, and Benjamin, and the primary concern of the novel is to reveal the reactions of the three boys to the conduct of their sister, Caddy.

The first section makes explicit the irony of the Shakespearean title: it is told by an idiot. Benjy cannot speak intelligibly; he can only bellow and moan when distressed; but we are called upon to follow his memory from about the time of "Damuddy's" (Grandmother's) death in 1898 down to the present, April 7, 1928. Inevitably, this is a strenuous exercise in comprehension. Benjy's mind is free of abstractions, concepts; he can only report, and interpretation lies solely with the reader. But we can see, at least upon rereading, that Benjy wishes to preserve his childhood relationship with his sister intact; and anything that threatens the order of his world is inimical, causing him to bellow in his distress. As we follow Benjy's memory back and forth over thirty years, we may suspect that a new perfume (Caddy smelled like "trees," and to Benjy this must not be changed) was as much of a threat to him as Caddy's seduction, but we are still not completely sure of what has happened.

With Quentin's section, dated June 2, 1910, the reader finds the past more explicitly revealed. He learns that a young man named Quentin Compson has told his father that he has committed incest with his sister, trying to redeem her from putative sluttishness by alleging an act of such transcendent evil that it will isolate her—and him—"amid the pointing and the horror beyond the clean flame." But Quentin has not committed incest with Caddy. She was seduced by a rural swashbuckler, Dalton Ames, and she was forced into a marriage to a Northern dupe to give her child a name. Having failed to preserve his pride in family, Quentin smashes his grandfather's watch, symbol of time and tradition, and isolates himself only, by suicide.

Quentin Compson loved death, Faulkner wrote in the appendix to *The Sound and the Fury* which he did for the Modern Library edition. He did not love his sister's body but "some concept of Compson honor. . . ." In his love of death and in his jealous protection of this "honor" he preferred incest (family sin) to promiscuity (public sin). He did not love the "idea of the incest which he would not commit, but some presbyterian concept of its eternal punishment: he, not God, could by that means cast himself and his sister both into hell, where he could guard her forever and keep her forevermore intact amid the eternal fires."

It is hard to construe this comment as other than an assessment of pride. For all Quentin Compson's gentleness to children, his love of the idiot Benjy, his agonizing over injustice, he is unwilling to leave God's business to God. He is the self-appointed guardian of his sister's honor—a meaningless honor, because it is not based upon inner worth or dignity but only "temporarily supported by the minute fragile membrane of her maidenhead."

Olga Vickery writes that Quentin has "constructed for himself a private world to which Caddy is essential, a world which is threatened and finally destroyed by her involvement in circumstance" (*The Novels of William Faulkner*, 1959, 36). He has no resources with which to defend his private world. The jaded determinism of his father, which has so far degenerated from Calvinist predestination as to amount almost to moral nihilism, leaves nothing for the boy but the equally degenerate code of honor which requires him to make a formalized defense of his sister's virginity. Lacking the physical hardihood to act according to the code, Quentin's last resource is only a memorized concept of the Presbyterian hell, which he hopes to create on earth by alleging the terrific act of incest. As Rabi points out, incest is associated with "the flight beyond the boundaries of time, and the escape from the world of suffering" ("Faulkner and the Exiled Generation," *William Faulkner: Two Decades of Criticism*, eds. Hoffman and Vickery, 1951, 131), but Quentin could not perform the act: he could only destroy himself, and thereby his tragedy becomes pathos.

Faulkner makes it easy to understand Quentin as a victim of neurosis; it is harder to understand the nature of his guilt; yet in his pride he is not a slaughtered innocent, as Rabi suggests, but a man who placed an empty code higher than love or duty. To judge his actions we have only to weigh them against those of Dilsey, the Negro servant who provides the ethical norm of the story. Dilsey assumes the burden of all the Compsons, misguided or vicious though they may be. Faulkner's cryptic remark about Dilsey is, "They endured"; but the endurance is not simply a patient, primitive stoicism but is compounded of a faith in providence and those qualities of love, compassion, and responsibility that Faulkner has emphasized in his more recent novels and his public pronouncements.

The technique employed in Quentin's section has been skillfully analyzed by half a dozen competent critics. Suffice it to say here that the structure is based upon a double pattern, the action of the present, in which Quentin goes through the events of his last day of life competently enough so that his friends suspect little of his plight, and that of the past, given through the stream of association. Unlike Benjy, Quentin is capable of conceptual thought and symbolic reference. The level of communication begins to move upward, and, to a degree, outward; but there are two more sections to explore before the process of gradual discovery is complete.

Jason's section, dated April 6, 1928, is absolutely transparent, but we are no longer in the Compson world. Jason is Compson become Snopes, so that all his actions and attitudes are predicated on the simple formula: "What's in it for me?" The description of Jason in Faulkner's appendix is somewhat misleading in emphasizing his role as a dutiful son, providing a house and food for his mother, his niece (named Quentin, after her dead uncle), and the Negro servants; Jason is efficiently damned out of his own mouth. He is the country cynic, assessing all humanity with the same faults and admitting none of the virtues. His speech and thought are unqualified, literal; yet they are marked by a certain cruel wit which reduces all values to the same level of expediency that governs his actions. There is no love in Jason, no compassion, not even trust. He has compacted within him all of the vindictiveness of the survivor, the tag end of a fated race. He sees all the world as Compsons, the fools of time, and, with survivor cunning, he becomes completely solipsistic. He depends upon nothing, no one, not even upon the progress that he has become a part of. He distrusts banks and hides his money. He distrusts any human motivation, regarding each human attempt at rescue as a snare set by something like a Compson. Yet Jason survives. As Faulkner wrote, he "not only fended off and held his own with Compsons but competed and held his own with the Snopeses."

From Jason, the one Compson without a haunted mind, we learn primarily what is happening in the present, the situation of the Compson household on Holy Saturday, the day that Quentin (the daughter of Caddy) takes his hidden hoard of money and runs away with a carnival barker. We have been carefully prepared for Jason in Benjy's and Quentin's sections. The cumulative characterization begins when he is a little boy running with his hands in his pockets so that he will not lose his treasure. So we see Jason as a materialist, ruled by logic. As Mrs. Vickery has written, "His is a world reduced to calculation in which no subjective claims are tolerated and no margin for error allowed" (*The Novels of William Faulkner,* 43). In a few years Faulkner was to reproduce this characteristic in one of his grandest and most enigmatic figures, Thomas Sutpen; but for the moment it has limited scope: it simply forms another perspective from which the Compson situation is viewed, and must be measured against the ethical norm which Dilsey provides in the last section of the novel.

The last section completes the movement outward. It opens with a detailed description of Dilsey, wearing a dress of purple. The date is Easter Sunday, April 8, 1928. Dilsey, who represents communion, just as surely as Benjy, Quentin, and Jason represent various forms of isolation, is the central figure. With communion comes the release from the burden of time. "I've seed de first en de last," Dilsey says as she sits "crying rigidly and quietly in the annealment and the blood of the remembered Lamb." But if redemption is suggested by this passage, the saving message is almost smothered among its attendant ironies. Benjy, who is emasculated and sent to Jackson when he is thirty-three, is the first of the several Christ figures who were to appear in Faulkner's novels, but he is Christ as victim, the test of our humanity, not Christ the redeemer; and of all who surround him, only Dilsey passes the test. The meaning of the book, finally, is not one that yields to abstract statement. It is imbedded in the structure, but at least we can say this. The redeeming force is there, even if it is found largely in the eloquence of a Negro preacher in a shabby church.

> With his body he seemed to feed the voice that, succubus like, had fleshed its teeth in him. And the congregation seemed to watch him with its own eyes while the voice consumed him, until he was nothing and they were nothing and there was not even a voice but instead their hearts were speaking to one another in chanting measures beyond the need for words, so that when he came to rest against the reading desk, his monkey face lifted and his whole attitude that of a serene tortured crucifix that transcended its shabbiness and insignificance and made it of no moment, a long moaning expulsion of breath rose from them, and a woman's single soprano: 'Yes, Jesus!'

This passage, not from any character but from the omniscient author, expresses the achievement of communion and transcendence—the hearts speaking without words and the transfiguration of the word itself, not the Word become flesh, but the flesh become Word: until "he was nothing and they were nothing and there was not even a voice." Yet the redemptive force is not final. After the sermon is over, we are thrust back into the Compson situation, Jason's discovery of the theft of his money, his frenzied pursuit of Quentin, and Luster's unfortunate turn *left* (the turn is usually *right*) around the Confederate monument while taking Benjy to visit the cemetery. Disoriented, Benjy bellows in appalling crescendo until Jason appears in a rage and turns the carriage about. Then Benjy's

> eyes were empty and blue and serene again as cornice and façade flowed smoothly once more from left to right; post and tree, window and doorway, and signboard, each in its ordered place.

This is a final irony. A timeless order had been suggested by the communion and transcendence in the sermon, but back in the Compson world of isolation, only temporal order is meaningful, and even that only to an idiot.

The year 1929 began a period of remarkable fecundity for Faulkner. About eleven months after the publication of *The Sound and the Fury* appeared the short novel, *As I Lay Dying* (1930). In it the techniques introduced in *The Sound and the Fury* were employed with such success that some critics have thought it his best novel. Again the device of multiple perspectives is used, but instead of four points of view, as in *The Sound and the Fury*, there are fifteen. Of these reflectors (the Jamesian term is in order here) seven are "interested" parties, the members of the Bundren family who are directly concerned with the death, the funeral journey, and the burial of the mother, Addie. Eight are neighbors, the voices of the outside world, involved in the Bundren situation in varying degrees. The reader must listen to the fifteen voices and decide for himself which are the true and which the false prophets. And he must make qualifications of the vision of each. Darl, regarded by the neighbors as strange, perhaps "touched," seems to have the gift of second sight. His intuitions regarding his brothers and sister have the primary certitude of revealed truth; but can his vision of his mother be trusted? He senses that he, the second son, the second violation of his mother's aloneness, is the alien in the family. He has no mother, he says; and if much of his madness (he is declared mad and sent to the asylum) is divinest sense, the reader must still hold himself in readiness for the other voices of the novel, not the least of which is that of Addie herself, dying.

Addie's predicament, revealed through her thoughts and memories, is one frequent in Faulkner, that of isolation coupled with a frantic longing for fellowship. Even before her marriage, instructed by her father "that the reason for living was to get ready to stay dead a long time," she hated the "secret and selfish thought" of the pupils in the class she taught, longing for the moment when they "faulted," so that she could whip them, feeling the welts and ridges in her own flesh. "Now I am something in your secret and selfish life, who have marked your blood with my own for ever and ever."

Searching for the communion of the heart, she married Anse Bundren, but she learned that he was a man of words, and that words are no good. What happened in the night was love to Anse; to her it was a violation, but though she was violated over and over, only when her children came did the violation take root in her thoughts and flower in the strange solitude of her mind. And the flower was despair. Addie's life was an attempt to break through the walls of her solitude and find some kind of meaning; but both the men with whom she was involved sexually, Anse, her husband, and Preacher Whitfield, the father of her third son, Jewel, were men of words, and to Addie, "words go straight up in a thin line, quick and harmless, and how terribly doing goes along the earth, clinging to it, so that after a while the two lines are too far apart for the same person to straddle from one to the other."

The separation of words and acts is Addie's analysis of the human predicament, but we should not quite credit her, as Mrs. Vickery seems to do, with the theme of the novel. There are other meanings. William Van O'Connor states that the theme, at least in part, "is the obligation to be involved, with involvement implying a commitment to violence" (*The Tangled Fire of William Faulkner*, 1954, 50), and to Hyatt Howe Waggoner, "behind" the story "lies a search for a lost center of value, a direct probing of ultimate questions, a continuation of Quentin's futile search for *human* meaning."

What we find in *As I Lay Dying* is a work of extreme structural complexity that does not lend itself easily to a unilateral interpretation. In his recent book Waggoner has explored the Christian references and symbolism of the novel, adding a new level of meaning to the several that have become current. In it he finds, centered in the character Cash (significantly, a carpenter, foreshadowing the "good" Isaac McCaslin in *The Bear*) "a sacramental view of nature—all nature—without a specific historical Incarnation: a religious view of life but not one that, in the historic sense of the word, can be called Christian." Without pushing the Christian symbolism quite as far as Professor Waggoner has, one can acknowledge his insight. Addie's dilemma is the dilemma of the seeker in a world without faith, a world in which the Word remains "just a shape to fill a lack." The communion of the heart achieved during the Negro sermon in *The Sound and the Fury* is never experienced in *As I Lay Dying*. Even with Jewel, the child dearest to her,

Addie can establish only a relationship of violent possessiveness. Darl says of Jewel, his mother is a horse. And so she is! Jewel's surrogate mother is a wild Texas pony, upon whom he lavishes love and violence in equal measure. All the other characters are distantiated in one way or another from each other and Addie. In the final journey through flood and fire to bury her, we are tempted to see a heroic commitment to the word that has been given to the dead. But we learn that each member of the group has his private reason for going on the wagon journey to Jefferson, with the putrefying corpse drawing buzzards like a lodestone. And so, in the end, the isolation of each is maintained. Darl is declared mad by his own family and sent to an asylum—ostensibly because he attempted to burn Addie's corpse in a barn which he fired, actually because he knows the secret heart of each. And Anse, the man of words, who has paid loud tribute to sorrow and duty, finds a new wife within hours after the funeral. He introduces a "duck-shaped" woman to his family, saying, "Meet Mrs. Bundren." These are the last words of the novel.

Though both *Sartoris* and *The Sound and the Fury* have connections with the other novels of the Yoknapatawpha series, *As I Lay Dying* comes to a dead end. The Bundrens do not appear significantly elsewhere. But it is in this novel that Faulkner reveals a complete mastery of his most characteristic form, the use of various reflectors to define a single action; and in it he shows a mastery of tone, ranging from pathos to grotesque humor. He accomplished this again and again in his later work, but never with more success than in *As I Lay Dying*.

After five novels, two of them among his best, Faulkner ought to have been considered a major writer, but his books did not sell. Understandably impatient at his lack of success with the public, he wrote in three weeks what was designed as a shocker—"The most horrific tale I could imagine," he has said. This was *Sanctuary* (1931), the most savage of the Yoknapatawpha novels. Apparently he had a change of heart, however, before the novel appeared. He did extensive revision on the galley proofs, which probably rescued a book that might have been far beneath his talent.

Deservedly *Sanctuary* has received less attention from the

critics than Faulkner's greater novels. The characters, at least the most "horrific" among them, are seen from the outside. Popeye Vitelli, the impotent gangster, has been said by Faulkner himself to be a symbol of evil. "I just gave him two eyes, a nose, a mouth, and a black suit. It was all allegory." Still, Popeye is not representative of all evil, only the specific evil of an industrial society. His hat is like a modernistic lampshade. His eyes are rubber knobs. In his tight black suit he seems stamped out of tin. He is terrified at the sights and sounds of nature, spits in a clear, bubbling spring, and shoots a harmless dog that snuffled at his heels. Product of a defective heredity and the slum environment of Memphis, he is almost as much a social case history as a symbol of evil; and Faulkner treats him with none of the compassion he usually expends on even his most depraved characters. To the reader, Popeye is like a particularly repellent worm, to be examined curiously but not to be understood.

Temple Drake, the University of Mississippi coed whom Popeye rapes with a corncob, is scarcely more human. Faulkner does give us a glimpse of her emotions prior to the rape, but there is no satisfactory insight into her motivation: why did she not escape from Popeye before the rape or even afterward? (Faulkner apparently felt this lack of motivation was serious enough to warrant explanation in a later work.) More seriously, why does Temple lie on the witness stand, sending Lee Goodwin to a horrible death at the hands of a lynch mob? Again, since we see her chiefly from the outside, we are not sure. Unlike Faulkner's other novels, *Sanctuary* has no characters whose views constitute some kind of ethical norm. Nearly all are depraved. Horace Benbow, the lawyer, who first appeared in *Sartoris*, is depicted as ineffectual, the one palsied champion in the lists against the overwhelming force of evil. Baptist ministers thunder from the pulpit, advocating lynch law for an innocent man. Politicians (Senator Clarence Snopes) sell information to the highest bidder. The district attorney, a club-footed go-getter who helped pay his way through college by cheating at poker, is alien to even the most rudimentary concept of justice. The women of Jefferson persecute Ruby Lamar, Goodwin's common-law wife, and her dying infant. *Sanctuary* is a world without light.

It is also a world turned socially inside out. The children of the best families, Temple Drake and Gowan Stevens, go to college in search of sensation—liquor and sex. In a grotesque parallel, the children of the rednecks, Virgil Snopes and Fonzo Winbush, go to Memphis to "barber" college, but actually wind up living in Miss Reba's whorehouse, which at first they think is a kind of girls' school or dormitory. (The girls' dormitory at the University of Mississippi is called the "Coop," both in *Sanctuary* and in actuality.) Miss Reba and her friends sit around in a kind of parody of a tea party, except that they are drinking beer. "Miss Reba's the perfect hostess," the thin one said. A little boy, Uncle Bud, raids the icebox, as children will, but he is looking for beer and gets drunk when he finds it. There is even a parody of a funeral ceremony, with the body of the slain gangster, Red, lying in state at a roadhouse. The mourners quickly get drunk, dance to the funeral music, and knock the coffin to the floor in a brawl, so that the wire of the flower wreath penetrates Red's cheek and the wax falls out of the bullet hole in his forehead.

In *Sanctuary* Faulkner's humorous episodes, so wildly grotesque that they have been called surrealistic, provide a commentary on the leveling out of values. The "best" people, who more than any others should be charged with the preservation of humanistic and religious virtues, behave like creatures from the slums; and the mobsters, madams, molls, and rednecks sedulously ape the manners of the elite of Jefferson. The sanctuary is violated, the temple is profaned, and the cry for justice is heard only from the mouth of a weak-kneed prophet, put upon by women, who tries to divorce his wife (whom he had got through adultery) because he cannot abide the smell of the shrimp that she regularly imports from New Orleans. Nowhere else in Faulkner is there so final an abandonment of the traditional virtues, and nowhere else such a strident assertion of depravity.

The voice of outrage that predominates in *Sanctuary* is muted in *Light in August* (1932), though the story, judged by events alone, is just as horrifying. The difference—and it must be judged as a qualitative difference in favor of the later novel—lies in the compassion that Faulkner has lavished on the most abandoned and desperate of the characters. Joe Christmas, the central figure, is in many ways the most tragic of Faulkner's studies of isolation. A humanized development from the Popeye of *Sanctuary*, Joe Christmas has been warped by both his childhood in an institution and his belief in his mixed blood. Lost between the two races, white and black, he repudiates both and isolates himself in brigandage on a long and narrow road at least partly of his own choosing, defending that road against enemies of both colors.

It is a temptation, particularly since Faulkner has paralleled Christmas in certain ways with Christ (C. Hugh Holman has shown that it is the "suffering servant" of Isaiah, the "despised and rejected of men," instead of the Messiah of St. Paul ("The Unity of Faulkner's *Light in August*," *PMLA*, LXXIII [1958], 158), to regard him solely as victim. Certainly Christmas is driven, from the age of five until his death, by self-appointed minions of morality who often usurped the authority of God Himself. His foster father, McEachern, demanded that "the Almighty be as magnanimous as himself." The mad grandfather, Eupheus Hines, justified his sadism and brutality because he was an instrument of God's will. Obviously Christmas is a victim of the Pharisees, but each character in *Light in August* is multidimensional. Joe Christmas is villain as well as victim. He is a sadist, a murderer, perhaps a latent homosexual, making Faulkner's achievement in arousing sympathy for him worthy of comparison with Dostoievsky.

Christmas, however "determined" his life course may seem to be, does not simply squirm in the naturalist's trap of heredity and environment. He has opportunities to move upward into light and communion. And his deliberate and brutal repulse of every attempt to establish some kind of human relationship with him is emphasized throughout the book—from his contemptuous refusal of Byron Bunch's proffered food to his deliberate decision to murder Miss Burden because she had begun to try to "save" him. Clearly there was an element of choice in Christmas's self-immolation to the god of his own pride. Faulkner makes explicit the curious affinity between Joe Christmas and Calvin McEachern, the most unbending of his persecutors. Even as McEachern can reject the temptations of the flesh in adhering to the rigidity of the Calvinist code, so Joe can reject whatever threatens his definition of himself.

His most striking acts of rejection are of food, the traditional symbol of fellowship and generosity. Give me bread, says the fainting pilgrim, and the traditional "good man" opens his larder. Three times Christmas refuses food, the first as a boy when he takes the hot meal Mrs. McEachern has prepared for him and deliberately hurls it to the floor. She is endangering his isolation, which can be maintained easily within the limits of the crime-and-punishment rule of his foster father. The second time he smashes dishes of food is when Miss Burden has locked the front door of her house against him and he has had to enter by the rear. Finding the food set out in the kitchen, he lifts the dishes and hurls them against the wall, thinking, *Set out for the nigger. For the nigger*—not remembering that to this woman who had inherited the burden of the Abolitionist conscience his Negro blood would have been a sight draft on the best she had to give. His third rejection of food is unqualified by foresight or afterthought. Byron Bunch, a traditional good man, his generosity uncomplicated by categories, offers to share his lunch with Christmas. "I aint hungry. Keep your muck——" is Joe's response.

One last time Christmas is given food. In his final flight, after he has driven out the Negro congregation and cursed God in the church, Christmas comes close to some sort of spiritual resolution, or at least a resignation. Then, in the symbolical act of the breaking of bread, he realizes his predicament. He has invaded a Negro cabin.

> Then there was food before him, appearing suddenly between long, limber black hands fleeing too in the act of setting down the dishes. It seemed to him that he could hear without hearing them wails of terror and distress quieter than sighs all about him, with the sound of the chewing and the swallowing. 'It was a cabin that time,' he thought. 'And they were afraid. Of their brother afraid.'

The belief that the course he has taken was of his own choosing, that he has wrought his own fate, brings Christmas closer to the situation of the tragic hero than Quentin Compson. Quentin is pathetic. His struggle scarcely engages our admiration. But Joe Christmas is both heroic and pathetic. He is heroic in his struggle to define himself as a human being existing in his own right, outside the categories and stereotypes of Southern Protestantism and racism; but he is pathetic as a victim of soul-warping forces beyond his control.

William Van O'Connor has made it clear that the Calvinist concept of inexorable punishment is the primary force that shapes Joe Christmas. Subject to this force from his cradle on through his formative years, Christmas was quite willing to accept it as the operative regimen of existence. It was simple, it was relentless, and it allowed him to define himself. But when ordinary, compassionate humanity (usually women) intervened between the crime and the punishment, the code broke down and there were no operational rules of behavior. He could in no way clear the record but could only allow the crimes to accumulate for eventual reckoning at some awful and deferred judgment.

Thus the women who try to save Joe Christmas commit an act of violation: they try to invade his privacy, compromise his self-wrought integrity. When, in his final renunciation, he murders Miss Burden, it is because she has tried to help him. The temptation to let her work her will was there, but pride forced him to reject it, thinking, "No. If I give in now, I will deny all the thirty years that I have lived to make me what I chose to be." She, womanlike in her desire to save, but more fanatic than woman, had asked him, " 'Do you realize . . . that you are wasting your life?' And he sat looking at her like a stone, as if he could not believe his own ears." A little later, failing as savior, she tries to become judge and even executioner, failing in both as Christmas slashes her throat.

Though the immediate motivation of Christmas's act of murder seems to be self-defense, its final cause is the code that allowed him to define himself as the archcriminal—even perhaps as Satan. "He believed with calm paradox that he was the volitionless servant of the fatality in which he believed that he did not believe. He was saying to himself *I had to do it* already in the past tense; *I had to do it; I had to do it.*" This was his thought *before* he used the razor.

If the crime-and-punishment code of Eupheus Hines and McEachern can be blamed for Christmas's feeling of fatality, the symbolic nature of his role as victim becomes clear. He, like Christ, is sacrificed by the Pharisees; and he "is despised and rejected of men, a man of sorrows, and acquainted with grief." But here the resemblance ends. The analogies with Christ are by no means conclusive, and even at the last, although Percy Grimm "crucifies" Christmas with gun and knife and there is a sort of ascension (Joe's black blood rises "soaring" into the memories of the lynch mob), one is likely to agree with O'Connor that the Christ-Christmas parallel is a monstrous irony.

Of the other characters in *Light in August* who, juxtaposed to Joe Christmas, assume their human burden or deny it, Gail Hightower, whose name suggests his role, is the most significant parallel. Two others are opposites. Lena Grove (her name is also meaningful, suggesting the light and freshness of the fecund earth) and Byron Bunch (Bunch is a family name in north Mississippi but may possibly signify here "group" or "crowd") have simple faith and humanity. Byron, at first defining himself within the limits of the religious code, flees the appearance of evil and with self-righteousness isolates himself from life. But with the advent of Lena Grove he assumes responsibility for another and thereby becomes a spokesman for humanity. Hightower at first makes a doctrinaire denial of any virtue in Bunch's act, but finally comes to an act of *caritas* himself. Delivering Lena's child, he thinks:

> This will be her life, her destiny. The good stock peopling in tranquil obedience to the good earth; from these hearty loins without hurry or haste descending mother and daughter. But by Byron engendered next.

Having performed an act of human responsibility, having breached the walls of his own prison, Hightower manages a kind of redemption. He had thought to make a bargain, a compact with time. He had bought and paid for his dream of the past, the past that became his prison. In his final recognition, however, he became aware of his solipsism, of how he had sacrificed his wife to his own desire to live in a dream world. "You took her as a means toward your own selfishness. As an instrument to be called to Jefferson; not for My ends but for your own." He had resigned his pulpit with the appearance of

a martyr's reasons . . . bearing in the town's sight and

hearing, without shame, with that patient and voluptuous ego of the martyr, the air, the behavior, the *How long, O Lord* until, inside his house again and the door locked, he lifted the mask with voluptuous and triumphant glee: Ah. That's done now. That's past now. That's bought and paid for now.

He had bought his ghost.

Ironically, Hightower's most complete vision of the past comes to him only after he has assumed the burden of his humanity, after he has learned in his soul that it was his ego that had been the instrument of his wife's despair and shame. Thinking this in agony, against his will, he feels the wheel of his thought turning on "with the slow implacability of a medieval torture instrument beneath the wrenched and broken sockets of his spirit, his life." He learns at last that for fifty years he "had not even been clay," but had been "a single instant of darkness in which a horse galloped and a gun crashed." Coming to this recognition, this *anagnorisis*, the torture wheel of his thought runs more easily. The imperial ego has been dethroned, and Hightower can endure his redemption. Dying, he thinks he should pray, but he does not try. Now he can think of someone besides himself.

With all air, all heaven, filled with the lost and unheeded crying of all the living who ever lived, wailing still like lost children among the cold and terrible stars . . . I wanted so little. I asked so little. It would seem . . .

The wheel turns faster now. The little he had wanted from the Almighty had been too much, because it had amounted to absolvement from time and responsibility. It had amounted to isolation within a heroic moment lived and done with.

Light in August is less obviously experimental than either *The Sound and the Fury* or *As I Lay Dying*. The reader is not required to adjudicate so strenuously among several points of view. Yet Faulkner does attempt to unify thematically, and to a certain extent on the level of action, three separate stories —Joe Christmas's, Lena Grove's, and Gail Hightower's. This attempt is in a sense a reconciliation of opposites, and critics have frequently drawn attention to the polarities of image, symbol, thought, and action in the novel. The most obvious polarity is between Lena Grove and Joe Christmas. Lena is a symbol of those who live in "obedience" to the earth. As Karl E. Zink has written, her "essential nature . . . is a tranquil rapport of mind and body, indifferent to time and change, quite distinct from the tragically frustrated and tortured natures of Joe Christmas and Gail Hightower" ("Flux and the Frozen Moment," *PMLA*, LXXI [1956], 293). Richard Chase has pointed out that the images associated with her are curves, as opposed to the linear images associated with Christmas. Thus Faulkner not only counterpoints the story of Lena Grove to that of Joe Christmas; he reinforces the contrast by the poetic devices of image and symbol—a technique used more extensively in this than in his other novels. One result is that *Light in August,* though not the most technically daring, is one of the most powerful of Faulkner's novels.

After seven novels, published within six years, Faulkner's creative production continued almost without a check, but the Yoknapatawpha tales appeared for a time only as short stories, some of them (*Wash, Spotted Horses,* and *The Hound*) to be rewritten and incorporated in *Absalom, Absalom!* and *The Hamlet.* In 1933 he published his second book of verse, *A Green Bough,* which, like his first, was tame and derivative, Eliot, Housman, and Thomas Gray being among the obvious voices echoed in the lines. In 1935 he turned momentarily in a new direction, with *Pylon,* a not wholly successful novel which Faulkner has said was an effort to find "a folklore of speed." It dealt with a weird group of aviators who made a precarious living racing and stunt flying.

If there was a falling off in *Pylon,* the next novel of the Yoknapatawpha series, *Absalom, Absalom!* (1936) is Faulkner on the heights. Over twenty years ago George Marion O'Donnell found in all of Faulkner's work a "striving toward the condition of tragedy" ("Faulkner's Mythology," *William Faulkner: Two Decades of Criticism,* 53). *Absalom, Absalom!,* which he calls an "action of heroic proportions," most nearly reaches that condition. In this novel the striving is explicit, at least in part: the tragic parallel is proposed by one of the characters. Mr. Compson, Quentin's father, whom we remember from *The Sound and the Fury* as the purveyor of a cynical

fatalism, projects the house of Sutpen against the dark background of the house of Atreus. Sutpen names his illegitimate
daughter Clytemnestra, but Mr. Compson says, "I have always
liked to believe that he intended to name Clytie, Cassandra,
prompted by some dramatic economy not only to beget but
to designate the presiding augur of his own disaster." Mr.
Compson sees Sutpen as an actor, "still playing the scene to
the audience, behind him Fate, destiny, retribution, irony—the
stage manager . . . already striking the set and dragging on
the synthetic and spurious shadows and shapes of the next
one."

Undoubtedly Greek tragedy, with its paramount situation
of the mighty but guilty family, with its symbolic actions of
incest and the slaying of kin, and with its terrifying manifestation of the guilty mind in the pursuing Erinyes, furnishes a
shadowy precedent for the plot of *Absalom, Absalom!* The
theme, however, is peculiarly Faulknerian, as is the Gothic
décor and the mode of narration.

As has been suggested more than once, the book's narrators,
of whom Mr. Compson is one, at different times play the roles
of chorus, witness, or messenger, and through their partial
knowledge, misinterpretation, or true reporting, the dramatic
irony becomes sharpened. The first narrator, and surely the
most misleading, is Rosa Coldfield. It is partly her "demoniz-
ing" that provides Sutpen with his larger-than-life dimension.
Through Miss Rosa's voice Sutpen materializes before Quentin's vision.

> Out of quiet thunderclap he would abrupt (man-horse-
> demon) upon a scene peaceful and decorous as a school-
> prize water color, faint sulphur-reek still in hair clothes
> and beard, with grouped behind him his band of wild
> niggers like beasts half tamed to walk upright like men.

That Miss Coldfield is an untrustworthy witness is soon apparent. Through the tortured rhetoric of her story, more
heightened, more Marlovian than the voice of any other
Faulkner character, Quentin gets, not the truth, but a kind of
irresponsible personal history which deprives him of the will
to endure because of the inescapable guilt handed down to
him from a tremendous and accursed past. Miss Rosa, seizing

upon the Sutpen story as *her* history of the South, gives Quentin a full measure of fatality.

Yes, fatality and curse on the South and on our family as though . . . some ancestor of ours had elected to establish his descent in a land primed for fatality and already cursed with it.

It is this feeling of fatality that destroyed the Sartorises, the Compsons, and would have destroyed the McCaslins (the third "great" family in Yoknapatawpha) if some of them had not possessed a capacity for penance almost as great as their pride. If guilt could be handed down, so could the right of expiation; so Isaac McCaslin (hero of the novelette *The Bear* and of two short stories, *The Old People* and *Delta Autumn*) repudiates his pride in blood and possessions along with his inheritance, and thereby foregoes a son. His wife, holding onto family and pride, admits him to her bed once to persuade him to keep the land. But he wishes to free his heir of ancestral guilt and is not persuaded. The son is never conceived, and his wife leaves him. Charles Mallison (*Intruder in the Dust*), bearing McCaslin blood, if not the name, balances the scale by saving his distant Negro relative, Lucas Beauchamp, from an undeserved execution. This is a complete reversal of Sutpen (and Compson) behavior. Charles is superior to the kind of fatality described by Miss Rosa and Mr. Compson because he feels moral responsibility and acts on it. Quentin Compson was never able to achieve such action because he was lost in the Sutpen-Compson legend of the past, interpreted for him by doom-ridden minds. Quentin felt only the responsibility to a nominal honor, an honor meaningless in time.

However, *Absalom, Absalom!* is not really Quentin's book, even though the story of Sutpen represents for him the meaning of history; and it certainly provides more motivation for his suicide than can be gleaned from *The Sound and the Fury* alone. But the story is really about Thomas Sutpen, and, as Cleanth Brooks has made clear, it is largely about Sutpen's "innocence." Sutpen is the character in Faulkner who most nearly possesses what the Greeks called *hubris;* he is the character who takes the scheme of things and remolds it to his heart's desire. He cannot conceive of ethical responsibility, only of justice in the purely rational, almost the purely economic, sense. With this blindness, this innocence—which, one fears, is the innocence of modern man—he makes the most heroic effort of all Faulkner's characters to conquer time, not by suicide (Quentin Compson) or by choosing his punishment (Joe Christmas), but by establishing a dynasty. The aspect of victim present in both Quentin Compson and Joe Christmas is absent in Sutpen; Faulkner allows him the panoply of the tragic hero; but the ethos is Renaissance rather than Ancient Greek, and Sutpen is modern man.

Coming from a primitive background (the mountains) where what a man can *do* is the measure of his worth, Sutpen is thrust into an established Tidewater society where the assessment of value is related not only to what one is but also to the history one represents. Sutpen assumes that, because he has courage, strength, and the will to success, he can establish himself within that society. All he has to do, he thinks, is get the land and the Negroes and the fine house. Then he would have made an ample definition of himself in the public world.

Through incredible courage he obtains a wife and fortune in the West Indies. A son is born, an heir apparent to the Sutpen barony; but then he discovers that his wife has Negro blood, so she cannot be "adjunctive" to his design. His first act of injustice is the abandonment of his wife and his child, relinquishing to her his estate, in what he considers fair payment for any wrong that he may have done.

At first it appears that Sutpen is going to succeed. By sheer will and courage, and by a liberal employment of the ruthless behavior that he does not consider injustice, Sutpen acquires his hundred square miles of land and his mansion. Then he chooses a wife, not out of the compulsion of any human emotion, but because in her impeccable respectability she will be "adjunctive" to the design (this drive for respectability ultimately became Faulkner's interpretation of Flem Snopes's behavior in *The Town* and *The Mansion*).

Very soon Sutpen, like Joe Christmas, becomes a solitary. Again, as in *Light in August*, this is symbolized by his shunning the fellowship of the table. When Sutpen's Coldfield kin come to dinner, he is always absent: he repudiates them. The repudiation of kinship is outrageous in the South, where "family" dinners are a social institution; but there is a deeper implication. Sutpen has no friends. People come to his hunts—loafers, hangers-on, satraps to the monarch—but only Quentin's grandfather (General Compson) stands in any definable human relationship to him. Determined to shape his own destiny, Sutpen has put himself outside of human fellowship.

When disaster catches up with Sutpen, it is of his own making. Charles Bon, the son of his first, deserted wife, comes to Oxford to go to school, whether through the maneuvering of his mother's lawyer (as Quentin's roommate, Shreve, suggests) or by chance, it is impossible to say. Henry, Sutpen's second son, meets Charles at the university and admires him, at first without knowing their relationship. He brings Charles home with him, but Sutpen refuses to recognize Charles as his son, by a word or even a clasp of the hand. This denial of kinship (at least in Shreve's interpretation) helps to bring about the final catastrophe. Judith, Sutpen's daughter, falls in love with her half brother. Henry appears reluctantly willing to permit the incest, but, when he finds out that Charles has Negro blood, refuses to allow miscegenation. At last, after four years spent with Charles in the Civil War, Henry becomes a fratricide and a fugitive, pursued like Orestes by the Erinyes of his own conscience.

But, just as Macbeth continues his course of evil even after the apparition of Banquo, so Sutpen ignores the manifest warning that his house is doomed. Now old and home from the war, he immediately sets about reclaiming his estate and begetting a new heir. He knows he has little time left, but he plans to use it efficiently. He will rectify, not his wrong, but his "mistake."

Operating under his simple businessman's code of justice, he proposes to bed with Rosa Coldfield. If the issue is male, he will make good his end of the contract with marriage. If it is a girl, the contract is null and void. Before this transcendent outrage Rosa retires to her demon-harrying for the rest of her life, bequeathing her demon to Quentin Compson.

Even this failure does not dismay Sutpen. He turns to the only available female, Milly, the fifteen-year-old granddaughter of Wash Jones, his tenant-farmer retainer, and buys her consent with candy, beads, and a new dress. True to his nature,

Sutpen pays cash on the barrelhead, but Milly's child is a girl, a "mare," and the mother, not having lived up to the unspoken contract in Sutpen's mind, is denied "a decent stall in the stable," to which the real mare, having foaled a horse, is thereby entitled. Wash Jones, enraged not by the seduction of his granddaughter but by this final denial of humanity, beheads Sutpen with a scythe, symbol of the eternal triumph of time. But at least it is a decapitation, the death of a monarch.

Like the doom of the house of Atreus, the fatality of the Sutpens outlives the progenitor. Charles Etienne St. Velery Bon, the only son of Charles Bon and an unnamed octoroon of New Orleans, is brought by Judith Sutpen and her mulatto half sister Clytemnestra (daughter of one of Sutpen's slaves) to live at Sutpen's Hundred. Unlike Joe Christmas, whom he resembles superficially, St. Velery Bon has no Calvinist code to live by and cannot determine the nature of his guilt. Lost between the two races, he banishes himself completely from the whites by taking for his mate a Negro woman whose physical and intellectual characteristics had made her an outcast even among her own people. He begets on her an idiot son, who is called Jim Bond. This boy the faithful Clytie cares for in a cabin at Sutpen's Hundred.

But the doom is not yet final. Henry Sutpen is still alive, still the heir apparent. In the closing pages of *Absalom, Absalom!* we learn that someone is out at the old mansion. Miss Rosa goes to find the secret dweller. It is Henry, old and sick. The ambulance that Rosa brings to get him is apparently mistaken by Clytie for a patrol wagon. Rather than submit him to the law, she burns down the house, and as it burns, Rosa and the driver think that they can see her, "the tragic gnome's face beneath the clean headrag, against a red background of fire," and they can hear Jim Bond, "the scion, the last of his race," howling about the ruins.

This is the terrifying close of the most formally realized of Faulkner's tragedies, with its theme of a titanic ego pitted against time itself. Sutpen's Hundred, like Tadmor and Persepolis, is left to the raven and the wolf, with the barely human survivor lurking in its ashes.

By the very completeness of the destruction *Absalom, Ab-*

salom! affirms the existence of a moral order above and beyond man. Tragedy does not make its affirmation of this moral order by statement but by its presentation of a man working his own doom. It is tragic irony that Sutpen never seems to recognize his fault; but if we remember that Faulkner, as moralist, is not writing of Sutpen alone or of the South alone but of something in the nature of modern civilization, Sutpen's failure to understand his guilt becomes necessary, because it is the failure of rational man to understand the moral universe.

Absalom, Absalom! is the fullest presentation of Faulkner's vision of the Old South, with each aspect of the collective myth subject to the irony that the method of narration enforces; but many people have taken the next novel of the Yoknapatawpha series, *The Unvanquished* (1938) as an uncritical acceptance of the myth. The novel is actually a collection of short stories, five of which had appeared in the *Saturday Evening Post* between 1934 and 1936, but it is unified enough in characters and theme to be considered a novel.

The selected bibliography published by *Modern Fiction Studies* in 1956 does not contain a single article devoted to *The Unvanquished,* and of the most recent critics, only Hyatt Howe Waggoner has considered the book worthy of extended appraisal; but we may be instructed by his insistence that in it the Sartoris "glamour" is given critical scrutiny and that Bayard Sartoris (Grandfather Bayard in *Sartoris*) in the process of maturing is "made . . . aware of the thin line between heroism and heroics." It is also instructive to compare the Sartoris legend as it is recalled in *Sartoris* and as it is *experienced* by Bayard Sartoris in *The Unvanquished.* The fabulous Colonel John Sartoris gradually dwindles from a more than life-sized hero to a man, and a not-very-large man at that. The Aunt Jenny of *The Unvanquished,* younger and more realistic than the creative fabulist of *Sartoris,* helps Bayard acquire a new perspective on the code that governed John Sartoris's actions, until he is able to retain the value of the code—courage—while foregoing its concomitant—violence. Bayard walks unarmed into the office of the man who murdered his father, proving his courage but rejecting the code's requirement of blood vengeance.

The Hamlet (1940) suggests a major change in the Yoknapatawpha series, which may be briefly described by saying that Faulkner's primary drive is no longer toward tragedy but toward comedy. The old themes reappear, it is true, in *Intruder in the Dust* (1948), *Requiem for a Nun* (1951), and *A Fable* (1954), but the passion declines. In Faulkner's work, Paradise cannot be regained, and his chronicling of the attempt to regain it is less compelling than his dramatization of the loss. His later work is, appropriately enough for comedy, often a kind of social criticism.

Like *The Unvanquished*, *The Hamlet* is a loosely knit series of episodes unified by common characters and themes; but, unlike the earlier novel, *The Hamlet* has a double focus. The episodes can be grouped, as Mrs. Vickery has shown, into love stories and stories of trade, but the counterpointing in this case does not constitute an absolute polarity, as in *Light in August*. Instead, there is a rough parallel.

Though various Snopeses have appeared briefly in previous novels, *The Hamlet* is Faulkner's first extensive treatment of Snopesism, which may be defined as the pure commercial instinct, the spirit of trade that Sidney Lanier attacked in *The Symphony* in 1875. Faulkner does not oppose love to trade in the same sense that Lanier did, but he does show that spontaneous natural emotion cannot survive in a world committed to the business ethic—in which all that is legal is right.

Flem Snopes is not without precedent in Yoknapatawpha. Both Jason Compson and Thomas Sutpen operated by the business ethic, but both had their passions. Flem is these earlier figures deprived of their humanity. Broad and impassive of face, with a tiny, predatory hooked nose and eyes like stagnant water, he is a symbol of obsessive greed; and the tales of trade in *The Hamlet* record his entry into the Frenchman's Bend section of Yoknapatawpha, his gradual rise through using the Varners, and his final victory over the representative of humanistic ethics, V. K. Ratliff. The stories of love are more various; but the more significant ones concern Ike H. Snopes, an idiot who loves a cow, and Eula Varner, a bucolic goddess so rife with fertility that men follow her like dogs, until she is finally impregnated by a wandering Pan (Hoake McCarron) in a yellow-wheeled buggy and traded as wife to Flem Snopes with the Old Frenchman Place as dowry. This is patent allegory: Eula, the lovely, fecund earth, fertilized in natural love, is traded to and owned by impotent economic man, Flem Snopes. This "Southern agrarian" theme in Faulkner, that man's right relationship to the earth and nature is one of love and veneration, was to be the burden of this and his next book, *Go Down, Moses;* but the mere presence of the unifying theme does not indicate the richness of Faulkner's treatment.

All Faulkner's skills as a comic artist reach fulfillment in *The Hamlet.* The account of Ab Snopes's horse trading is written in the tradition of the tall tale, deriving from such sources in Southwestern humor as A. B. Longstreet's *The Horse-Swap.* There is comic fantasy (like Benet's *The Devil and Daniel Webster*) in Ratliff's tale of Flem outwitting the devil, and there is country-store ribaldry in the ludicrous anticlimax of Mrs. Varner's response to the news of Eula's pregnancy, matched only by the rank vulgarity of her husband, Will, over the same event.

Highly figurative country wit, embracing both hyperbole and litotes, and even (in the voice of Ratliff) puns and deliberate ambiguities, is an element in the comic texture of *The Hamlet;* but, as in most great comic masterpieces, there is pathos too. The compassion with which Faulkner treats Ike Snopes, the idiot, Mrs. Armstid (whose very language is a masterpiece of folk idiom arousing pity instead of amusement), and even the venomous little murderer, Mink Snopes, is equal to that found in his greatest work.

Perhaps Faulkner's most striking rhetorical achievement in *The Hamlet* is his transformation of the Ike-cow episode, a sordid tale of rural sodomy, into a love story that suggests the passion of the gods when the world was young. It is easy to consider this a tour de force, Faulkner flexing his verbal muscles, but, as T. Y. Greet has said, the style "elevates the lovers into symbols, encouraging the reader to seek in myth and legend for its rationale" ("The Theme and Structure of Faulkner's *The Hamlet,*" *PMLA,* LXXII [1957], 784).

The next Yoknapatawpha chronicle was also a collection of stories, first printed as *Go Down, Moses, and Other Stories* (1942) and then simply as *Go Down, Moses.* Here Faulkner returns to one of his old subjects: the guilt of the white in relation to the black race, and introduces what might be called the "wilderness matter." The first McCaslin in the· territory, old Carothers, incurred the guilt, and it remained for Isaac McCaslin, his descendant, to assume the penance for his ancestor's passion.

Isaac is reared in a proper relationship to the wilderness, the natural order of God, by the old half-Indian, half-Negro hunter, Sam Fathers. Sam initiates him into manhood by marking his face ritualistically with the blood of the first deer he kills; and the initiation is completed when the boy sheds the accouterments of civilization (rifle, watch, and compass), and faces the ancient bear, a kind of wilderness god, in awe and humility. The slaying of the bear by Boon Hogganbeck, the least worthy of the hunters, symbolizes the abrogation of the old relationship between man and nature, and ultimately, between man and man. The great wilderness is soon to be gone. Ike repudiates his McCaslin inheritance, not only because he must expiate the guilt of his ancestor Carothers, but also because he refuses to participate in the corruption of the old relationship with the land. The ultimate fate of the land, of course, is to become the property of a Snopes, who will neither work it nor love it but use it only for commercial transaction. Such a fate Isaac regards without approval, and so, we presume, does Faulkner.

But with all his conscience, Isaac McCaslin follows a pattern of repudiation rather than responsibility. He gives up his patrimony, he assumes an avuncular relationship to the children of the entire community, and he ends as a pathetic figure, slightly comic, certainly ineffectual. Apparently for Faulkner there is no true sense of responsibility in any of the older generation.

But in the younger generation, in Charles Mallison of the McCaslin line, he finds a hope that he seemingly almost denied in his great novels on the tragic theme. *Intruder in the Dust* (1948) was attacked by Elizabeth Hardwick as a "states' rights, leave-us-alone, don't-be-coming-down-here-and-telling-us-what-to-do pamphlet which falsifies and degrades his fine comprehension of the moral dilemma of the decent guilt-ridden Southerner" ("Faulkner and the South Today," *William Faulkner: Two Decades of Criticism*, 249). But Miss Hardwick has missed the point: the novel is about the growing up of Charles Mallison. Gavin Stevens, though characterized as a morally sensitive intellectual, speaks as character, not as author. He represents a perspective—a perspective that is severely qualified by the loyalty and sense of responsibility of the boy Charles and the intuitive vision of that most splendid of Faulkner's old maids, Miss Habersham. By saving Lucas Beauchamp, Charles Mallison and Miss Habersham defy not only the wrath of the murderous Gowries (Beat Four moonshiners) but also shake the entire structure of Yoknapatawpha's attitude and belief in regard to the Negro. Charles assumes responsibility by deed and not by word, thus invoking the moral principle of *As I Lay Dying*.

Requiem for a Nun (1951), even if it could be hailed for nothing else, is a daring experiment. It is in the form of a three-act play, but each act is preceded by a kind of prologue, too long ever to be spoken on the stage, recapitulating the history of Yoknapatawpha. Furthermore, the book is written in two entirely different styles. The prologues are in Faulkner's familiar lyrical, evocative rhetoric; but, as Hyatt Howe Waggoner has put it, the dramatic sections sound as if Faulkner were trying to out-Hemingway Hemingway.

The novel (or play) is a sequel to *Sanctuary*. Temple Drake is still central to the story, and we find out what we should have known in *Sanctuary:* that she invited her rape by Popeye and that she thoroughly enjoyed her stay in the house of prostitution. Gowan Stevens, the lover who abandoned her in *Sanctuary*, has married her in an access of repentance. Now they live in Jefferson, seemingly a model couple, equipped not only with the bungalow and two children but also with the "liberal" ideas of the cocktail-party set. Temple employs Nancy Mannigoe, an ex-dope-fiend Negro whore (whom Faulkner has picked up from his short story, *That Evening Sun*), as maid—publicly as a gesture of rehabilitation, but privately because Nancy can talk the same language, the language Temple had learned in her happy days in Miss Reba's whorehouse. But still Temple is bored, and when Pete, the younger brother of her Memphis lover Red (killed by Popeye) appears, to blackmail her with her obscene letters to Red, she offers him the money on condition that he take her too. Nancy, as a last stratagem to keep the family together, murders one child so that the home will be preserved for the other—surely the most insane solution to the problem of a broken home ever presented in fiction.

Yet Nancy, dope fiend, whore, and murderess, is the urgent voice of morality in the play; and Temple, Gowan, and even Gavin Stevens must submit to her instruction. The lesson, hitherto implied in Faulkner's work, finally becomes explicit: you have to sin, but you must trust God, who gives you a chance to suffer penance. Faulkner, in Nancy's speeches, comes about as close to orthodox Christianity as one can get without citing chapter and verse. Man is a fallen creature, subject to the sinful passions of his fallen estate. But if we must sin, we are given the free will to suffer penance, and through this suffering even the least of us, the despised and rejected, will be saved.

The long prologues—*The Courthouse, The Golden Dome,* and *The Jail*—represent man's stratagems to rise from his fallen condition, to perfect himself by law and social organization; but underneath the brick veneer of the jail, the first public building in Jefferson, are "still the old ineradicable bones, the old ineradicable remembering: the old logs immured intact and lightless between the tiered symmetric bricks and the whitewashed plaster." And beneath the smooth façade of man's civilization, the whitewashed plaster of his public face, lie the ancient bones of his depravity and the sinful passions of his recalcitrant heart.

Requiem for a Nun is Faulkner's most direct statement of his moral position, but, as always, when message becomes dominant in the work of the artist, the art itself suffers. *Requiem,* establishing the need of penance, is inferior to the great novels portraying the passions; and the rebellious corporal of *A Fable* (1954), an explicit Christ, even to the twelve disciples and a Judas Iscariot, is shadowy beside the solitary demon and victim of *Light in August,* Joe Christmas.

Faulkner's last two volumes of the Snopes trilogy, *The Town* (1957) and *The Mansion* (1959), also show a decline when measured against *The Hamlet.* Gavin Stevens and Ratliff are the self-appointed champions of Yoknapatawpha against Snopesism, but Stevens becomes increasingly futile and garrulous. His rivalry with Manfred de Spain over Eula Varner Snopes is low comedy, as is his later rivalry with Matt Levitt over Linda, Eula's daughter.

Eula herself is diminished. She is no longer the Olympus-tall earth goddess of *The Hamlet,* towering a full head over her froglike husband, but merely the local Semiramis or Helen —still too much, it seems, for any one man. Flem Snopes, too, is changed. He is no longer the embodiment of the soulless, commercial spirit, a fit opponent for the devil, but only a country boy striving with all his might toward something beyond wealth—social respectability! He even becomes an agent of civic virtue, driving out of the community the most reprehensible of his kinsmen so that the Snopes name may rise in respect. *The Town* is good entertainment, rarely dull, often hilarious, but it lacks the rich variety of *The Hamlet;* and it leaves us wondering whether Faulkner in his new tolerance may not ultimately find Snopesism acceptable.

The Mansion completes the trilogy. Linda Snopes's fortunes are pursued to Greenwich Village, where she marries a Communist sculptor; to Spain, where she goes to fight with the Communists (her husband is killed there); and back to Yoknapatawpha, where she outrages the community by engaging in various reformist activities and perhaps outrages the reader by assisting in the murder of her foster father, Flem.

Flem Snopes, now respectable, at last receives his comeuppance, but by this time we scarcely think that he deserves it. It is as if in these last two novels Faulkner finds himself with indignation gone, all passion spent. The outrage that marked his earlier work has become toleration, the compassion not even pity, but a kind of twinkling acceptance. Only one character in *The Mansion* strikes the old fire. In the portrait of Mink, who murders Flem, the prose attains the beautiful and poignant lyricism of Faulkner's great works. As Mink muses over the patient and enduring earth that will soon receive his bones, the Faulkner of *Light in August, Absalom, Absalom!* and *The Hamlet* reappears in the splendid poetry of the reverie. In these last few pages, at least, Faulkner recaptures his language and vision, plumbing the mystery of the abiding earth and entreating compassion for even the least of its creatures. And if he does break his pencil after *The Mansion*, as he has threatened, he may rest content in having achieved in his Yoknapatawpha saga a work of the imagination scarcely to be paralleled in modern times.

"THE DARK, RUINED HELEN OF HIS BLOOD": THOMAS WOLFE AND THE SOUTH

BY C. HUGH HOLMAN

Thomas Wolfe was born and grew to young manhood in Asheville, North Carolina. When he went North after his graduation from the University of North Carolina, he went as a Southerner, to write of Southern subjects in George Pierce Baker's "47 Workshop" at Harvard, and to compose his first novel out of the Southern scenes of his childhood with an autobiographical candor and an accuracy shocking to the residents of his native city. Yet Thomas Wolfe never returned for long to the South, once he had left it—indeed, he declared that "you can't go home again"—and the portrait that he drew of his native region in his first novel elicited from his former Chapel Hill classmate Jonathan Daniels the charge that "in *Look Homeward, Angel*, North Carolina and the South are spat upon." Some critics have believed, as Maxwell Geismar suggested, that Wolfe "was born in the South, but he shared with it little except the accident of birth" (*Writers In Crisis*, 1942, 196).

Upon his native region he heaped a Gargantuan scorn in his sprawling, loosely constructed tales and novels, condemning what in *Look Homeward, Angel* he called the Southerners' "hostile and murderous intrenchment against all new life . . . their cheap mythology, their legend of the charm of their manner, the aristocratic culture of their lives, the quaint sweetness of their drawl." In *The Web and the Rock* he expresses his anger at "the old, stricken, wounded 'Southness' of cruelty and lust," at men who "have a starved, stricken leanness in the loins," and at the lynchings that end with castrations, betraying his mingled disgust and sense of shame. The Southern intellectual fared little better in Wolfe's novels. He had contempt for the Agrarians whom he called in *The Web and the Rock* "the refined young gentlemen of the New Confederacy . . . [who] retired haughtily into the South, to the academic security of a teaching appointment at one of the universities, from which they could issue in quarterly installments very small and very precious magazines which celebrated the advantages of an agrarian society." And he wrote with feeling in the same novel of "the familiar rationalizing and self-defense of Southern fear and Southern failure: its fear of conflict and of competition in the greater world; its inability to meet or to adjust itself to the conditions, strifes, and ardors of a modern life; its old, sick, Appomattoxlike retreat into the shades of folly and delusion, of prejudice and bigotry, of florid legend and defensive casuistry . . ."

This South was feminine to him—what he called once *"the female principle—the earth* again . . . a home, fixity"—and in his thinking he opposed it to the father principle, which, in *The Story of a Novel,* he called "the image of a strength and wisdom external to his need and superior to his hunger, to which the belief and power of his own life could be united." From the maternal and subjective South, "the dark Helen of his blood," he turned to storm the male citadels of the North and to find in the "enfabled rock" of the Northern city a defense against the web of the South. Yet this South beat in his brain and pounded in his veins. "Every young man from the South," he said in *The Web and the Rock,* "has felt this precise and formal geography of the spirit," in which South and North are sharply dichotomized autonomies; and the qualities in young Southerners brought to the North "a warmth you lacked, a passion that God knows you needed, a belief and a devotion that was wanting in your life, an integrity of purpose that was rare in your own swarming hordes. They brought . . . some of the warmth, the depth, the richness of the secret and unfathomed South. They brought some of its depth and mystery. . . . They brought a warmth of earth, an exultant joy of youth, a burst of living laughter, a fullbodied warmth and living energy of humor." Wolfe could proudly boast in a letter to James Boyd, "I'm a Long Hunter from Bear Creek, and a rootin', tootin', shootin' son-of-a-gun from North Carolina"; and he could write Maxwell Perkins that "The people in North Carolina . . . are rich, juicy, deliberate, full of pungent and sardonic humor and honesty, conservative and cautious on top, but at bottom wild, savage, and full of the murderous innocence of the earth and the wilderness." What he said of his character George Webber is true of Wolfe himself: "He was a Southerner, and he knew that there was something wounded in the South. He knew that there was something twisted, dark, and full of pain which Southerners have known all their lives—something rooted in their souls beyond all contradiction." But all his knowledge of her darkness and damnation could not stifle his love for the lost and ruined and burning Helen in his blood.

That his vision of his native region was both obsessive and ambiguous was not surprising. Wolfe was born to a Northern father and a Southern mother, and the division of life into male and female, North and South, wanderer and homebound, was a simple extension of what he saw daily as a boy. He grew up in a Southern mountain town, but at a time when it was changing into a resort city, flourishing in the shadow of the baronial estate of the Vanderbilts, the pseudo-French château, "Biltmore," and literally mad for money. He went to college at Chapel Hill, a Southern state university, but at the time when that school was beginning the pattern of liberalism that made it the symbol of New South progressivism, completely opposite to the agrarianism of Vanderbilt University. Furthermore, at the feet of a locally famed teacher of philosophy, Horace Williams, he imbibed a form of Hegelian dialectic that made him see all life in terms of opposites and gave his work the fundamental structure of thesis and antithesis in sentence, paragraph, and scene as well as in its more obvious oppositions, such as South and North, female and male, Jew and gentile, mother and father, the web and the rock.

Ambiguous and contradictory though his views of his native region were, the South was a theme and a subject matter for much of Wolfe's work, and it existed for him in a sensuous, irrational emotional state of mutual attraction and repulsion. And this contradiction and ambiguity, this co-existing intense love and passionate hatred are characteristic not only of Wolfe's attitudes toward the South but also of his total work. His published writings consist of four novels (two of which appeared posthumously and were prepared for the printer by an editor), two volumes of short stories and sketches (one published posthumously), a play, and a few other items—plays and sketches in magazines—which are of minor importance. The six volumes of novels and short stories represent the significant corpus of his work, and they were carved out of a vast and complex outpouring of words.

The term most often applied to these works is "formless," for their structure is difficult, diffuse, uncertain. *Look Homeward, Angel* and *Of Time and the River* are the adventures of Eugene Gant in his growth from childhood to maturity, and Eugene Gant is an embarrassingly direct portrait of Wolfe himself. *The Web and the Rock* and *You Can't Go Home Again*, the posthumously published novels, trace the similar story of George Webber and carry it on through his love affair with Esther Jack and his success as a novelist. Webber is seemingly as autobiographical as Gant. The stories in *From Death to Morning* and *The Hills Beyond* were all—or almost all—written originally as episodes in the great "book," of which the four novels are parts. Here, in these millions of words, then, is the intensely felt experience of a single person, the author, presented almost entirely without benefit of formal plot or traditional structure. Subjectivity has seldom more totally dominated a major work, and it is difficult to read Wolfe without feeling the justice of Robert Penn Warren's wry comment: "It may be well to recollect that Shakespeare merely wrote *Hamlet;* he was *not* Hamlet" ("A Note on the Hamlet of Thomas Wolfe," *Selected Essays*, 1958, 183).

But imprisoned within this vast body of words are hundreds of sharply realized scenes, dozens of characters who have an authentic existence—W. O. Gant, Eliza Gant, Bascom Pentland, Helen Gant, Francis Starwick, Esther Jack, Judge Rumford Bland, Nebraska Crane—and literally thousands of descriptive passages of such lyric intensity and sensuous directness that they impinge upon the senses of the reader and achieve for a moment in his consciousness a concrete reality.

Few American novelists have projected more ambitious programs or had more demanding plans for their novels. The task Wolfe set himself was, he once wrote in a letter, the representation of "the whole consciousness of his people and nation

. . . every sight sound and memory of the people." In order to formulate this vast subject, he sought encompassing themes. He concocted a three-part theory of time, which he found inherent in his materials: actual present time, past time, and "time immutable," and saw in their simultaneous projection in a work of fiction a "tremendous problem." He attempted to express the essential loneliness and isolation of all human existence. He borrowed Greek myths, sketching characters to fill the roles of Antaeus, Heracles, Poseidon, Kronos, Gaea, Helen, Jason—seeking to find in the patterns of their lives a controlling myth or metaphor for the meanings he wanted to convey. His letters are filled with the outlines of vast projects before whose scope Balzac seems limited and Faulkner cautious. As he himself once wrote in a letter, "The book on which I have been working for the last two or three years is not a volume but a library."

The motive force of his works seems to have been his desire to express the elements of a universal experience, and this universal experience was for him closely tied up with the national, the American experience. To a remarkable degree Thomas Wolfe was using himself to describe and to define both this universal experience and his native land, to produce the American epic, to create the egalitarian and generic hero. In a letter to Perkins he once said, "My conviction is that a native has the whole consciousness of his people and nation in him; that he knows everything about it, every sight sound and memory of the people." Much of his career was a search for America, and he came to see fairly early that, as he expressed it in *The Story of a Novel*, "the way to find America was to find it in one's heart, one's memory, and one's spirit."

And thus he fell in with the powerful epic impulse that has motivated much American writing since the eighteenth century: the attempt to encompass in a fable or narrative the spirit and the nature of the land, to represent the soul of a people through a representative hero and archetypal actions. As Tocqueville suggested, over a century ago, in an egalitarian democracy the traditional heroes of the aristocratic plots and literary genres are forbidden to the artist, and somehow he must find in the common man the center of his patriotic art.

Walt Whitman, feeling the demands of the epic impulse, attempted a solution by celebrating his own generic qualities.

One's-self I sing, a single separate person,
Yet utter the word Democratic, the word En-Masse.

This self of Whitman's became the spokesman of his nation by its ability to witness all things imaginatively and to participate vicariously in all actions.

For Wolfe the center of his art was in a similar view of the self, but the method was different. Like Whitman, he believed that the writer "ought to see in what has happened to him the universal experience." All the people, events, images, and visions that crossed his experience became a part of him, and were to be transmuted into a "final coherent union" in which America was to be embodied. For Whitman this embodiment was expressed in chants. The embodiment would be for Wolfe, as he said, "a story of the artist as a man who derived out of the common family of earth and who knows all the anguish, error, and frustration that any man alive can know." To find an adequate experience, an effective language, and a unifying structure for this man became for Wolfe the obsessive task of the American artist. He said in *The Story of a Novel:*

> . . . in the cultures of Europe and of the Orient the American artist can find no antecedent scheme, no structural plan, no body of tradition that can give his own work the validity and truth that it must have. It is not merely that he must make somehow a new tradition for himself, derived from his own life and from the enormous space and energy of American life, the structure of his own design; it is not merely that he is confronted by these problems; it is even more than this, that the labor of a complete and whole articulation, the discovery of an entire universe and of a complete language, is the task that lies before him.

In his efforts to accomplish that tremendous task, to realize the self as generic American and make his personal pilgrimage the national odyssey, Wolfe functioned with uneven effectiveness. He magnificently realized individual scenes and sections of his mammoth work, especially in the form of short novels, but he only imperfectly formed the faint outlines of the larger task. That the elements which made up his all-encompassing effort were woven from the filaments of his self and that that self was both woven and torn by his Southern heritage should be beyond dispute; but in the interest of illuminating a little of both Wolfe and the literature of his region it may be worth while to point to some of the Southern qualities in his work.

The urge to represent America, to embody it in a work of art, although by no means unique to the region, has been persistent in Southern literature. The Southerners of the antebellum period often raised their voices in support of a native literature and stood with the "Young America" group of critics in their intensely nationalistic demands for art in the 1840s and 1850s, despite the serious political differences between them and the New York critics. They distrusted the "internationalism" of New Englanders like Longfellow and of New Yorkers like the editors of the *Knickerbocker Magazine*. Yet these Southerners were aware that the nation could better be represented by drawing its particularities than by picturing the whole. In 1856, for example, William Gilmore Simms, of South Carolina, had written: ". . . to be *national* in literature, one must needs be *sectional*. No one mind can fully or fairly illustrate the characteristics of any great country; and he who shall depict *one section* faithfully, has made his proper and sufficient contribution to the great work of *national* literature" (*The Wigwam and the Cabin*, 1856, 4–5). This view is not far from Wolfe's own, when he insists upon the representation of his unique self as the proper subject for a national art. Wolfe was like Thoreau, who said, "I should not talk so much about myself if there were anybody else whom I knew as well. Unfortunately, I am confined to this theme by the narrowness of my experience." However, for Wolfe, the observation of his fellow men was a basic part of that experience, as it was not for Thoreau.

It is also typical of the Southern writer that this epic portrayal of America should constitute a project of great magnitude and tremendous complexity. Wolfe's letters and *The Story of a Novel* carry the evidence of the vastness of scope and the complexity of design of the "work in progress" on which he expended his days and hours and which he left incomplete. It is startling to one who has accepted the standard view of Wolfe's work as the spontaneous and unpremeditated overflow of the author's powerful feeling, recollected in abnormal intensity, to find him writing to Maxwell E. Perkins, "I think you may be a little inclined to underestimate the importance of arrangement and presentation, and may feel that the stories can go in any way, and that the order doesn't matter much." In the light of his efforts to get on paper the theme, the argument, the structure of the large work as he labored on its parts, such a statement—although it does not redeem his novels from formlessness—makes poignant and telling Wolfe's protests against the publication of *Of Time and the River* in the form in which Perkins sent it to the press.

This large design would have traced the history of the Pentlands (or, later, the Joyners) from the Civil War to the present, emphasizing the Southern roots of the generic hero. It would have included thousands of characters and episodes—the whole, Wolfe said, to be "seen not by a *definite personality*, but haunted throughout by a consciousness of *personality*," and that personality was to be the perceptive "self" through which the writer could know and express his America. Before a work of such magnitude as he projected, time became the great enemy. The scope of his ambitious plan—which was to be no less than the record of his nation and his people told through one representative man—merits in its magnitude comparison with the master projects of literary history, with Balzac and Zola and with Tolstoy. To embark upon such vast projects has also been typically, although by no means exclusively, Southern, perhaps because the Southerner tends to distrust abstraction and to doubt that one can see a "world in a grain of sand,/ And a heaven in a wild flower." Whatever the reason, twentieth-century Southern writers have tended to plan work of enormous scope, such as James Branch Cabell's many-volumed and incomplete record of Poictesme; Ellen Glasgow's fictional record in thirteen volumes of Virginia's social history from the Civil War to the 1940s (whether such a structure was her original intention or a design she imposed after a good portion of the fact); and William Faulkner's vast and growing record of Yoknapatawpha County. Wolfe, like these other Southerners, set himself a task that staggers the imagination and defies'the reality of time. Little wonder that Faulkner considers him among the greatest of American writers because he dared the most!

Near the beginning of his first novel Wolfe wrote, "Each of us is all the sums he has not counted: subtract us into nakedness and night again, and you shall see begin in Crete four thousand years ago the love that ended yesterday in Texas. . . . Each moment is the fruit of forty thousand years." This concern with time grew more intense as his career developed. The artist's problem, he believed, is the resolution of a threefold consciousness of time into a single moment so that scenes can represent "characters as acting and as being acted upon by all the accumulated impact of man's experience so that each moment of their lives was conditioned not only by what they experienced in that moment, but by all that they had experienced up to that moment," and with these actions set somehow against a consciousness of "a kind of eternal and unchanging universe of time against which must be projected the transience of man's life, the bitter briefness of his day." Whether or not Wolfe is indebted to Proust and Bergson for these ideas, he certainly envisions his characters as set in a complex fabric of time, and their actions as having remote roots and immeasurable forward extensions. Louis D. Rubin, Jr., has noted elsewhere in this book that "The interplay of past and present, of the historical and the contemporaneous, causes all the modern Southern writers to be unusually sensitive to the nature and workings of time." This interplay is one of the basic materials of Wolfe's fiction.

Wolfe shares with many Southern writers his concerns with the reality of the past in the present and with the nature of time. One can find examples of the Southern writer's concern with time and his belief that it is, not only fact or sequence, but, more important, a key to the nature of human experience in Robert Penn Warren, particularly in *The Ballad of Billie Potts* and *World Enough and Time;* in Ellen Glasgow; in William Faulkner, with his elaborate dislocations of time sequence in many of his narratives; in Tate's *Ode to the Confederate Dead;* in William Styron's inverted structure in *Lie Down in Darkness;* and in many other places. It is not surprising that one of Wolfe's best-known short stories should be *Chickamauga* and that the novel fragment on which he was working at the time of his death, *The Hills Beyond,* deals with his Southern ancestors in the nineteenth century. Among twentieth-century American novelists only the Southerners have with any frequency treated the past outside the pattern of romance and adventure. William Faulkner, Robert Penn Warren, Ellen Glasgow, and James Branch Cabell have written extensively with a historical orientation.

The mixture of styles in which Wolfe wrote is also not uncommon in Southern writing. On one level Wolfe illustrates with great effectiveness the concrete, the immediate, the sensuous. He accurately described himself when he wrote in *The Story of a Novel,* "The quality of my memory is characterized, I believe, in a more than ordinary degree by the intensity of its sense impressions, its power to evoke and bring back the odors, sounds, colors, shapes, and feel of things with concrete vividness." It is this quality in his work that gives many of his pages an intensity which almost approximates direct experience. This lyric aspect of his writing, in which the object is evoked with such power that it seems to be rubbed against the reader's exposed nerve ends, this ability to make "the world's body" vividly real, succeeds again and again in giving the reader new insights; in Wolfe's terms, in making "the utterly familiar, common thing . . . suddenly be revealed . . . with all the wonder with which we discover a thing which we have seen all our life and yet have never known before." A passage from *Of Time and the River* will illustrate the centrality of the concrete in Wolfe's writing. Eugene Gant is daydreaming and not worrying about where the money to fulfill his dreams is to come from.

> If he thought about it, it seemed to have no importance or reality whatever—he just dismissed it impatiently, or with a conviction that some old man would die and leave him a fortune, that he was going to pick up a purse containing hundreds of thousands of dollars while walking in the Fenway, and that the reward would be enough to keep him going, or that a beautiful and rich young widow, true-hearted, tender, loving, and voluptuous, who had carrot-colored hair, little freckles on her face, a snub nose

and luminous gray-green eyes with something wicked yet loving and faithful in them, and one gold filling in her solid little teeth, was going to fall in love with him.

Here, where he is mocking Eugene's stereotype dreams, the rich young widow is made concrete and detailed; the lucky purse is found in a particular place. This use of the particular, this tendency to distrust the conceptual and abstract, is one of the most widely recognized characteristics of Southern writing. As Robert Penn Warren has pointed out, the Southerner lives in "the instinctive fear . . . that the massiveness of experience, the concreteness of life, will be violated . . . [in] the fear of abstraction" (*Segregation*, 1957, 15). Virginia Rock has noted that the Southern poet feels "not only a rage for order but also a rage for the concrete, a rage against the abstract" ("Agrarianism in Southern Literature: The Period Since 1925," *The Georgia Review*, XI [1957], 157). Even in criticism, Southerners have concentrated their attention on particular works of art and have not formulated abstract systems. As Allen Tate put it, "There was no Southern criticism; merely a few Southern critics" ("The New Provincialism," *On the Limits of Poetry*, 1948, 290).

Closely associated with this concern for the concrete is Wolfe's delight in folk speech, dialect, and speech mannerisms. His works are full of accurate transcriptions of vivid speech. His characters seem sometimes to talk endlessly, but they always talk with vigor and with great distinctiveness of diction, syntax, and idiom.

Yet the same writer who displays these startlingly effective qualities of lyric concreteness and speech accuracy is also guilty of excesses in both quantity and quality of rhetoric perhaps unequaled by any other American novelist. With the power to evoke a particular object, scene, or character with remarkable clarity, he is unwilling to let these creations speak for themselves, but must try by the sheer force of rhetoric to give expression to the peculiar meanings that they suggest, to define ineffable feelings, to formulate the inchoate longings and the uncertain stirrings of spirit which he feels that all men share. These qualities are manifest in the following passage from *Of Time and the River*, where he is trying to define the "fury" that drives Gant toward the North and away·from the South.

It is to have the old unquiet mind, the famished heart, the restless soul; it is to lose hope, heart, and all joy utterly, and then to have them wake again, to have the old feeling return with overwhelming force that he is about to find the thing for which his life obscurely and desperately is groping—for which all men on this earth have sought—one face out of the million faces, a wall, a door, a place of certitude and peace and wandering no more. For what is it that we Americans are seeking always on this earth? Why is it we have crossed the stormy seas so many times alone, lain in a thousand alien rooms at night hearing the sounds of time, dark time, and thought until heart, brain, flesh, and spirit are sick and weary with the thought of it; "Where shall I go now? What shall I do?"

Set beside some of the apostrophes from *Look Homeward, Angel*, like the one to Laura James at the end of Chapter 30, this passage seems restrained, yet it represents pretty clearly that rhetorical groping toward understanding and expression which is a very large element in Wolfe's work. He is fascinated by language, enchanted by words, carried away by rhetorical devices. A kind of primitive logomania is in him: if the word can be found and uttered, vast forces are unleashed and great truths miraculously uncovered. The artist's search, Wolfe declared in *The Story of a Novel*, is the search for a language, for an articulation. "I believe with all my heart, also, that each man for himself and in his own way, each man who ever hopes to make a living thing out of the substances of his one life, must find that way, that language, and that door—must find it for himself as I have tried to do."

The drift toward rhetoric is the aspect of Wolfe's work most frequently called Southern. Alfred Kazin observed of Wolfe and Faulkner: "It is their rhetoric, a mountainous verbal splendor, that holds these writers together . . . the extravagant and ornamental tradition of Southern rhetoric" (*On Native Grounds*, 1942, 468). Wilbur J. Cash believed that it was their use of the rhetorical tradition that tied Faulkner and Wolfe to earlier Southern literary traditions, and Joseph Warren

Beach felt that "Wolfe's inclination to extravagant and ornamental writing" should be associated with "something in the tradition of Southern culture" (*American Fiction, 1920–1940*, 1948, 211). As Floyd Watkins has asserted, "Wolfe must be viewed as a Southern rhetorician" ("Rhetoric in Southern Writing: Wolfe," *The Georgia Review*, XII [1958], 82). Certainly the passion for the sound of the word, the primitive desire to give the name, the sense of the power present in the magic of incantation, show up with alarming frequency in Southern writing. The particular linguistic combination that Wolfe used—the combination of concrete detail, accurate speech, and incantatory rhetorical extravagance is also present to a marked degree in the works of Faulkner, particularly since 1932, and in the novels of Robert Penn Warren.

Wolfe likewise shares the Southerner's willingness to accept and find delight in paradox. At the heart of the riddle of the South is a union of opposites, a condition of instability, a paradox: a love of individualism combined with a defense of slavery and segregation, a delight in polished manners and at the same time a ready recourse to violence, the liberalism of Thomas Jefferson co-existing with the conservatism of John C. Calhoun. Such paradoxes bother Southerners less than they would bother their Northern neighbors, for while they hunger for order and are moved by a rage for tradition, they can at the same time accept instability as a permanent aspect of human existence and the unresolved contradiction as a part of man's condition. Southern writers often value paradox as a primary element in art. Cleanth Brooks, for example, finds the meaning in poetry in the paradoxes that are to be found in word, image, and structure. The Fugitive poets, notably John Crowe Ransom, find the full meaning of an incident in the comprehension of its persistent ironies. Allen Tate sees the meaning of a poem in the "tension" created by the conflict between its intension and extension.

Wolfe saw his world and himself through an only semilogical application to life of the Hegelian dialectic. He seemed to need to define a thing's opposite before he could comprehend the thing, and to have a naïve faith that somehow the meaning was manifest if the opposites were stated. Hence, there is in his work on practically every level—sentence, paragraph, scene, theme, large project—a structure of paradox. But all these attributes of Wolfe's work individually are essentially superficial qualities of his "Southernness." So strong a combination of these attributes as he displays does not often occur in America outside the South; yet these qualities suggest rather than define a distinctively Southern quality. In certain other respects, however, Wolfe seems definitively Southern. One of these is his attitude toward capitalistic industrialism; another is his sense of the tragic implications of experience; and a third is his deep-seated sense of human guilt.

That Wolfe had little patience with the group of Southern writers known as the Agrarians is obvious from what has already been quoted. He regarded their intellectualism as false, their devotion to the life of the soil as pretentious and unreal, and he heaped scorn on them more than once, calling them by the opprobrious name "New Confederates." Yet one has the feeling that much of his contempt rested on ignorance of what the Agrarians were advocating, and that he would have been pretty much of their party if he had known what the party really was. However, he belonged loosely to the New South school, which saw in industrial progress the key to a new and better life and believed that the South must emerge from its retreat into the reality of the modern world. In *The Web and the Rock* he wrote:

> There was an image in George Webber's mind that came to him in childhood and that resumed for him the whole dark picture of those decades of defeat and darkness. He saw an old house, set far back from the traveled highway, and many passed along that road, and the troops went by, the dust rose, and the war was over. And no one passed along that road again. He saw an old man go along the path, away from the road, into the house; and the path was overgrown with grass and weeds, with thorny tangle, and with underbrush until the path was lost. And no one ever used that path again. And the man who went into that house never came out of it again. And the house stayed on. It shone faintly through that tangled growth like its own ruined spectre, its doors and windows

black as eyeless sockets. That was the South. That was the South for thirty years or more.

That was the South, not of George Webber's life, nor of the lives of his contemporaries—that was the South they did not know but that all of them somehow remembered. It came to them from God knows where, upon the rustling of a leaf at night, in quiet voices on a Southern porch, in a screen door slam and sudden silence, a whistle wailing down the midnight valleys to the East and the enchanted cities of the North, and Aunt Maw's droning voice and the memory of unheard voices, in the memory of the dark, ruined Helen in their blood, in something stricken, lost, and far, and long ago. They did not see it, the people of George's age and time, but they remembered it.

They had come out—another image now—into a kind of sunlight of another century. They had come out upon the road again. The road was being paved. More people came now. They cut a pathway to the door again. Some of the weeds were clear. Another house was built. They heard wheels coming and the world was *in,* yet they were not yet wholly of that world.

Yet Wolfe was also keenly aware that industrial progress and the things associated with it could have damaging effects on American and Southern culture. Writing to his mother, in May 1923, he condemned "progress" and commerce in scathing terms:

I will not hesitate to say what I think of those people who shout "Progress, Progress, Progress"—when what they mean is more Ford automobiles, more Rotary Clubs, more Baptist Ladies Social unions. I will say that "Greater Asheville" does not necessarily mean "100,000 by 1930," that we are not necessarily 4 times as civilized as our grandfathers because we go four times as fast in automobiles, because our buildings are four times as tall. What I shall try to get into their dusty little pint-measure minds is that a full belly, a good automobile, paved streets, and so on, do not make them one whit better or finer,—that there is beauty in this world,—beauty even in this wilderness of ugliness and provincialism that is at present our country, beauty and spirit which will make us men instead of cheap Board of Trade Boosters, and blatant pamphleteers.

He defined the "essential tragedy of America" as "the magnificent, unrivaled, unequaled, unbeatable, unshrinkable, supercolossal, 99-and-44-one-hundredths-per-cent-pure, schoolgirl-complexion, covers-the-earth, I'd-walk-a-mile-for-it, four-out-of-five-have-it, his-master's-voice, ask-the-man-who-owns-one, blueplate-special home of advertising, salesmanship, and special pleading in all its many catchy and beguiling forms." Certainly for him, capitalistic industrial progress had as little appeal as it did for the Agrarians; for him, as for the Twelve Southerners who wrote *I'll Take My Stand*, the modern industrial world had become a perversion of the American dream. The Twelve Southerners declared, "If a community, or a section, or a race, or an age, is groaning under industrialism, and well aware that it is an evil dispensation, it must find the way to throw it off. To think that this cannot be done is pusillanimous. And if the whole community, section, race, or age thinks it cannot be done, then it has simply lost its political genius and doomed itself to impotence" ("Introduction," *I'll Take My Stand*, 1930, xx). George Webber shared these sentiments when he said, in *You Can't Go Home Again:*

"America went off the track somewhere—back around the time of the Civil War, or pretty soon afterwards. Instead of going ahead and developing along the line in which the country started out, it got shunted off in another direction —and now we look around and see we've gone places we didn't mean to go. Suddenly we realize that America has turned into something ugly—and vicious—and corroded at the heart of its power with easy wealth and graft and special privilege. . . . And the worst of it is the intellectual dishonesty which all this corruption has bred. People are *afraid* to think straight—*afraid* to face themselves —*afraid* to look at things and see them as they are. We've become like a nation of advertising men, all hiding behind catch phrases like 'prosperity' and 'rugged individualism' and 'the American way.' And the real things like freedom, and equal opportunity, and the integrity and worth of the individual—things that have belonged to the American dream since the beginning—they have become just words too. The substance has gone out of them—they're not real any more."

Admittedly, this sounds more like Sidney Lanier's condemnation of "trade" than Donald Davidson's advocacy of the agrarian way, yet the enemy that all three faced was an enemy well known to the South and commonly confronted by Southerners.

Wolfe looked upon himself as a radical, even, as he once called himself, a "Revolutionary," and he angrily expressed his hatred of the gross injustice and inhumanity that the depression produced. But to him the solution was never material; indeed, the substitution of the material for the spiritual was the cause for his belief "that we are lost here in America," and only his confidence that ultimately America would put aside the material for the spiritual made it possible for him to add, "but I believe we shall be found."

Wolfe is peculiarly Southern, too, in the degree to which he sees the darkness, pain, and evil in life, and yet does not succumb to the naturalistic answer of despair. "The enemy," he tells us in *You Can't Go Home Again*,

> is old as Time, and evil as Hell, and he has been here with us from the beginning. I think he stole our earth from us, destroyed our wealth, and ravaged and despoiled our land. I think he took our people and enslaved them, that he polluted the fountains of our life, took unto himself the rarest treasures of our own possession, took our bread and left us with a crust.

Wolfe seemed to feel, as George Webber did, "the huge and nameless death that waits around the corner for all men, to break their backs and shatter instantly the blind and pitiful illusions of their hope." He was supremely the novelist of death in American literature, for the ending of life was an obsessive theme with him. All his characters come to face the fact of death; as he expressed it, "They knew that they would die and that the earth would last forever. And with that feeling of joy, wonder, and sorrow in their hearts, they knew that another day had gone, another day had come, and they knew how brief and lonely are man's days." And the end, at least in its physical sense, was ugly. In *Of Time and the River* he described it this way:

> This was the sickening and abominable end of flesh, which infected time and all man's living memory of morning, youth, and magic with the death-putrescence of its cancerous taint, and made us doubt that we had ever lived, or had a father, known joy: this was the end, and the end was horrible in ugliness. At the end it was not well.

In *The Story of a Novel* Wolfe is explicit about this darkness and evil in life. "Everywhere around me . . . I saw the evidence of an incalculable ruin and suffering," he said, and enumerated the "suffering, violence, oppression, hunger, cold, and filth and poverty" he saw, so that through "the suffering and labor of [his] own life" he shared the experiences of people around him.

This sense of evil and suffering is more typical of Southern writers than of other Americans, for a variety of reasons: the South's distrust of progress, its refusal to believe in perfectibility, its experience of compromise and paradox—all culminated in the defeat in the Civil War and its long and bitter aftermath. As C. Vann Woodward has cogently argued, the South is the only American region where the principles of progress and the concept of perfectibility are demonstrably false. "Nothing," he asserts, "about [its] history is conducive to the theory that the South was the darling of divine providence" ("The Irony of Southern History," *Southern Renascence*, ed. Louis D. Rubin, Jr., and Robert D. Jacobs, 1953, 65). This sense of defeat could lead Ellen Glasgow to say that she could never recall a time when "the pattern of society as well as the scheme of things in general, had not seemed to [her] false and even malignant" (*The Woman Within*, 1954, 42), and the same feeling found expression in the dark damnation of Faulkner's world and the ambiguous calamities of Robert Penn Warren's.

When, however, the nation as a whole began to experience the cataclysms of the twentieth century and to react to scientific and philosophic views of man that were less optimistic,

the American artist outside the South tended to turn to programs of Utopian reform, or satiric correction, or naturalistic
despair. The Southern writer on the other hand, older in the
experience of calamity and defeat, saw the tragic grandeur
of man, the magnificence of his will in the face of disaster,
and the glory with which he maintained the integrity of his
spirit in a world of material defeat. Southern writers have often
used their history to make a tragic fable of man's lot in a
hostile world, and to celebrate the triumph of the human spirit
when challenged by an idea or a responsibility. As Ellen Glasgow asserts, "One may learn to live, one may even learn to
live gallantly, without delight." And as Ike McCaslin says in
Faulkner's *Delta Autumn*, "There are good men everywhere,
at all times. Most men are. Some are just unlucky, because
most men are a little better than their circumstances give them
a chance to be." This view of man changes defeat into tragic
grandeur and touches the spectacle of suffering with the transforming sense of human dignity.

The Southern writer is often obsessed with a sense of guilt
and the need for expiation. Robert Penn Warren calls this feel-

ing by its theological name in his poem *Original Sin,* and sees
it as the inevitable result of our lost innocence; in Allen Tate's
The Wolves it is a threatening evil to be faced always in the
next room; in William Faulkner it may be symbolized by the
vicariously shared guilt which Quentin Compson must assume
and die to pay for in *The Sound and the Fury,* or the inheritance of the father's which Ike McCaslin vainly tries to
repudiate in *The Bear.* This sense of guilt may be the product
of the pervasive Calvinism of the region; it may be the product
of the poverty and suffering that the region has known; it is
certainly in part the result of the guilt associated with slavery
in the nineteenth century and the Negro's second-class citizen-
ship in the twentieth—a guilt most thoughtful Southerners have
felt. In any case, it appears to be a hallmark of the serious
twentieth-century Southern writer. And it is a hallmark that
Thomas Wolfe's work certainly bears.

He states his own sense of guilt explicitly in *The Story of a
Novel.*

> And through the traffic of those thronging crowds—whose
> faces, whose whole united and divided life was now in-
> stantly and without an effort of the will, my *own*—there
> rose forever the sad unceasing murmurs of the body of
> this life, the vast recessive fadings of the shadow of man's
> death that breathes forever with its dirgelike sigh around
> the huge shores of the world.
>
> And *beyond, beyond*—forever *above, around, behind*
> the vast and tranquil consciousness of my spirit that now
> held the earth and all her elements in the huge clasp of
> its effortless subjection—there dwelt forever the fatal
> knowledge of my own inexpiable *guilt.*

In *You Can't Go Home Again* he explicitly links this sense
of guilt with the South, and in turn sees the South as a symbol
and in a sense a scapegoat for the national hurt.

> Perhaps it came from their old war, and from the ruin
> of their great defeat and its degraded aftermath. Perhaps
> it came from causes yet more ancient—from the evil of
> man's slavery, and the hurt and shame of human con-
> science in its struggle with the fierce desire to own. It

came, too, perhaps, from the lusts of the hot South, tormented and repressed below the harsh and outward patterns of a bigot and intolerant theology. . . . And most of all, perhaps, it came out of the very weather of their lives. . . .

But it was not only in the South that America was hurt. There was another deeper, darker, and more nameless wound throughout the land. . . .

We must look at the heart of guilt that beats in each of us, for there the cause lies. We must look, and with our own eyes see, the central core of defeat and shame and failure. . . .

Thomas Wolfe did not live to complete his representation of his America through the portrait of himself as generic man, and out of the novels, short stories, and letters we piece out the pattern he was trying to follow and we guess at meanings and intentions. One thing seems clear: Wolfe was a Southerner, torn by the tensions and issues that thoughtful Southerners feel, oppressed as they tend to be with the tragic nature of life, and feeling as they often do a sense of guilt that demands some kind of expiating action. The work he completed had demonstrable Southern qualities; the total work, had he lived to complete it, would probably have had these qualities too. The South did, indeed, burn in his blood and on his pages like a "ruined Helen"—beautiful, passionate, and dark with violence and guilt.

ROBERT PENN WARREN

BY ELLINGTON WHITE

I

During one of those university parties that traditionally terminate the campus visits of celebrated writers, Robert Penn Warren (so the story goes) was handed a student poem and asked for his comments. It had been a long day and in the course of it Warren had read and commented on many such poems. To spring on him still another, while he sat resting in the oasis, struck some of the guests as being stupid and cold-blooded, but if Warren felt this way he did not show it. He received the poem politely and holding it far out in front of him—head cocked, one eye closed—scrutinized it in silence for several minutes. "Well, it's a poem," he said. "I can see that. But it's like a wall, like a wall. I can't seem to get a foothold."

Probably the story is apocryphal, as such stories usually are, but even so, its appeal remains, if for no other reason than because the wall is such an appealing image to apply to Warren's own work, which is heavy and sturdy—with footholds, yes, but with footholds so placed that one will never get to the top without a good deal of stretching. There are other modern writers, of course, who demand that their readers do a little stretching, and the result is that they are written about in the quarterlies and elsewhere avoided. But with Warren the case is different. He has accomplished what all writers want to accomplish: respect and popularity too. While the reviews have been turning out essays about him, Hollywood has been turning his novels into motion pictures. One of his novels has joined the Modern Library and parts of another book were printed in *Life* magazine. Thanks to *Life* and to Hollywood and to the Modern Library, Warren is now able to support his family on what his books alone bring in, and that, in the literary world, makes him about as rare as a whooping crane. Warren's work has a solid intellectual structure and is clearly the product of a writer who has thought long and hard about his craft. He is bawdy and often crude. There is considerable violence in his novels, and in some of his poems too. His plots are usually spectacular and his language and his style are both very close to the earth. Added to these qualities is a very real concern with the public affairs of men, a fact readily borne out by simply counting the number of governors and senators and meaty-jowled politicians who inhabit his novels. I don't mean by this that Warren is a political writer. He shows little interest in "issues" as such and, with the exception of Willie Stark in *All the King's Men,* his politicians are usually quite incidental as characters. But the fact that they are there at all, and so numerously there, says something about the kind of society that generally prevails in his fiction. Certainly it is a different society than the society one encounters in the novels of Henry James, for example, or Marcel Proust, where the fictional world is confined to the self or to the household. Warren's society belongs to the world. It is *public.* And by public I mean, to quote the dictionary, "Of or pertaining to the people; relating to, belonging to, or affecting a nation, state, or community at large;—opposed to *private.*" A public society is the society one enters when he leaves either himself or his home. Here he must act and move, because by leaving himself he has entered history, and history is movement. It is here too —for Warren, at any rate—that one encounters knowledge— knowledge, paradoxically, of the self—and since the search for knowledge is one of the "burdens" that man's human nature has imposed upon him, eventually he must do what Jack Burden does at the end of *All the King's Men*—"go out of the house and go into the convulsion of the world."

Readers of *All the King's Men* (1946) will recognize this house as being located in Burden's Landing, where Jack Burden was born. They will further recognize the person who will "go out" of it with him, Anne Stanton, as his childhood sweetheart, with whom he had once refused to make love because love was an act that would plunge Anne Stanton "into the full dark stream of the world." Yet now, now that Willie Stark has touched both their lives, he is willing for Anne Stanton to cross the threshold with him—not away from but into the world. Why? The answer of course lies with Willie Stark and what he represents. Embracing the chief characteristic of political man, namely a huge capacity for action and movement, Willie Stark *is* the world, and as such he has already happened to Jack Burden and to Anne Stanton. Through him they have already entered the public realm, with its hazards and horrors. Call Willie Stark an agent if you like, but an agent very much alive, with a character all his own.

In *Night Rider* (1939), Warren used an historical incident rather than a person to draw his protagonist into the world's flood. *Night Rider* is the story of a tobacco war that took place in Kentucky at the turn of the century, and of a group of farmers who organized to protect themselves against a monopoly of buyers. Percy Munn, the central figure, is a country lawyer and farmer; when the book opens, he is arriving in Bardsville, Kentucky, for a rally being held by the Association of Growers of Dark Fired Tobacco. The train he is riding is crowded, and he feels "disgust" for the "dead hot weight of flesh which would plunge against him and press him." He resents "the pressure that was human" and wishes he were home again, where things were pastoral and removed. He thinks of his wife "as he had seen her last that morning, in a white dress, standing on the porch, at the other end of the row of sugar trees, and waving to him as he got into the buggy that was to take him down to the crossing where he could flag the local." The local that was carrying him away from the privacy of the farm into the pressures of the world finally reaches town, and there he meets Mr. Christian, whom he had known before, and on whose account he is eventually drawn into politics.

Mr. Christian and other Association members persuade him to join the board of directors. At first he declines. He cries, "No!" and wonders afterward what "secret but violent promptings" had thrust the word from his lips. Something more than modesty had been involved. This he knew. But what precisely this was he could not say, "though it moved him powerfully." As the book progresses, Percy Munn is drawn deeper and deeper into the affairs of the world without any clear idea, one feels, of what is happening to him or where he is going. One of the faults of *Night Rider* is that Percy Munn's will is too easily annihilated in the world's forward rush.

I mention the book here simply to show that at this early stage in Warren's career he was already concerned with this question of the private versus the public. Percy Munn's inability to understand his reluctance to enter politics is no different from Jack Burden's inability to understand why he was not willing to plunge Anne Stanton into the world. Both instinctively draw away from the world because of the world's power to draw them out of the comfortable darkness of themselves, where they, like most of us, would rather remain. Jack Burden describes the interior life as "a clammy, sad little foetus you carry around inside yourself"—clammy and sad, yes, but also safe. That is why Jeremiah Beaumont prefers it to the world, as does his wife: "I hate the world," she says, "it will take you away." It is also the reason for the following description of the world from *Band of Angels*. The speaker is Amantha Starr.

> But the world was there, creeping in like cold air under a door, collecting like lint in the corner, crowding in on us like the camel in the tent, the people, the words, the papers, the letters . . .

But first, *World Enough and Time* (1950). Like *Night Rider*, it is based on an historical incident, a murder that happened in Kentucky, and, like Percy Munn, Jeremiah Beaumont, the protagonist of *World Enough and Time*, is also asked to enter politics. His reply is not too different from his predecessor's.

> Almost violently, he [Jeremiah] shook his head, saying "No. No."
> But Mr. Madison [who had asked Jeremiah to run for the state legislature] was looking directly at him with his grey, severe eyes, saying earnestly, "But it is your duty. If you can subdue your natural modesty and preference for the private life. It is your duty."

The private life is the life, up until this point, which Jeremiah had been living with Rachael Jorden, whose hand he had won by promising to kill Cassius Fort. Jeremiah does make an attempt to kill Fort, but at the last moment he takes pity on the old man, who was once his friend, and the opportunity passes, and he and Rachael withdraw from the world into what Jeremiah terms "a winter dream," a retirement from involvements into the privacy of the self and the home. (Jack Burden's name for a similiar period in his life is "the Great Sleep.") At Mr. Madison's request Jeremiah enters the public realm and before leaving it becomes so entangled with politics that in the end he does kill Fort—not, as he thought, to fulfill his promise to Rachael, although that plays a part in his "resolve," but because Fort's violation of Rachael was used as a political weapon by the opposing party. In other words, the action is forced on Jeremiah by the world; for, as Jack Burden says, "Politics is action," and action is a characteristic of the world.

Before killing Fort, Jeremiah had viewed his oath to Rachael as "an appeal to the world," and once the deed is done, once he has been tried and found guilty, he returns to the death cell, a pitlike opening in the ground. "He wanted to go down, down into that quietness and dark and hear no voices." He calls the pit his "private darkness" where he "had thought to embrace" his "peace," and when peace is denied him here and he and Rachael are imprisoned on a boggy island in the swamps he thinks of the island as peace, the "black inwardness and womb of the quagmire."

> It was a peace with no past and no future, the absoluteness of the single, separate, dark, massive moment that swells up fatly like a bubble from the deep mud, exists as a globe of slick film housing its noxious gas, then pops and is gone, and then, with the regularity of the pulse of the blood, is followed by another that goes, and then by another, forever.

Thus removed from history, Jeremiah sinks into a kind of natural life, fishing, hunting, lying in the sun. Though nature has its attractions, they are dangerous attractions, akin to those of sleep and death. In an essay on Hemingway (*Kenyon Review*, Winter, 1947), Warren equates "Nature-as-all" with moral chaos, an idea frequently encountered in his own fiction. Thus, left alone with nature, Lilburn and Isham Lewis (*Brother to Dragons*) are turned into animals; and thus the "natural chill" that R.P.W. senses in the same poem when, standing among the ruins of the old Lewis house, a snake appears from a "black aperture among the stones."

And suddenly the head thrust forth, and the fat, black
Body molten flowed, as though those stones
Bled forth earth's inner darkness to the day.

Another "black aperture" is the scene of Warren's most recent novel, *The Cave* (1959), which is about a man, Jasper Harrick, who finds an opening in the ground and dies exploring it. *The Cave* is Warren's most symbolic book and in many ways his most puzzling. To say that it is about Jasper Harrick is not strictly true. We never actually see him as a person, and though he is the motivating character, the main characters are those assembled outside the cave. All we know of Jasper is what we learn about him from other people—his mother and brother, in particular—and they tell us that he was a person who never came to grips with life, "working a little for just enough money for shotgun shells, sitting alone and singing his songs, drifting down the river for days and nights, off into the mountains, in winter, alone, with or without a rifle, hunting or not hunting, crawling into the caves, off and gone, without ever a word."

Not only in his nearness to nature is Jasper Harrick like Jeremiah Beaumont, but he expects to find something like peace in a cave, as did Jeremiah. When his mother asked him to explain his cave explorations, he answered, "Well, in the ground at least a fellow has a chance of knowing who he is." If we take Jasper's answer at its face value, it would seem to be a reversal of the idea found elsewhere in Warren that one knows "who he is" only after an engagement with the world. But since Warren introduces the novel with a quotation from Plato's celebrated cave image, another possibility suggests itself. What Plato says is that the cave houses only shadows and that before one can know the real, the true, he must turn around and face the painful glare of the sun. Monty Harrick's song to his brother, sung at various times in the book, ends with variations on the refrain, "Oh, bring him out and let him in the sunshine stand!" But this appeal goes unanswered and Jasper dies. In view of this, since the cave seems to represent the interior life, just as it did for Jeremiah Beaumont, it would seem that, contrary to what Jasper told his mother, he failed in his search for self-knowledge because he was looking for it in the wrong place. As for the "aboveground folks," however, Jasper's father, his mother, and Ikey Sumpter, they do learn about themselves and what they learn is Warren's book.

One of the things Jasper liked about the cave was the absence there of winter and summer, the absence, that is, of history, and as this is true of the cave, so is it true of Jeremiah Beaumont's "winter dream" and Jack Burden's "Great Sleep." It is also true of the West, to which Jack Burden flees, following the discovery that Anne Stanton is Willie Stark's mistress. In Warren's long poem, *Brother to Dragons* (1953), Charles Lewis also goes West: "I fled the intolerable World that I had made and that had made me." And so does Amantha Starr in *Band of Angels* (1955) after the collapse of her husband's ideals—"failing westward," as she describes it. Percival Skrogg (*World Enough and Time*) hides from the world in intellectual abstractions, one of Warren's chief hatreds.

> . . . he was perfectly fearless because the world outside himself was not real. . . . What was real was an idea inside himself, and all outside the idea which was his true self—both the wide world and his own meager body—was nothing but chaos which could become real only in so far as it was formed by his idea.

In *All the King's Men*, Adam Stanton has constructed around himself such a cozy idea of the world that when the real world—the affair between Willie and his sister—breaks it down, he hasn't the means to reconstruct it and so abandons the world altogether in a suicidal act of revenge. Notably, when Jack Burden asks him to direct Willie's new hospital, which would mean involving himself in the public world, he reacts as Percy Munn and Jeremiah Beaumont did—he shakes his head. A romantic, Jack Burden calls him, who "has a picture of the world in his head, and when the world doesn't conform in any respect to the picture, he wants to throw the world away."

This is true of Adam Stanton, but it is likewise true of Jack

Burden himself. "The world was full of things I·didn't want
to know," he says at one point; and one of these things is his
mother, whose marital behavior so much offended him that
in rejecting her he rejected the world by fleeing into the past.
In the past he encounters Cass Mastern, whom he fails to
understand, and so flees one step farther, this time into the
"Great Sleep," when you "stop going to sleep in order that
you may be able to get up, but get up in order that you may
be able to go back to sleep." Willie Stark arouses him, however—literally arouses him, with a ringing telephone—and Jack
Burden again enters the world. At least he moves in the world,
thanks to Willie Stark, who imparts some of his own energy;
but moving through it his thoughts still go out to animals
("Time is nothing to a hog . . .") and to that traditional de-
fender of the private life, the housewife.

In this respect his sympathies belong more to Lucy Stark,
who finally leaves her husband and retires to a farm, than to
Willie. But without Willie, Jack Burden would be powerless
to act, and without this capacity he would have no identity,
at least not in any public sense, and for Warren that is the
only sense in which identity is possible.* As Jeremiah says in
World Enough and Time: "If a man lives by what he feels to
be the truth in him, and discovers in a single instant that the
tongue of the world says differently of him, there comes the
fear and shame that what he had held to be the truth in him
may not be the truth after all and there may be no truth but
the terrible truth now given him by the tongue of the world.
And if a man is robbed of his truth, and of a sudden, how can
he know what he is?" Amantha Starr says much the same thing
in *Band of Angels:* "If I could only be free, I used to think,
free from the lonely nothingness of being only yourself when
the world flees away, and free from the closing walls that
would crush you to nothingness." As for Jack Burden, the walls
of the self do not fully open until Judge Irwin's suicide, which

* The search for identity, it might be noted, is what drives Sue
Murdock in *At Heaven's Gate* (1943) to Sweetwater, a labor agi-
tator. Though a public figure like Willie Stark, Sweetwater has
none of Willie's real concern for the public good. He is cynical
and self-seeking and eventually fails Sue Murdock, as had her
father before him, her father's protégé, Jerry Calhoun, and Slim
Sarett, a homosexual poet.

he was responsible for because of his political involvements, and which leads ultimately to the discovery that Judge Irwin was his father. Fittingly enough, he was asleep at the time.

I came out of the sleep and popped straight up in the bed. I was wide awake. The sound that had awakened me was still ringing in my ears. I knew that it had been a scream. Then it came again. A bright, beautiful, silvery soprano scream.

The scream belongs to his mother, and following it, Jack Burden learns not only the truth of his origins, but, more important, he learns that, contrary to what he had once thought, actions are not all blind, presided over by the "godhead of the Great Twitch," but are a human activity and as such receive their meaningfulness, or their blindness, from man himself, who as a political animal both creates and discharges them.

II

Because of his concern with man as a political animal Warren stands outside the mainstream of modern literature. With few exceptions, our modern writers have gone underground, with the understanding that it is here, apart from worldly illusions, that man must discover himself. No one any longer doubts that they have chosen the right direction. The public world has for so long now and for so many reasons been suspect, that the idea of a man turning to it rather than to himself for any real sense of human fulfillment is totally foreign to us, however aware we might be of that moment in history, millions of years ago, when men did turn joyfully to the sun's blinding light. I am referring, of course, to the Greeks, and what the public realm meant to them. The Greeks engaged in the *vitae activa*, a term used by Hannah Arendt in her book *The Human Condition* to mean a life devoted to public-political matters, because that is what they were expected to do as human beings. To quote Miss Arendt: "In ancient feeling the privative trait of privacy, indicated in the word itself, was all-important; it meant literally a state of being deprived of something, and even of the highest and most human of man's capacities. A man who lived only a private life, who like the slave was not permitted to enter the public realm, was not fully human" (*The Human Condition*, 1958, 38). The Greeks looked upon necessity as belonging to the household; freedom resided in the *polis*, where men were given the opportunity to display their capacities and so show to the world who and what they were. I mention this because something of the sweet simplicity inherent in this idea runs throughout Warren's work. In *Brother to Dragons*, for example, there is a long monologue by R.P.W. in which a boy, having shot a wild goose, ran

> *Three miles to town and yelled for joy and every*
> *Step cried like a baby and did not know why.*

R.P.W. remarks:

> *Even without the goose you might have found*
> *The image you'll need when you reach forty*
> *And have to learn the single lesson left*
> *To learn worth learning, and that lesson is*
> *That the only thing worth learning you had learned*
> *Long back before you laid your BB down*
> *For the .12 gauge. And that lesson is that the only*
> *Thing in life is glory.*

There is nothing metaphysical about this concept of glory, no more than there is anything metaphysical about a goose. It is solely a product of the world, and for this reason can be achieved only in terms of the world—that is, through action.

So the Greeks left the household to slaves, who were not considered human, and gave their undivided attention to the world. Originally, Miss Arendt remarks, they did this "in order to embark upon some adventure and glorious enterprise," but later it was done "simply to devote one's life to the affairs of the city" (*The Human Condition*, 36). To devote his life to the affairs of the city Jack Burden leaves Burden's Landing. And so does Percy Munn leave his farm and Jeremiah Beaumont his "winter dream." Jack Burden alone, however, goes willingly, and not even he has any fixed idea of glory before him. But since glory is one of the aspects of knowledge, and knowledge one of the burdens of being human, eventually man who is not a slave has to reckon with it. If he is a slave, then he had better do what R.P.W. advises: sit down

> To the careful cultivation of cirrhosis,
> For drink's a kind of glory too, and man
> Can't live without some glory after all,
> Even a poor kind.

A fundamental difference between Warren's view of the political realm and that held by the Greeks is that for them it was characterized by persuasion, where for him it is continually exploding into violence. Action contains both the sword and the word, and the age must decide which to use. We have chosen the sword; so the presence of violence in Warren's fiction, since it is a worldly fiction, seems to us only natural. Violence, of course, is not confined to Warren. We find it in most Southern writers. Perhaps this is because Southern writers are also possessed with history and consequently are aware of the connection that exists between history and action. As Miss Arendt notes, without action we would have no history to begin with, by which she means that since action is engaged "in founding and preserving political bodies" it incidentally "creates the condition of remembrance." You can't have one without the other, any more than you can have action without violence.

Percy Munn is shot down, as is Willie Stark; Jeremiah Beaumont is decapitated, and Amantha Starr, after witnessing and surviving any number of violent acts, fails westward with her broken husband. At the end of his long journal, Jeremiah Beaumont asks a question: "Was all for naught?" But long before this question Jeremiah had glimpsed the shades of nothingness closing around his world. The same shades hang over *Night Rider* and *At Heaven's Gate* and *All the King's Men*, and were later to fall over *Band of Angels*. Here, as elsewhere, Warren's thought is strongly existential. He insists that time and bones have bound man to the earth and that consequently his knowledge must likewise be rooted in the ground; and again, like the existentialists, he assumes that man's essence is acquired *after* his existence rather than before it. William Barrett (*Irrational Man*, 1958, 90) quotes Ortega y Gasset as saying that "man has no nature, only a history," and that is what Warren is also saying.

To think to find it [reason] as a given condition of man
Would be but to repeat, I now see,
My old error. I have suffered enough for that.
Oh, no, if there is to be reason, we must
Create the possibility
Of reason, and we can create it only
From the circumstances of our most evil despair.
We must strike the steel of wrath on the stone of guilt,
And hope to provoke, thus, in the midst of our coiling darkness
The incandescence of the heart's great flare.

The speaker here is Thomas Jefferson, but the thought belongs to Warren, who would use the same voice to answer Jeremiah's question: "Was all for naught?"

For nothing we had,
Nothing we were,
Is lost.
All is redeemed,
In knowledge.

CEREMONIES OF BRAVERY: JOHN CROWE RANSOM

BY ISABEL GAMBLE MAC CAFFREY

The poetry of John Crowe Ransom is a small but accurate mirror of the modern sensibility. In it are reflected the miraculous virtues of contemporary verse at its best: its combination of delicacy with strength, of fervor with restraint, of elegance with earthiness. One needs only to glance at the critical writing about Ransom to see how perfectly apt, for his poetry, are the favorite words of this generation's critics. He has been celebrated, rightly, as the poet of perilous equilibrium, of dichotomies and irony, of tension and paradox; his verse portrays, Randall Jarrell once wrote, "the composed and inexhaustible ambiguity of things" ("John Ransom's Poetry," *Sewanee Review*, LVI [1948], 383). In addition, Ransom's poetry illustrates with beautiful clarity the interdependence of form and matter; his style emerges from the exigencies of his subjects, which are completed and composed by its perfect fidelity.

In his own Poetics—for he is preceptor as well as practitioner—Ransom has done much to convince us of the worthiness—indeed, the necessity—of these modernist virtues, and the attitudes which lie behind them. They are the attitudes, we should like to think, of a civilized man: courtesy, manners, regard for the individual as an individual, refusal to simplify the complex, insistence on balanced judgment, proper respect for the facts of life, and a determination to triumph over them whenever possible. Ransom's imaginary kingdom, like that of another civilized man, E. M. Forster, is Love, the Beloved Republic,

> *Where the men or beasts or birds*
> *Exchange few words and pleasant words.*

Somewhere is such a kingdom, though not here, not now.
Forster and Ransom are, indeed, a congruent pair, sharing a
good many points of view; Forster's essay, "What I Believe,"
might stand as a manifesto for both. "My law-givers are
Erasmus and Montaigne, not Moses and St. Paul," he writes;
and we remember that St. Paul fares but poorly under Ransom's scrutiny as well (see "Our Two Worthies"). The saint
was a devotee of the Pure Idea, a Platonic notion to which
the sceptical empiricist cannot subscribe.

> *Plato, before Plotinus gentled him,*
> *Spoke the soul's part, and though its vice is known*
> *We're in his shadow still.*

Ransom and Forster foregather instead under the banner of
Aristotle, "pulling steady on the bottle"; if, indeed, they will
accept a banner at all—for, they keep reminding us, they do
not believe in belief. They believe in personal relationships and
the whatness of things.

These attitudes produce the special style we have chosen to
call modern, although actually it is a recurrent style, reappear-
ing as the cycles of history move around. Its characteristics
are adumbrated in the critical terms listed above. The refusal
of belief demands an ironic style (both Ransom and Forster
are masters of it), a necessity of the double vision, which
wishes to say one thing while suggesting another. Allegiance
to Aristotle, the natural father of poets, requires in addition
a sense of the complexity of things. For the Aristotelian, beauty
is not the Pure Idea, but (as one of them has said), "in the
flesh it is immortal." Spirit is incarnate in flesh and our mortal
condition is ambiguous, amphibious. Rejecting the Platonic
universal, distrusting the grandeur of generality, the modernist
chooses instead to render the unique, the precious object. This
choice enforces an oblique style, since the vocabulary of directness, smoothed by too many tongues, fits the body of the object loosely and shrouds its particularity. Ransom has declared
positively that "the direct approach is perilous to the artist,
and may be fatal." Circumlocution may take the form either
of a dramatic-symbolic style, where images enact ideas; or of
linguistic dislocation, the formation of a dialect at once thick-
ened and subtilized until it can present the object in a fresh and

therefore (so our theorists assert) a truer light. The style of Gerard Manley Hopkins is a greater exemplar of this second manner (his term "inscape" is an earlier name for the precious object); Ransom's is a diminished but scarcely less effective instance.

Devotion to the individual, the particular, imposes special burdens on the poet, which affect not only his idiom but his subject matter. Ransom's highly personal style and his consistency of tone have driven critics almost irresistibly toward an attempt to describe his "major subject." It is usually stated in terms of "dichotomies," such as science versus poetry, reason versus imagination—in short, "the divided sensibility." There are, indeed, divisions in almost all of Ransom's poems. But if we are to use so clumsy a concept as "major subject" at all, we must use it to signify some special preoccupation that is always present in the poet's consciousness, the chasm that yawns beneath all slighter ditches. The predicaments of the divided sensibility, though serious, are less fundamental than the division persistently recorded by Ransom. It can be stated quite bluntly; best, perhaps, by another poet, who had also weighed Plato against "solider Aristotle" and, in some moods at least, found him wanting.

> Man is in love and loves what vanishes,
> What more is there to say?

This realization lies behind almost all of Ransom's poetry; his subject is the war of death with life.

Death has a special menace for the anti-Platonist, who has denied the Pure Idea and the great complacent universals that can resist time. He has lost the consolation of the unchanging and placed his values in the precarious purlieus of mortality. As Yeats wrote in another place: "Everything that man esteems/ Endures a moment or a day." No longer permitted to love universal beauty, the sorrowful modernist must learn to love each new incarnation of it. "Perilous and beautiful" becomes an inevitable formula, recording the frailty of beauty's earthly vessels. Thus Hopkins laments the felling of an ash tree: "seeing it maimed there came at that moment a great pang, and I wished to die and not to see the inscapes of the world destroyed any more." His poetic memorial to this incident is in *Binsey Poplars*.

> *After-comers cannot guess the beauty been.*
> *Ten or twelve, only ten or twelve*
> *Strokes of havoc unselve*
> *The sweet especial scene.*

Just as the dozen strokes havoc the poplars, so Ransom's "lady of beauty and high degree" is unselved "after six little spaces of chill, and six of burning." It is a commonplace that one mark of the modern consciousness is an awareness of time's pressure; but this comes to the surface in every age when men are forced for one reason or another to love what vanishes. Elizabethan poetry is a long lament for the brightness that falls from the air; the seventeenth-century prose writers—Ralegh, Browne, Jeremy Taylor—give sonorous instruction in the rules of dying. As Hopkins sadly observed,

> *It is the blight man was born for,*
> *It is Margaret you mourn for.*

It is this dilemma, sharpened to acuteness in our age that has nothing to cling to except the personal, which gives Ransom's poetry its persistent elegiac tone and dictates its intention. Following Hopkins, he writes *Of Margaret*.

> *Virgin, whose image bent to the small grass*
> *I keep against this tide of wayfaring,*
> *O hear the maiden pageant ever sing*
> *Of that far away time of gentleness.*

The poems are a series of images preserved against the tide of wayfaring, the dark sweep of time. They are little histories of mortals who are to be overcome by encroaching night; Ransom's books are populated with gallant but dying gentlemen and a bevy of blue girls akin to Wallace Stevens' Susanna. Reading him, we confront "a dream of ladies sweeping by"—and cry out to save it.

> *Let them alone, dear Aunt, just for one minute*
> *Till I go fishing in the dark of my mind.*

Wordsworth, the first "modern" poet in so many respects,

also saw his poetry as a preserving medium for the talismanic "spots of time" which together make up a life. Ransom has written that "the tense of poetry" is past. "We ask what the specific poems, the ones that we cherish as perfect creations are doing. I should say that they are dramatizing the past."

"Mortal" is one of Ransom's favorite—or, at any rate, most necessary—words. "The cold hearts in us mortally return"; "we are mortals teasing for immortal spoils"; and "instructed of much mortality." To number his poems on the subject of mortality is almost to make a complete index of Ransom's work. There is the little cousin, "dead, by foul subtraction," and his counterpart, John Whiteside's daughter; Miss Euphemia, who "sits with us only, Till next Pentecost"; the lady young in beauty besieged by the gentleman in a dustcoat; Emily Hardcastle: "Right across her threshold has the Grizzled Baron come"; and Conrad in Twilight, Captain Carpenter, Grimes "subsiding slowly To the defunctive posture of the stained dead," the Old Mansion ruining quietly, Janet's hen descended to "the forgetful kingdom of death," Margaret mourning for the dead leaves and Miriam Tazewell for "her lawn deflowered" by a "villain" world, the aging lovers in *Fall of Leaf*, the aging South in *Antique Harvesters*, and a lady who is celebrating her birthday:

> *Sure eyes, you have observed on what hard terms*
> *Beauty has respite from voracious worms;*
> *Her moment comes; thereafter fast or slow*
> *Her daily funerals go.*

The celebration of daily funerals gives Ransom's poetry its depth of sadness. He is constrained to be a perpetual mourner because he is a perpetual lover.

> *Assuredly I have a grief,*
> *And I am shaken; but not as a leaf.*

Ransom's elegies are not only for the death of the body, but also for the thousand little deaths of the soul whose daily funerals escape eyes less surely instructed in mortality. There is the death of parting—"A cry of Absence, Absence, in the heart." There is the death of love, frail as the hollow tree in *Vaunting Oak*, slain by "silences and words" in *Two in August*, riding away "up the hill forever" on the messenger's bicycle in *Parting, without a Sequel*. Absence of love, or denial of love, is indeed death in Ransom's world, for life can flourish only in the Beloved Republic.

> *Heartless lovers are as dead*
> *That walk the earth unburied.*

One of his saddest little poems is a dirge for a marriage, *In Process of a Noble Alliance*.

> *For now in funeral white they lead her*
> *And crown her queen of the House of No Love:*
> *A dirge, then, for her beauty, musicians!*
> *Ye harping the springe that catches the dove.*

Spectral Lovers and *The Equilibrists* memorize the doom of those whose lives were never fully realized, "whose songs shall never be heard" because their love remained unfulfilled.

What is there to set against all this grief? Only the acceptance of brutal fact: that the perilous closeness of death is a sign of life, that "life is not good but in danger and joy"—in a word, courage. The frail mortals celebrated by Ransom are, in Marianne Moore's phrase, forms "steeled straight up" with defiance; they "accede to mortality," but with honor. The poet exhorts the birthday lady, in the face of funerals: "Dear love, rise up and proudly sing," reminding her of soldiers:

> *They fling sweet oaths on high, not honouring*
> *The dismal nearing Thing.*

Ransom makes elegies for the hopeful, courageous blue-eyed people.

> *Devising for those gibbeted and brave*
> *Came I descanting.*

Gibbeted and brave are Captain Carpenter with his "sweet blue eyes," and the dying Grimes, the "fortress," in *Puncture*:

> *Blue blazed the eyes of Grimes in the old manner.*

"Blue" is a word invoked by Ransom to counter his other key word, "mortal." It is the color of life, of hope, of bravery.

Jane Sneed, one of the speakers in an Eclogue on death, dreams wistfully of faithful lovers united against night, "the dark and fathomless." "The flame of each to the other's flame cries Courage!"

> *So unafraid they keep the whole night through,*
> *Till the sun of a sudden glowing through the bushes*
> *They wake and laugh, their eyes again are blue.*

Here all of Ransom's plus terms—life, love, courage, blue eyes—converge. Miss Euphemia, who is about to die, nevertheless ventures out to count her tulips:

> *Out of the frore escaping*
> *To the blue upper arch.*

The dead lady in *Blue Girls* now has "blear eyes fallen from blue," but once "was lovelier than any of you." In another poem, Ransom praises a lady's "eyes of an extravagant hue: *viz.*, china blue." They blaze out defiantly against the turning seasons.

> *Where does she keep them from this glare*
> *Of the monstrous sun and the wind's flare*
> *Without any wear?*

The lovely miller's daughter has eyes "which are a blue still-water." And ducks, courageously building their nests, "dangerous at the earth-heart":

> *will rise and go*
> *Where Capricornus dips his hooves*
> *In the blue chasm of no wharves.*

In *Painted Head*, body's love is invoked to "colorify" "the big blue birds" of the head. The cows who come alive joyously in *Little Boy Blue* have "hooves and horns of blue." One of Ransom's characters wakes in the morning with a feeling of joy and a desire "to be singing not talking." "Blue air" is swimming "all round his bed"—the same blue air that "rinses the pure pale head" so unwillingly loved by the Man without Sense of Direction. In *Prelude to an Evening*, one of his best poems, Ransom juxtaposes his contrary themes in a single stanza—the blue of life and love, the undertone of danger and death—as the foreboding wife listens.

> *Freshening the water in the blue bowls*
> *For the buckberries with not all your love,*
> *You shall be listening for the low wind,*
> *The warning sibilance of pines.*

A final example of blue comes more ambiguously in an earlier poem, *Hilda,* which mourns still another of Ransom's dead girls.

> *O Hilda, proudest of the ladies gone,*
> *Wreathing my roses with blue bitter dust,*
> *Think not I would reject you, for I must*
> *Weep for your nakedness and no retinue*
> *And leap up as of old to follow you,——*
> *But flesh hath monstrous gravity, as of stone.*

A fume of life rising upon the bitter air is the only thing left when all the nymphs have departed. But it is significant that Ransom should still insist on recognizing the "monstrous gravity" of flesh. In that two-pronged phrase he compasses the sadness of earth, and its earthiness as well—its mass and inertia, weighing heavily on the human spirit, but part, too, of its very life. It is a measure of Ransom's own courage that he has never refused to record the brutality and evanescence of life. For the poet in love with what vanishes, the temptation is strong to give his keepsakes the unreality of tombstone art. Shall he lay them up in lavender? Shall he make of them golden birds to set upon a golden bough? For a single stanza, he almost succumbs.

> *Bring proper gifts to Beauty then:*
> *Bring topaz, emeralds, gold, and minerals rare,*
> *Musk that will ever be sweet on mortal air,*
> *Bright stiff brocades outlasting the short ken*
> *Of usual mortal men.*

But this is the stiffness of death, not life. And so the poet who seeks to preserve his precious objects from time's tide is forced into a paradox. Change *is* life, so they must be allowed to change, lest they find in art a death more final than any other. Their deaths must be renewed a thousand times, in homage to their vitality. As Virginia Woolf wrote, "Beauty must be broken daily to remain beautiful." "The artifice of eternity" will not serve. Ransom, in a phrase that might be a retort to Yeats, has only dispraise for "the extravagant device of art," castigating it

> For having vinegarly traduced the flesh
> Till, the hurt flesh recusing, the hard egg
> Is shrunken to its own deathlike surface.

The enduring is what has never been alive, the deathlike surface of abstraction. So the poet of inscapes is left with his daily funerals, his perpetual recognition of the peril, the swiftness, the vulnerability and gravity of flesh.

The surfaces of Ransom's poetry are far from deathlike; they are as shifty, as startling and shiny, as the living things reflected in them. The poet's devotion to beauty immortal in the flesh produces, as we have suggested, his special manner, with its combination of brutality and bravery, its diction compounded of bluntness and elegance. He celebrates "ceremonies of bravery," and, like an earlier poet of "brutall terminations," Sir Thomas Browne, devises a style which draws on the resonances of our double language to reproduce their solemnity and transience. Just as "foul subtraction" might have been written by Browne, so Ransom might have composed "brutall terminations," or, "Diuturnity is a dream and folly of expectation." Both of them exploit the precision and formality of Latin, which has the stiff beauty of the golden bird, to fix their diuturnities against a background of austere eternity. Both combine with this background a foreground of love and sadness, embodied in the common English words that have a hold on our emotions. Thus the timeless and the temporal, the abstract and the concrete, spirit and flesh, intelligence and feeling, are joined to compose our mixed unity. Ransom's *Vaunting Oak* is a fine example of this technique; the poem, as usual, is about transience, and the dilemma emerges through its very language. So on one side there are words like "concumbent," "eruptive," "susceptive," "eminent," "profuse," "testified," "traversed," "instructed," "dolorous," "reverberance"; and, on the other, shapes of earth, fashioned in an earthly tongue: "a flat where birdsong flew," "daisies and yellow kinds," "the singing of bees; or the coward birds that fly," and a flock of simple words—"frail," "mad," "young," "bitter," "tall," "green," "steep," "brag," "knobs," "boomed," "sped." A few sentences from *Urn Burial* will show how Browne, who called man the great amphibium, records his predicament in the same ambidexterous medium.

> Sense endureth no extremities, and sorrows destroy us or themselves. To weep into stones are fables. Afflictions induce callosities, miseries are slippery, or fall like snow upon us, which notwithstanding is no unhappy stupidity. To be ignorant of evils to come, and forgetfull of evils past, is a mercifull provision in nature, whereby we digest the mixture of our few and evil dayes, and our delivered senses not relapsed into cutting remembrances, our sorrows are not kept raw by the edge of repetitions.

Ransom and Browne are alike, too, in the stateliness of their styles; both are believers in ceremony. And we remember, again, Yeats, with his "ceremony of innocence."

> *How but in custom and in ceremony*
> *Are innocence and beauty born?*

One might add, how else are they to be kept alive? Ransom's tone, uniformly severe and ironic, is a product of his belief in the necessity of ritual for civilized life. His essay, "Forms and Citizens," in *The World's Body*, is the prose locus for this belief; his verse is the enactment of it. It is his own form of defiance, matching the courage of his personae. Ritual masters transience by imposing an order upon it. And ritualism in poetry is, also, a mastery of emotion. It is one type of oblique style, fending off the assaults of sentiment inherent in the direct approach. "Our sorrows are not kept raw"; they are made less piercing, and at the same time are lent dignity and depth, by acquiring a pattern. Ritual, or ceremony, exposes the paradox of feeling, which gathers strength the more firmly it is controlled. The paradox was phrased by Yeats when he wrote:

I might have had no friend that could not mix
Courtesy and passion into one.

Ransom could have been such a friend. His style, like that of Yeats, is high talk, combining the courtesy of a courtly tongue with the heart's passionate outcry. And, like Yeats, Ransom draws strength for his rituals from an awareness of tradition, his sense of being "rooted in one dear perpetual place," even though the perpetuity may be only relative.

It is true that Ransom cannot cry out as loudly as Yeats; that the elder poet is the greater because he is capable, when the necessity arises, of abandoning obliqueness and ceremony for a terrible naked directness. True, too, that Ransom often seems too elegiac, too much concerned with dramatizing the past, and incapable of the fierceness, the positive joy and gusto that could make Yeats' Self triumphantly outshout his Soul, turning toward the future to cry,

I am content to live it all again
And yet again . . .

and to end, with Blakean ecstasy, "Everything we look upon is blest." Nevertheless, though we may conclude that Ransom errs on the side of too much courtesy, and may grow weary at times of his restraint and good manners, we have more need today of courtesy than of passion, of control than of abandon. Forster, in the essay quoted earlier, has reminded us of the dangers that attend great men. So, though we may agree that Yeats and D. H. Lawrence are greater than Ransom and Forster, we must also admit that they committed dreadful errors of judgment and taste, that they were extravagant as human beings, politically naïve, and inclined to take themselves too seriously. They are necessary for our health; but two are enough for one generation, and it is equally imperative that we produce the minor excellence that is the best fruit of civilization—an aristocracy, as Forster has said, "of the sensitive, the considerate, and the plucky." To this aristocracy, famous for its foolhardy allegiance to humanity in the face of darkness, Ransom belongs.

ALLEN TATE: THE ARROGANT CIRCUMSTANCE

BY LOUIS D. RUBIN, JR., AND ROBERT D. JACOBS

Among the makers of literature of the modern South, Allen Tate holds a distinguished position. Poet, critic, biographer, and novelist—he has exhibited a versatility unusual even among that group of extraordinary talents that brought out *The Fugitive* in Nashville in the 1920s. But it is as a poet, he once said, that he would like to be remembered, a sentiment that may sound strange to anyone aware of the range and depth of his literary and social criticism, and the comparative slenderness of the volume of poems he has chosen to preserve. Tate has written many fewer poems than Robinson or Frost or Cummings; his work has not had the sweeping impact of Eliot's; and he has as yet produced nothing of the proportions of Hart Crane's *The Bridge* or Robert Penn Warren's *Brother to Dragons.** For the untutored reader, sometimes even for the sophisticate, his poems are difficult to understand; and he shows small concern over it, unless his essay "Narcissus as Narcissus," which is still the most useful analysis of his best-known poem, *Ode to the Confederate Dead,* be construed as concern over possible misunderstanding. Yet it is difficult to imagine that American poetry could have come to be as it is today without Allen Tate. His poems and criticism, though not, like Eliot's, the center of a vogue, have been profoundly influential. It is

---

* However, he has for some years been engaged upon a long poem, three portions of which have appeared under the titles, (I) "The Maimed Man" (*Partisan Review,* XIX [1952], 265–67), (III) "The Swimmers" (*Hudson Review,* V [1953], 471–73), and (VI) "The Buried Lake" (*Sewanee Review,* LXI [1953], 175–80). A somewhat different version of "The Buried Lake," from which the quotations in this essay are taken, appears in *The Criterion Book of Modern American Verse,* ed. W. H. Auden, 1956, 197–202.

no exaggeration to say that the tastes and perhaps even the attitudes of a whole generation of poets and readers have been affected significantly by his work.

I

Born on November 19, 1899, in Clark County, Kentucky, on the edge of the famous bluegrass region, Allen Tate was sent, like his two brothers before him, to Vanderbilt University. The place and time were propitious, for with him on the campus by some fortunate dispensation were John Crowe Ransom, Robert Penn Warren, Donald Davidson, and Merrill Moore. It was this group which, with certain others, brought out *The Fugitive,* and thereafter the course of American poetry was materially altered.

As poet and critic Tate matured quickly. Soon he was contributing verse, reviews, and critical articles to magazines all over the country. But his other concerns were soon to be manifested. With Ransom, Warren, Davidson, and eight others he joined in a symposium, *I'll Take My Stand* (1930), in which Southern life and attitudes were closely examined. Tate's own essay, "Remarks on the Southern Religion," initiates the attack on scientific rationalism that was to be fairly constant in both his social and literary criticism. First he examines religion in general as it is affected by rationalism, pragmatism, instrumentalism—the various "isms" he subsumes under the label "positivism" in later years. Next he examines the failure of the Southern religion and traces it to the "Jeffersonian formula," the rationalism the Southerner inherited instead of a genuine religious tradition. It is the "qualitative" instead of the "quantitative" evaluation of experience that Tate calls for in 1930, and this demand, modified only as the subject and method of discourse change, reappears in most of his later writings.

I'll Take My Stand was followed by another volume of social essays, *Who Owns America?* (1936), edited by Tate and Herbert Agar. In both books, the South was urged to forsake the ways of industrialism and to return to the predominantly agrarian pattern of the past. But the call for a resurgent agrarianism and a vital religion were by no means Tate's only contribution to the understanding of Southern culture. Two biographies of Southern leaders, *Stonewall Jackson: The Good Soldier* (1928) and *Jefferson Davis* (1929), examine the qualities—and the defects—of leadership when the Southern way of life was on trial; and a novel, *The Fathers* (1938), is involved thematically with the meaning of tradition.

But it is primarily with Allen Tate's poetry that we are concerned here. If one examines his poetry, written over the course of more than three decades, one sees that it falls into four phases. First, the youthful work of his student days and immediately afterward. Second, the period of *I'll Take My Stand* and the Agrarian writing, during which his poems, in subject matter, were involved with the South and with American history. Third, a period during which Tate became less interested in regionalism, and in which his poetry was occupied with the theme of a search for religious belief. Fourth, and most recent, the period of his conversion to Roman Catholicism, during which he has been at work on a long poem, as yet incomplete.

II

Of the early verse, published in such magazines as *The Fugitive, The Double Dealer, Hound and Horn,* and collected in *Mr. Pope and Other Poems* (1928), relatively few poems were included by the poet in the volume which contains all the work he wished to preserve, the *Poems 1922–1947* (1948). One of the earliest in this volume is *The Progress of Oenia,* dated 1922–23 and written when the author was less than twenty-five years old. It is a love poem in five parts. The first two, entitled "Madrigale" and "In Wintertime," celebrate the young man's worship of his love in a manner somewhat reminiscent of Dowson with his roses and passion. Part III, "Vigil," a bit tougher in fiber, surveys the prospect of death and the end of love. Part IV, "Divagation," records disillusionment and its pain, while Part V, "Epilogue to Oenia," is a wry commentary upon the experience. It is all quite *fin de siècle* in tone. A youthful romanticism replete with world-weariness runs throughout the poem, an attitude almost entirely foreign to the temper of Tate's later poetry. The language, however, is not quite so old-fashioned as the sentiment. Some of it reminds us of the early Cummings, but also here and there is the authentic note of Allen Tate.

> *Seed in your heart, warm dust transmuted*
> *Gold, blooms in flakes of radiance*
> *Arched in your face whereon my days,*
> *Brinks of silence, glance.*

> *Dream-emptied by some shifting*
> *Monna Bice, you I resume:*
> *Continually suffer the habitual*
> *Cobra of my slightest gloom!*

The Cummings-like motif is apparent in both of these stanzas; one image, however—that of the cobra—is significantly Tate's own. It is too startling, too savage for Cummings; indeed, it is rather out of place in the context. The violence, the baldness with which it is exhibited jar the otherwise gentle romantic tempo of the first part of the poem. Its use anticipates Tate's later style, in which there is scant room for flakes of radiance, Monna Bices emptied of dreams, and the like. For the most part *The Progress of Oenia* is pleasantly lyrical, containing lines as unlike Tate's mature mode as "Your mouth is more passionate than any summer"; "I will gather up the whispers you came after"; "your eyes careless of yesterday"; "The madness of scaling/ a certain dusk to the first small star" (this last is almost genuine Cummings). One can hardly imagine the author of *The Mediterranean* and *Seasons of the Soul* devising lines like the following:

> *Pardon me! if turning over*
> *In the reminiscence of a lover*
> *The leaves of a dessicate romance,*
> *I can but wonder if a chance*
> *Invasion of a handsomer look*
> *Than mine began you another book?*

We shall not encounter such mannered ruth in Tate again. However, toward the close of the final section, there are traces of an attitude characteristic of the later verse. Leaving the immediately personal situation, the poem touches on the contrast between vulgar modernity and a more decorous past:

Yet sad that the modern bawd, grown dim,
Obscures the hotel cherubim
Whose red neckties had honored this page
In a hotter, less barbaric age.

Here Tate uses the same device which Eliot handles so skillfully in *The Waste Land,* the juxtaposition of colloquial terms
with more traditional imagery, in order to draw a contrast—
"hotel cherubim," "red neckties had honored," and so on. The
lines are immediately followed by six more which presage
Tate's later manner:

For now the languid stertorous
Pale verses of Propertius
And the sapphire corpse undressed by Donne
(Prefiguring Rimbaud's etymon)
Have shrunk to an apotheosis
Of cold daylight after the kiss.

Although this is close to Tate's later work, the last line does
not have the irony of the mature style. Nevertheless, the literary allusions—Propertius, Donne, Rimbaud; the learned vocabulary—stertorous, etymon, apotheosis; the unhesitating use
of complex imagery—"the sapphire corpse undressed by
Donne"; the daring alternation of Latinate with colloquial
words; the general apocalyptic tone—these are distinctive
Tatean devices.

The very last line of the poem shows the trace of another
strong force at work on Tate's poetry at this time, the example
of his fellow Fugitive John Ransom:

No glories of your breast and thighs
Shall these poor verses advertise——
Only the dry debility
Of a spent wind in a winter tree.

In *The Progress of Oenia* Tate adopted Ransom's habit of
concluding with a simple, muted nature image that by a contrasting inaction produces a final effect of stasis; yet the difference between the two men's manner is readily apparent.
Ransom would never have used the image in the next-to-last
line of Tate's poem. "Dry debility" is much too final, too com-

mitted, to be whimsically ironic. In Ransom, violence is always mocked by perfect decorum of attitude and diction, while Tate leaves it absolutely unqualified. The image of "dry debility" is typically Tate's own in its clash between the neutrality of the abstraction and the savage context in which it is imbedded.

How fast Tate's style was maturing can be seen by comparing *The Progress of Oenia* with a poem first published only two years later, *The Death of Little Boys*, which in her essay on Tate's work Miss Vivienne Koch rightly singles out both as a very good poem in its own right and one of its author's most characteristic as well. One will search its five quatrains in vain for perceptible echoes of Cummings, Ransom, or Eliot. The world-weary lover is gone. The poem is all Tate in method, language, and attitude, although there are a few thoroughly assimilated echoes which we shall have occasion to discuss in a moment.

The opening quatrain has the power and intensity of imagery and meaning of Tate's best work; he uses his adverbs and adjectives with a complete economy of violence.

> *When little boys grow patient at last, weary,*
> *Surrender their eyes immeasurably to the night,*
> *The event will rage terrific as the sea;*
> *Their bodies fill a crumbling room with light.*

The poet demands of his reader full attention to unravel the apparent paradox and take in the exact nature of the situation. What the event is, is not immediately proclaimed in the poem (although the title gives it away), but there is no reluctance to proclaim the full horror of the occasion. The contrast between the "patient" stillness of the boy (universalized by the plural) and the profound effect upon the sensibility of the watcher is recorded in the imagery of natural calamity. The phrase "the event," almost shockingly neutral, draws up the various aspects of dying into a unity; and its strong contrast to the verb "rage," intensified by the adjective "terrific," dramatizes the emotional impact of the occurrence upon the observer. This same contrast suggests the disparity between the reaction of the outside world, to whom the death is a mere "event," and the reaction of the involved observer.

The apparent contradiction of the bodies filling the room with light places a new and sinister interpretation upon the word "light," even while it serves the more obvious hyperbolic purpose of dramatizing the fixed attention of the observer. The body, drawing the eyes as would a light in darkness, becomes itself a source of light and by implication postulates another kind of light—the "enlightenment" of our understanding of the fact of death proceeding from the very corpse. These lines, with their careful contrast of the neutral and weighted terms, their skillfully managed ambiguities, embody the boldness and authority of a confident, self-assured poetic craftsman.

The onlooker stares at the bedside, then looks through the window at the outside world, framed in what is now inanimate terror:

> *As the windowpane extends a fear to you*
> *From one peeled aster drenched with the wind all day*

then back at the bed, noting how the enveloping covers "mount to the teeth, ascend the eyes, press back the locks," while the stillness of the child's body forcibly recalls to the viewer the life that has left it. The desperate nature of the moment sinks in:

> *Till all the guests, come in to look, turn down*
> *Their palms, and delirium assails the cliff*
> *Of Norway where you ponder, and your little town*
> *Reels like a sailor drunk in a rotten skiff.*

In these lines appear the assimilated echoes previously mentioned. It is highly probable that Edgar Allan Poe's *A Descent into the Maelstrom* and *The Narrative of A. Gordon Pym* lie behind the cliff-boat-drunken sailor configuration of the imagery. The first of these tales opens on a cliff of Norway, a "sheer unobstructed precipice of black shining rock," where a feeble, white-haired man is telling of "six hours of deadly terror which . . . have broken me up body and soul." To find the "sailor drunk in a rotten skiff," we must move to *The Narrative of A. Gordon Pym*. Pym and his companion Augustus sail from an old decayed wharf in a small sailboat, which had to be bailed free of water. After they are well out of the harbor, Augustus reels away from the tiller and falls to the bottom of the boat. Pym discovers that he is "beastly drunk—he could no longer either stand, speak or see." Yet prior to his collapse Augustus had appeared rational, which was, in Poe's words, "the result of a highly concentrated state of intoxication—a state which, like madness, frequently enables the victim to imitate the outward demeanour of one in perfect possession of his senses." This "mad" rationality, a characteristic of Poe's work, has a special import for Allen Tate. "No other writer in England or the United States, or so far as I know, in France," Tate has written, "went so far as Poe in his vision of dehumanized man" ("Our Cousin, Mr. Poe," *The Forlorn Demon*, 1953, 89). And it is dehumanized man, the Cartesian thinking machine, who figures as a major concern in Mr. Tate's poetry and much of his criticism.

This central concern appears urgently in *The Death of Little Boys*. Our confrontation of the fact of mortality without a saving myth is the subject of the poem. In the reading of John M. Bradbury, the last lines of the poem are ironical:

> *There is a calm for you where men and women*
> *Unroll the chill precision of moving feet.*

Thus, "absorbing oneself in a mechanistic world where men and women are automata . . . will make of the death a statistic," an "event" to be reported in the obituary column (*The Fugitives*, 1958, 61). Poe's old man emerges from the Maelstrom because he preserved a preternatural rationality in the face of grief (for his drowned brothers) and death; and Tate's observer finds calm from the violence of his grief through action, by behaving like a machine. Images from Poe's tale, so perfectly assimilated that they have escaped notice completely, and the serious import to Tate of Poe's writings have combined to produce some of the most startling imagery of modern poetry.

The dehumanization achieved by Poe's heroes is by no means complete in the protagonist of *The Death of Little Boys*, however. There, in the unexpected event of the child's death, there is chaos, the completely irrational happening, giving the lie to orderly processes of personal adjustment, of social convention. It is a moment of absolute terror—unreason.

> The bleak sunshine shrieks its chipped music then
> Out to the milkweed amid the fields of wheat.

The synaesthesia here is perfectly managed so as to convey the disorder of the moment. The derangement of the senses parallels the emotional chaos of the protagonist; and equilibrium is not restored until others invade the isolation and force at least the semblance of sanity in the formal poses—the meaningless ceremony of the funeral—the chill precision of moving feet.

In this poem, as Vivienne Koch points out, Tate voices firmly what is to be the principal attitude of all his best poetry: the rejection of the present as a time of sterile forms and meaningless conventions. The realization and contemplation of chaos and irrationality have not been banished; they have only been externally sublimated to the demands of custom and decorum, while in the mind the terror is the more real for the contrast between the imaged actuality and the specious resignation, the mechanic calm of the civilized gestures required by the occasion.

From *The Death of Little Boys* onward we shall watch Tate do increasingly sharp battle with modern times, and his verse will consist of ever deeper inquiry into man's plight in a world of materialism and fragmentation of belief.

A later poem that may be singled out here for special attention along the same lines as these is *The Last Days of Alice*. The Wonderland of Alice becomes a metaphor for the modern world: "The All-Alice of the world's entity."

Unlike *The Death of Little Boys*, this poem is relatively straightforward. The first five stanzas, which develop the analogy between the Alice of Dodgson's absurdly logical Wonderland and the collective inhabitants of our modern wonderland of science and mathematics, has a humor much more savage and direct than the Ransomic wit of the early poems.

> Bright Alice! always pondering to gloze
> The spoiled cruelty she had meant to say
> Gazes learnedly down her airy nose
> At nothing, nothing thinking all the day.

But once the analogy has been explored, the tone changes to one of the utmost seriousness, and the language carries the Latinate dignity of Tate's celebrated *Ode*. The next three stanzas of the poem use the language of science in contrast to traditional value terms to expose the emptiness of the positivist's universe.

Alone to the weight of impassivity,
Incest of spirit, theorem of desire,
Without will as chalky cliffs by the sea,
Empty as the bodiless flesh of fire:

All space, that heaven is a dayless night,
A nightless day driven by perfect lust
For vacancy, in which her bored eyesight
Stares at the drowsy cubes of human dust.

We too back to the world shall never pass
Through the shattered door, a dumb shade-harried crowd
Being all infinite, function depth and mass
Without figure, a mathematical shroud.

But the fourth makes a direct exhortation rare in Tate's earlier poetry.

Hurled at the air—blessèd without sin!
O God of our flesh, return us to Your wrath,
Let us be evil could we enter in
Your grace, and falter on the stony path!

Thus in this poem Tate continues the attack upon abstraction (as symbolized by mathematics) that he launched in his essay "Remarks on the Southern Religion." "For abstraction is the death of religion no less than the death of anything else," he had written in the essay. Now in the poem he uses the very language of the enemy against him, and manages it with great poetic tact. John M. Bradbury has noted that "Tate's abstractions are constantly driven toward their concretions in images, while the images or situations are driven toward their abstract significances" (page 158). Nowhere is this more true than in the two poems just discussed.

Some years later Mr. Tate wrote, "As I look back upon my own verse, written over more than twenty-five years, I see plainly that its main theme is man suffering from unbelief; and I cannot for a moment suppose that this man is some other than myself." *The Last Days of Alice* is one of the clearest statements of this theme. The forms that it was to assume in the poems to come would be varied; the theme itself would remain constant.

III

In the middle 1920s Allen Tate had found that, along with John Ransom, Donald Davidson, Andrew Lytle, and others of his Nashville friends, he was becoming increasingly interested in the life and culture of the region in which he had been born and reared. When the writers of *I'll Take My Stand* looked around them at their own country, they saw a South which at last was beginning to emulate in earnest the ways of the industrial society. In their view this meant that the South, in order to gain the material possessions of the commercial and industrial community, was deliberately turning its back on a life that was agrarian, traditional, religious, which emphasized the whole man in right relationship to nature.

In *I'll Take My Stand*, John Ransom stated the proposition concretely in the declaration of principles to which all the contributors gave assent. "Of late, however, there is the melancholy fact that the South itself has wavered a little and shown signs of wanting to join up behind the common or American industrial ideal. It is against that tendency that this book is written. The younger Southerners, who are being converted frequently to the industrial gospel, must come back to the support of the Southern tradition. They must be persuaded to look very critically at the advantages of becoming a 'new South' which will be only an undistinguished replica of the usual industrial community" (x–xi).

What matters here is not what the choice between agrarianism and industrialism might mean for the South but what it meant for Allen Tate's poetry. In the legend of the Old South, Tate found an image of belief and spiritual existence that he could contrast sharply with the unbelief and materialism of the modern world he saw about him. In exploring the image, Tate entered upon a period of sustained poetic accomplishment. To borrow Eliot's term, Tate discovered in the Southern tradition the "objective correlative" for his feelings about man and the natural world. The result was a large body of his best poems.

One such poem is *The Mediterranean,* which Tate chose to begin his *Poems 1922–1947.* The poem describes the search of the poet for his tradition, which first led him from the New World to the Old World and the historical past. Using the theme of Aeneas as exemplar, Tate describes a journey to a strange country.

> *Where we went in the small ship the seaweed*
> *Parted and gave to us the murmuring shore,*
> *And we made feast and in our secret need*
> *Devoured the very plates Aeneas bore*

Here he resorts, as he frequently does in his verse, to a classical allusion, that of the Seventh Book of the *Aeneid,* in which the wandering Trojans recognize that they have at last arrived at their destination because in their hunger they have eaten not only their scanty bread but the tables as well, thus fulfilling Anchises' prophecy. For the poet, it is a matter of discovering the classical past, "the famous age/ Eternal here yet hidden from our eyes," the origins of Western civilization, before he is able to grasp the true meaning of the present. Only through his tradition may the poet find his theme, experience the natural world, and create his art.

> *Now, from the Gates of Hercules we flood*
>
> *Westward, westward till the barbarous brine*
> *Whelms us to the tired land where tasseling corn,*
> *Fat beans, grapes sweeter than muscadine*
> *Rot on the vine: in that land were we born.*

So the poem concludes, with an image of the real world of nature through which the poet can work his art. But it is not an abstract place; it is a particular place, the South—"in that land were we born." The poet's return, as a man, as an artist, is to the place of his origins, and he achieves it through his tradition.

Another striking poem of this period is *Aeneas at Washing-*

ton, in which Tate again uses the theme of the Trojan wanderer to describe his present situation. The poem is a monologue spoken by Aeneas, in which he first describes his flight
from Troy.

> *That was a time when civilization*
> *Run by the few fell to the many, and*
> *Crashed to the shout of men, the clang of arms*
> *Cold victualing I seized, I hoisted up*
> *The old man my father upon my back,*
> *In the smoke made by sea for a new world*
> *Saving little—a mind imperishable*
> *If time is, a love of past things tenuous*
> *As the hesitation of receding love.*

Now the fleeing Aeneas looks back, in memory, at the land
that was.

> *I saw the thirsty dove*
> *In the glowing fields of Troy, hemp ripening*
> *And tawny corn, the thickening Blue Grass*
> *All lying forever in the green sun.*

Troy, it turns out, is also suspiciously like the old bluegrass
of Kentucky, and the sack of Troy, "a time when civilization/
Run by the few fell to the many," is reminiscent of nothing
so much as the War between the States as seen by a Ken-
tuckian. So we are not surprised that as Aeneas

> *stood in the rain, far from home at nightfall*
> *By the Potomac, the great Dome lit the water,*
> *The city my blood had built I knew no more.*

The capital of the Republic is no longer the place or the
ideal that this Southern Aeneas had envisioned; it has changed,
until the meaning it held for the people has become lost.

> *Stuck in the wet mire*
> *Four thousand leagues from the ninth buried city*
> *I thought of Troy, what we had built her for.*

In *Aeneas at Washington* Tate once again uses Southern
history to portray modern man's rootlessness and degradation.
But his most famous poem of this period, one included in al-

most every anthology of American poetry, and probably the most accomplished of all his poems, is the magnificent *Ode to the Confederate Dead.*

Tate began the poem in about 1926. Published in *Mr. Pope and Other Poems*, it underwent several revisions over the course of the next decade before its author was finished with it. He subsequently described the writing of the Confederate Ode in a brilliant essay, "Narcissus as Narcissus." Its theme, he declared, "is 'about' solipsism, a philosophical doctrine which says that we create the world in the act of perceiving it; or about Narcissism, or any other *ism* that denotes the failure of the human personality to function objectively in nature and society."

The poem begins with a man standing at the gate of a Confederate cemetery.

> *Row after row with strict impunity*
> *The headstones yield their names to the element,*
> *The wind whirrs without recollection;*
> *In the riven troughs the splayed leaves*
> *Pile up, of nature the casual sacrament*
> *To the seasonal eternity of death*

The man at the gate watches the graves, and muses over the incessant way of time.

> *Think of the autumns that have come and gone!*
> *Ambitious November with the humors of the year,*
> *With a particular zeal for each slab,*
> *Staining the uncomfortable angels that rot*
> *On the slabs, a wing chipped here, an arm there:*
> *The brute curiosity of an angel's stare*
> *Turns you, like them, to stone,*
> *Transforms the heaving air*
> *Till plunged into a heavier world below*
> *You shift your sea-space blindly*
> *Heaving, turning like the blind crab.*

The figure of the crab is of a creature with mobility but no direction, energy but no human purpose for it. "The crab," Tate declares, "is the first intimation of the nature of the moral conflict upon which the drama of the poem develops:

the cut-off-ness of the modern 'intellectual man' from the world." The image of the Confederate graves is juxtaposed with the modern observer's helplessness in time, his isolation within the walls of self, sealed off from meaning and purpose. Tate contrasts this condition with the ability of the dead Confederates to act in the world.

> You know who have waited by the wall
> The twilight certainty of an animal,
> Those midnight restitutions of the blood
> You know—the immitigable pines, the smoky frieze
> Of the sky, the sudden call

The Confederate soldiers had purpose. They knew what they were fighting for—to use a popular slogan—and, knowing, could act with conviction.

> You who have waited for the angry resolution
> Of those desires that should be yours tomorrow,
> You know the unimportant shrift of death
> And praise the vision
> And praise the arrogant circumstance
> Of those who fall
> Rank upon rank, hurried beyond decision——
> Here by the sagging gate, stopped by the wall.

But the modern watcher at the gate cannot be partner to that earlier certainty; the vision is shut off from him by the egocentricity of the present world. He returns to the refrain running through the poem, symbolizing the impossibility of the watcher's finding any meaning for himself in what he sees. All he can know is the sight of the leaves being blown about the tombstones in autumn.

> Seeing, seeing only the leaves
> Flying, plunge and expire

The vision of the dead Confederates and their certitude will not stay with him. He cannot find reality for himself in what they believed or achieved.

> You hear the shout, the crazy hemlocks point
> With troubled fingers to the silence which
> Smothers you, a mummy, in time.

What, he asks, can we say of our own existence, in terms of what they did? What truth can the modern watcher at the gate achieve for himself, what knowledge can he derive from the memory of the dead Confederates and their day of battle? How can the certainty and resolution that the soldiers possessed be gained by the modern man for his own time and situation?

> *What shall we say of the bones, unclean,*
> *Whose verdurous anonymity will grow?*
> *The ragged arms, the ragged heads and eyes*
> *Lost in these acres of the insane green?*
> *The gray lean spiders come, they come and go;*
> *In a tangle of willows without light*
> *The singular screech-owl's tight*
> *Invisible lyric seeds the mind*
> *With the furious murmur of their chivalry*

The watcher at the gate sees "only the leaves/ Flying, plunge and expire"; he is cut off from them in time, walled in by the present. The vision is lost; all that remains is the self, the body, and death.

> *Night is the beginning and the end*
> *And in between the ends of distraction*
> *Waits mute speculation, the patient curse*
> *That stones the eyes, or like the jaguar leaps*
> *For his own image in a jungle pool, his victim.*

All that the modern intellectual man, hemmed in by his own subjective prison, can know for surety is physical existence and death. In Tate's words, "autumn and the leaves are death; the men who exemplified in a grand style an 'active faith' are dead; there are only the leaves." If death is the only certainty, shall it then be courted, as the only way to flee the subjective walls of self? The watcher at the gate knows through his tradition what meaning and certainty can be, but cannot apply them to himself in the modern world; shall he then

> *set up the grave*
> *In the house? The ravenous grave?*

No, that will not do either. He can neither find belief in life nor, by courting death, deny that a meaning exists.

The final vision is that of one absolute: time. If the Confederate graves can impart no other truth for the modern man, still, the cemetery itself constitutes one meaning, which is that man is inextricably involved in time; and on that note the watcher leaves the graveyard.

> Leave now
> The shut gate and the decomposing wall:
> The gentle serpent, green in the mulberry bush,
> Riots with his tongue through all the hush—
> Sentinel of the grave who counts us all!

The closing image is the ancient symbol of time, the serpent, which remains there in the mulberry bush by the cemetery after the modern observer turns away, and the graves of the Confederate dead lie among the leaves.

A brief analysis such as this cannot hope to do justice to the *Ode to the Confederate Dead*. It is a complex poem, embodying all of Tate's critical notions of what a poem should be, as set forth in his critical essays. It requires and rewards careful, close reading. Though there are other fine poems written during Tate's "Southern period"—*Retroduction to American History, Causerie, To The Lacedaemonians, The Oath, Emblems, The Trout Map*, among others—still, when all is done, the Confederate *Ode* is probably Allen Tate's most perfectly realized achievement in poetry. Later work, such as the *Seasons of the Soul*, might be more complex, but for felicity of expression and acuteness of perception, the Confederate *Ode* remains unsurpassed. The Southern tradition, with its Confederate memories, provided an image for a stirring commentary on the state of modern man. Later poems would isolate the causes of the dilemma more precisely, perhaps; they would not state it more eloquently.

IV

Toward the end of the 1930s, Allen Tate's poetry was changing. All along it had been developing, but during these years—one might label them the end of his Agrarian period—

the poems show a sharp shift in subject matter and perspective. The South and its history begin to be used less often. Instead, a religious motif begins to assume primary importance. The two *Sonnets at Christmas* (1934) can be seen in retrospect as the key transitional poems. Perhaps, as Vivienne Koch has conjectured, the writing of Tate's historical novel, *The Fathers,* served to drain off his historical and regional interests into the more flexible form of fiction. At any rate, though Tate was not for some years to lose interest in the Southern tradition as subject matter for his poetry, regional self-consciousness ceases to be as important in his poetry as the 1930s draw to a close.

There are critics who see this as something of a retreat, a rejection, and who gleefully point to the fact that neither Tate, Ransom, nor Warren lives in the South today as a sure sign of their infidelity. In so doing they display a lack of familiarity with Tate's poetry, as well as an ignorance of the nature of poetry. In Tate's poems the South and its history were never more or less than an important symbol. The essential theme of his work has always been the fragmentation of modern man, and his loss of belief. For ten years the symbol of the Old South was able to serve as correlative for Tate's notion of a traditional, purposeful society, making possible a harmonious life. This is its importance as far as Tate's poetry is concerned —this and no more.

The value of the South as such a poetic symbol cannot be overestimated, provided that its symbolic nature is understood. The Old South provided Tate with material for some of his best work. On a level of thematic usefulness, it could be said that thus far he has never found anything else to take its place. But for all that, in his poetry Tate was not writing *about* the South; he was using the region to symbolize the plight of modern man as he saw it. That is the theme that remains the central image in his work, and the shift in topical material that began taking place in the middle 1930s did not in the slightest represent abandonment of that theme. Rather, Tate began to visualize the condition of modern man in predominantly religious rather than historical imagery. There had always been a strongly religious bent to his work, but it had been but one of several important tendencies. Now the cut-off-ness of the modern "intellectual" man from the world began to seem more and more a religious problem. We see it stated clearly in the first of the two *Sonnets at Christmas*, which describes a man musing over the fact that he cannot perceive the spiritual implications of the Christmas season, cannot find spiritual meaning for himself amid the holiday preparations.

> *But I must kneel again unto the Dead*
> *While Christmas bells of paper white and red*
> *Figured with boys and girls spilt from a sled,*
> *Ring out the silence I am nourished by.*

In the second sonnet the man surrenders to the religious implications entirely, but it is not an experience of joy. Rather, he thinks back on the past, and of past sins, and he is overcome by the consciousness of guilt.

> *Deafened and blind, with senses yet unfound,*
> *Am I, tutored to the after-wit*
> *Of knowledge, knowing a nightmare has no sound;*
> *Therefore with idle hands and head I sit*
> *In late December before the fire's daze*
> *Punished by crimes of which I would be quit.*

For the next decade and more, Tate's chief poetic concern was to be this sense of man, oppressed by his guilt, seeking the religious faith. From *Sonnets at Christmas* through *Seasons of the Soul*, his poems are concerned with this theme.

Seasons of the Soul, perhaps Tate's major long poem, appeared in book form in *The Winter Sea* (1944). Composed during wartime, it represents a personal stocktaking, in which the poet examines his own spiritual situation as it reflects Western man caught up in a period of barbarism and savagery. The regret and irony over "the failure of the human personality to function objectively in nature and society," which he had voiced in the Confederate *Ode,* has become desperation. Beginning his poem with a quotation from *The Inferno*, Tate equates the present-day dissociation of sensibility with the medieval Hell.

> *Allor porsi la mano un poco avante,*
> *e colsi un ramicel da un gran pruno;*
> *e il tronco suo gridò; Perchè me schiante?*

The passage is from the Seventh Canto, in which Dante visits a wood where the souls of lovers who took their own lives have become trees upon which Harpies eternally feed. The poet severs a twig from a thornbush and the trunk shrieks, "Why do you tear me?" In the poem that follows, Tate explores the rending of the modern soul.

The poem is in four parts: Summer, Autumn, Winter, and Spring. The four seasons correspond to the four elements of ancient man, chronicling man's four ages in relation to the four aspects of the universe. Summer is the present,

> *a gentle sun*
> *When, at the June solstice*
> *Green France was overrun*
> *With caterpillar feet.*

It is a time of fear, and brings to mind past summers in the innocence of childhood, as well as the summer of the past, of classical antiquity.

> *When was it that summer*
> *(Daylong a liquid light)*
> *And a child; the new-comer,*
> *Bathed in the same green spray,*
> *Could neither guess the night?*

The second season, Autumn, is one of death, of growing isolation, in which modern man's rootlessness and selfishness are uppermost. The image is of a world peopled by ghosts, in which the protagonist imagines himself down a well and in a house that is familiar, because it is that of his childhood.

> *I could see*
> *I had been born to it*
> *For miles of running brought*
> *Me back where I began*

But he cannot regain that past self, and cannot resume therefore his past identity.

> *My father in a gray shawl*
> *Gave me an unseeing glint*
> *And entered another room!*
> *I stood in the empty hall*

And watched them come and go
From one room to another,
Old men, old women—slow,
Familiar; girls, boys;
I saw my downcast mother
Clad in her street-clothes,
Her blue eyes long and small
Who had no look or voice
For him whose vision froze
Him in the empty hall.

His parents walk by without seeing him; his individuality as their son is gone; their love is denied him; he stands alone in an empty hall.

In the third section, Winter, the poet considers love. He urges Venus to return to the world. Religion, Christianity, are dead, he says; all that is left is the pagan concept of love.

All the sea-gods are dead.
You, Venus, come home
To your salt maidenhead,
The tossed, anonymous sea
Under shuddering foam

But the sea rages on; pagan delight of itself is no solution.

Eternal winters blow
Shivering flakes, and shove
Bodies that wheel and drop

Only lust results from love without faith.

The pacing animal
Surveys the jungle cove
And slicks his slithering wiles
To turn the venereal awl
In the livid wound of love.

Finally comes Spring, but without regeneration. Only death exists. Man is at his ultimate despair, and he can place his hope only in an unknown hereafter. Whether it will mean animal extinction, or the rebirth of the spirit, he does not know.

> *In time of bloody war*
> *Who will know the time?*
> *Is it a new spring star*
> *Within the timing chill,*
> *Talking, or just a mime,*
> *That rises in the blood—*
> *Thin Jack-and-Jilling seas*
> *Without the human will?*
> *Its light is at the flood,*
> *Mother of silences!*

Man is compared with the inhabitants of Plato's cave, who knew no reality save the shadows cast upon the walls by the outside light. Who is the "mother of silences"? Is it the image of the Virgin, or is it oblivion? Whichever it is, he waits.

> *Then, mother of silences,*
> *Speak, that we may hear;*
> *Listen, while we confess*
> *That we conceal our fear;*
> *Regard us, while the eye*
> *Discerns by sight or guess*
> *Whether, as sheep foregather*
> *Upon their crooked knees,*
> *We have begun to die;*
> *Whether your kindness, mother,*
> *Is mother of silences.*

The poem ends without answering the question, for the poet does not himself know the answer.

Seasons of the Soul is a poem of last resorts. Modern man, finding meaning neither in pagan delight, the past, society, knowledge, physical love, awaits the outcome—whether for death or resurrection, he does not know. All devices, concerns, pursuits are negated by this ultimate riddle. With its pronouncement in *Seasons of the Soul,* the theme that runs throughout Tate's work from earliest days reaches its climax. Up through this last major completed poem, Tate's work can be viewed as a steady stripping away of the layers of symbolic reference in which that question had been veiled—first the early romantic notions of the young poet, then the historical and social context embodied in the *Ode to the Confederate Dead* and other poems of the "Southern period," until finally what is left is the stark religious issue: God or no God; belief or unbelief. The theme of man suffering from unbelief has been given its sharpest utterance.

V

After the poems contained in *The Winter Sea*, Tate published no more verse for some years. In his own life the period was one of turmoil, culminating at last in his decision to follow his first wife, the novelist Caroline Gordon, into the Roman Catholic Church. In 1946, after two distinguished years as editor, he gave up the directorship of *The Sewanee Review*, having converted that rather amorphous publication into one of the two or three outstanding literary publications in the United States. In 1951 he succeeded his fellow Fugitive, Robert Penn Warren, as professor of English poetry at the University of Minnesota, a position he has retained ever since.

It was not until 1953 that new verse appeared by him. In that year Tate published three parts of a long poem. The work represented a significant change in his poetic outlook. Though the major work of which they are part has not been completed, the three sections differ from all of Tate's earlier work in that they are religious poetry, written openly out of faith, not unbelief. They are in *terza rima*, the rhyme scheme of the *Divine Comedy*, and the frame of reference is strongly religious. The lines in the first published section, "The Maimed Man," serve to exemplify the new attitude.

> *Teach me to fast*
> *And pray, that I may know the motes that tease*
> *Skittering sunbeams are dead shells at last.*
> *Then, timeless muse, reverse my time; unfreeze*
> *All that I was in your congenial heat*

To judge from what has so far been published, the poet looks at childhood again, and perhaps his whole life, through the new perspective of religious faith. A second published section, "The Swimmers," recounts a childhood occurrence in which five youths, out swimming in a creek, encounter a posse searching for a lynched Negro. Twelve men are in the posse, but only eleven ride back.

> *eleven same*
> *Jesus Christers unmembered and unmade,*
> *Whose corpse had died again in dirty shame.*

The youths watch the sheriff, who is the leader of the posse, at work with the corpse, until suddenly

> *A single horseman came at a fast lope*
> *And pulled up at the hanged man's horny feet;*
> *The sheriff loosed the feet, the other end*
> *The stranger tied to his pommel in a neat*
> *Slip-knot. I saw the Negro's body bend*
> *And straighten, as a fish-line cast transverse*
> *Yields to the current that it must subtend.*
> *The sheriff's God-damn was a facile curse*
> *Not for the dead but for the blinding dust*
> *That boxed the cortege in a cloudy hearse*
> *And dragged it towards our town.*

The scene is patterned after that in the Gospel According to St. John, in which Joseph of Arimathea and Nicodemus retrieve Christ's body from the cross and take it for burial. Tate is not just describing five Kentucky boys who see a lynched Negro; the Passion is being re-created. The young watcher recoils from the scene in horror, but not from knowledge of its religious consequences. Rather it is the horror of innocence first encountering evil. The religious level awaits the adult's newly regained moral perspective.

The third published portion, "The Buried Lake," which Tate lists as Part VI of the projected long poem, concerns a haunting dream of the past, going far back into childhood.

> *The way and the way back are long and rough*
> *Where Myrtle twines with Laurel——*

These age-old symbols of death and art symbolize the path to be re-explored. "The Buried Lake" is psychological in nature, written with a pervading awareness of dream symbolism. The narrator relates how he

fumbled all night long, an ageing child,
Fled like a squirrel to a hollow bole
To play lead soldier, Tiny Tim, and, mild

In death, the Babes with autumn leaves for stole——
The terror of their sleep I could not spell
Until your gracing light reduced the toll.

In the dream he finds his way to an empty room lined with benches, and prepares to play a violin. A dancing girl emerges and locks up the fiddle, after which the narrator first sees an old friend, then finds himself.

guilted on a moving stair

Upward, down which I regularly fell
Tail backwards, till I caught the music room
Empty, like a gaol without a cell.

A beautiful woman laden with sorrow appears, but as the narrator embraces her she turns into

Another's searching skull, whose drying teeth
Crumbled me all night long, and I was dead.

Then the narrator walks in the dark, until he comes to a radiant woman.

Santa Lucia! at noon—the prudent shore,
The lake flashing green fins through amber trees——
And knew I had not read your eye before
You played it in the flowing scale of glance:
I had not thought that I could read the score.

At first the narrator welcomes her lucent aid and his new-found power to make music, but then he resents her playing, and wishes to remain in the dark. This too passes, however, and he accepts the vision. He

thought of ways to keep this image green——
Until the leaf unfold the formal cherry——
In an off season, when the eye is lean
With an inward gaze upon the wild strawberry,
Cape jasmine, wild azalea, eglantine,

And the sad eclogue that will then be merry;
And knew that nature could not more refine
What it had given in a looking-glass
And holds there, after the living body's line
Has moved wherever it must move—wild grass
Inching the earth; and the quicksilver art
Throws back the invisible but lightning mass
To inhabit the room

Particularly for anyone acquainted with the poet's literary career, the dream constitutes an apt symbolic reckoning. The poet tries to work his art in an empty house of death, but a girl—the flesh, the carnal—prevents him from doing so, only to disappear as the poet finds himself falling—an ancient symbol of physical love. When he seeks to embrace a beautiful woman, she turns into a skull—the decay of the flesh, the negation of sensual love. Then a period of wandering, until a religious symbol, the Virgin, appears. The poet resents her appearance, but then accepts her song, though at first he sought to interpret it through nature imagery (we remember the image of the real world, the South, in *The Mediterranean*). But then he realizes that the natural world, no matter how attractive, can only reflect and can never originate the innermost beauty of the vision. With this realization, the poem closes.

The dream is over and the dark expired.
I knew that I had known enduring love.

The religious symbolism is clearly stated. The dream is analogy of the search for illumination—art, "knowledge carried to the heart," belief, approached in various ways but fully realized at last only in a religious acceptance. In the three parts of Tate's uncompleted poem, the theme is still man suffering from unbelief, but told now from a perspective of belief.

Tate has published no new poetry since 1953. The long poem remains uncompleted. How many additional sections Tate will publish, if any, remains to be seen. However, one is not at all convinced that Tate's poetry is concluded. Though one of the elder statesmen of modern poetry, he has only just turned sixty. Certainly the three portions of the long poem published thus far evidence no falling off of his poetic imagination. More complex than any of his previous work, they show a mastery of various modes of poetic expression.

Whatever else may be said, this much is sure: Allen Tate's accomplishments have earned him a place as one of the seminal poets of the twentieth century. His impact on the verse of his time has been far-reaching. The sources upon which he has drawn—the English metaphysicals, the classical poets—have through his example become a vitalizing force in poetry today. Reinforced by a rigorous critical foundation put forth with vigor and brilliance in a number of influential essays, his work has been example and model for the best younger poets of his day. If the best poetry of this century is firm and unified, composed in verse both texturally rich and structurally coherent, standing of its own self and making its own case, then the credit must go to Allen Tate as much as to any poet alive.

DONALD DAVIDSON

BY RANDALL STEWART

Donald Davidson is best known for his social criticism, which is a trenchant criticism of the modern notion of industrial "progress," the most trenchant and fearless we have had since Thoreau. For Thoreau, too, was skeptical of industrial progress. "Will the division of labor never end?" he cried out in *Walden*. He was regarded as an eccentric, a crank, in the New England of his time, that region being then full of industry and progress. A hundred years later, he is a diagnostician and prophet, the region's economy having changed meanwhile from "young" to "mature." By the same token, Davidson has been regarded as a bit "out of step" by many Southerners since the South has begun to hum industrially. He is today, I imagine, more widely and sympathetically read in New England than in his native South. But the whirligig of time will continue to bring in his revenges.

Davidson was one of the chief figures in the neo-Agrarian movement which dates from the publication, in 1930, of *I'll Take My Stand*, "by Twelve Southerners." In the chapter which he contributed to that volume, "A Mirror for Artists," he regarded industrialism as the foe of art. "The making of an industrialized society," he said:

will extinguish the meaning of the arts, as humanity has known them in the past, by changing the conditions of life that have given art a meaning. For they have been produced in societies which were for the most part stable, religious, and agrarian; where the goodness of life was measured by a scale of values having little to do with the material values of industrialism; where men were never too far removed from nature to forget that the chief subject of art, in the final sense, is nature.

"The kind of leisure provided by industrialism," he said, "is a dubious benefit." "Mass-production, if applied to the arts," he maintained, "must invariably sacrifice quality to quantity." He saw, with industrial progress, "a gradual corruption of integrity and good taste."

In 1952, in response to a questionnaire sent by the *Shenandoah* magazine to the contributors to *I'll Take My Stand,* Davidson reiterated his indictment of industrialism.

> Industrialism [he said] has increased its sway. It has provided more and better automobiles, airplanes, refrigerators, and weapons of war—including the atomic bomb. And it has also become a party to the infliction of war, death, and destruction on an unprecedented scale. It has wasted our resources to the point of danger. It has degraded society, perverted education, and undermined religion. It has invaded, abridged, and all but destroyed our constitutional liberties, and now threatens to convert our government into a totalitarian regime. It has spread confusion, and suspicion; it has begotten corruption and treason; it has reduced millions to a state of groveling servility and fear.

The only qualifying criticism of *I'll Take My Stand* which Davidson would make twenty-two years later was that "the term 'agrarian' was too narrow a description of the society that the 'Agrarians' were advocating." "The emphasis," he said, "should have been put, more firmly, upon religion." The question came up during the Fugitives' reunion, held at Vanderbilt in May 1956. There seemed to be general agreement as to the inadequacy of the "agrarian" tag. As Frank Owsley put it, "Everybody thought we ought to go out and plow" (*Fugitives' Reunion,* 1959, 206). (The same sort of symbolic misreading occurred in Thoreau's case when genteel readers objected to living in a cabin with only a pumpkin to sit on.) Reviewing the matter once more, in the Lamar Lectures in 1957, Davidson said, "I believe we would now be justified in defining the so-called Agrarian Movement not only in terms of its first gropings and tentative beginning, but also in terms of its ultimate broader direction and general fruitfulness of application. For brevity, I might call it the cause of civilized society, as we have known it in the Western World, against the new barbarism of science and technology controlled and directed by the modern power state."

Davidson said in the *Shenandoah*, "There can hardly be such a thing as a 'society,' in any true sense, without religion as the all-pervasive arbiter of value." And in religion, he prefers, I think, the Christian salvational religion—not the social gospel, which is secondary and organizational, and still less the "religion of science." Granted that the machine is here to stay (or until total destruction, which appears to be something more than a possibility), does it follow that one should fall down and worship it? Our *attitude* toward the machine is perhaps the crux of the whole matter. Henry Adams was tempted to pray to the Dynamo. The mass of lesser men in our time have succumbed to that temptation, indeed looking to the Dynamo and its surrogates for salvation.

A special objection by Davidson to industrialism is that its spread tends to make the whole country uniform, whereas he cherishes the local peculiarities. He argues that these persist hardily, despite the strong trend to national uniformity. He insists upon the necessity of our "recognizing the principle of diversity in American life," and goes on (in his essay "Still Rebels, Still Yankees") to give two illustrations of diversity— Brother Jonathan of Vermont and Cousin Roderick of Georgia. Both portraits are drawn from life (the author has lived in both communities), and engagingly drawn. They contain just the right balance between the classic and the romantic, the general and the particular, the representative and the idiosyncratic. Although it must be confessed that Davidson seems a little more at home in Georgia (despite many summers' residence in Vermont), both portraits are sympathetic, and almost equally so. The author's thesis is simply that "the unity of America must rest, first of all, on a decent respect for sectional differences."

The good writer must give to airy nothing a local habitation and a name. He cannot escape the urgency of place; if he does, he vanishes in sheer vapidity. In his essay "Why the

Modern South Has a Great Literature" Davidson points out the importance to a writer like Faulkner or Warren of the Southern inheritance, of places as places, people as people.

> Thus it is [he says] that in the moment of self-consciousness the Southern writer is able to bring to bear, not only his personal view, but also the total metaphysic of his society. He is therefore unlikely to indulge in the exaggerations and over-simplifications that are the mark of a divided sensibility. From him the people in the bend of the creek are not only sharecroppers representing a certain economic function. They are complete persons with significant personal histories. In fact, they are Joe and Emma, who used to work on old man Brown's place, but left him for reasons unknown. The banker is not merely a banker. He is Mr. Jim, whose wife's mother was somebody's grandmother's double first cousin.

And the author goes on to speculate on the ways *All the King's Men* would be different if it had been written by, say, Sinclair Lewis. Confidence in one's inheritance, belief in one's instinctive knowledge ("knowledge carried to the heart," Davidson says, quoting Tate's *Ode to the Confederate Dead*), faithfulness to one's artistic vision—these are the qualities which distinguish the good writers of the modern South, the author believes—and indeed, one could add, good writers of any time, any place.

The love of old places, old customs, old histories is found everywhere in Davidson's writings (recalling Thoreau's love of the local histories of eastern Massachusetts). Take the meticulous, detailed reconstruction of the history of the Tennessee Valley (his unfriendliness to TVA was owing to the sacrifice by inundation of hundreds of homesteads and thousands of acres of rich bottomland—it *was* quite a sacrifice!—to the erection of a vast electric power plant). Or take this account of such a rural homestead (in "The Two Old Wests") as Davidson himself may have known as a boy in Lincoln County, middle Tennessee.

> Let there be a fence around the grove, with a gate that opens upon a boxwood walk leading to a high-columned

porch. And between fence and road let there be a pasture for the horses, with a creek flowing in it, and limestone outcroppings, and iron-weed scattered about (who cares?) and blackberries in the fence corners. Let there be fields of corn to left and right, and beyond them a high hill, well forested, a range for turkeys only half tame, and for 'possum and 'coon that are wholly wild.

Or take the folk operetta *Singin' Billy* (Davidson wrote the words, Charles Bryan the music), which has an authenticity and a poignance lacking in most attempts of this kind. Or take his moving account of the White Spirituals in "The Sacred Harp in the Land of Eden." From scenes like these, he seems to say, our country's grandeur springs.

Davidson, obviously, is a traditionalist, and the oldest literary tradition, he emphasizes, is the oral: the ancient epics were recited for many generations before they were written down; Shakespeare's plays were composed to be spoken. "The admission of modern poetry to the textbooks of school and college classes," he says in "Poetry as Tradition," "may be in a sense as much an entombment as a triumph; this is for poetry a kind of death-in-life, to exist only on the printed page, not on the lips of men, not carried by their voices, and therefore almost never in their memories, rarely in their hearts." Poetry is doomed to ultimate extinction, he believes, unless a way is found to restore something of its former oral character. "This is a problem for our civilization," he adds, "no less than for our poetry. No civilization of the past has ever lived without poetry, and ours can hardly be an exception."

Davidson is enamored of ballads (the South has been especially rich in this field) and his special understanding of balladry and folklore enables him to contribute important new insights. In his essay "The Traditional Basis of Thomas Hardy's Fiction," for example, the author focuses attention on the folk element; seen from this viewpoint, Hardy was a ballad maker turned novelist, and it is just as much beside the point to call a Hardy novel "pessimistic" as it would be to apply that adjective to "Edward" or "Johnny Armstrong." In the literary essays (collected in *Still Rebels, Still Yankees and Other Essays*), the author is always looking closely at backgrounds, traditions, the inherited ways of the folk. He likes "the tones of the speaking voice" which ring throughout Stark Young's *So Red the Rose*, and "the unified personality" of Hugh McGehee, contrasting with the modern fragmented world, where men are incomplete with the terrible division of their age. He discounts the blueprints of the sociologists, which can't explain Faulkner, or Shakespeare either—for both, he reminds us, were country boys from "backward" regions, and both belong among "the world's incomparable originals."

Davidson's prose, as searching as it is, should not be allowed to obscure his verse. For it was as a poet that he began, and it may very well be (as so often happens to a good poet) that he will be longest remembered for his verse—poetry, generally speaking, being literature's immortal part.

He began with the Fugitives. (Davidson himself has given a charming, idyllic account of the beginnings in "The Thankless Muse and Her Fugitive Poets.") He was not a "minor" Fugitive, as Mr. John Bradbury seems to think, but a "major" one, as Mrs. Cowan abundantly shows in her book on the Fugitive Group. He was not as "modern" as the others. He seems to have escaped almost completely Eliot's influence, and Pound's. He lacks the metaphysical density of Tate, the starkness of Warren, the nuanced ambiguity of Ransom. Miss Gamble quotes Ransom as saying that "the direct approach is perilous to the artist," and goes on to speak of Ransom's "oblique style," which "fends off the assaults of sentiment inherent in the direct approach." Well, Davidson is comparatively direct, and isn't afraid of sentiment. There is sentiment aplenty (but not sentimentality, which is properly defined, I think, as feeling in excess of clear cause).

I should like to mention (without attempting much more) some of the characteristics of the verse, as it strikes me.

First, there is the classical influence. Davidson, like the other Fugitives, is grounded in the Greek and Roman classics. This influence comes out not only in quotation and allusion but in purity of language and in the severe, astringent imposition of restraint upon emotion.

Second, there is a pervasive sense of the past, an ancestral past. This past is not merely a Southern, or even American experience; it goes back indefinitely in the history of the race; it takes on a mythical, and finally a mystical, quality; it is remembered in the blood. The meeting of the lovers in *Epithalamion* suggests earlier lovers' meetings, when men in gray halted by an Ohio farmhouse; and a still earlier meeting

> *Brief by the Frisian coast, when the fair-haired Goths*
> *Came aharrying over the path of the whale . . .*
> *Young was the herald of Goths. The light of his eyes*
> *Burned in the crowded hall. And the eyes of a girl*
> *Met his warm through the spears.*

Third, there is an unusual talent for narrative verse, a form which has appeared only sporadically since Chaucer. Narrative verse seems to be in critical disfavor at the present time. Not that a modern poem doesn't tell a "story"; but the story must be ferreted out, constructed from the images (as in Warren's *Original Sin: A Short Story*). Davidson is capable of a straightforward narrative remarkable for verve and movement. A short segment of *The Sod of Battle-Fields* will illustrate the quality.

> *And there was a tale of Jim Ezell and the Yankees,*
> *How he licked ten of them—fifty maybe——*
> *All by himself. Oh, he was a Forrest scout*
> *And a Chapel Hill boy, you know. The Yankees*
> *Heard he was lying wounded and in bed*
> *At old Dad Smiley's farm up by the creek,*
> *So they sneaked up, all ten of them (maybe fifty),*
> *And the first thing he knew he was surrounded.*
> *Then Jim rared out of bed like a young colt,*
> *Kicked up his heels, spit bullets in their faces,*
> *That-a-way, this-a-way, lit in his saddle fighting,*
> *Bang through the fence and splash in the creek,*
> *And up the dirt road with his shirt-tail flapping.*
> *The Yankees yelled and shot their guns. No use!*
> *None of your butter-fingered Yankee cavalry*
> *Ever could touch Jim Ezell. It took*
> *Ten Yankees anyhow to lick a Southerner,*
> *Even to make him run.*

Perhaps the best-sustained narrative is *The Running of Streight,* where Bedford Forrest chased Streight and his federal cavalry out of Alabama. The following excerpt gives a real sense of movement through the countryside:

That running went to the Black Warrior River,
That running went over the rocks and fallen trees,
By crossroads and by field, by land and water
They gnawed and nagged and shot and charged him down,
And soon by country stores and villages
Came fast and hard, while women and old men
Waved from porches, whooped at roadside gates.
Without a rest for the spent fox, without
A spell to tighten girth or breathe a horse.
They left him not a shady place to lie in,
They cut him off from every telegraph,
They drove him from his oats, his corn, his pasture,
They harried Streight to hell in Alabama.

Fourth, there is everywhere (in the verse as in the prose, for Davidson is all of a piece) the old agrarian-industrial antinomy. He sees the Civil War as a struggle between the rural and urban economies, and, as a corollary, between local self-government and the rule of the power state. In *The Deserter: A Christmas Eclogue,* one of the interlocutors declares:

Nashville was occupied by Federal troops
In eighteen sixty-two. They hold it still!
The only difference is, they do not wear
Blue uniforms.

Many of the images throughout Davidson's verse—if they were tagged and classified—would be found to fall in one or the other of the two antinomies. In the poem just quoted from, there is the ever present smoke: "But soot means money./ More smoke, more trade." Rural scenes have retreated to a remote distance: ". . . down the hollow through the pasture, past/ The big spring." City and farm, of course, are symbols. They symbolize guilt and innocence, respectively. But in Davidson's poetry they are more than symbols; they are facts.

There is, fifth, the religious bias. In *The Breaking Mould,* the narrator speaks of himself as one

Who learned of a gentle mother the Ten Commandments
And read the Good Book through at the age of twelve,
Chapter by chapter. The hymns of country choirs
Haunt my tongue. The words of stately men
Speaking from ghostly pulpits forbid me still
From shameful things. And youthful prayers arise
Unbidden to my lips in hours of dread.
Woman is sacred still, and wine is a mocker,
The words of God are written in the Book
Which I will keep beloved though earth may speak
A different language unto those who read her.

In the same poem, the narrator says that he is "three men": the one just described; another, "with pagan blood"; and a third, "born to weigh the sun." But the reader feels that the old-fashioned Christian is the most real, for the paganism is partly something read about, and the scientism something imposed by the Age of Science. Not that Davidson is a "churchman": he is critical of the clergy's doctrinal softness; of the church's adoption of business methods; of the big neon sign "Jesus Saves" in front of an old downtown church. But the religious bias goes deeper than current churchly aberrations. ". . . if I pass you by, O House of God, [he says]/ It is not now in scorn. I would not sit/ In the seat of the scornful or walk in the way of sinners."

Two of the better poems, readers will agree, are *Lee in the Mountains* and *Fire on Belmont Street*, which can be read as two modes of prophecy.

The image of Lee grows into symbol. It is an accretion of parts which finally glow in a single incandescence. The parallel between his career and his father's is a contributing part; the re-creation of Civil War battles is another; the "acceptance" of the new era of "little men," another. These and other elements are interfused to make the complex symbol that is Lee. Lee's going to the mountains extends the symbolic dimension. He had formerly been identified with the Tidewater, while the more "puritan" Jackson had stood for the Blue Ridge. But now Lee comprehends them both, and other places and times as well. Toward the end, he speaks to the young men about the God of their fathers.

Young men, the God of your fathers is a just
And merciful God Who in this blood once shed
On your green altars measures out all days,
And measures out the grace
Whereby alone we live;
And in His might He waits,
Brooding within the certitude of time,
To bring this lost forsaken valor
And the fierce faith undying
And the love quenchless
To flower among the hills to which we cleave,
To fruit upon the mountains whither we flee,
Never forsaking, never denying
His children and His children's children forever
Unto all generations of the faithful heart.

The words have the tone of prophecy. Whatever virtue there was in the Lost Cause—whatever valor, faith, love—will have a rebirth, when the fullness of time shall have come. The prophecy is quiet, confident, long-range.

Fire on Belmont Street is imminent and alarmist. The predicament comes closer home today than the poet could have foreseen when he wrote the poem two decades ago. He asks the contemporary question:

Who can quench }
The white-hot fury of the tameless atoms }
Bursting the secret jungle of their cells? }

One is reminded of Cassandra, who had the prophetic gift but was fated to be disbelieved.

Davidson's more recent poetry (for he has continued to write, though there has been no collected volume since 1938) is less explicitly partisan, less admonitory. It is as if, with Wordsworth, he "will grieve not, rather find/ Strength in what remains behind."

One source of "strength" is the old friendships. This is expressed with nostalgic beauty in *Lines Written for Allen Tate on His Sixtieth Anniversary.*

So, Allen, you have kindled many an evening
When the creed of memory summoned us to your fire.

I remember that blazon, remember firelight blessing
Owsley's uplifted head, Ransom's gray eye,
The Kentucky voice of Warren, until that household's
Oaken being spoke like a plucked lyre . . .

Another source is nature and religion. *Gradual of the North-*
ern Summer is a case in point. The "nature" is in Vermont,
where the Davidsons have a summer home, near Middlebury.
This is not a new note, for Vermont nature had received due
appreciation in the early essay, "Still Rebels, Still Yankees,"
but the Catholic aura perhaps is, the "gradual" being a portion of the Mass. The author gives a religious particularization
to certain aspects of nature: ". . . vesper deer come forth to
browse"; and

> *The little, naked red fox peers*
> *With prayerful face and upright ears,*
> *Then genuflects, with sweep of paw,*
> *To mark the rigor of God's law.*

These are of course not identities, but only analogies; the
poem does not say that God and nature are one; the deer and
fox are fellow creatures, endowed by "pathetic fallacy" with
worshipful attitudes. The road connecting the highway and
the author's house is rough and steep.

> *Whoso would turn to our abode*
> *Must take the narrow, rain-scraped road*
> *And learn by one-way steeps and grooves*
> *God loves best where he unimproves.*

The old polemic about "improvements" persists.

The disposition of the present world of neo-conformism is
to go along servilely with the prevailing, statistically demonstrated trends—whether in space exploration, or organization
monopoly, or leveling nationalism, or whatnot. The key word
of our age is "adjust." Ours not to reason why. Davidson (in
both poetry and prose) is one of our few living writers who
fixes the responsibility unmistakably and precisely where it
belongs—upon each individual. "I do not surrender to the servile notion," he says, "that the existence of a powerful 'trend'
is a mark of its 'inevitability.' All the works of men result from

human choices, human decisions. There is nothing inevitable about them. We are subject to God's will alone; we are not subject to any theory of mechanical determinism originating in 'social forces.'" Only by such a steadfast position can we hope to maintain a culture worthy of our loyalty and the world's respect.

POETS AND CRITICS

BY JOHN EDWARD HARDY

What principally distinguishes the Southern men of letters is just the exclusiveness of their concern with *literary* values. In contemporary America they are the chief if not the
only defenders of the word in its ultimate freedom.
The intrinsic values of eloquence which Faulkner, pre-
eminently, in the opposition of his influence to that of Hemingway (the original "man of few words") has championed
in his novels and short stories—Cleanth Brooks, John Crowe
Ransom, Allen Tate, and Robert Penn Warren have upheld
in criticism and poetry.* Insofar as the careers of these men
have reflected a commitment to *regional* values, it is only to
the extent that Southernism has seemed to them identifiable
with a greater tradition of Western letters, and a philosophy
of literary practice, according to which the imaginative use of
language is one of the basic activities of civilized man, self-
sustaining and self-justifying, and not properly subservient,
either as art or as academic discipline, to the interests of politics, religion, commerce, or "science." In some of the more
enthusiastic regionalist pronouncements of one or another of
them—as, notably, in the essays of *I'll Take My Stand*—the
identification (of "the South" and its traditions with the literary tradition) may have been over- or misstated; but the intent
with which it was made, the direction of emphasis, upon the
universal, literary values, rather than upon the geographical
and historical region as such, should always have been clear
to any unprejudiced reader.

* Warren, of course, is also a distinguished writer of fiction.
But for the purposes of my concern here, the fiction can safely
be taken just as a part of the "poetry."

I trust it is by now commonplace to observe that the region-alism has never had anything to do with a provincialism of interest. For example—at the same time that he has been the most ardent and articulate of Southerners, it would be difficult to think of any modern writer in America or Europe who is more thoroughly *urbane* than Allen Tate. Although it would be a mistake to regard it *merely* as stratagem, as professional pose, one has observed nothing of the basic, ironic strategy of Tate's poetry and prose if he has not seen how the provin-cialities of subject and style are always deliberately contrived as a foil to the urbanity.

One of the most important aspects of the urbanity is Tate's classicism. He, as well as Brooks, Ransom, and Warren, was educated in a Southern system that held on longer than the schools in any other part of the United States to the study of the classical languages as the basic humanistic discipline. And the shaping influence of that education is evident everywhere in his poetry and criticism.

As a matter of poetic "strategy," the recurrent ironic effect of which I have spoken, with the provincial setting and con-cern of the poem played off against the protagonist's conscious-ness of man's past grandeur—the effect of the "Tennessee ac-cent to the classic phrase" (not to equate Tate in any other way with the speaker of Warren's line!)—the function merely of the classical allusions, to "muted Zeno and Parmenides," etc., of the *Ode to the Confederate Dead*, will serve well enough as example. It is an effect similar to, and, no doubt, though masterfully, to some extent imitative of, the strategy with which we are familiar in the work of Eliot and Yeats. But in many more subtle ways too, in his own English verse as well as in his distinguished translations, the entire rhetoric and metrics of Tate's poetry are informed by his classical studies.

And in his critical essays, on a variety of subjects, and whether always overtly or not, a deploring of the decline of classical studies in modern education is an almost obsessively recurrent theme. It is not simply that the contemporary uni-versity student no longer knows how to read poetry because, not having studied Latin, he has no conception of grammar (*vid.*, "Is Literary Criticism Possible?"). The cultural decay

of which the specific corruption of literary studies is representative, Mr. Tate's argument runs, has affected all aspects of
our society, robbing us, for example (*vid.*, "What Is a Traditional Society?"), of that capacity of the "historical imagination," the "genius for dramatizing themselves at their own particular moment of history" which sustained the statesmen of
the early American Republic, however "lower" the myth of
the Ciceronian character which they chose for themselves than
others they might have taken, in a political and economic freedom, a wholeness of manhood in their public life and utterance, that is quite beyond the conception of the contemporary
positivists in governmental affairs.

Mr. Tate has always been careful to maintain the inde-
pendence of letters (*vid.*, "The Man of Letters in the Modern
World," and "To Whom Is the Poet Responsible?") and to
express his own doubt that merely a superior literary-critical
acumen on the part of the politicians before World War II—a
taste for Dante instead of Arthur Hugh Clough on Churchill's
part, or, on that of the continental leaders, a knowledge of
Proust or Kafka—could have saved Europe from its collapse.
Literature, and the knowledge of it, is not the *cause* of either
the growth or the decay of societies.

But the substitution of *communication* for *communion* as
the end of language studies, of jargon for rhetoric and logic,
is part and parcel of the same positivistic spirit that has destroyed the other humane institutions (political, religious, economic, social, and scientific) of our culture. One can, and
must, distinguish the parts of a culture, one from another, and
the limits of the various professional responsibilities—of the
man of letters, the politician, the scientist, and so forth—but
to distinguish is not to disjoin or to argue that there is no
significant, historical relationship among them.

There are, perhaps, in his tendency to associate the "cause"
of letters and literary scholarship in the modern world with
that of classicism, and the latter in turn with the traditionalism
of the South, grounds for convicting Mr. Tate the polemicist
of negativism. There is something a little morbidly self-
apologetic about many of the essays, a rather tired, all too
gentlemanly awareness that they are all lost causes, lost values,
that he espouses, a suggestion that he has espoused them,

perhaps, *because* they are lost—and fears that an approach to any of the problems more hopeful and positive must necessarily smack of the positiv*istic*. But if, as Marcus Cunliffe has suggested, there is sometimes the same tone in his poetry, "an edge of asperity or despair, as in 'Aeneas at Washington'"—and if it is yet somewhat to misread the unified poetic effect to observe in qualification that, "however, his classical urbanity *comes to his relief*" (italics mine)—(*The Literature of the United States*, 1954, 332)—it is a tone, a feeling or attitude, that as such cannot damage the poem. For, unlike the critical essay, the poem, as Tate himself has so often argued, is to be held responsible only for adequate expression, an effective and convincing representation, or "dramatization," of its adopted attitude. The poet's choice of attitude is unarguable.

By all odds the most vigorous of the group, and the most varied in his talents, has been Robert Penn Warren. His career alone—as professor, editor, novelist, poet, and critic—is sufficient proof of the falsity of any suspicion that the gentility of the Southern traditionalist, and especially of the Southern academic, must involve a quality of the effete and jaded.

And that career, I would argue, for all its variety of effort, is all of a piece. The virtues of the professor and editor (notwithstanding the intimation of Mr. John Aldridge, say, that such a situation is impossible) are those of the novelist and poet. The same themes, and the same implicit system of values, appear in the poetry and the fiction. Warren as apologist for regionalism (the theory of which he has done as much as Tate, for example, to distinguish from provincialism) is identical with Warren as objective critic of Hemingway, Conrad, Shelley, Coleridge, and the Metaphysicals, and with Warren as lecturer on Shakespeare.

In his earlier work, as for example in the novel *At Heaven's Gate*, the voice of the professor often strikes through rather too prominently and self-consciously. By the time of *All the King's Men*, some three years later, he had managed to incorporate the lecture into the fable—so effectively, indeed, that it required the critical offices of Robert Heilman to inform the reading public that the book *was* a tragedy in the traditional form. And something of the same observation might be made on the poems. Derivative and overstrained in both directions, in the colloquialism on the one hand and the "intellectuality," the effort at the traditional grand manner on the other, poems like *Pondy Woods, Pro Vita Sua, Original Sin: A Short Story,* etc.—by contrast to the best things in his latest volume, *Promises*—must seem now less to have achieved the effects of irony they aimed at than simply to have produced them, according to the "prescription" implicit in some of the analyses and study questions of the first edition of *Understanding Poetry*.

But my point is just that Warren *has* managed, more and more successfully in his later work, to unify his interests and preoccupations. Without any loss of strength in any one direction, without abandoning one concern for the sake of another, he has moved steadily nearer a final synthesis. I suppose that the synthesis will come, if it does, in his fiction; the novel appears to provide him the form in which he is most effective. His first promise as a dramatist has so far come to little. And he has, I believe, recently quit teaching. But this latter decision, at least, was probably dictated simply by considerations of personal convenience—*All the King's Men* alone remains as sufficient evidence that he did not have to leave the academic life in order to write a good novel. And, all along, his published criticism, unquestionably to a great extent shaped by his experience in teaching, has provided the best available commentary on his own poetry and fiction.

Perhaps simply because he has had his success as poet and novelist to sustain him, Warren has been able more than most critics to afford the luxury of choosing subjects according to his felt affinities and disaffinities. Often, as in the comparative savagery of his strictures on Thomas Wolfe, or in the cautiously qualified appreciation of Hemingway, the motive of adverse self-criticism, the intent to provide opportunity for detached judgment of questionable tendencies in his own work, is as apparent as the more positive sympathy of his concern with Faulkner, say, or Conrad and Coleridge.

But he is at his critical best, I think, in the latter role, as explicator of his enthusiasms. We may take his comments on Faulkner as an example. Warren has some preliminary reservations to make, as anyone must, on the inconsistency of quality in Faulkner's work, but essentially his attitude is one of open and intense admiration. And Warren was the first among American critics, if not to discern, at least to articulate fully, two essential truths about Faulkner which are also fundamental to his own art. I mean, the relationship between the realism and the legend in Faulkner's treatment of "the South," the way in which Yoknapatawpha County functions as the world's stage—and the relationship between past and present, the fact that for Faulkner "the 'truth' is neither of the past nor of the future . . . [but] of both" ("William Faulkner," *Selected Essays*, 1958, 67).

With these two observations alone, on his great, older contemporary, Warren has (or, at any rate, *should* have) not only cleared away the most prevalent and fundamental critical misconceptions of Faulkner's work but has also provided the key to the central design of the two novels that are his own greatest accomplishments to date—*All the King's Men* and *World Enough and Time*. They are, of course, closely related truths. It is, so to speak, *in order to* discover that *All the King's Men* is the tragic legend suggested by the nursery-rhyme title, and not just a more or less accurately realistic account of the politics and sociology of Huey Long's Louisiana, that one must rightly assess the role of Jack Burden, and the significance of the discoveries he makes through his "research" into the old, aristocratic order of politics represented by the Irwins and the Stantons. And, similarly, that *World Enough and Time* is not an "historical novel," that secondary type of the merely contemporary and realistic in fiction, but also, like *All the King's Men*, a romance and a tragedy, is discernible only to the reader who has observed the dramatic opposition of *styles* in the book—that of the modern, not quite omniscient narrator, Warren, and the superbly re-created, period style of the internal hero and narrator Jeremiah Beaumont.

But perhaps it matters little where or in what direction one starts, so long as he grasps the fundamental fact of the *verbal order*, of a world not simply told about, but re-created, in wholeness and intelligibility, through language. Individually in his various fictions, and in the total pattern of his work as poet-novelist *and* critic, we have in Warren perhaps the most complete, contemporary American image of *man* as man of letters. And that image is identical with the character of the Southern *regionalist* as I have meant to interpret it—i.e., simply of the man who has had to make a world of language, because, he was given the intelligence to discover, language is all that is left to him.

John Crowe Ransom is, theoretically, the principal source of the basic ideas on the nature of poetic language, and the relationship of poetry to religion and to science, that are held in common by the Southern group. Tate, Warren, and Brooks were all his students, and as defenders of the objectivity and substantiality of poetic truth, of the wholeness of the individual work of art, of the concreteness of language against the threat of abstractionism, of "orthodoxy," of the world's body, they all derive their first inspiration from him. Insofar as there may be supposed to exist a larger, national and international, movement or school in modern criticism to which the Southerners owe allegiance, it is Ransom who first defined it—or, at least, gave it a name. But enough and more has been said about all that.

More important, perhaps, for indicating the strength and scope of the alliance which these men formed under Ransom's leadership is an emphasis upon the ways in which they have often disagreed, and most sharply with the master himself. There is surely none of them who will thank him now for the tag of the "New Criticism." (*Vid.*, Mr. Tate's comments on this subject in "A Note on Critical 'Autotelism'," *The Forlorn Demon*). As editor of the *Kenyon Review*—and perhaps it is in this role, through his acceptances and rejections, a career the history of which could only be put together in some unlikely future collection of his letters to contributors, that he has had his greatest influence on modern literature—Mr. Ransom does not seem to me especially to have furthered the common causes of the group. The direction of his thinking in the last fifteen or twenty years has led him into positions on fundamental issues of poetic theory that are acutely at variance with those of his earlier disciples. His disagreement with Brooks on the question of the function of metaphor and the logical unity of a poem—hardly to be resolved by the tactics of such a piece as "Why Critics Don't Go Mad"—will serve as example. And so on.

In short, the doctrines to which the members of the group have commonly adhered are of a kind calculated precisely to encourage the greatest freedom and individuality of development. And the career of Ransom, the original leader, provides the best example of such individuality.

Ransom seems at times to feel not obliged even to agree with *himself*, much less with his former pupils. Besides the numerous radical shifts, if not of fundamental persuasion, at least of interest, in the course of his critical writing, there is, I feel, a curious absence of the kind of clear coherence of purpose that unifies the work of Warren, for contrary example, as poet and critic.

For one thing, there is an oddly abstractionist tendency in much of his poetry, both early and late. There is, even in such a late piece as *The Painted Head,* a great sharpness of concrete *detail* in the imagery. But the images, if I may put it so, are chosen, ordered, or arranged according to an abstract dialectic. They are there at the *demand* of the dialectic. And the same tendency is apparent in the allegory and the carefully wrought antinomies of poems like *The Equilibrists* and *Antique Harvesters.* The "characters" of many of his little dramatic-lyric, semi-dialogue pieces are only rather stiff and formalized personifications of terms in a dialectic opposition. I do not say that this quality is necessarily bad—although I happen to prefer the poems in which it is least apparent, those less pretentious ones with more of a definite human story or situation and setting, such as *Janet Waking,* and *Blue Girls,* and *Dog,* and the exquisite *Prelude to an Evening,* and believe that it is on such as these that his reputation will rest most securely. But, if in itself neither a fault nor a virtue, the tendency I have noted is worth pointing out as at least a curious qualification, in the poetic practice, of the anti-abstractionist doctrine expressed in his critical writings.

It is in its theological emphases that I find the effect of his critical writing most questionable. His definition of the metaphorical character of religious truth, for example, seems to me ultimately to risk falling into a simple reversal of the old Arnoldian error. And I have never understood what could possibly be meant by an "orthodoxy" that urges—"with *whatever* religious institution a man may be connected, let him try to turn it back towards orthodoxy"—(italics mine)—(*God Without Thunder*, 1930, 327).

But, however all this may be—and perhaps in this group it is Ransom's greatest distinction as a critic that he has been the most intellectually restless, daring, has been willing to *take* the most risks, of whatever kind—at least, as I have observed with reference to Mr. Tate, the poet's choice of attitude is unarguable. Ransom's poems are certainly, always, fully realized. They are entirely and unmistakably his own, in no danger ever of becoming "dated." And if the same cannot be quite so confidently said of his critical writing, still, it is impossible to conceive what the history of modern Southern letters would have been without it.

It is just to say that Cleanth Brooks has made more sense about more poems than any other American critic of our time. His peculiar virtue as a critic, as I see it, is his singular devotion to the poem, the one, unique, indivisible whole of the particular work.

Brooks is original much more as reader than as theorist. It is true also that he has consciously devoted himself to the education of a generation of readers. A good half of his writing has been in textbooks, deliberately and directly tied to his professorial interests. The three *Understanding* anthologies have indeed been primarily effective, if not ultimately causative, in bringing about a pedagogical revolution.

(His devotion to the duty of teaching has been, in fact, so strict, that he might seem to have asked for final obscurity, for submergence in his cause. Not only—unlike Tate, Warren, and Ransom—has he confined himself, at least since his early career, almost exclusively to critical writing, but the manner of his criticism too has discouraged due consideration of his originality. And it is just because so little, relatively, has been written on his work that I feel justified in treating it here at greater length than that of the others.)

And if the textbooks, dedicated to creating a more critically responsible professoriate that, it must be hoped, will perpetuate itself, seem *calculated* to produce "competition" for their authors, both in the classroom and in editors' and publishers' offices, I think the volumes of essays Mr. Brooks has published are, after all, hardly less likely to do so. Mr. Brooks really has no theory of Poetry. He has a theory of the structure of poems, but that in effect is the same thing as a methodology. A systematic aesthetic theory has a certain sanctity, but a methodology is not inviolate. It invites, even demands, constant testing in practical application, and thereby risks reduction to the status of technique, available to everyone, and subject to facile, careless apprentice imitation of effects.

The revolution is so well accomplished—indeed, the explication fad in criticism, as fad, so long overworked already—that we very badly need now some means of distinguishing between the genuine and original contribution, such as all Brooks's readings still are, and the merely doctrinaire imitation. But the means are, actually, ready to hand, if seldom taken; the difference is remarkably simple, if rigorous.

It is the difference between approaching a poem as an architectural problem or as an engineering problem. It is perfectly true, as some of his critics are fond of pointing out, that the terms of Mr. Brooks's theory which refer properly to principles of form are often used as if they referred to structural materials. But they are not so used by Brooks. He has done nothing by his own example to encourage the view that one might learn to read or write a poem in some sort of literary Strength of Materials course—with lessons in the tensile strength of paradox, the relative virtues of cast and wrought irony, the flexibility of reinforced concrete.

It is the difference between looking for what holds specific effects together in the whole of a particular poem and having a facile eye only for the effects as such. The context is all for Brooks. He has never in any sense been concerned with effects, but with all devices as manifestations of an informing and unifying principle in any poem. And for Brooks, the principle, the form itself, always emerges, as John Crowe Ransom has observed, out of the poem's "own metaphorical energy."

Ransom speaks of Brooks's determining sometimes a dominant image in a poem and then "wrestling" the poem into the terms of that dominance. The figure of the wrestler is good. One might conceive of Brooks's terms—paradox, irony, and so on—as so many practiced holds that he applies in an encounter with a poem. He is wrestling a Proteus, to be sure. Brooks is insistently interested in the "common structural properties" of various poems of all periods, in "universals"—this insistence is an essential part of his quarrel with the historical scholar-critics. But if each poem is but one shape of the many that the ultimately single, wily opponent may take, still, that particular form, of the individual poem, has at least an immediate, active reality that had better be respected if he *is* to be held fast, and made at last to prophesy, to tell of what is beyond the present and particular. How the holds are to be applied in each instance will effectively depend upon whether he chooses to appear a man or a serpent for the moment.

There is the difference, further, between knowing and not knowing what one is rejecting when he strips the poem to read it "as poem." I am not sure that it is good, or even that it is possible, to be a scholar first, before one is a critic. It may be that one may choose only between a responsible or an irresponsible critical attitude, that every scholarly undertaking is shaped by a previous critical judgment, good or bad, controlled or uncontrolled. But assuredly it is desirable to acquire habits of scholarly competence *along with* the practice of criticism. And Mr. Brooks is a scholar; the breadth of his scholarship, through the twenty-odd years of his work, has increased constantly with that of his critical insight, not to alter the essential purpose of the criticism, but to strengthen and confirm it in an always richer and at once more rigorous definition. When Brooks proposes to read a poem *sub specie aeternitatis,* he knows fully the cultural matrix, the biographical facts, the situation of textual doubt or certainty from which he is releasing the poem. And he never approaches a reading without first clearing the ground, assessing the critical history of the poem. If anyone tries to practice the exegetical method simply because he is ignorant of the techniques and results of other approaches, it is not Mr. Brooks—and if the word I have of those who have labored for a Ph.D. under his direction is trustworthy, it is not his students either.

But besides those who have too narrowly adopted Mr. Brooks's method, there are others who have, from varying motives, attempted to adapt it. Now there is little question that a *rapprochement* of some kind between the method of structural analysis and other philological disciplines is desirable; I am inclined to think it is also possible. But there is a question of procedure in getting them together, so that the unique purposes of one or the other, or both, may not be lost in the process.

Almost every respectable, publishing scholar now finds it at least politic to support the "facts" of his research on any literary work with a plausible effort now and again at structural analysis. But even when the motive is more than one of expediency, the effort is made too often without attention to the fact that structure is total structure. Mr. Brooks has not, perhaps, always succeeded in accommodating a poem to this view—and the fault may be, in one instance or another, either his or the poem's, or both—but the view is, as we have observed before, that the poem generates its own principle of form, and that the final test of validity in the reading of any aspect of a poem is the taking of the aspect as organic *part*, and submitting it to the question of what impulse it bears from and imparts to all other parts. If one takes "structure" to mean anything else, he is not speaking Mr. Brooks's language. It is well to understand that the vocabulary and the rhetorical tricks of the analytical method may be adapted without any real grasp of its principle.

I think this is what has happened in a good many instances of the grinding of old axes against the new stone. They are axes, and they are old, though usually fitted now with new handles. Biographical criticism, for example, of the sort that used to be practiced especially on Milton and the Romantics, whereby poems were made out to be transcripts or allegories of the personal life experience of the poet, has been pretty well discredited. But it, or something essentially very similar to it, begins to appear again in the guise of what might be called intellectual biography, an effort to plot from the development of habitual rhetorical practices and intellectual concerns in the work of a particular poet an over-all *system* of his poetic, what is spoken of most cautiously as a consistent personal myth, or most rashly as a personal metaphysic, in terms of which every particular poem must be understood. The older kind of biographical study, taking literature more or less frankly as a reflection of life and largely indifferent to the internal order of the image, the text, concerned with pinpointing relationships between particular aspects of poems and particular life experiences of the poet, lacking the system, could not be easily accommodated to the view of a poem that demands an account of the functional interrelationship of all its parts. The revamped approach, on the other hand, does confine itself largely to texts, the conscious utterances of the poet, for its materials. Ostensibly, at any rate, it gives to the poetic text a status at least equal to that of letters and whatever formal, critical statements the poet might have made. And having a system, so developed, a logical structure of categories into which the several aspects of all the poems can be fitted and shown to function thus and so within the frame of that logic—such an approach can much more readily read its order into any particular study with an appearance of its being an account of the total order of the poem—or the order, for purposes of relative evaluation of poems, that the poem seeks but perhaps fails to attain.

Now, there is some justification for such a procedure. Certain poets—Wordsworth, Yeats, Donne, Milton even—especially yield themselves to at least one notion that is central here (emphasis varies with the practitioner): that of the career in which all the many poems are but partial representations of the one poem, the poem that maybe never got written at all in its single, whole perfection. And perhaps my remarks on Brooks as wrestler with Proteus might be seen to imply that he is doing the same thing on a larger scale—envisioning the One Poem, not just Wordsworth's one poem or Yeats's one poem, but everybody's, of which all particular poems are shapes.

Brooks would probably turn away in horror at the first sight of such an image of himself as mystic. But if there is anything at all to it, I am inclined to think that the difference of scale is *all* the difference. The broader the vision, the conception one has of the ultimate reality, in literary criticism as in religion and politics, the more respectful one is of particular and immediate realities. It is the very, seeming nearness of the possibility that a totality may be grasped, the mind of the individual poet, the whole form of his thought defined, which seduces the kind of critic I have been talking about into impatience with the particular form of the single poem. And granted that there is something grand and lordly in such impatience, a fine and assured contempt in the relegation of the structural analysis to the status of example or proof—"I can *do* this, of course, but I am after something so much bigger" —granted that there is something stodgy and schoolmasterish, maddeningly patient about Brooks's procedure—"What is *this* poem saying, what is *its* dominant image? Read *that* line over before you make up your mind finally about this one"—still, we ought to see clearly that if the consideration of the single form *is* merely accessory, it is a *different* thing from what Brooks does, not the same thing in a larger context. And I would further suggest, as an admonition to the impatient seeker for wisdom in his essays, that Brooks is probably at his most serene when he appears at his grubbiest—a kind of monk devoutly spading the abbey garden.

But finally, to leave the question of what the tendencies and alliances of his work are and are not in the whole context of modern criticism in English, it might be interesting to see what can be made of Brooks as a Southerner. He is sometimes identified with the spirit at least of the Fugitive and Agrarian groups, although he is younger, of course, than the original leaders of these vaguely allied movements. He has written a few essays, on the South and poetry, and the South and Protestantism, that show an affinity with the Agrarian philosophy. He has at various times given his voice to the defense of the doctrine. He has been directly, critically interested, in a fashion that takes account of its theoretic regionalism, in the poetry of the Fugitives. Certainly also his editorial alliances have fostered these interests. And it may be significant that the first book of his single authorship on an individual writer is the study of William Faulkner now in progress.

And yet, here as in the larger context, it is clear that his work has put the emphasis upon the poem and the story, removed from consideration of its cultural origins and influence. Or, if "cultural" is too large a term here, certainly he has been consistently less interested, in his published work, than any of the other Southern critics with whom he is usually

associated—Tate, Ransom, Davidson, and so on—in the *social*
implications of his critical ideas.

But it is, I think, a fact essentially significant in the development of his criticism, not accidental or incidental or simply a
matter of temperament and the habits of friendship, that
Brooks is a Southerner. The task he set himself was different
from that of any of the other Southern critics, but neither
more nor less surely calculated to drive him eventually into
exile than theirs, its difference in no way a matter of its being
less Southern. Brooks saw no more clearly than many others,
perhaps, that the greatest, or possibly the only hope for the
South to survive or to be redeemed, to flourish as a distinct
cultural reality, lay in the practice of letters—belles-lettres, our
lady had to be, or else, there was no other way, submit more
and more willingly to the role of happy housewife, indulged in
an occasional charming excess of sentimentality, to a nation
accustomed to think of literature and its history as a branch
of advertising. But what he either did see more clearly than
most, or has kept more constantly in mind, is that critical integrity in regionalism depended upon a rigorous refusal to have
the region confused with the historical and geographical and
social and political province. That the regional work might
be understood as work of art, and not document of provincial
life or dream, it was, first, essential that one understand the
nature of *a* work of art, the principle of form by which it always works through but transcends the particulars of its
maker's time and place. And, within the boundaries of the
common language, the search for the principle seemed most
likely to succeed if it ranged as far and wide as possible.

Further, it seems to me there is something, not universally,
to be sure, but peculiarly Southern, in the way itself that
Brooks looks at a poem. Not every Southerner, nor even every
literary Southerner, but more certainly still, hardly any non-
Southern American critic, could take quite so seriously this
view: that not only does the poem exist, but that such things,
things existing in and for themselves, have a right to exist, and
that it is a proper end of man's intellectual endeavor simply to
study that existence.

Brooks, then, is fairly easily convicted of Southernism—almost as easily as Tate, Warren, and Ransom. But it is a South-

emism, again like theirs, and more pronouncedly so, that takes the whole English literary world as its province, that proposes no restrictions upon either its legitimate area of study or its audience.

EUDORA WELTY: THE SENSE OF PLACE

BY ROBERT W. DANIEL

Grandfather Ponder's heart attack leaves Daniel, his youngest child, the richest inhabitant of Clay, Mississippi, with a big house, a Studebaker, and a cook who drives it. His niece Edna Earle, nearly as addlepated as he is, tells the story of his second marriage, his wife's death and funeral, and his trial for her murder. Edna Earle is not so addlepated, though, as to be unaware of the wide social gap separating her uncle and his new in-laws. "The Peacocks," she observes, "are the kind of people keep the mirror outside on the front porch, and go out and pick railroad lilies to bring inside the house, and wave at trains till the day they die." Yet Edna Earle's only response to the marriage is to soothe Judge Clanahan, who is upset by it. "People get married beneath them every day," she tells him, "and I don't see any sign of the world coming to an end. Don't be so small-town."

Far from bringing the world to an end, the marriage creates hardly a ripple of disapproval—and this calm is typical of the way in which *The Ponder Heart* surmounts the underlying improbability of its situations. The improbability is concealed by two powerful agencies: the unmistakable voice of Edna Earle as she tells the story, and the authenticity of the settings, which are real enough to touch. Take the Peacocks' shack, where the funeral is held: we already know, from the sentence introducing them into the story, what kind of place it will be. The details of it, observed by Edna Earle during the funeral, individualize it unforgettably. Outside, the tire with red verbena growing in it; on the porch, portulaca in pie pans and, of course, the mirror; inside, cracks in the floor and chickens under your feet. And all of it authenticated by the broom standing behind the door! How could skepticism greet a story that happens in such undeniably real places? It succeeds as Eudora Welty shows that Faulkner's *Spotted Horses* succeeds: A "harlequinade-fantasy," she calls it, in whose "shining fidelity to place lies the heart and secret of its comic glory."

The sentence occurs in a condensation of the lectures she gave at Cambridge in 1954, published since as an essay, "Place in Fiction" (*South Atlantic Quarterly* [January, 1956], 57–72). And certainly her best stories have grown primarily out of their settings. While the tone of her work ranges from the broad satiric comedy of "Petrified Man" to the delicate pathos of "The Bride of the Innisfallen," and its historical time from the present to the days of Aaron Burr, its author's strong sense of place endows it with a common center, despite its surface variety. "Experience has ever advised us to base validity on point of origin," she remarks in her essay, and it is by means of the geographical region re-created in her fiction that its major themes are validated.

Born in Jackson, Mississippi, on April 13, 1909, Eudora Welty was still living there twenty-seven years later when a magazine called *Manuscript* brought out her first published story, and she lives there today. Excursions to the University of Wisconsin, New York, San Francisco, England, and Italy have provided exotic settings for some of her stories, but the greater number—and the most distinguished—take place in Mississippi. Sometimes she writes of the middle-class world of beauty parlors and card parties that presumably is Jackson; oftener she takes her readers into the Delta, the western fringe of the state between Memphis and Natchez, a region of plantation houses, struggling farms, and sleepy villages. Beyond all these, in her stories, lie the encompassing woods and rivers, or else the primeval wilderness, when she writes of the region as it was a century and more ago. "It is both natural and sensible," as the essay asserts, "that the place where we have our roots should become the setting, the first and primary proving ground, of our fiction."

It happened, however, that by 1936, when "Death of a Traveling Salesman" appeared in *Manuscript*, Eudora Welty's place, her literary proving ground, was already well populated. Faulkner in particular had begun to create his own version of

Mississippi with the publication of *Sartoris* seven years earlier; and by the time she turned from newspaperwork and photography to the writing of fiction, Faulkner's "parable or legend of all the Deep South" was complete in its main outlines. On the young Southern writer this emblem of the Southern experience exerts an almost irresistible spell. If he is to write about his own region—and that he will is virtually inevitable, as "Place in Fiction" suggests—one of the first questions he must face is how to avoid rewriting Faulkner.

To say that Faulkner's books were appearing at the time Eudora Welty began to write is not, of course, to say that she read them. True, she shares Faulkner's preoccupation with the purity of the wilderness, with the simplicity of small farms and hamlets, with the moral ambiguities of plantation houses and cities. But the parallels may have resulted as much from a common upbringing as from direct influence. "Mississippi has two cities," runs the proverb, "Memphis and New Orleans." It comes natural to Mississippi writers to see life as countryside and county seat, consisting of a present saturated with the past, and achieving its ultimate degradation in the cities beyond the state's boundaries. Faulkner's work may have helped Eudora Welty to an understanding of the historical process in which many of her characters are enmeshed, but this influence is distinctly subordinate to the strikingly original foreground of her stories. Her fiction at its best abounds in characters, settings, vocal rhythms, and feelings which—they compel us to believe—only she could have created.

These qualities appear in even her first published story, and though "Death of a Traveling Salesman" is a story of contrasts —between two kinds of life and the attitudes appropriate to them—the characters are treated with a most un-Faulknerian charity. The story also introduces what was to become its author's most characteristic theme: the counterpoint of human love, in the prelapsarian state of the hill couple, and human loneliness, represented by the salesman, R. J. Bowman, who is brought by the action of the story to envy their primitive existence. That both motifs are presented without a vestige of sentimentality may be ascribed to the strength of Eudora Welty's sense of place: the characters of Sonny and his wife are developed out of the "shotgun house, two rooms and an open passage between, perched on a hill," that they inhabit; and Bowman is created by the lonely hotel rooms in which he has passed his recent life. When the moment of comprehension comes, he is led in reverie to exclaim, "I have been sick and I found out then, only then, how lonely I am. Is it too late? My heart puts up a struggle inside me, and you may have heard it, protesting against emptiness. . . . It should be flooded with love."

"Death of a Traveling Salesman" is one of seventeen stories that in 1941 became Eudora Welty's first book, *A Curtain of Green*. Throughout her career, collections of stories have alternated with longer works; *The Robber Bridegroom* (1942), her own "harlequinade-fantasy," was followed by *The Wide Net and Other Stories* (1943) and then the novel *Delta Wedding* (1946). *The Ponder Heart* (1954) separated *The Golden Apples* (1949) and *The Bride of the Innisfallen and Other Stories* (1955), her most recent book. *A Curtain of Green* is made up of stories of the present day; in tone they range from the pathos of the two about salesmen to the best of her early humorous pieces, "Petrified Man" and "Why I Live at the P. O." They show that, from the beginning, Eudora Welty could write as well about Negroes (in "A Worn Path," for instance) as about whites. Poor farmers, simple-minded villagers, and decayed aristocrats predominate among the characters; and *The Wide Net*, published two years later, draws in part upon the same material. The best things in it, however, are the scenes laid in the great forest at the beginning of the nineteenth century, the times of Aaron Burr, Audubon, and the highwayman Murrell.

If the world of these first two collections lacks a middle class, the deficiency is supplied by the stories in *The Golden Apples*. These concentrate upon characters who grew up in the town of Morgana, Mississippi, a few years ago, and belong to the class that can afford servants and music lessons for its children, though not always easily. *The Golden Apples* also differs technically from its predecessors: its parts are independent, yet the same characters appear in most of them. The book gives the reader a sense of knowing not only the life of Morgana in its entirety, but even the later lives of some of the people who leave it. Apart from its pervasive melancholy, *The Golden Apples* might be called a Mississippi *Cranford*.

"Music from Spain" in *The Golden Apples* shows Eudora Welty moving beyond her native scenes. As might be expected from "Place in Fiction," which suggests that a writer who restricts his choice of settings to his own region is suffering from "spiritual timidity or poverty or decay," the stories of Mississippi in her latest collection are overshadowed by those that take place in New Orleans, the harbor of Naples, and a train moving across Wales. This development affords a new source of interest—yet *The Bride of the Innisfallen* is a disappointment. The Mississippi stories lack novelty; "Kin" in particular contains too many echoes of *Delta Wedding;* and the title story, which is the best of the others, though brilliant in observation and in delicacy of feeling, is marred by the obscurity of its theme and its uncertain conclusion. The memorable aspect of Eudora Welty's fiction remains the world she has created out of her experience of the American South.

If instead of the chronology of her publications we consider the places which make up that world, her stories fall into four main groups. "First Love" and "A Still Moment" concern the Natchez Trace and the nearly untouched forest of a century and a half ago; these are the stories involving historical characters. They dramatize the era in her world that may be described as Before the Fall. In it nature is paramount, or at least man and nature are equal, reverencing one another. The incidents are narrated gravely, as befits the subject, in a controlled style marked by words chosen with great deliberation. The characters are dignified, free from the quirks that usually identify her characters of more recent times. The action, even when violent, is gently disclosed, its point often being rendered by a symbol. In general it may be said that the farther back the era on which her imagination is working, the more symbolically she writes. Whereas her stories of the recent past report directly on what she seems to have herself observed, symbols carry the weight of the meaning when she is working on what she has read or been told about. The essential quality of the wilderness stories is found in the scene from which "A Still Moment" takes its name. As Audubon is about to shoot a white heron, he reflects: "The gaze that looks outward must be trained without rest, to be indomitable. It must see as slowly as Murrell's ant in the grass, as exhaustively as Lorenzo's angel of God, and then, Audubon dreamed, with his mind going to his pointed brush, it must see like this, and he tightened his hand on the trigger of the gun and pulled it, and his eyes went closed. In memory the heron was all its solitude, its total beauty. All its whiteness could be seen from all sides at once, its pure feathers were as if counted and known and their array one upon the other would never be lost. But it was not from that memory that he could paint."

The stories concerned with the countryside in recent years are far more numerous. Their characters, ranging from the absurd to the heroic, are depicted sometimes with sly humor, sometimes with a most moving pathos. There are the unfortunate couple of "The Whistle," who sacrifice even the bedclothes to save the tomato crop; Old Phoenix, in "A Worn Path," with her December journey in search of medicine for her grandchild; and, in the two stories about traveling salesmen, the guitar player and the tenant farmers, who support their lot with grace and dignity. " 'Same songs ever'where,' said the man with the guitar softly. 'I come down from the hills . . . . We had us owls for chickens and fox for yard dogs but we sung true.'" Then there is a whole group of naughty characters—William Wallace Jamieson, Livvie, Ruby Fisher, Mattie Will Holifield—who are busily escaping from the trammels of marriage and asserting their untamable humanity.

A third group of stories, those set in the towns, must be subdivided. Some of them concern the dwellers in the big houses, the ruined mansions; others, the townspeople who work for a living. The division is underscored by a technical difference: where the stories about average people are filled with bustle and movement, the immobile lives of the aristocrats are often suggested by a device that may reflect Eudora Welty's earlier interest in photography. This is the arrested moment, the scene that is, as it were, caught by a click of the camera's shutter, where the very stillness of the scene is essential to its meaning. In "Asphodel," for instance, three old maids picnic near six white columns, which, with a fragment of the entablature, are all that remain of a Doric portico. Behind it the house has burned and become a habitation only for goats. " 'This is Asphodel,' they repeated, looking modestly upward to the frieze of maidens that was saturated with sunlight and seemed to fill with color, and before which the branch of a leafy tree was trembling." In other stories the well-born characters include Mr. Marblehall, who has two wives and a son by each, and Clytie, who cares for her paralyzed father, drunken brother, and half-mad sister. Clytie at last drowns herself in the rain barrel, "with her poor ladylike black-stockinged legs up-ended and hung apart like a pair of tongs." The working class of the towns is represented by the family in "Why I Live at the P. O.," a dramatic soliloquy that has enlarged the boundaries of American humor; by several of the characters in "Lily Daw and the Three Ladies"; and by the traveling salesmen, Tom Harris and R. J. Bowman. These two stories, among the finest that Eudora Welty has written, juxtapose town and country characters in a manner entirely her own. Like Bowman in "Death of a Traveling Salesman," Harris, the salesman in "The Hitch-Hikers," reflects the pathos that lies in the lonely rootlessness of modern life. "Walking over to the party, so as not to use his car, making the only sounds in the dark wet street, and only partly aware of the indeterminate shapes of houses with their soft-shining fanlights marking them off, there with the rain falling mist-like through the trees, he almost forgot what town he was in and which house he was bound for."

A fourth setting that Eudora Welty has occasionally employed, particularly in her newest collection, is that of the metropolis: New Orleans, San Francisco, New York. Such stories as "Flowers for Marjorie" and "No Place for You, My Love" develop further the sense of exile, of human beings on whom inhuman lives are imposed. These stories, though no admirer would rank them among Eudora Welty's best, complete her view of the modern world. "Music from Spain" was first published separately, by the Levee Press, and seemed then to lack force and point. Read as part of The Golden Apples, it makes clear what Morgana stands for: the little town from which all but its more vegetable inhabitants must from time to time consider fleeing. Yet in the loneliness of exile, Eugene MacLain looks back with longing to the comparatively primitive life of his boyhood. Morgana, with all its simplicity, was an organism, to which its people could feel that they belonged. It must, however, be written of in the past tense: most of the incidents in *The Golden Apples* take place in 1910 or a little later.

Eugene MacLain's life was transformed by his moving to San Francisco. For those who remain, as his twin brother Randall does, the transformation occurs in the people and the towns themselves. The high point of Randall's story is his seduction of a girl on an iron bedstead in a tourist cabin (in "The Whole World Knows"). The incident recalls the coarseness of the women in "Petrified Man," which had appeared in Eudora Welty's first book, but this time the story is told with compassion, in place of the horrified amusement that the women's absurdity inspires. Taken together, the stories of the modern city and the modern town imply the level of existence to which humanity is drifting, across the span of years that extends from the death of the white heron to the present day. The simplicities of life in Morgana, Mississippi, caught at the moment that its organic life is dissolving, represent perhaps the midpoint of the process.

The title of *The Golden Apples* recalls the Greek myth, and the first story compares its hero to Zeus; but the action is firmly grounded in the ordinary life of a Mississippi town some forty years ago. (Not that its dominant episodes are ordinary occurrences.) It affords countless examples of Eudora Welty's ability to catch the absurd but authentic mannerisms of her characters, as in Mrs. Morrison's answer when her daughter asks her if she could have learned the piano: "'Child, I could have *sung*,' and she threw her hand from her, as though all music might as well now go and jump off the bridge." Lightly told as most of the stories are, the theme of *The Golden Apples,* like that of "A Still Moment," is the loss of innocence, the journey from childhood to maturity, or, in keeping with the Hellenic title, we should more properly say the Golden vs. the Silver Age.

The most ambitious and most successful of these stories is "June Recital," a story of points of view, which was perhaps inspired by the famous passage in James's preface to *The Portrait of a Lady:* "The house of fiction has in short not one window, but a million . . . at each of them stands a figure with a pair of eyes, or at least with a field-glass, which forms, again, and again, for observation, a unique instrument, insuring to the person making use of it an impression distinct from every other." One of the windows in "June Recital" belongs to the younger Morrison child, Loch, who is spending a summer afternoon in bed with malaria. His boredom explains his interest in the house next door, visible from his window; and because he has malaria he is permitted to use his father's telescope. His fever also produces a slight distortion in what he alone can see occurring in the other house, both because he has the telescope and because there is nothing to distract his attention. As the story develops, these circumstances are seen to be symbolically related to Loch's innocence of sex, love, and the pathos of a lonely old age.

In the next room, meanwhile, Loch's sister Cassie, who is less ignorant about at least the first of these, is dyeing a scarf to wear this night on a hayride. Loch cannot get her attention on the strange activities that he is watching in the other house, an almost abandoned old house, inhabited only by a night watchman, who sleeps in the afternoon. Loch has seen a sailor carry a girl in at the back door and make love to her on a bare mattress in a room upstairs, but that interests him less than the old woman who enters at the front door and begins to festoon the living room with newspapers. (She has escaped from her keepers and intends to set the house on fire.) Then she goes to the piano and plays the opening bars of a piece called *Für Elise*—which brings Cassie to her window.

Cassie looks toward the other house, but in the sunlit afternoon she cannot see inside. The tune, however, takes her thoughts back to the events that led up to the present degradation of the girl and the old woman. The woman is Miss Eckhart, who once gave music lessons in the room that she is now trying to destroy, and Virgie Rainey was her only talented pupil. *Für Elise* was Virgie's particular piece—though at the annual recital she played concertos by Liszt and even harder selections. She was the consolation of Miss Eckhart's bitter and lonely existence, yet on finishing high school she has become the piano player at the local picture show.

The fascination of "June Recital" is that it invites the reader to combine the limited points of view of Cassie and Loch.

Cassie, who fully recalls the past incidents that lead up to the present, cannot see into it; for one thing, she "was practicing on her ukelele again so she could sing to the boys." Loch, at the other window, sees the present fully, but is too inexperienced to understand it. When Miss Eckhart throws the metronome, a symbol of time, into the yard, he climbs down a branch outside his window and retrieves it. But he does not know what a metronome is. He imagines, half seriously, that it is a bomb. Returning to his bed, he falls asleep as the sun sets. "A cloud lighted anew, low in the deep sky, a single long wing. The mystery he had felt like a golden and aimless bird had waited until now to fly over."

When Cassie comes back from the hayride, her thoughts return to Miss Eckhart and Virgie Rainey; and as she too falls asleep she grasps at least a part of the mystery. "Both Miss Eckhart and Virgie Rainey were human beings terribly at large, roaming on the face of the earth. And there were others of them—human beings, roaming, like lost beasts."

If "June Recital" and other parts of The Golden Apples show Eudora Welty's serious writing at its best, her humorous treatment of small-town life reaches its climax in The Ponder Heart. In many ways, Edna Earle is the same woman as Lily Daw's three ladies and the speakers in "Why I Live at the P. O." and "Shower of Gold." But in theme The Ponder Heart belongs with The Golden Apples and some of the earlier serious stories, as may be seen by comparing it with its stage version, the work of Joseph Fields and Jerome Chodorov, who ruthlessly blunt its point. Both versions end with the acquittal of Uncle Daniel, but in their ways of reaching this denouement they differ considerably. The stage Daniel, when at last he understands that he is the accused, pleads guilty—on the grounds that his return to Bonnie Dee caused her heart to burst with love. The jury does not even find it necessary to retire before deciding to acquit, and Daniel leaves the courtroom in triumph with his late wife's younger sister.

Eudora Welty's novel, on the other hand, is related to "Death of a Traveling Salesman." There are likenesses of detail: the town of Beulah, for instance, is R. J. Bowman's destination, and Mr. Springer, a salesman, pays frequent visits to Edna Earle while she is managing the Beulah Hotel. A far more important likeness, however, is that *The Ponder Heart* recalls the contrast between Bowman's world and that of the hill couple. The novel, to be sure, reverses the point of view, so that the town of Clay is revealed from within rather than approached from without, as is the hill couple's life. But Clay is nonetheless contrasted with that world which has produced Bowman: declaring her uncle's innocence, Edna Earle says that " 'he wouldn't have done anything to anybody in the world for all you could give him, and nobody, you'd think, would do anything to him. Why, he's been brought up in a world of love.' " It is, in short, an Eden—or has been until Bonnie Dee's death and the arrival of the Evil One in the shape of the lawyer, Gladney. Although Gladney loses his case, his symbolic victory is complete: Daniel, who has managed to draw out all the Ponder money, secures his acquittal by scattering it over the courtroom. At the end of the novel "that money has come between the Ponders and everybody else in town," and Daniel, expelled from his Eden, finds himself as lonely as Bowman.

To dwell long on the theme of such a masterpiece of the comic imagination as *The Ponder Heart* is to risk distorting it. Its theme is here emphasized to show the continuity that runs underneath the surface variety of Eudora Welty's stories. The essential point about them is neither the reality of their settings nor the abstract worth of their themes and attitudes, but the relationship of the one to the other. The presiding genius of her work is her sense of place; it is what makes her feelings trustworthy. And the fusion of setting and theme, to conclude with yet another quotation from "Place in Fiction," has been nowhere better described than by a sentence in that essay. "The moment the place in which the novel happens is accepted as true, through it will begin to glow, in a kind of recognizable glory, the feeling and thought that inhabited the novel in the author's head and animated the whole of his work."

ANDREW LYTLE

BY THOMAS H. CARTER

When Andrew Lytle published a novel called *The Velvet Horn* in 1957, what some critics had maintained all along became evident to a large audience: that this fifty-eight-year-old Tennessean is one of the most original and accomplished fiction writers of his time.

Even a sensitive reader may have missed the full impact of Lytle's accomplishment. His novels have been few and slow to come. Aside from the obvious ability they all reflect, they bear no superficial resemblance to one another. Since Lytle varies his texture to suit his story, they do not even have a common style. Lytle's development has been slow, not in talent (which was always plain) but in increasing awareness. Writing, like living, is a process of learning, a progressive understanding of oneself and one's culture. As an artist, Lytle has been steadily growing, and new knowledge suffuses each novel. This is a critical, not a biographical, fact, apparent from the fiction; yet biography is important.

Andrew Lytle has taken part in the most important literary association, in America, of this century, the Fugitive–Agrarian conjunction at Vanderbilt. (At the Fugitives' reunion at Vanderbilt in 1956, those presiding attempted to dissociate the two, but it could not be done.) Lytle was born in Tennessee in 1902 and attended Vanderbilt, graduating in 1925. There he knew the Fugitive poets, who were arguing about aesthetics and poetry and publishing *The Fugitive*. Although Lytle wrote little verse, he was elected to the editorial board of the magazine just before it ceased publication. The Vanderbilt writers were deadly serious about the arts, a thing almost unheard of in the South at that time. Moreover, the Old South, doomed since at least the Civil War and now changing inexorably into the New South, was generating that special awareness that sometimes results in literature; Allen Tate has called it a looking two ways. This is a fit subject for a writer, but one that Lytle has never taken for his own, even though he has stated that the Vanderbilt writers showed him his true occupation.

After graduation, Lytle managed a cotton farm for his father, then spent two years under George Pierce Baker in the Yale School of Drama. He lived a year in New York, acting for a living, while he did the research on his Civil War biography, *Bedford Forrest and His Critter Company* (Tate and Warren also wrote Civil War biographies). It is difficult to assess just what Lytle learned from his drama apprenticeship. The plays he wrote have not been published. But in his earliest fiction he is master of what Henry James called "the scenic art"; he can structure a scene deftly and dramatically, giving it the air of felt reality. His 1947 novel, *A Name for Evil*, is a succession of quick scenes, always under control, driving rapidly toward a climax.

When he returned to Tennessee, Lytle became involved with the Vanderbilt-centered Agrarian symposium *I'll Take My Stand* (1930), whose essays were written by former Fugitives Ransom—who, on stylistic evidence must have composed the introduction—Davidson, Tate, Warren, and other recruits, some of whom, like Frank Owsley, felt passionately concerned. Lytle contributed a well-researched cry of the heart defending the agricultural South against encroaching industrialism. But it is possible, as I shall suggest presently, to make too much of Lytle's Agrarianism.

Lytle taught college history, edited the *Sewanee Review*, and, alone among the Agrarians, attempted to farm—which, predictably, he found "incompatible" with writing. Since he was forced to choose between farming and writing, he chose the latter. He has since taught creative writing—and, naturally, written.

Certainly there is a relationship between Lytle's predilection for Agrarianism and his fiction. However, the fact that Lytle couldn't farm *and* write is without significance; the Agrarians never claimed that agriculture was productive of the literary arts. What they did assert was that the life of the soil offered the most humane existence, and that the South, incompletely industrialized, provided a vantage point for an attack on the prevailing national tendency. They wrote of self-sufficiency, a clearly defined culture deriving from England and Western Europe, a generally humanistic religion, and a highly developed code of manners. They implied a civilization, rich and self-contained—as opposed to the chaotic existence resulting from a money-controlled industrialism.

Many of the Agrarians have modified their views. In 1930 Agrarianism was a topic that exercised Lytle a great deal; it is not clear whether it does still. Occasionally he issues provocative, enigmatic notes and brief essays that suggest the South still has much to teach. (To accuse Lytle of an uncritical defense of the South is absurd; unfortunately, he has never bothered to write out a systematic account of his opinions in a book.) But his Agrarianism has not had an overpowering effect on his fiction. Lytle has chosen to express himself as an artist; he has been concerned that the story find its form, and that the technique reveal the meaning. He never spells out his themes. And a cut-and-dried Agrarianism has never been his subject.

Lytle's first novel, *The Long Night* (1936), is only partially concerned with the Civil War; its initial theme, eventually overwhelmed by the immense presence of the war, is reminiscent of an Elizabethan revenge tragedy. Young Pleasant McIvor, his father maligned and then murdered by a conspiracy of slave stealers, attempts to kill off the criminals one by one.

Before *The Velvet Horn*, whose massive and interlinked action obviously dictates its unique and necessary shape, Lytle appears always to have selected a specific convention for each novel, calculated to reveal the reality investing the presented surface. But in *The Long Night* the revenge motif serves awkwardly—one youth to dispose of some fifty men—and it strains credibility. It is folklore, a tall tale, a story to be told by firelight, not the skeleton of a realistic novel. We are conscious, as we never are in the later work, of the author's manipulating hand.

It seems clear that Lytle himself realized he was in trouble. The story opens in the first person, to establish a listener to old Pleasant McIvor's history; it is taken up by the voice of Pleasant McIvor himself, recounting what has happened—but not for very long. When the quest for revenge is begun, there is a switch to the third person, from which the story is thereafter told. When *The Long Night* was published, Mr. John Ransom objected that this switch was aesthetically jarring, a violation of point of view. (The form of *The Long Night,* as Lytle later remarked, was suggested by the *Odyssey,* which not only has an episodic plot but is very free with its point of view.) But it must have been plain to Lytle, as he saw more deeply the nature of his story, that the objectivity of the third-person approach was necessary. In all, Pleasant kills—often with a knife—some fifteen men. Yet we see him neither as the youth who lived with his parents nor as a kind of sympathetic monster. He is made rigid and unswerving by vengeance. We can watch him in action; we can share the report of his senses; but clearly we cannot share his state of mind.

Lytle employs an impressive variety of skills to make this half of the novel successful. He relies heavily on the enveloping action, all the lives that go on simultaneously with that of his protagonist, resulting at worst in a living texture, at best in a confrontation that forces meaning at a climactic point. To make us believe in the reality of an avenger we can't credit, Lytle puts the woods where Pleasant hides—its sights, sounds, and smells—concretely before us. He presents vignettes of the doomed men; he sketches in sparse but effective detail the lives of the innocent men and women about to be touched. He gains in variety and, more important, in that illusion of life which makes us present at the scene, almost participants in the act. But in his protagonist, he cannot make us believe.

At the beginning of the Civil War, Pleasant enlists in the Confederate Army. His original purpose is blunted, and when he tries to return to it, he deliberately fails on a scouting mission, and his best friend is lost. (For Lytle, friendship is an enduring value.) Pleasant, feeling that he has betrayed his friend to death, immediately deserts.

But Pleasant's fate scarcely matters. What suddenly does matter, for author and reader, is the war. Lytle has found his true subject. Although the Agrarians have been accused of doing so, Lytle does not wave an old flag; he simply brings to bear on the Battle of Shiloh the same immense and careful skill he brought to bear on Pleasant's life in the forest. It is a virtuoso performance. He employs the panoramic view and the short vivid scene, shifting from Johnston's headquarters to the men in the line, whirling the reader backward and forward but never letting him become confused.

Lytle can make men of history accessible to our perception without diminishing their magnitude. (Whether Johnston is the man Lytle says he is, is for historians to determine, if they can.) In the rapidity of the battle scenes, Lytle characterizes his soldiers and officers in less than a paragraph. The enveloping action takes the foreground, and Pleasant recedes, as do many others, to a post of observation. Lytle's achievement is to make the battle instantly immediate, as it is seen by the observing officers, and as it is seen by the soldiers in the broil of combat. The second half of *The Long Night* is a triumph of controlled point of view.

I have lingered so long over Lytle's first, imperfect novel because it demonstrates its author's early skill at "rendering," and, after an initial confusion, of the handling of point of view; as well as, of course, his acute sense of pace.

The Long Night also hints at many of Lytle's constant pre-occupations: with death—often with violent death, handled compassionately—as one of the mysteries of life; with nature, as one of the definitive factors in human destiny; with history, though ultimately more with private than public history; with what goes to make up a man and his culture (part of the subject of *The Velvet Horn*); with love, as one of the basic forces that make a man human (it influenced Pleasant McIvor to rejoin humanity); and, finally, with kinship, the sense of family, the family unit as a shaper of society. There is, further, Lytle's genuine but unobtrusive idealization of woman, first hinted at in the character of Pleasant's mother.

Lytle learned from *The Long Night*; his technical control grew surer, and his second novel, *At the Moon's Inn* (1941), has an aesthetic and narrative unity, though its conclusion, the death of de Soto, does not bring the subject to entire articulation. De Soto's death, one feels, results from the inevitable failure of his nearly unconscious attempt to elevate his human will to a Godlike eminence—which is, after all, central to the theme which informs the novel. If the beginning of *At the Moon's Inn* seems overlong—one does begin to wonder just what the author is about—the conclusion, in its prose texture, is murky; but these blemishes appear minor when conjoined with the brilliant, lengthy middle section, which in depth and seriousness is quite unlike anything else in modern fiction.

The subject of *At the Moon's Inn* is historical, the story of Hernando de Soto's "conquest" of Florida, a land barren of the gold he so avidly sought. The novel has something of the nature of a late medieval chronicle, and it is apparent that Lytle did a thorough job of research. But research will go only so far; the main burden always falls on the imagination.

At the Moon's Inn opens with a "prologue" in Spain, before the expedition, which acquaints us with the principal characters. De Soto is the point of focus, and, later it is his determination that holds the expedition together. We are not told his thoughts; we know him as we know an acquaintance—by watching his actions and hearing him talk. His wife tries to persuade him not to go to Florida; her plea simply makes no impression on him, and he makes love to her that night, despite her protest. At once his character is established: he will have his way and will automatically overcome objections by force or guile.

He makes an excellent commander; his will subdues and unites the soldiers he leads into Florida. Once the expedition is begun, the story is told from the point of view of Tovar, previously second-in-command to de Soto but now reduced in rank. This reduction serves Lytle well; Tovar reflects the opinions of both officers and ordinary soldiers. He is devoted to de Soto; his feeling of closeness to the commander humanizes a figure who has abstracted himself to a single purpose. Tovar, despite his experience and skill, could not have led the expedition as successfully as de Soto, for he accepts the world and himself; he heeds—perhaps rashly—his senses. Unlucky in love, he knows the value of love; in Florida he marries an Indian woman.

Although de Soto hears no reports of gold in Florida (he has been dreaming of another Peru), he determines to move inward. There is an epic march. This is naturally limited to the short view; but there can be no long view when men are continually breaking new ground. Hence we see most of the invasion through Tovar's eyes. Our attention is held by the enveloping action; but above the broil of the march we are aware of de Soto's will overcoming obstacle after obstacle. Lytle's narrative gift, shown as early as *Bedford Forrest and His Critter Company* (revised edition, 1960), sustains him now; the pace is rapid, but not too rapid to reveal the discomfort of the invaders; the incidents are varied; and one intense scene stands for many.

Lytle's handling of the Indians shows a rare literary tact. They are portrayed at home, living their everyday lives, and also as they appear to the invaders, as uniquely bloodthirsty savages. To the Spaniards they represent an incomprehensible, alien culture from which they instinctively recoil. De Soto has come both to seek gold and—always the paradox—to bring salvation at the point of the sword. In the end he is overwhelmed by the strangeness of Florida and its inhabitants. Lytle is too sure an artist to take sides. It would be facile to say that the Indians are early Agrarian victims of capitalistic exploitation; but Lytle carefully keeps himself within the range of Tovar's awareness.

De Soto does face a peculiarly modern predicament arising from the heart of the medieval world. After the battle of Mauvilla, which the Spaniards won at the cost of their gear, de Soto is attending Mass, his head reverently bowed, when the priest abruptly halts the ceremony and orders him by the authority of the Host to leave Florida. De Soto is stunned. He has never doubted the teachings of the Church, or his own piety; he has believed it the will of God that this savage land be pacified. Lytle has deliberately, perhaps symbolically, kept at a distance from de Soto, as though none of the soldiers could understand their commander's fierce determination. The strain shows on the commander's person. De Soto decides; he takes the Host from the priest, and in so doing takes the spiritual power upon himself.

He has not wanted to; the issue has been forced upon him. It was the Church, in the person of this priest, which had decided to influence temporal matters. De Soto has only his unchecked will to fall back on. The meaning of a novel lies in the relation of all its parts, but this scene is the decisive climax of *At the Moon's Inn,* and it prefigures the modern dilemma in which spiritual and temporal authorities confusedly usurp one another's realm.

Lytle's third novel, *A Name for Evil* (1947), is a slight and puzzling volume. The novel resulted from Lytle's reading again *The Turn of the Screw* and asking himself: What would happen if adults rather than children were placed in a similar situation? The novelist began to experiment with the form of James's novel, as poets sometimes experiment, say, with a sonnet. But after thirty pages or so, the story took over.

Stylistically, *A Name for Evil* appears to be Lytle's least distinguished work. The narrator is a modern man called Henry Brent; and while Lytle's acute and solid observation is still present, this time it seems as lifeless as a catalogue. However, Lytle means his style to be more functional than ever; events, striking and important, tumble pell-mell after one another until the reader becomes unaware of the actual writing except as a medium to register the action. But soon—and this is one of the devices by which Lytle characterizes—the style begins to reflect a mind seriously disturbed, with moments of ominous calm or, worse, a somehow sinister elation. We have been deceived by the lack of color in the style; its factual transparency establishes a norm by which to measure the later disturbance. Tone and texture create a world in which a ghost story may take place.

Conceivably the novel may be interpreted in many different ways, which is to say that it is ambiguous, and deliberately so; but we must begin with what Henry Brent sees, or thinks he sees. His head full of Agrarian notions, Henry Brent wants to buy and restore The Lodge, the ruined country estate of a dead connection, Major Brent. His fragile wife, Ellen, agrees, and the purchase is made. The couple begin immediately on the restoration, but it appears almost hopeless. The attempt at restoration is the initial enveloping action, but its importance grows progressively less; attention is focused on the main action—a drama isolated from the outside world.

Henry Brent encounters the figure of Major Brent, who must be long dead; it is evident that the figure does not desire the restoration and, more especially, has designs of some nature on Ellen. Without confiding in her, Henry Brent tries ineffectually to protect his wife, who is disturbed by *his* violent and unusual manner. Shortly after revealing that she is pregnant, Ellen is accidentally killed by falling through the rotten timbers of the springhouse, frightened, perhaps, by the appearance of her husband, or, as he sees it, lured on by Major Brent.

There can be no question that *A Name for Evil* is that hardest thing to write: a successful ghost story. The events all seem native to The Lodge; and when we begin to know the narrator, they seem inevitable. But what actually happens? Is Major Brent *really* Major Brent, as the narrator believes? Or is he the lingering spirit of malicious evil able to manifest himself only through others? Does he "possess" Henry Brent, who lives in his house and works in his fields, making him terrible enough to frighten a delicate lady to her death? The past will make itself felt. Henry Brent feels it too strongly. Is Henry Brent obsessed, even mad, at times? This would account for his wife's pathetic efforts not merely to pacify him but to live the kind of life he wants. Again, the theme of love.

A Name for Evil, representing a solid yet quicksilver reality, is infinitely richer for its ambiguity. Although it deals with the South and makes use of Agrarian ideas, its use of these ideas is dramatic, not propositional, and the story could as well have happened in New England. Sphinxlike, it refuses to comment on Agrarianism and the South. Henry Brent is deranged, for whatever reason; he represents an extreme case. And he is a daft Agrarian. He meant literally to restore the past, and when that happens, the result is always a Major Brent.

Andrew Lytle's most impressive achievement to date, an end and a beginning, is *The Velvet Horn*, which he spent nine years in writing. Technically it is smoothly joined and all of a piece, though the opening section is a little jammed. At the same time, it is infinitely varied and complex; it offers the richness and confusion of life. An entire subculture, that of the Cumberlands hill country of the late nineteenth century, is dramatized.

The story deals with self-knowledge. Apparently the protagonist is young Lucius Cree, and the determination of his fate closes the book. In fact, the narrative device employed is that of the "roving narrator"; the dominating, and evaluating, intelligence is that of Lucius's uncle, Jack Cropleigh; and Lytle keeps him so constantly in the reader's attention that actual, brief shifts from mind to mind are unobtrusive. Of *The Velvet Horn*, Lytle has written: "Everybody was the hero and heroine, but only Jack Cropleigh, the brother and uncle, could represent them, for Jack, the spiritual hermaphrodite, contained them all in his mind. He alone could suffer the myth" ("The Working Novelist and the Mythmaking Process," *Daedalus*, Spring, 1959).

The myth that Jack suffers is that of the Garden of Eden, and his special awareness—to his nephew Lucius he is both tutor and the living, approachable past—forces on him the role of an enigmatic Hamlet; unavoidably, he talks too much. But most of it is good talk.

Lytle has never spent more time on the enveloping action, which occupies an unusual amount of space. This is essential, for at times of crisis secondary characters, more closely linked to Lucius than he expects, step forward to fill their appointed roles in the main action. Everything, including the precise imagery, fits together without any apparent contrivance. Lytle's gaze is clearer than ever, he never misses the telling detail; the pace is sure; the time shift is used, not—as in much of Lytle's previous work—for suspense, but for revelation.

As far as he knows, Lucius Cree is the son of Captain Joe Cree, a respected businessman. While Lucius's Uncle Jack is on the mountain to witch a well, and Lucius himself has taken to the nearby woods with Ada Belle Rutter (the indigent, shiftless Rutters that neither the Crees nor the Cropleighs, his mother's people, can accept socially), Captain Joe Cree deliberately puts himself in the path of a falling tree. Lucius, when he is informed, realizes that it must have been suicide.

As uncle and nephew return home on a wagon, there is a time shift in Jack's consciousness, the technical skill of which recalls Ford Madox Ford. Its burden is the youth of the orphaned Cropleighs and their attempt to maintain a primeval innocence beyond its season. Predictable disaster strikes when, on a hunt, the Cropleigh brothers find their sister Julia—in time, Lucius's mother—asleep in the arms of Pete Legrand. Duncan, half wild anyway and loving Julia more than any of the brothers, engages Legrand in a knife duel in which the latter is fearfully slashed, but lives to nurse a dreadful, patient love for Julia.

The more civilized of the brothers, Dickie and Jack, resort to convention: Julia must marry Cousin Joe Cree, who has asked for her hand. As a person, Duncan is permanently ruined, but the danger is apparently circumvented. Lucius is raised as Joe Cree's son; and it is to the fact that he is not, as Legrand inadvertently blurts out after Captain Cree's death, that he must adjust. Learning the truth (perhaps only a half truth), Lucius knows immediately that he is not what he has always assumed himself to be; he must achieve a personal identity.

Love has always been a central theme for Lytle. But there is something unworldly in the Cropleigh children's love for each other. Their love was freely felt and freely given, but it was a willed love, ignoring time and the world (as brother Beverly, who fled to the wilderness, tried to ignore mankind). No one can remain innocent and a child forever; but still, without clear knowledge, they tried. (Their attempt, as Lytle has pointed out, is archetypal, existing outside of time, but recurrent within it. Naturally, the innocence and wholeness of Eden, before Eve was drawn from Adam's side, cannot be restored.) Sympathetic as Lytle is to their bond, he does not attempt to disguise the abyss they skirted and finally fell into. Julia spent twenty years of marriage with Joe Cree, with Lucius as their son (certainly *her* son), but when Jack is murdered, she rejects Lucius. The bond is too finely drawn.

The reader must conclude that it was Duncan himself, in his despair, who first violated their innocence and is consequently Lucius's real father. This Lucius never learns, though it is Joe Cree's knowledge of it that makes him walk under the falling tree. For Lucius, the sudden belief that he is Pete Legrand's bastard is sufficient shock to make him look inward, to see who, as a person, he really is.

Here we have two generations, two stories, the mother's directly affecting the son's; but the two generations cannot forcibly be welded together. Lucius is left with only partial knowledge. And the bloody events of one time are pale to a later. Yet the action hinges on the question of Lucius's paternity. As a problem in sheer technique, it is immensely difficult.

Lytle's resourcefulness is especially apparent as he twines the two stories together. He uses the time shift and the conversational reference; but it is his use of Jack's wide and encompassing awareness—in a sense, Jack, with no life of his own, has, like Tiresias, foresuffered all—that finally makes both stories seem contemporary and equally important.

Lytle divides his dramatization of the Eden myth in *The Velvet Horn* into three stages. First, there is Adam alone, the creature entire and innocent. When Eve is extracted from his side, the perpetual conflict begins; incest is the symbol. Incest represents the attempt to restore to unity a violated being. (Hence the deceptive label on the dust wrapper: "A novel of man's search for wholeness.") The third stage is the effort to fit the parts into a whole that will constitute knowledge; the symbol is the serpent, "the old intruder"—here, Pete Legrand.

The "velvet horn" itself is, of course, the controlling symbol. Animals are not horned by sexual classification. A buck with velvet still on his horns is, in his way, innocent, suggesting another sort of hermaphrodite. When he does rub off the velvet against a tree, he has instinctively readied himself for definitive male action.

One point must be made. A symbol, by definition, is a sign, like a traffic light; a myth, or if one prefers, a *false* myth, can be merely a pretty tale. Their bodily importation into fiction guarantees nothing; it often hints of sham. Lytle's own conception is organic: "myth: symbol: archetype—the structure: the image: the conflict of the ever recurring human experience."

Lytle's symbols have a literal counterpart, as all symbols must; they are grounded solidly in the text itself, and the reader automatically proceeds on a level of literalism. The prose texture itself determines what he makes of what he reads. The myth of the Garden dominates the structure of the story; Lytle has made it, for the duration of *The Velvet Horn* (which is all one can ask of myth "incarnated" in fiction), important as primeval or recurrent insight into human life; but any novel must stand or fall by its naturalistic surfaces. And *The Velvet Horn* demonstrates a mastery of naturalistic surface. (Cf., for a relevant example in which so fundamental a necessity is utterly ignored, the failure of Faulkner's *A Fable*.)

"The feeling and knowledge [Jack] suffers," Lytle writes, "pass progressively through the three phases of the Garden's drama, renewing through the nephew, the inheritor, the same perpetual cycle." Surely not. The recurrence of the myth has been dramatized in terms of highly singular circumstances. *The Velvet Horn*, though Lucius does finally elect to build his own house from the timber of the tree that crushed Captain Cree, scarcely suggests that Lucius must suffer, in his turn, the full force of the myth. This does not, of course, invalidate the novel, or even weaken it. Perhaps, by isolating Lytle's one-sentence explanation from the context of a lengthy essay, we read it too strictly.

Even a cursory reading of *The Velvet Horn* makes plain that what Lucius inherits is simply the human condition, one manifestation of which Lytle has brought sharply to focus. That the myth of the Garden, as an archetype, may or may not recur, is off the point; I cannot see its recurrence for Lucius, in recognizable form: it would require new circumstances and a rather different character.

Lucius lacks a sense of place, therefore of identity. His urgent need is to be somebody in himself, not just somebody's son. His first step is to marry the illiterate but womanly Ada Belle Rutter. She is pregnant, and he vows that his child will have *his* name. He undertakes to cut the stand of timber which Captain Cree's men had been felling at the time of his death. At first Lucius is bewildered, lost, but finally he begins to hope. He senses, without words, the truth Lytle has expended his skill preparing for. Gradually, despite his uncertainty, Lucius is himself becoming a man.

And suddenly we see that *The Velvet Horn* dramatizes, among other things, a rigorous but not unique initiation rite: Lucius is the extreme case of a universal need. A legitimate name, inheritance, help a man, and they mold him too. Lucius is free. He has been shaped by circumstances; he cannot escape the tug of his blood; but he can know these for what they are. In the beginning, when he and his Uncle Jack were off on a lark to witch a well, he had whispered, "I can be anything I want." Now, waiting for the murdered Jack's words perhaps to turn to knowledge, he can hope, even if the hope is raw. He can be his own man.

The superficial reader, we may note in closing, tends to assume a resemblance in the work of Lytle and Faulkner, at least in those fictions of Lytle's concerned with the South. Often Lytle and Faulkner deal with the same society; they know its composite appearance well. But their interpretations, a "metaphysical grasp" like that of the historian's, are totally unlike. The "styles" of the two men—Faulkner comes much closer to having an overriding style than Lytle, though neither man is trapped by style, as Hemingway is—are completely dissimilar; their subject matter seldom overlaps; and their basic attitudes toward life—what Tate, in a justly famous phrase, has called "knowledge carried to the heart"—are very nearly at opposite poles.

I have tried to indicate that Andrew Lytle is as unique as he is important among contemporary writers of fiction. Always he has followed his own bent; it has led him down strange paths, like that to Peru ("Alchemy"). He is a Southern writer because he was born in the South and knows it intimately, yet he is not obsessed with its predictable burdens; he has an active intelligence that worries with a subject until he has understood it. Like Lucius Cree, he is his own man; and his novels, issued over the years, amply document that fact.

KATHERINE ANNE PORTER AND
HISTORIC MEMORY

BY RAY B. WEST, JR.

In describing Miranda, the little girl in the short story entitled "The Grave," Katherine Anne Porter wrote: "Miranda, with her powerful social sense, which was like a fine set of antennae radiating from every pore of her skin." Miranda appears as a character in "Old Mortality," "Pale Horse, Pale Rider," and in the short stories which open *The Leaning Tower*. In general, Miranda is the mask for the author when the short story is fashioned from autobiographical material and told from the author's point of view. Insofar as the short stories are concerned—as short stories—this fact is of no importance. Insofar, however, as we are concerned with Katherine Anne Porter as a Southern author, the fact is necessary information. Miss Porter's talent consists of just such a sensibility as she attributes to Miranda. She herself has said that her method of composition is to write from memory. When a remembered incident strikes her as having meaning, she makes a note; then, as details accumulate, she adds other notes. At some point in the process, all the individual details seem suddenly to merge into a pattern. With her notes about her, she sits down and writes the short story. Many of her notes begin simply: "Remember."

How such moments occur we can deduce from another passage concerning Miranda in "The Grave," where Miss Porter says: "One day she was picking her path among the puddles and crushed refuse of a market street in a strange city of a strange country, when without warning, plain and clear in its true colors as if she looked through a frame upon a scene that had not stirred nor changed since the moment it happened, the episode of that far-off day leaped from its burial place before her mind's eye." What "leaped," of course, was not merely the episode, but the full composition of the picture—the events with their pattern of meaning. "The Grave" is the story of how Miranda and her brother Paul discovered a gold ring and a small silver dove, which had once served as a screwhead for a coffin, in the emptied grave where her grandfather had lain before his final transfer from a home burial plot to the big new public cemetery; it is also about how Paul killed a rabbit which was just about to give birth to young, and how the knowledge of the young unborn bodies lying within the womb of the dead animal was first a secret between them, then finally forgotten, until it was suddenly remembered years later "in a strange city of a strange country." "It was a very hot day and the smell in the market, with its piles of raw flesh and wilting flowers, was like the mingled sweetness and corruption she had smelled that other day in the empty cemetery at home: the day she had remembered always until now vaguely as the time she and her brother had found treasure in the opened graves."

This "memory," as it became a short story in "The Grave," is much more than the remembered incident. It is a story about birth and death, about the beginning of life and the corruption of life. The words "innocent" and "evil" do not appear in the story, except symbolically and by implication, but the story is one of the initiation of the innocent by knowledge. The gold ring which Miranda received from her brother in exchange for the small silver dove symbolizes knowledge and suggests qualities which that knowledge possesses. It is about the time "she and her brother found treasure in the opened graves," and by the end of the story, when this passage occurs, we recognize the double intention of the words: the innocent "treasure" of childhood and the sweet, mysterious, guilty "treasure" of maturity.

How did the incident come to take on this burden of meaning? No complete answer can be given, of course. We must begin vaguely by saying that Katherine Anne Porter's creative sensitivity, like Miranda's, is a "powerful social sense," which detects special and subtle meanings in experience and translates them into fiction. By this, we mean that her senses, "like a fine set of antennae," detect meanings in experience which are then transformed into aesthetic experiences, where the meanings are made available through their embodiment in recognizable images, characters, and events. What we are to be most concerned with in this account is the nature of the experience upon which that sensibility operates.

Katherine Anne Porter was born in Texas in 1894, of a family which traced its ancestry to Daniel Boone, the Kentucky pioneer. If we take the account of Miranda's background in the stories from *The Leaning Tower* as being roughly autobiographical, we can say that the family had moved, within the lifetime of Miss Porter's grandmother, from Kentucky into Louisiana, and from there to Texas. As with most Southern families, it had retained a strong sense of family unity as well as an awareness of its place in the framework of Southern history and Southern society. The grandfather, although he had died before the family left Kentucky and even though the move itself was mainly necessitated by his imprudence, moved with the family each time they were uprooted, for his grave "had been twice disturbed in his long repose by the constancy and possessiveness of his widow. She removed his bones first to Louisiana and then to Texas as if she had set out to find her own burial place, knowing well she would never return to the places she had left."

Miss Porter's experience, then, is not only of the fixed, almost absolute values of Southern society, but also of our relationship to them in the face of a history of movement and of change. In addition, the family was Scotch and Catholic, inheriting a rugged stubbornness as its national inheritance, a determined set of moral values from its religion. When the grandmother talked about "all the important appearances of life, and especially about the rearing of the young," she "relied with perfect acquiescence on the dogma that children were conceived in sin and brought forth in iniquity. Childhood was a long state of instruction and probation for adult life, which was in turn a long, severe, undeviating devotion to duty, the largest part of which consisted in bringing up children."

I realize the dangers of talking about events from a literary work as though they were autobiographical facts. I think the danger in the case of Katherine Anne Porter is lessened, however, by the fact that so much of her subject matter lies within the areas of her own experience: her Southern background, her travels in Mexico and Europe, her Roman Catholic upbringing, and her interest in liberal social causes. Also, in describing once how she had come to write the short story "Old Mortality," her tongue slipped, so that instead of saying, "Miranda's father said. . . ," she made the remark, "*My father* said . . ." In talking with her once about her stories, I asked her about the character Laura in "Flowering Judas." I had been puzzled by this character, because so many of the background facts concerning Laura were similar to those in Katherine Anne Porter's own experience: the strict Catholic upbringing, the interest in modern social causes, and the fact that Miss Porter had taught in Mexico and that when she returned she had brought with her an exhibition of paintings by Mexican school children. Why, then, wasn't this character called Miranda? Was Laura also an autobiographical figure? I asked. No. Laura was modeled upon a friend with whom Miss Porter had taught school in Mexico—but of course she was not merely a portrait of that girl; she was, Miss Porter supposed, a combination of a good many people, just as was the character Braggioni, in the same story. At the same time, the events of "Pale Horse, Pale Rider" —which is a Miranda story—were many of them actual events which happened when Miss Porter was working as a reporter on the *Rocky Mountain News* in Denver during the first war.

The danger arises, of course, when a character possesses traits similar to those belonging to Miranda. But the important thing to notice is that in all cases, Katherine Anne Porter's characters possess qualities which have some point of similarity with her own experience. If they are Irish or Mexican, they are also Roman Catholic—or they are political liberals. They are usually Southerners. I don't mean to suggest this as a serious limitation, but it may help to account for the relatively small amount that Miss Porter has written. At the same time, it may also account for the consistently high level which her work represents, a level probably unsurpassed by any writer of her time. When necessary, she exhibits a range of perception of ordinary manners and mannerisms which is almost uncanny; but usually such qualities, as in the character of Mr. Thompson in "Noon Wine," are attached to a person well within the limits of her own experience. The whole atmosphere of the Thompson place, which is a Western Texas farm in the years between 1896–1905, seems to suggest that such an event must actually have occurred, even if not precisely as it is related in the story, and that the author knew very well the kind of people Mr. and Mrs. Thompson were, even if she did not know exactly these same persons. Mr. Helton, in the same story, who is a Swede and who came from North Dakota, is an interesting and successful character, but he does not occupy so prominent a position in the story and so does not bear so heavy a burden of probability. The events of "Noon Wine" center upon Mr. Thompson's guilt—the psychological effects of an unpremeditated killing; and we can imagine that the story began from a memory either of the event or of the character of Mr. Thompson, or both, in the mind of the author, who was probably about seven or eight years of age at the time of the murder and suicide. It could have begun from the events alone, and the character could have been supplied from other memories; but however it happened, the character at the center of the story was of a type that Miss Porter must have known well, while the less familiar Mr. Helton got into the story because he was necessary to the events.

The important point is that such memory as we are talking about in discussing Miss Porter's talent is not "mere memory," not only memory of something that occurred, but something that occurred within the long history of personal, family, and regional events—finally, within the history of mankind. In referring to the friendship between Sophia Jane, Miranda's grandmother, and her Negro maid in "The Old Order," Miss Porter writes: "The friendship between the two old women had begun in early childhood, and was based on what seemed even to them almost mythical events." Miss Porter treats her memories also as "mythical events."

Myth is, of course, a form of tribal memory, preserving events of the past as a means of justifying and explaining its views of the present. Every society adapts "myth" to its own purposes, either myths which it has transported from elsewhere and uses as a means of organizing its memories, or myths which it has created from events of its own past. Colonial America, as Constance Rourke has pointed out in her book on American humor, created its concept of the typical Yankee, which is as true of the frontier peddler as it is of the modern G.I.—and as untrue. The society of the South was particularly inclined toward the creation of myths—partly, I suppose, because of the amount of Latin influence in its history, partly because of the amount of Anglo-Catholicism, partly because of its Negroes, but mainly because of its closeness to nature and because of the rural nature of its plantation society. The Latin background gave it a regard for manners and romance; the Anglican, a respect for ceremony; while the Negroes fused the two with primitive magic. In addition, the aristocratic and paternalistic structure of the plantation represented a means not only of creating regional and family myth but also of preserving it in a more or less unbroken chain from earliest times down to at least the period of the Civil War.

There have been bitter quarrels with the nature of the Southern myth, but few deny its reality or its importance to the society which it reflected. We may say that the South spent the first years creating its myths, a few important years defending them (even in battle), and its most recent years utilizing them as the subject matter for literature. Perhaps their most complete use is represented in the novels and short stories of William Faulkner, where the timeless world of eternal values of the Southern past is posted against the fluid and pragmatic present. In one way or another these contrasts have got into most Southern writing, whether the poetry of Allen Tate, John Crowe Ransom, John Peale Bishop, Robert Penn Warren, and Donald Davidson, or into the prose fiction of Ellen Glasgow, Caroline Gordon, Stark Young, Eudora Welty, Peter Taylor, Carson McCullers, Tate, Warren, and Katherine Anne Porter. With a special emphasis, it is to be found in the writings of Truman Capote, Elizabeth Hardwick, William Goyen, Tennessee Williams, and Leroy Leatherman. With an inverted emphasis, it is utilized by Erskine Caldwell, Lillian Hellman, and most of the Negro writers of our time.

Yet each author poses a separate problem—not the least of them Katherine Anne Porter. She is less the self-conscious "professional" Southerner than either Donald Davidson or Truman Capote; she shares somewhat in the tendency toward inversion —the liberalism—of Erskine Caldwell. The question of how much an author owes to his region has been discussed endlessly and is now seen as a futile preoccupation, at least insofar as an evaluation of his work is concerned. Even as it concerns the author himself, it has only a limited and often questionable value. But it is tantalizingly present as a puzzle in personality. Just what kind of writer might Katherine Anne Porter have been if she had been born and raised in a Fundamentalist, Protestant New England family in, say, Rutland, Vermont? The question is hypothetical and nonsensical, but it does emphasize the importance of Miss Porter's Southern, Roman Catholic background. How much her sensibility was affected either by her place or her religion must remain a puzzle, but her sensibility is her *self*—including her memory, which she would have had in any case, and she herself *did* grow up in the South of a family with a long history of living in the South; she *was* Roman Catholic; and she did, as the result of an unusually perceptive mind, recognize the importance of that background, not only as subject matter for her works, but also as representing a point of view toward all experience.

Herman Melville has spoken of "historic memory," implying that it is at least one quality of the artist's general "prescience." I can think of no better phrase to describe Miss Porter's special sensibility than to call it "historic memory." Such memory, though it does, as Melville stated, go "far backward through long defiles of doom," begins with the specific present: the young girl finding a carved dove in an abandoned grave and trading it for a gold ring, another remembering the image of a dead aunt preserved in a family photograph and the family memory and contrasting them with the living present, the memory of illness and death during the influenza epidemic at the time of the First World War, the memories of Mexican revolutionaries, of moving-picture companies on location, of Mexican women and West Texas farmers stirred to violence by passion. Partly these memories are controlled by a Catholic sensibility, which seeks out the ceremony and order in the events, partly by a Southern habit of thought that metamorphoses reality into "romance"—not the romance of inferior Southern authors, who see the events as picturesque and quaint manifestations of a peculiar social order, but something nearer the "romance" that Hawthorne sought in his *The House of the Seven Gables*, a romance that links man of the present with the long, legendary concepts of man in a continued and continuing past.

The creation and utilization of myth is, then, in Katherine Anne Porter's work, both subject matter and method. Neither as a Southerner nor as a Catholic is she orthodox—that is, she does not mistake the myth for the reality; for her it is merely another kind of reality. Hawthorne called it "the truths of the human heart." Today, I suppose we should prefer a term such as "psychological truth." The important thing in a short story like "Flowering Judas" is not that Laura fails to escape the conflict between a conservative upbringing and the desire to assist in liberal political causes, but that such a conflict is at the bottom of the whole idea of man's Christian redemption; that there is something Christlike about such a dilemma. The important thing in "Pale Horse, Pale Rider" is not that a young Southern girl found the war horrible or that she suffered from influenza and lost her lover to it, but that the sequence of events mirrored the relationship of man to good and evil. The important thing about "The Jilting of Granny Weatherall" is not merely that a proud and stubborn old lady dies, unable to forget the jilting of a long-lost lover, but that the story reflects a particular, but common, attitude toward death.

Perhaps the most complete instance of a short story which utilizes a specifically Southern background and memory for the creation of this larger, more generalized "truth" is "Old Mortality," where Miss Porter's subject matter is Southern attitudes as expressed through family history, and where the theme is concerned with the nature of reality—particularly with self-definition. The story is told from the point of view of Miranda between the ages of eight and eighteen, and its details agree with all of the other Miranda stories insofar as they detail events in a family which had moved from Kentucky to Louisiana and from there to Texas. At the center of the story are the memories of a girl, Amy, about whose long courtship and brief marriage to "Uncle Gabriel" the aura of "romance" has accumulated. We meet her first in a photograph in the family parlor, "a spirited-looking young woman, with dark curly hair cropped and parted on the side, a short oval face with straight eyebrows, and a large curved mouth." The family legend represents her as a vivacious, daring, and extremely beautiful young girl, against whom the beauty and grace of later members of the family are forever being judged. It tells of her using her cruel beauty to tantalize Uncle Gabriel until he despaired of ever winning her, of her precipitating events at a ball which caused a family scandal and disgrace. It tells of her sad suffering from an incurable illness, of her sudden and romantic marriage to Gabriel, and of her early death.

But the legend, which is more than just a romantic memory of Aunt Amy, is also a reflection of the family's attitude toward all events of the past—memories which Miranda cannot share and an attitude which she cannot adopt because of discrepancies which she senses between such stories, as related by the family, and the actual facts which she perceives in the people and events which surround her in the everyday life of the present. In the photograph of Amy, for instance, "The clothes were not even romantic looking, but merely most terribly out of fashion"; in the talk about the slimness of the women in the family, Miranda is reminded of their Great-Aunt Eliza, "who quite squeezed herself through doors," and of her Great-Aunt Keziah, in Kentucky, whose husband, Great-Uncle John Jacob, "had refused to allow her to ride his good horses after she had achieved two hundred and twenty pounds"; in watching her grandmother crying over her accumulation of ornaments of the past, Miranda saw only "dowdy little wreaths and necklaces, some of them made of pearly shells; such moth-eaten bunches of pink ostrich feathers for the hair; such clumsy big breast pins and bracelets of gold and colored enamel; such silly-looking combs, standing up on tall teeth capped with seed pearls and French paste." Yet despite these disappointing incongruities, the child Miranda struggled to believe that there was "a life beyond a life in this world, as well as in the next"; such episodes as members of her family remembered confirmed "the nobility of human feeling, the divinity of man's vision of the unseen, the importance of life and death, the depths of the human heart, the romantic value of tragedy."

Another view is suggested in the second section of the story, when Miranda and her sister have become schoolgirls in a New Orleans convent. During vacation on their grandmother's farm, they had read books detailing accounts of how "beautiful but unlucky maidens, who for mysterious reasons had been trapped by nuns and priests in dire collusion, 'were placed' in convents, where they were forced to take the veil—an appalling rite during which the victims shrieked dreadfully—and condemned forever after to most uncomfortable and disorderly existences. They seemed to divide their time between lying chained in dark cells and assisting other nuns to bury throttled infants under stones in moldering rat-infested dungeons." In Miranda's actual experience at the convent, no one even hinted that she should become a nun. "On the contrary Miranda felt the discouraging attitude of Sister Claude and Sister Austin and Sister Ursula towards her expressed ambition to be a nun barely veiled a deeply critical knowledge of her spiritual deficiencies."

The most disheartening disillusion came, however, during this period, when Miranda came actually to meet the legendary Uncle Gabriel for the first time. His race horse was running in New Orleans and her father had taken her to bet a dollar on it, despite the fact that odds against it were a hundred to one. "Can that be our Uncle Gabriel?" Miranda asked herself. "Is that Aunt Amy's handsome romantic beau? Is that the man who wrote the poem about our Aunt Amy?" Uncle Gabriel, as she met him, "was a shabby fat man with bloodshot blue eyes, sad beaten eyes, and a big melancholy laugh like a groan. His language was coarse, and he was a drunkard. Even though his horse won the race and brought Miranda a hundred unexpected dollars—an event which had the making of a legend in itself, Miranda saw that victory had been purchased, not as a result of beauty, but at the price of agony; for the mare when seen close up "was bleeding at the nose," and, "Her eyes were wild and her knees were trembling."

In legend, the past was beautiful or tragic. In art, it might be horrible and dangerous. In the present of Miranda's experience, it was ugly or merely commonplace. In the first two sections of "Old Mortality," we get first the view of the past as seen through the eyes of the elders with their memories of the past, not as it actually was, but as they wanted it to be. In section two, we get the view of it through the eyes of Miranda herself, who judges it merely as it is reflected in her present. By section three, Miranda is eighteen. She has eloped and married, but she is still struggling to understand her own relationship to the past. To her, her elopement seemed in the romantic tradition of Aunt Amy and Uncle Gabriel, although we soon learn that it is, in actual fact, a failure. We meet her on the train, returning home for the funeral of Uncle Gabriel. His body has been returned to lie beside Amy's, as though in a final attempt to justify the dream, even though he has married again, and (it is hinted) there are better and more real reasons for him to be buried beside his second wife, who had shared the bulk of his wandering, homeless, and meaningless existence. On the train, Miranda runs into Cousin Eva, also returning for the funeral, whose own life had been burdened by a constant comparison with the legend of Amy. While Amy was beautiful, thoughtless, impulsive, and daring, Cousin Eva had been homely, studious, and dedicated to high purposes. Amy had died and had been preserved in the romantic legend; Eva had lived to develop a character and a reputation as a fighter for women's rights. In a sense, Cousin Eva's good works, too, were part of her legend of homeliness and dedication. At bottom, Miranda finds her a bitter, prematurely aged woman; but it is Cousin Eva who provides her with a third view of the legend of Aunt Amy. She hints that it was nothing but sublimated sex that caused the young girls of Amy's day to behave as they did. " 'Those parties and dances were their market, a girl couldn't afford to miss out, there were always rivals waiting to cut the ground from under her. . . . It was just sex,' she said in despair; 'their minds dwelt on nothing else. They didn't call it that, it was all smothered under pretty names, but that's all it was, sex.' "

The old, then, had two ways of looking at the past: the romantic way of Miranda's father and of other members of the family, and the "enlightened" way of Cousin Eva. Each way was different, and each was wrong. But the old did have something in common; they had their memories. Thus, when the train arrived at the station, it was Cousin Eva and Miranda's father who sat together in the back seat of the automobile and talked about old times; it was Miranda who was excluded from these memories and who sat beside the driver in the front. Yet Miranda feels that she has a memory now and the beginning of her own legend—the legend of her elopement. Strangely enough, neither Cousin Eva nor her father will accept it. When reminded by Miranda of it, Cousin Eva says: "Shameful, shameful. . . . If you had been my child I should have brought you home and spanked you." Her father resented it. When he met her at the train, he showed it in his coldness. "He had not forgiven her, she knew that. When would he? She could not guess, but she felt it would come of itself, without words and without acknowledgment on either side, for by the time it arrived neither of them would need to remember what had caused their division, nor why it had seemed so important. Surely old people cannot hold their grudges forever because the young want to live, too, she thought in her arrogance, her pride. I will make my own mistakes, not yours; I cannot depend upon you beyond a certain point, why depend at all? There was something more beyond, but this was a first step to take, and she took it, walking in silence beside her elders who were no longer Cousin Eva and Father, since they had forgotten her presence, but had become Eva and Harry, who knew each other well, who were comfortable with each other, being contemporaries on equal terms, who occupied by right their place in this world, at the time of life to which they had arrived by paths familiar to them both. They need not play their roles of daughter, of son, to aged persons who did not understand them; nor of father and elderly female cousin to young persons whom they did not understand. They were precisely themselves; their eyes cleared, their voices relaxed into perfect naturalness, they need not weigh their words or calculate the effect of their manner. 'It is I who have no place,' thought Miranda. 'Where are my people and my own time?' "

Miranda is not merely a Southern child, in Southern history, reflected through the sensibility of a Southern author—even though she is—partly, at least—all these things. She is any child, anywhere, seeking to come to terms with her past and her present—seeking definition. Katherine Anne Porter's Southern history, whether legendary or actual, provided the concrete experience through which her "historic memory" could function. Thus when she wrote the concluding sentence of "Old Mortality," she was expressing, not the dilemma of Miranda alone, but the dilemma of all of us who seek understanding.

" 'At least I can know the truth about what happens to me,' " Miranda thinks, "making a promise to herself, in her hopefulness, her ignorance."

It is out of hopefulness and ignorance combined that myths are constructed and self-definition achieved, from a sense of social need and a vision of a society which expresses both the hopefulness and the need. Southern society represented the proper conditions for the perceptive talent of an artist such as Katherine Anne Porter, who responded both critically and with a warmth of admiration to her memories, thus transforming them, finally, into something more than mere memory.

ART AND MISS GORDON

BY WILLIAM VAN O'CONNOR

Caroline Gordon belongs to the generation of writers who spent at least part of their youth in Paris. The gods of the nineteenth century had fallen, but these young people found another: Art. Like most gods, Art had many guises, and was sometimes called Poetry, sometimes The Novel, and sometimes Modernism. Art had innumerable prophets, but in its guise as The Novel the chief of these prophets were Flaubert, James, and Ford Madox Ford. Miss Gordon has expressed great reverence and respect for each of them, and was fortunate enough to be personally acquainted with Ford.

Intervening generations, younger than Miss Gordon by ten or fifteen or twenty years, have also believed in Art. Anyone who aspired to write knew that it was impious not to believe in Art. In the years between the two wars, the poets, novelists, and critics who amounted to anything in the eyes of their fellows were true believers. Art was sacred. A great many sermons or homilies were given about technique and structure and point of view.

After World War II, Art continued to be respected, but some of the young writers occasionally protested. When drunk they might even say, "Let's get off this crap about Art—ya gotta have something to say!" or, "Look, kid, if you can't invent, you can't write," or, "This technique stuff, stow it!"

The older writers, like Miss Gordon, knew the pendulum swung back and forth, toward Art, then toward Life, and they would try patiently to explain that they were not opposed to Life's getting into literature; there was no other way of serving Art. But Art had to be served. And the younger writers, rather shamefacedly, would admit, "Yeah, ya gotta serve It." Despite the seeming unanimity a schism had begun, although a rather lax theologian might say, "The differences are merely matters of emphasis. Nothing is wrong, provided each of us serves Art in his own way."

Miss Gordon, the author of many articles and books on fiction, and, like Katherine Anne Porter, a writer's writer, has served Art faithfully. She has been to school under the masters. In one of her textbooks she makes this comment on Anton Chekhov:

> Chekhov presented difficulties to his first English readers. Imaginations "conditioned" by the Victorian novelists' leisurely pace were not athletic enough for the collaboration he demanded. And, indeed, his achievements surpassed anything the Victorians had imagined. He may well be compared to the great Pointillist painter, Seurat, on whose canvas every fleck of paint, when viewed in the proper perspective, unites with a neighboring fleck of paint to make the color the artist had in mind. There are no "dead" spots on Chekhov's canvases. Each detail not only vibrates with a life of its own but "acts" upon the neighboring detail. The result is a scene of extraordinary animation. The actors' speeches and gestures are lifelike in the extreme and they move through their roles with consistent boldness, but in addition, the whole scene seems to be bathed in a living air. Reading a Chekhov story one feels often as one does on an early autumn day when fields, woods, mountains, lakes and rivers show more brilliantly for the luminous light which shimmers between us and them.

The best of Miss Gordon's stories are like that; the details are vibrant. "The Brilliant Leaves" is a good example. A boy watches the girl he loves fall to her death from a ledge they had been climbing. The two had arranged a tryst in the woods. She insists on climbing high into the rocks near a waterfall called Bridal Veil. She slips on a rock and falls. In the hands of certain writers the horror would be the story. Miss Gordon does much more. The woods are life and adventure, the waiting future; and the dazzlingly brilliant leaves are passion and also death. Human lives are in nature, and to live well is to live adventurously, aware of love against death, aware that death is the mother of beauty.

In the same story there is also the "death" of the women who sit gossiping, ghostlike, apart from love. They live in the little white houses that seem staid and permanent and secure. Perhaps the young man should run away with his girl—we are not told. The women on the porch have gossiped about Sally Mainwaring, now a bitter old spinster, whose young man, fearing her father, had deserted her. The boy has often heard the story, but it has not upset his sense of the equilibrium of the world. The death of his beloved shows him how precarious that equilibrium has been.

> He ran slower now, lurching sometimes from side to side, but he ran on. He ran and the brilliant, the wine-colored leaves crackled and broke under his feet. His mouth, a taut square, drew in, released whining breaths. His starting eyes fixed the ground, but he did not see the leaves that he ran over. He saw only the white houses that no matter how fast he ran kept always just ahead of him. If he did not hurry they would slide off the hill, slide off and leave him running forever through these woods, over these dead leaves.

"The Forest of the South" and "Old Red" also show Miss Gordon's unwillingness to describe essentially inert situations, to create what Joyce called "mere literature." She not only wants the reader to look into the eyes of the characters—she wants the characters to look back at the reader, to have a light radiating from the page.

"The Forest of the South" describes the total destruction of a Southern household, Clifton, in the Civil War. The Yankee victor, Lieutenant Munford, falls in love with the daughter, Eugenie. There is a mysterious yet beautiful light in the girl's eyes, and Munford, still loving her, realizes she is mad, and the reader realizes that her madness is the madness of the destruction itself.

Even more skillful is the whole texture of details in "Old Red," undoubtedly one of the finest short stories written in our time. Its protagonist, Aleck Maury, who appears prominently in a number of Miss Gordon's stories, is a man who tries to unveil nature's secrets. He looks into the burning eyes of a possum, and he studies the soft colors in streams and lakes with the quiet intensity of a Buddhist monk. He is a scholar, and he learns to respect classic simplicity—but he loves life, not death, and hunting and fishing become the center of his pursuits. He refuses the blandishments of the ghostly ladies who sit on the porches of the white houses. In the process he alienates his wife, and she dies after having kept her illness secret from him.

The central symbol in "Old Red" is the fox. Mr. Maury, trying to fall asleep one night, finally realizes that he and Old Red are being pursued and will eventually be caught. But when he is caught, it will be because he can no longer run. The identification of fox and man comes gracefully and unexpectedly into the story, like an ancient tale of metamorphosis.

If he allowed his mind to get active, really active, he would never get any sleep. He was fighting an inclination now to get up and find a cigarette. . . . The young men would hold back till Uncle James had wheeled Old Filly, then they would all be off pell-mell across the plain. He himself would be mounted on Jonesboro. Almost blind, but she would take anything you put her at. That first thicket on the edge of the woods. They would break there, one half of them going around, the other half streaking it through the woods. He was always of those going around to try to cut the fox off on the other side. No, he was down off his horse. He was coursing with the fox through the trees. He could hear the sharp, pointed feet padding on the dead leaves, see the quick head turned now and then over the shoulder. The trees kept flashing by, one black trunk after another. And now it was a ragged mountain field and the sage grass running before them in waves to where a narrow stream curved in between the ridges. The fox's feet were light in the water. He moved forward steadily, head down. The hounds' baying grew louder. Old Mag knew the trick. She had stopped to give tongue by that big rock and now they had all leaped the gulch and were scrambling up through the pines. But the fox's feet were already hard on the mountain path. He ran slowly, past the big boulder, past the blasted pine to where the shadow of the Pinnacle Rock was black across the path. He ran on and the shadow swayed and rose to meet him. Its cool touch was on his hot tongue, his heavy flanks. He had slipped in under it. He was sinking down, panting, in black dark, on moist earth while the hounds' baying filled the valley and reverberated from the mountainside.

Miss Gordon has a fine ear for conversation, even to the shifts one hears in the speech of an educated Southerner. For example, when Aleck Maury is talking to his daughter, his language is formal. " 'Well,' he said, 'I'd better be starting.' " In the woods, thinking to himself, he says, " 'Ain't it funny now? Niggers always live in the good places.' " Miss Gordon's own prose has the simplicity of good taste. It is never pretentious. When, occasionally, it does rise toward rhetoric, the rhetoric is always justified by the action itself.

Her subject matter, too, is essentially simple. For the most part, she writes about the relationships of men and women. Ideally, she seems to say, a woman should give herself to a man, wholly and without question, and he should not betray her faith. The stories frequently have to do with betrayal, by the man, the sudden intrusion of nature (violence or death), or the breakdown of the society (the Civil War). Sometimes the failures are the woman's. By and large, Miss Gordon's subject is not a complicated one, and the grave simplicity of her style is in accord with her subject.

The Women on the Porch is in treatment and subject a fairly typical Gordon novel. A young stallion provides the central symbolism, and there is a clearly discernible pattern of imagery drawn from water and cloud and leaves. The writing, quietly beautiful, hardly calls attention to itself. Theme and subject have to do with masculine failures and women's frustrations. Because of accident, weakness of character, or possibly the period in history in which the characters find themselves, the men fail to satisfy the female need for loyal, courageous, forthright action, for love. The novel has that firmness of surface and impersonality to which Miss Gordon's writing aspires. The story opens:

The sugar tree's round shadow was moving past the store. At five o'clock when the first leaves were withering on the burning macadam the storekeeper raised his eyes to the fields across the road. The heat rose somewhere between the road and those distant woods. Always at this hour he looked, expecting to see it rise out of that far cornfield and always when he looked it was there. Only a light shimmer now above the green, but the shimmer would deepen as the field brimmed over. In a few minutes the first waves would beat against the porch. He got up and, walking to the end of the porch, lifted the lid of the red metal ice-chest.

"How about you, Ed?" he asked.

The man at the other end of the porch leaned forward, felt in his trousers pocket until he found a nickel, and pitched it to the storekeeper.

This description immediately involves the reader in the action, as though the author, Joyce-like, had dissolved into the atmosphere. It is reminiscent of the skillful opening paragraphs of *The Red Badge of Courage* and *A Farewell to Arms*. The atmosphere, of dust and heat and ennui, with occasional relief, is maintained throughout the novel.

There is lore or learning of various sorts—about flowers, mushrooms, horses, painting, local history, even architecture and literature. For the most part, all this knowledge functions unobtrusively. The story itself is about the search for love. A male reader, incidentally, might easily feel that Miss Gordon's idyll of peace deep in the forest of time, death, and danger is a woman writer's dream. She seems to ask of the male more understanding, courage, and tenacity than most mortals, male or female, possess. And the same reader, especially if he does not share Miss Gordon's respect for the "cold pastoral," for Art, might feel that something is being put over on him. The right place for cold, eternal truths is the "cold pastoral" of an urn. The poor male, with all his weaknesses, could wish that the artist had not dissolved into the atmosphere. There are a couple of questions he would like in all fairness to put to the author.

Being, for the moment, a little hard on Miss Gordon, we

ought to take a look at yet another novel, *None Shall Look Back*, in which, ironically, her very artistry seems to deaden the subject. There are many beautiful, skillfully evoked scenes, but they are so numerous that one finishes the book feeling that he has seen too many pictures—of forts, cannons, gunboats, staring corpses, gutted houses, handsome young soldiers tall on their sturdy horses, and young women crying in their darkened rooms. One gives *None Shall Look Back* a sort of credence —but only the sort given to an excellent book of Civil War pictures.

Miss Gordon's Southern piety too may have interfered with the dramatic possibilities of the subject. There is not enough in the book about the human heart in conflict with itself. Faulkner quarreled with his heritage and produced *Absalom, Absalom!* Miss Gordon brought too much respect and too little skepticism to her Civil War novel.

But Miss Gordon deserves to be judged by her best work. At least two of her novels, *Penhally* and *Aleck Maury, Sportsman,* are first-rate. Ford Madox Ford said of the former that he thought it the best novel that had been produced in modern America. This may be, and probably is, too great praise. *Penhally* is, nonetheless, a very fine novel. *Aleck Maury, Sportsman* is a masterpiece.

Both novels deal with the struggle to stay the hand of time. *Penhally* has what *None Shall Look Back* lacks: an inner life growing out of two ideas in conflict. In *Penhally*, nostalgia about the old ways, the ante-bellum world, is in conflict with change, and the latter inevitably has the victory, ironic and bitter though it turns out to be.

Aleck Maury, Sportsman is about an individual man, fully aware that his enemy is time. Day after day, Maury increases his skill as a fisherman and his artfulness in dodging those who would waste *his* time. His drama is not less poignant for being quiet. For seventy years his head has been filled with the sound of clocks which are stilled only when he is standing in a stream, casting, or sitting peacefully on a smooth lake. The reader comes to share his every success, his every failure. Miss Gordon's style, touched with a detached and loving irony, has never served a happier subject. In Aleck Maury, skillful, thoughtful, and sensitive men win at least a temporary victory —all they have ever hoped to win.

Most of the critics who have written about Miss Gordon have discussed her as a Southern writer—and of course she is. Some of her characters are deracinated Southerners or Middle Westerners, usually intellectuals who have left home. They are invariably unhappy; trouble and disorder trail along their foreign paths and remain with them when they occasionally return home. Miss Gordon has also written many passages, even whole novels, about the land and its healing moral power, which gives one a sense of belonging. She especially likes land that has not given up its fruits and rewards too easily; one appreciates what one has sweated to achieve.

Is Miss Gordon's preoccupation with Art also Southern? Perhaps, but her style is closer to Willa Cather's than it is to Southern rhetoric, even the quiet rhetoric of Katherine Anne Porter. Respect for form is in part Southern—for example, in manners, which cover and control personal likes, dislikes, drives, and ambitions; possibly too in a fairly general disregard for scientific principles and a preference for the arts that bear on personal relationships; and in a more open respect and liking for "elegance." But change comes on apace, and the Southern world of Miss Gordon's youth is no longer what it was. North and South grow more, not less, alike, and at least one or two of her novels seem to acknowledge that this is so.

Miss Gordon's art, as we suggested at the beginning, is related to the nineteenth-century European heritage. In her fiction, and explicitly in her many critical discussions of the novel and short story, she has clearly identified herself with the tradition of such men as Flaubert, James, Chekhov, and Stephen Crane, and with their successors—Joyce, Ford, and Hemingway.

Did she, in choosing to be a part of this literary heritage, choose well? It is presumptuous to answer such an Olympian and possibly impertinent question. But, having posed it, we must answer. Chekhov, in one of his letters, says, "One must write about simple things: how Peter Semionovich married Maria Ivanovna. That is all." When Miss Gordon writes about American Marias and Peters, she can be, and often is, an excellent fiction writer. She is always excellent in writing about the Aleck Maurys. She is better when the subject matter arouses her sympathy and her humor than she is when the subjects arouse her anger or lead her into large theoretical conclusions about men and women or the social order.

Miss Gordon has written enough good stories—at least two novels of a very high order and a half dozen excellent short stories—to have won a permanent place for herself in the hierarchy of American letters. Recognition has come slowly but it has come, and it continues to grow. Miss Gordon has served Art well, and, by and large, it has not betrayed her.

NOTES ON ERSKINE CALDWELL

BY ROBERT HAZEL

In books about our writers, whether in transition, mid-, or uneasy passage, we usually find an essay about Erskine Caldwell tacked on to the end like the little red caboose behind the train. A procession of our novelists would not be complete without that smudged and inherently funny little car, yet we seem embarrassed by its presence and the need for it.

This attitude toward the necessary but unwanted has always perplexed me. My experience with Caldwell was, from the first, one of almost constant delight. I am not embarrassed about, by, or with Caldwell. My reaction to him involves both exasperations and admirations, and this may explain certain excellences and defects, but not explain them away. Likewise, they may have to do with Caldwell's Southernness, or lack of it, but neither does Caldwell's Southern background explain them away.

I

Caldwell "can't write," in the sense that Dreiser couldn't write but James could. Style seems to elude certain men. It is really an easy distinction to draw. It is meant simply that Caldwell's language as language does not possess a very interesting life. Language is no particular friend of his, and he has to go it alone, the hard way of a writer who has not found within him the capacity to love language. This does not mean a lack of ear, for Caldwell has heard accurately and put down the living speech of his men and women. It means, in practice, that the world of men and women which Caldwell creates lacks that final rhetorical dimension which transfigures the worlds of writers such as Wolfe and Faulkner. Scottsville does not lie for us amid peaks of language as do Altamont and Jefferson. This is not even to say that one wishes it did. Rather, one is content that Caldwell, having a more immediate sociological concern than Wolfe or Faulkner, and further removed thereby from conditions which had nourished an heroic grammar, eschewed an English rhetoric of a sort which has lingered, which has even been caused to linger, by the Agrarians, who had certainly no genuine concern with plain speaking. Caldwell could and did stake out his acre and work it. Any literature, and certainly Southern literature as a body, is a group effort. And without Caldwell's reportage this marvelous country of his would have been lost, another "country not heard from."

I am not saying that it is better to be given a world in whatever language than not to have been given it at all. An immediate sociological concern may have assigned to Caldwell a language true to his task. In this he diverges from a group of Southerners who remain suspicious not only of sociology as such but of a mode of operation based upon the semi-science. What occurs, at any rate, in the writer who has not addressed himself to the problem of language for its own sake is that stresses are created which must be absorbed elsewhere and reasserted within the particular mode. In Caldwell, the solution, reportage as mode, forces him into one of the excellences of journalism. Caldwell made a great virtue of dialogue as a carrier of action. His local speech advances his narrative cleanly. In Caldwell we have a functionalism of action rather than of diction, of mythos rather than melody. It would seem—and I say this with genuine amusement—as if the persons who buy millions of his books must have agreed with Aristotle that action is most important in a work. Such a statement, of course, requires modification. For in our understanding of language in relation to the world of action, we must insist upon the fact that the created world is a function of the language itself. Given this slightly different, but not invalidating, twist to our understanding, we can conclude that the nature of the action in Caldwell is precisely what its language makes it, and that the world is, among other things, one of plain speech, of local idiom, of vulgar rather than fine motivations and actions, of a uniform levelness, of a consistent and impressive monotony—

a desiccated world where the lifting of a hand or foot seems to be arduous and significant, a world lacking in poetry. When poetry wants to steal into this world, it is not realized—as in the instance of the girls with eyes like morning-glories who work in the mill—it is impregnated with sentiment only. In the world created by the language of Caldwell, there is no valid occasion for poetry. There are only poetized attitudes about all the chimney sweepers who come to dust. There is a difference. The most poetically resonant novelistic languages seem to be written by men who contain in themselves not enough poetry to be poets, but enough so that, working assiduously, they create Baroque prose. Caldwell lacks this resonance. Stylistically, Caldwell is not a Southern writer.

II

This section might be called character as exaggeration, or caricature. The particular exaggeration is innocence, a peculiar and grotesque and malignant innocence which Caldwell alone has been able to fill his world with. (Faulkner has certain indestructably innocent characters, but on no such scale, or to such metaphysical degree, as Caldwell.) Caldwell seems to make a world culpable, not its particulars, to make large forces guilty, not persons. The social (I use the word loosely) attitudes of the twenties and thirties had developed strongly enough so that Caldwell could produce, as others did, the guiltless man. With the infallible innocence of the simple man he moves God's little acre from place to place. Ty Ty is irascible and indestructible, but above all innocent. Perhaps it is because he has no consciously realized, turned and weighed values. He has not even the rudimentary and static love of land which is Jeeter's most nearly conscious value. Jeeter Lester loves the worn-out clay of Tobacco Road, but Ty Ty Walden doesn't even stop to consider why he wants to strike gold on his farm. He is a mindless slave of processes, not ends. And from evidences of behavior in the body of Caldwell's work, we can infer safely that if Ty Ty had found gold he wouldn't have known what to do with it any more than a child would. Caldwell's people live that unexamined life which is not worth living, except of course to the tenacious egos themselves, if only because they subsist on animal faith, the final value in a world where all else is ruin. It seems that a character such as Ty Ty is able to sense the ruin. "There was a mean trick played on us somewhere. God put us in the bodies of animals and tried to make us act like people." But here he is out of character. Caldwell says this, not Ty Ty. Only when Caldwell lets Ty Ty return to his digging does he restore the character.

In force feeding ideas of impersonal nature into his fiction, Caldwell has departed from the stream of Southern writing and taken to the brush, to a jungle of forces, not the intensely personal and dramatic area of guilt and expiation which has bounded a remnant and vestigial society, a society driven in upon itself and forced to look at motives, a process of intensification which has helped put Southern writing in its present position of leadership. Caldwell has laid his emphasis elsewhere. He has dealt with submen who are beyond good and evil as truly as are the supermen of the *Künstlerroman*. Caldwell's characters are certainly beyond tragedy. To show Caldwell's divergence more clearly, we can note an interesting instance in which Faulkner chose to make his persons innocent and a society guilty—*The Wild Palms*. He attempted a tragic action, but in choosing an antagonist named society, an impersonal, amorphous, faceless, characterless force, he failed. And he didn't try again in this vein. It has been said of another Faulkner novel, *As I Lay Dying*, that he singularly denied his persons tragedy, whereas in his other work he permits his characters tragic status. The inference was that in this novel the characters were *below* tragedy and, one might add, were too nearly like Caldwell's submen to achieve tragedy. At any rate, whether the persons of *As I Lay Dying* are tragic or not, we do note that in this work Faulkner came his closest to poaching on Caldwell's acre. There are other parallels and approximations, here significant in a picture of Southern literature, which Faulkner and Caldwell share. But the shared areas are largely reduced to particularity, not scheme. Both writers share the mules, the plowlines, and the rednecked men, but their unifying schema are as far apart, and as near, as tragedy and comedy, as terror and laughter. Given their different contexts and visionary designs, one cannot interchange particulars, cannot, for example, say *incest* and mean both writers at once. The Snopeses and Bundrens are cousins to Ty Ty. A third-generation Snopes might own a textile mill where Ty Ty's son-in-law would go on strike. This Snopes probably wouldn't let Ty Ty come to his house in town to visit. Jason Compson rides an old Ford, a camphor rag about his neck. Caldwell's people ride old cars or crack up new cars, so they become old —he insists upon a junk-filled world where men bale newspapers without a market for the bales—the agrarian South is shown in passage between the mule and the Model A, unable to afford, but purchasing for a spree, a new car, meeting the jangling industrial South emerging in mills, urban and rural elements juxtaposed and productive of the crackling ironies which are germane to Caldwell's situation humor.

The innocence of which I speak is related in simplest terms to an attitude found generally in the world of Caldwell's people: a man ain't to blame. "If you've got a rooster, he's going to crow." It is an attitude which is pre-psychological and expressive of a certain large and bland tolerance and negligence and not much questioning. This attitude, in contrast with the more inquisitive and energetic attitudes held by most of us in the audience, provides an important lever for Caldwell's humor. The boy ain't to blame if he wants to chuck a ball against the side of the house, or drive a car without oil. Another boy ain't to blame because his sister-in-law is so beautiful that he just has to have her. A man ain't to blame if he can't feed his niggers because he's got important things on his mind, has to dig holes in the ground looking for gold. I say pre-psychological, and this necessitates one refining explanation. The reason why these persons are pre-psychological is not that they are guiltless for being what they are. Psychologists do not hold any man guilty of his desires, his impulses, or even certain rather destructive acts. But Caldwell's characters are pre-psychological insofar as they do not, need not, and will not alter the patterns of their desires or the patterns of fulfillment. In their innocence, they do not know enough to wish to change or to seek means to divest their acts of destructive power. Again the unexamined life, pre-psychological. A candidate for the office of county sheriff ain't to blame if he instructs other men where to find an albino and how to rope him, as long as they don't get too rough. Here is one of the cruel paradoxes that give a sting, a poisonous and vivid inflammation, to the humor of Caldwell. He lances social sores, boils, cancers. The laughter produced is as fire. It burns the throat. In examining this matter, we are touching tender skin on us and our time. We do not feel like laughing any more at a Negro boy who is forced to climb a tree to silence woodpeckers and who is pecked on the head in the dark, the birds mistaking his skull for the wood. We do not feel it is appropriate to laugh sadistically at the evil in ourselves, projected, or at the expense of other persons. It is one of Caldwell's particular virtues as a humorist that he confronts us with symbols which start laughter only to smother it in the pain of sympathy or revulsion. His is a humor of the preposterous, often free enough of pain, involved merely with such attributes as sloth (Pluto's lazy vote counting) or stupidity (Ty Ty's insistence that his gold digging is carried on scientifically), but when the preposterous becomes outrageous the humor adds another dimension, becoming doubly pathetic.

If Caldwell's world is without tragedy, it contains pathos—often of an irritating sort. The irritation may perhaps be an encompassing emotion within us, which does not often come to the surface to disturb our enjoyment, a feeling that there is no excuse, finally, for the life lived in that world. This may be our feeling. It has nothing to do with Caldwell's success or failure. Caldwell's problem was to create a world, not to prejudge it. Here one must except the kind of prejudgment inherent in the naturalistic method and its variants, and, further, the kind of judgment which inevitably precedes any creative act.

III

A humor of situation, which is also a humor of the preposterous, is what Caldwell has given us with such overwhelming success that it bears further scrutiny. There is little need to comment on its gusto, or the "Rabelesian" or "Chaucerian" labels which have adhered to it. Suffice it to say that these words contain quite precise meanings, more than tag words ordinarily do. Certainly the humor is gusty, uniquely gratifying, a largess, a bounty, for which one always thanks the giver. We cannot thank Caldwell too much or too often for giving us the robust and depraved and homely and vulgar tomfoolery as no one else has given in our time. His literalities, equivalents, and approximations, particularly concerning the sex content in the lives of his people, come forth genuinely incorporated and derived from the traditional and popular mind-body of the rural South. Can anyone, especially those who know the region, ever forget or stop laughing at Ty Ty's praise for beautiful Griselda, remembering the thousand times he has heard it from a thousand obsequious adorers of a profaned virgin. The laughter is immense, but with just enough truth and sadness in it to keep it from being utterly coarse. And when sadness falls on Caldwell's humor, the gusto, which we associate with health, diminishes—as in the scene involving Will Thompson, when he declares he has to take his sister-in-law because when he first saw her he promised himself some of that and he just can't break his own promise. Gusto plays on the surface but is engulfed finally in our deeper apprehension of Will's sickness, and an entire landscape caving under the sickness which has produced him. As far as the eye sees, there stretches the ultimately humorless inferno of Caldwell. That the animal fails to attain humanity is not finally laughable. Or is it? Take either point of view, and Caldwell has provided amply for you. Or admit no yes-or-no answer, and Caldwell has provided a world complex enough. I do not know, certainly, how Caldwell himself feels about that world of his creation. It doesn't matter. We can know, from his stated preoccupations with certain social problems, how he must have felt about the actual world to which his fictional world bears some relation. The relation may be put thus: satire is the name of the relation of the real world of fiction to the actual world of fact. But satire is a too-easy name, too easily pronounced and let pass. We must, in observing the relation between those actual and real worlds, account for the sums and multiplications of particular elements and their alignments in given instants, otherwise how could we honestly say that Caldwell's world is funnier than ours *and* crueler *and* sadder?

The world Caldwell makes is a Southern world. It is not simply a world economically determined and which could be anyplace. Although various determinisms, compatible with and suitable to Caldwell's scene, are at work, they no more provide full explanations of that work than of any other work of stature. (Take Dreiser, for example, who was fond of determinism as method. The fact that Clyde Griffiths' mother didn't buy the child ice cream cones when he wanted them is not an adequate explanation for Clyde's crimes. The determinisms of the writers of the thirties offer keys to their gardens, as it were, but not to their houses. If we were dealing with Zola or Hardy, when naturalism was still in a relatively pure condition, it would be quite another matter.) Caldwell's contextual obligation to the Southern land and what grows and dies on it is incontestable. Here he is a Southern writer. I quote a friend's recollection of Georgia country after a trip across the state several years ago. ". . . the retinal highway shimmering in the brain, the dust-laden roosters, the laddered growth of corn southward, the claypowdered broad leaf tapering into pecan signs and turpentine pine, into the rutted swamp bridges, then the exotic verdure. The cold grease clotted grits, the thin etherized coffee. The 25c straw hat, the sullen, evasive eyes above beard stubble, the clay-red roadmapped neck. Hadacol, Mail Pouch peeling off the barns, J. C. Penney and Piggly-Wiggly, overalls—Lee and Headlight, brass studded. The sunset town: the all-nite Greek's in a sputter of neon, the leaner outside, the protuberant adam's-apple, the quid, the wen, the new baby-shit Florsheims . . ."

What my friend wrote was a description of an actual world, but it is also obviously, and without conscious intent, a description of Caldwell's real world. The description leads us to believe—for the moment, at least—that the relation between the worlds is nigh identity—until we reflect on the grotesque alignment of particulars from the actual world, which distinguishes the real. From this actual description, we could not even begin to predict the variants, the singular monads reflected by their fictional universe, that one stubbled face would belong to a Pluto Swint, another to a man who was tricked into paying money to copulate with his own wife. No, the real world is as different as it is superior. It permits combinations of elements in mixtures not actually possible. Caldwell permits us to be surprised. He also inures us to surprise by building consecutive layers of surprise. When we see Ty Ty digging for gold, we are surprised. When Pluto suggests an albino to divine the lode, we are surprised. But by the time Darling Jill drives away in Pluto's car, we are prepared. And, if in *God's Little Acre,* a man should walk on the scene and offer to buy the souls of dead Negroes, would the reader be surprised? I think the answer is no. Such is the construction of Caldwell's world as to support such goings-on.

IV

To build a world demands an inclusion of vigorous terms, and to build an infernal world of instinctual human life, without the purity of the instinct of animals, requires Caldwell's terms, his special troupe of irrational puppets, his dusty stage hung with burlap. In his zeal to make ample provision, Caldwell runs the risk of overstocking, of the needless multiplication of examples, of displaying the same set of objects in a too-little-varied action. But this is to err on the right side. Many "tests" of a novelist have been put forward. I suggest that, among these tests, one which is of first importance is: How adequate, how complete is a writer's projection of a world? To apply this criterion we must disregard the nature of that world. The failure of critics as a tribe to effect this separation between the completeness of and the nature of worlds has resulted in impossible hopes for and demands upon our writers. It is customary for the critic to hold up the fictional world to *the* actual world (as though he knew what *the* world is) and to judge by the mirror theory. But no writer can project *the* world (nobody can write a description even of a mule as it actually appears, much less describe *the* world) and the illusory hope that some writer can, and that all writers should try, leads to such absurdities of thought as enabled us to speak once of the Great American Novel. We do not even re-create *the* world; we create worlds. A writer creates a world and populates it with a set of objects—forces, ideas, persons, etc., and signifies these things by an elaborate system of signs—or he fails to do so. From the drift of these notes, I hope it will be supposed that Caldwell created a world abundantly and successfully, a world sufficient unto itself, which bears significant relation to other fictional worlds (to the Southern worlds, particularly) and, further, a world indispensable to the constellation we call Southern literature.

THE THEME OF SPIRITUAL ISOLATION
IN CARSON McCULLERS

BY OLIVER EVANS

As the novels of Carson McCullers made their separate appearances, the casual reader may have been more impressed by their differences than by their similarities. Even to some professional critics it seemed almost inconceivable that the same consciousness that created *The Heart Is a Lonely Hunter* (Mrs. McCullers' first novel, written when she was twenty-two) should have produced four years later a book as apparently dissimilar as *Reflections in a Golden Eye*. The critics realized from the beginning that they were dealing with a writer of unusual honesty and imagination, who, in spite of her youth and professional inexperience, nevertheless possessed an enormous technical skill—in short, that they were dealing with a first-rate literary talent. But they looked in vain for a subsisting pattern, for a characteristic philosophical attitude or point of view.

Such a pattern does exist, however. Once it has been discovered, all the major works of this remarkable writer, now in her early forties, will be seen to exhibit it. Indeed, the homogeneity of her work, viewed as the projection of a particular attitude to life, is really extraordinary—which is not to say that Mrs. McCullers has merely repeated herself; for the theme, as I shall attempt to show, is one which permits infinite variations.

The essential loneliness of the individual in a world full of other individuals as lonely as himself is a paradox which intrigued Carson McCullers from the first and which has ended by becoming an obsession. From this paradox, first set forth in *The Heart Is a Lonely Hunter* (a title suggested by the publishers in the hope that it would furnish a clue to the book's meaning), the author has developed an entire philosophy. It is in this sense the seed of all her work; her concept of the nature and function of love, which receives magnificent treatment in *The Ballad of the Sad Café* (1951), derives directly from it; and it accounts also for her preference for situations which inevitably lead to frustration, for her interest in adolescent characters and in characters deformed both physically and psychologically, and for the curious blend of compassion and irony which is her predominant attitude toward these characters.

Mrs. McCullers herself has used the phrase "moral isolation" to describe this universal condition of mankind (*Theatre Arts Monthly*, April 1950). However, "spiritual isolation" is probably a better term, as the moral implications are by no means the only ones. Every person, Mrs. McCullers believes, is imprisoned in the cell of his own being, and any practical attempt at communication, such as speech, is doomed to failure. (Speech, indeed, only leads to further confusion, frustration, and loneliness: it is worth noting that the two most articulate characters in *The Heart Is a Lonely Hunter*, Dr. Copeland and Jake Blount, are also the most miserable; and that Singer, the central character and the only happy one in the book, is a *deaf-mute.*)

The only force which does not make for spiritual isolation is love, or ideal communication. Love is the machinery by which men strive to escape from their cells, but their escape is seldom entirely or permanently successful, since love, powerful though it is, is subject to time and diminishes with the death of the love object—besides which, no love is ever a completely mutual experience. Even Singer's happiness is short-lived, and when the half-witted Antonapoulos, of whom he is incongruously enamored, dies, he commits suicide.

It is ironical that Singer, who is loved by almost everyone in the community, should choose as the object of his own love the depraved and demented Antonapoulos; but the irony increases when we realize that the reason Singer is so beloved is that no one really *knows* him—a point the author drives home repeatedly. It is exactly because he cannot make himself fully known to them (being mute) that they love him, for each of them is free to imagine that he is what they would like him to be. And—still further irony—it is perhaps because they cannot make themselves fully known to him (since he is also deaf) that he has achieved with them such a happy relationship. The situation is thus not so much a comment on the futility of communication as it is on its undesirability.

In *The Heart Is a Lonely Hunter*, love is either unreturned, unrecognized, or mistaken for its opposite. What we have in this novel is a number of persons, each pursuing, but never attaining, the object of his love: Singer writes letters which he never mails to Antonapoulos in the mental institution, and when he talks with him, he does not even know whether Antonapoulos understands him or not; Mick adores Singer, who never realizes that he is the object of her adolescent yearnings; Mick does not know that the middle-aged widower, Biff Brannon, whom she despises, loves her with a wistful affection which is part paternal, part maternal; the Negro, Dr. Copeland, loves his people, who do not understand him; Lucile loves Leroy, who has deserted her. Each of these lovers is alone in the sense that he never attains the love object, though perhaps he is less alone merely because he strives for it. Singer, after all, is happy (for a while), even though his love is not returned. There is the suggestion here of an idea which later receives more emphatic statement in *The Ballad of the Sad Café*: that love does not have to be a reciprocal experience to benefit the lover. Its chief value is to the lover, in helping to release him from his cell. Singer's letters are a case in point; but even Singer's love had a limit. Though it could survive Antonapoulos' indifference, it could not survive his death; and Singer could not achieve complete release except in suicide.

I do not think it has been sufficiently realized what a rich and thoughtful book *The Heart Is a Lonely Hunter* is. That all these meanings should be contained and objectified so expertly by a woman of twenty-two is, of course, little short of miraculous; but it is the meanings, after all, which are important, and many critics have overlooked the book's profundity in praising its precocity. There is no denying that these meanings are melancholy in the extreme, but the pessimism which informs them is a mature pessimism. If Mrs. McCullers reveals herself in this first novel as a pessimist, it is because she cannot accept an easy optimism. The predicament of Mick, who had dreams of becoming a concert pianist but who, on reaching womanhood, must work at Woolworth's and cannot even save enough to buy a piano, is really the predicament of all frustrated humanity, and the very desperation with which she still clings to her impossible ambition is the measure of her conviction that it is all in vain.

But maybe it would be true about the piano and turn out O.K. Maybe she would get a chance soon. Else what the hell good had it all been—the way she felt about music and the plans she had made in the inside room? It had to be some good if anything made sense. And it was too and it was too and it was too and it was too. It was some good.

All right!

O.K!

Some good.

Obviously more than a piano is involved here. Mick is trying, in the face of all the evidence to the contrary, to persuade herself that life has some meaning, that it "makes sense." But she is by no means certain that it does.

Mrs. McCullers' second book, *Reflections in a Golden Eye*, was a disappointment to many, who saw in it a mere "grotesquerie," a collection of artfully interwoven case histories out of Krafft-Ebing—impressive technically, but lacking the depth and emotional impact of her first novel, with which it appeared to have no connection. Some critics expressed alarm over what was taken to be the author's excessive preoccupation with abnormality, both mental and physical. There was a strong hint of this preoccupation in *The Heart Is a Lonely Hunter* (Singer and Antonapoulos are both deaf-mutes, besides which, Singer is homosexual and Antonapoulos a half-wit), but there it was subordinated to the total intention and did not seem out of proportion. Captain Penderton, in *Reflections in a Golden Eye*, is not only homosexual; he is also a sadist, a kleptomaniac, and a drug addict. Of the six other characters, all but two, Major Langdon and Leonora—his mistress and the captain's wife—are abnormal in some way, and Leonora herself is described as "a little feeble-minded." (Someone once observed that in this novel not even the horse, Firebird, who plays an important part in the story, is normal.)

This book earned for its author a reputation for sensationalism that unfortunately still survives—unfortunately, since it is not justified. I have said that Mrs. McCullers' basic theme is the spiritual isolation of the individual. Now, it should be obvious that any kind of deviation, whether physical or psychological, naturally tends to increase this sense of isolation. On a merely realistic level, it is certainly difficult to accept this novel, with its bizarre situations and twisted characters, as a truthful statement about life, but then, the book is not intended to be read on a merely realistic level. These characters are all symbols—just as the homosexual deaf-mute is a symbol—symbols of spiritual isolation and loneliness. As in The Heart Is a Lonely Hunter, all of them strive for release through love, but with each of them love takes a different form, the form determined by the nature of the lover. And this novel too ends in frustration and tragedy for all concerned. Captain Penderton's slaying of the soldier, whom he loves, in a situation involving the captain's wife, whom he does not love, comes as an appropriately ironical conclusion to the terrible fable. Though Reflections in a Golden Eye is a slighter work than The Heart Is a Lonely Hunter, its theme is exactly the same, only it is presented much more obliquely, after the manner of a fable or parable. Tennessee Williams, in his introduction to the New Directions reprint of this book, rightly calls attention to its technical excellence and to its affinities with Greek tragedy in the simplicity of its design, the economy of its presentation, and the swiftness and inevitability of its action.

In her third novel, The Member of the Wedding, Mrs. McCullers treats the isolation theme more overtly. The novel is simple in its design, and the classical unities are observed with a scrupulosity rare in modern writers. There are only three main characters—the adolescent Frankie Adams, her little cousin John Henry, and a Negro cook named Berenice—and the book consists largely of a series of dialogues among them. The language of these dialogues is remarkable. It is authentically Southern, giving the book a folk quality, and it is characterized also by strategic repetitions which suggest refrains in music. The total effect is reminiscent of the chanting in

Greek tragedies—or, more accurately, the group singing of certain folk ballads in the South.

Frankie is an unforgettable character, reminding us of that other marvelous adolescent, Mick, in *The Heart Is a Lonely Hunter*. The phenomenon of adolescence has a peculiar fascination for Mrs. McCullers (she has also explored it in the short story "Wunderkind"), and this too has its explanation, for at that age the sense of individual isolation is stronger than at any other. Adolescence sets one apart just as effectively as does a physical or mental aberration: one is no longer a child, nor yet an adult. Even one's sexual identity is ambiguous. (In *The Heart Is a Lonely Hunter* Biff Brannon muses about Mick as follows: "She was at the age when she looked as much like an overgrown boy as a girl. And on that subject why was it that the smartest people mostly missed that point? By nature all people are of both sexes. So that marriage and the bed is not all by any means. The proof? Real youth and old age. Because often old men's voices grow high and reedy and they take on a mincing walk. And old women sometimes grow fat and their voices get rough and deep and they grow dark little mustaches.") Adolescents do not *belong* anywhere, and thus constitute excellent symbols of spiritual loneliness. Frankie and Mick are symbols, just as are Singer, Antonapoulos, and Captain Penderton.

Frankie, we are told, is an "unjoined person who hangs around in doorways." Doorways—that is, always on the threshold of things, but never, because of the isolation which is a product of the condition of adolescence, really inside them. She suffers acute loneliness because she is not a *member* of anything. Her mother is dead; her father is too busy to spend much of his time with her; she belongs to no club. The action springs from her desire to identify herself with something outside herself. In the approaching marriage of her older brother, a soldier, she sees her opportunity. Marriage is a big thing, a glamorous thing, and a thing which *ties people together* (there is symbolism here too); so she decides that she will be a member of the wedding, thus identifying herself with it and with them (bride and groom). After the ceremony, she hopes, they will invite her to live with them, so that the identification will be permanent.

In terms of Freudian analysis, Frankie is unconsciously, though with all the awkward intensity of her age, seeking a love object, but it is not to a particular person, or even to a particular object, that she wishes to be joined: she wants something not only outside herself but also "bigger" than herself and more inclusive. She does not wish to be joined to a person but to *that which joins all people*—to the *we* of people, as she puts it.

The trouble with me is that for a long time I have been just an "I" person. When Berenice says "we" she means her lodge and church and colored people. Soldiers can say "we" and mean the army. All people belong to a "we" except me. . . . I know that the bride and my brother are the "we" of me. . . . So I am going with them and joining the wedding and after that to whatever place they will ever go. I love them so much because they are the "we" of me.

What Frankie is seeking is nothing less than the common denominator of all humanity. Elsewhere she says, "All these people and you don't know what joins them up. There's bound to be some sort of reason or connection. Yet somehow I don't know." And Berenice answers her, "If you did you would be God. Didn't you know that?"

Berenice and John Henry, almost as lonely as Frankie herself—though for different reasons—are the only people she sees much of. She clings to them out of necessity, in a kind of desperate compromise, but they bore her almost as much as she bores herself. (The kind of world she would like to move in can be inferred from the name she has given to herself in her daydreams: F. Jasmine Adams.) And although she is sick to death of the "ugly old kitchen," the scene of their curious dialogues, she is somehow powerless to leave it for very long, because it is inhabited by the only two companions she has in the world. Again, more is meant here than meets the eye. Frankie's dependence on companions who bore her, who for one reason or another are unequipped to give her the release she desires, is actually the situation of most men, forced into an unhappy compromise between the ideal romantic relationships for which they long and those humdrum and unsatisfactory substitutes that are available to them. And for *kitchen,* read *world*—a monotonous and sordid world from which there is no escape for most of us. "They sat together in the kitchen, and the kitchen was a sad and ugly room. . . . And now the old kitchen made Frankie sick. The name for what had happened to her Frankie did not know, but she could feel her squeezed heart beating against the table edge. 'The world is certainly a small place,' she said." Berenice asks her, "What makes you say that?" and she cannot explain. But it is clear that Frankie here has connected the kitchen with the world: both are small places, and both are "sad and ugly." And from both of them there is no escape. There is a certain superficial resemblance between the situation in this novel and that in Sartre's play, *No Exit,* where three characters are condemned to bore one another throughout eternity in a single comfortably furnished room—an unorthodox but oddly convincing concept of Hell.

Frankie's brother and his bride do not, of course, invite her to stay with them on their honeymoon, and this story too ends in frustration. It is a frustration from which, with the elasticity of her age, Frankie quickly recovers, and the experience has helped to mature her: in the last four or five pages we meet a new Frankie, a young lady who says "braids" for pigtails, who is "just mad about Michelangelo," and who has a friend at last, Mary Littlejohn, with whom she is planning to travel around the world someday. It has been thought that, because Frankie's disappointment is so short-lived, *The Member of the Wedding* ends on a more "positive" note and is less pessimistic in its implications than are the earlier novels. Perhaps this is true, but a thoughtful reader cannot escape the suspicion that at the end of the story Frankie merely replaces one impossible ambition with another one, and that her desire to travel around the world (which reminds one a bit of Mick's ambition to be a concert pianist) will never see fulfillment. When that dream collapses, another will take its place, and so on. On the whole, it is easier to view the book as yet another parable about the essential loneliness of man and the eternal futility of escape.

Eloquent as these variations are, Mrs. McCullers has given her theme its most impressive statement in *The Ballad of the*

Sad Café. This extraordinary novella contains in a bare sixty pages all the philosophy of her early novels, together with a fully developed theory of the nature of love—a theory which, consciously or unconsciously, she has slowly but steadily evolved from her chosen theme and which is naturally consistent with it. It will be helpful to summarize the story, laid in the author's favorite setting, a Southern mill town.

"The town itself is dreary," reads the first sentence. "If you walk along the main street on an August afternoon there is nothing whatsoever to do. . . . These August afternoons when your shift is finished—there is absolutely nothing else to do; you might as well go down to the Forks Falls Road and listen to the chain gang." The very first sentence establishes the tone of boredom and loneliness, and the chain gang (to which Mrs. McCullers returns in a kind of epilogue) is important in a way I shall presently show. We are introduced to a Miss Amelia Evans, a woman who lives all alone in a large house in which all the windows but one have been boarded up, a woman with a face "like the terrible dim faces known in dreams—sexless and white, with two gray crossed eyes which are turned inward so sharply that they seem to be exchanging with each other one long and secret gaze of grief."

But the house has not always been silent: it had originally been a kind of general store, run with an iron hand by Miss Amelia herself, a grim, masculine giantess with a habit of absent-mindedly fingering her powerful biceps. The town's richest woman, she was once married to Marvin Macy, a handsome ne'er-do-well whose love for her had had, in the beginning, a reforming influence upon his character. But Miss Amelia's motive in marrying had apparently been merely a desire for companionship; when Marvin attempted to make love to her on their wedding night, she repulsed him furiously, and thereafter, during the brief ten days he stayed with her, hit him "whenever he came within arm's reach of her and whenever he was drunk." She finally turned him off the premises altogether. After putting under her door a letter threatening revenge, Marvin left town, returned to his old wild habits, became a hardened criminal, and at last was sent to the penitentiary.

In the meantime Miss Amelia receives a visit from a hunchbacked dwarf, Cousin Lymon, whom she has never seen before but who claims to be a distant relation. The hunchback is tubercular and inverted sexually, but Miss Amelia falls in love with him from the very first. She closes her shop the day following his arrival, giving rise to rumors among the townspeople (who were certain that she would show Cousin Lymon the door) that she has murdered him for something he was carrying in his suitcase. Actually Miss Amelia has given herself a holiday to celebrate the beginning of a new chapter in her life, and a delegation of mill workers, who come to investigate Cousin Lymon's "death," find him decked out in a lime-green shawl, "the fringes of which almost touched the floor," and very much alive. Cheered by some of Miss Amelia's best liquor and amused by the antics of the dwarf, who is sociable in the extreme, the delegation stays on; and the session is so convivial that Miss Amelia decides to start a café on the premises.

For six years all goes well. Miss Amelia showers favors upon Cousin Lymon; he has the best room upstairs; and nothing is too good for him. Though it is apparently unreturned, her love causes a general transformation of character in Miss Amelia: she loses much of her old grimness and becomes in every way more amiable. Then Marvin Macy, released from the penitentiary, returns. Cousin Lymon is fascinated by him: though Marvin treats him with contempt, he dogs his footsteps, hangs upon his every word, plies him with Miss Amelia's liquor. In short, he falls in love with Marvin, thus becoming the instrument of the latter's revenge upon Miss Amelia. Night after night Cousin Lymon treats Marvin at the café, and even invites him to live with him upstairs, while Miss Amelia moves to a cot on the first floor. Miss Amelia endures all this because her love for the dwarf is large enough to include his love for Marvin, even though the latter is her deadly enemy. If she drives Marvin away, she knows Cousin Lymon will leave too, and she cannot bear the thought of that. "Once you have lived with another it is a great torture to have to live alone . . . it is better to take in your mortal enemy than face the terror of living alone."

Cousin Lymon, knowing her dependence upon him, exploits it to the utmost: he even mocks her publicly by imitating her walk, while Marvin looks on and laughs. But this only causes Miss Amelia to hate Marvin the more. The mutual hatred of these two one day explodes in a scene as ludicrous as it is terrible: a slugging match between them which is witnessed by the whole town (who have sensed that it was imminent), and which Miss Amelia wins. But at the precise moment that she pins Marvin to the ground and is presumably about to throttle him, the hunchback alights on her back and claws at her throat, forcing her to let Marvin go. After that Cousin Lymon and Marvin disappear together, but not before they have destroyed Miss Amelia's still, wrecked her café, and stolen her private belongings (she 'has locked herself and her grief in her study). They even try to poison her, leaving on the café counter a plate of her favorite food "seasoned with enough poison to kill off the county."

Thereafter Miss Amelia's hair turns gray and her eyes become increasingly crossed. For three long years she waits in vain for the hunchback to return; then, a broken woman, she hires a carpenter to board up the premises and becomes a recluse. The story closes on the same note of loneliness and boredom with which it began, and there is the same ballad-like use of repetition which we noted in *The Heart Is a Lonely Hunter* and which is here even more effective. "Yes, the town is dreary. On August afternoons the road is empty, white with dust, and the sky above is bright as glass. . . . There is absolutely nothing to do in the town. . . . The soul rots with boredom. You might as well go down to the Forks Falls highway and listen to the chain gang."

Near the beginning of *The Ballad of the Sad Café* there is a passage in which Mrs. McCullers, momentarily abandoning the narrative for the expository vein, discourses briefly on the nature of love. The effect is that of a text at the beginning of a sermon, which is precisely the author's intention, though the sermon itself is presented in the form of the story—or parable —which follows. (Indeed, all of Mrs. McCullers' books are parables in this sense.) She writes: "There are the lover and the beloved, but these two come from different countries. Often the beloved is only a stimulus for all the stored-up love which has lain quiet within the lover for a long time. And somehow every lover knows this. He feels in his soul that his love is a solitary thing. . . . Let it be added here that this lover about whom we speak need not necessarily be a young man saving for a wedding ring—this lover can be man, woman, child, or indeed any human creature on this earth. Now the beloved can also be of any description.. The most outlandish people can be the stimulus for love. . . . The preacher may love a fallen woman. The beloved may be treacherous, greasy-headed and given to evil habits. Yes, and the lover may see this as clearly as anyone else—but that does not affect the evolution of his love one whit. . . . The value and quality of any love is determined solely by the lover himself."

She concludes: "It is for this reason that most of us would rather love than be loved. Almost everyone wants to be the lover. And the curt truth is that, in a deep and secret way, the state of being beloved is intolerable to many. The beloved *fears and hates* the lover [italics mine], and with the best of reasons. For the lover is forever trying to strip bare his beloved. The lover craves any possible relation with the beloved, even if this experience can cause him only pain."

One can see here still another reason for Mrs. McCullers' choice of "outlandish people": not only do they serve as symbols of isolation, but they prove her thesis that "the value and quality of any love is determined solely by the lover himself." The more outlandish the characters, and the more incongruous the matches they make (one remembers Singer's love for Antonapoulos), the more eloquently they illustrate this truth. Cousin Lymon is outlandish enough for anyone's taste: he is a dwarf, he is hunchbacked, he is tubercular, and he is homosexual. His relationship with the manlike Amelia constitutes one of the saddest and most grotesque situations in fiction. (Observe the care with which the author has selected these two personalities, whose association can end only in frustration: indeed, a physical union between them—as she is careful to make clear—is out of the question, which, of course, only adds to the poignancy of the situation.)

Love need not be reciprocal to benefit the lover: so much we learned from *The Heart Is a Lonely Hunter*. And now this concept has been developed even further: the beloved actually fears and hates the lover. Cousin Lymon despises Miss Amelia, and we are shocked by his treatment of her; it is not, however, *in spite of* her love for him that he despises her (as it somehow seems more congenial for us to imagine), but *because* of it. There is dreadful justice in the fact that in the past she has herself treated Marvin Macy in the same way and for the same reason. One can trace the beginning of this idea as far back as *The Heart Is a Lonely Hunter,* where Mick hated Biff Brannon, but with the important difference that she was not aware of his love for her. There it was merely suggested, perhaps unconsciously; here it is the very center of the story, the melancholy burden of the ballad itself.

The Ballad of the Sad Café must be among the saddest stories in any language—not merely on the surface level of narrative, the level of "realism," but also, and far more importantly (because it makes a generalization about mankind), on the level of parable. Love, it will be remembered, is the only means by which man can hope to escape his loneliness. In the early novels escape was still *possible,* even though their outcome showed how difficult it was to achieve. Escape was possible in theory, if not in actual practice, so long as the only obstacles were time and imperfect reciprocity (for *relatively* reciprocal relationships could, after all, still be attained). But now the difficulty is not merely that in any relationship one person must always love more than the other, nor even that one of the persons may exhibit the indifference of an Antonapoulos. Now the obstacle is much more serious, so serious as to be insurmountable: the beloved *hates* the lover. This, according to Mrs. McCullers in *The Ballad of the Sad Café,* is the terrible law of nature that has sentenced man to a life of perpetual solitary confinement. There is no longer even a possibility of escape.

But although escape is impossible, there is still some advantage in making the attempt. The impulse to love is a good impulse, even though it is doomed to end in frustration. Singer's one-sided love for Antonapoulos sustains him so perfectly that the whole town is impressed by his air of poise and wisdom; Marvin Macy's early love for Miss Amelia has a brief refining influence upon his character; Miss Amelia's love for Cousin Lymon transforms her whole personality. It is true that these changes are temporary, but they are valuable while they endure. Some joy exists even in the midst of pain, though it is adulterated by the knowledge that it cannot last. (One is reminded of Keats's *Ode on Melancholy:* "Aye, in the very temple of Delight / Veiled Melancholy has her sovran shrine.") The lover realizes this intuitively, with the result that even such temporary escape as he contrives for himself must be imperfect: "And somehow every lover knows this. He feels in his soul that his love is a solitary thing." Love paroles man, and the tragedy is that he must return to his cell through no defection of his own.

Miss Amelia's love for Cousin Lymon contains a strong element of pity. This is especially obvious in the scene of their first meeting, when the circumstances are such as to arouse it most successfully, and it characterizes her attitude to the dwarf throughout. Part of the story's terrible effectiveness lies in the fact that Cousin Lymon returns the goodness of pity as well as the goodness of love with the evil of spite and hatred. Miss Amelia can pity the dwarf because her own abnormality affords her special insight into his predicament: he too is a deviate and suffers isolation. The same mixture of love and pity characterizes other grotesque relationships in Mrs. McCullers' fiction: Singer and Antonapoulos in *The Heart Is a Lonely Hunter,* Anacleto and Mrs. Langdon in *Reflections in a Golden Eye,* and Martin Meadows and Emily in the short story "A Domestic Dilemma."

It is perhaps significant that the townspeople mistake Miss Amelia's intentions toward Cousin Lymon at the beginning. They are certain she has murdered him, when she has instead fallen in love with him. Love, as has been noted, is frequently misunderstood and even mistaken for its opposite in Mrs. McCullers' work: one will remember Mick's attitude toward Biff Brannon in *The Heart Is a Lonely Hunter.* In this connection it should be noted that the author has been at some pains to give these suspicious neighbors the identity of a *group.*

All at once, as though moved by one will, they walked into the store. At that moment the eight men looked very much alike—all wearing blue overalls, most of them with whitish hair, all pale of face and all with a set, dreaming look in the eye. . . . Except for Reverend Wilkin, they are all alike in many ways as has been said . . . all having taken pleasure from something or other, all having wept or suffered in some way. Each of them worked in the mill, and lived with others in a two or three room house for which the rent was ten dollars or twelve dollars a month. All had been paid that afternoon, for it was Sunday. So, for the present, think of them as a group.

These men are an abstraction: they are suspicion itself. But they are also surprisingly human for an abstraction, and Mrs. McCullers has been careful to emphasize their normality, their "averageness," at the same time that she has used them as a symbol of suspicion. The inference is clear and characteristically melancholy. Most men *are* suspicious, quick to supply others with evil motives and slow to credit them with good ones, unable to recognize love when they see it. And this, of course, constitutes yet another obstacle to their escape.

The epilogue, simply and significantly entitled "The Twelve Mortal Men," describes a chain gang at their backbreaking task of repairing a highway. The meaning here is richly symbolic. The work of the "twelve mortal men" is hard work, and there is no escape from it because they are chained at the ankle. But while they work they sing. "One dark voice will start a phrase, half-sung, and like a question. And after a moment another voice will join in; soon the whole gang will be singing. The voices are dark in the golden glare, the music intricately blended, both somber and joyful. The music will swell until at last it seems that it does not come from the twelve men on the gang, but from the earth itself, or the wide sky. It is music that causes the heart to broaden and the listener to grow cold with ecstasy and fright. . . . And what kind of gang is this that can make such music? Just twelve mortal men, seven of them black and five of them white boys from this county. Just twelve mortal men who are together."

The twelve mortal men, of course, represent all mankind, and they are prisoners because they cannot escape the universal fate of spiritual isolation. There is paradox and irony in the fact that *what joins them together is exactly what keeps them apart*—that is, the predicament of their loneliness. They escape temporarily through their singing (love), which, significantly, they do *together*, in an attempt to resolve, or rather dissolve, their individual identities; but their music is "both somber and joyful" (love, that is, mixed with despair). The effect of this music of chained humanity upon the casual listener is also paradoxical, a mixture of "ecstasy and fright."

There is other symbolism in the work. Perhaps Miss Amelia's eyes are the most striking example; after the hunchback's departure, they become increasingly crossed, "as though they sought each other out to exchange a little glance of grief and lonely recognition." The physical defect becomes more pronounced as the isolation that it symbolizes increases.

It should be clear by now that the same fundamental pattern exists in all Mrs. McCullers' major prose works. It is more elaborate in *The Ballad of the Sad Café* than elsewhere, but its beginnings are recognizable in her first novel and its evolution has occupied her whole literary career. It is a closed pattern, and one that many readers will view with a reluctance which is the measure of their suspicion that it is, after all, authentic—like Mick, the would-be pianist in *The Heart Is a Lonely Hunter*. But it is a pattern with a strange beauty and justice. Few artists have woven it half so well, and it is doubtful whether any artist has been concerned with it so exclusively. There is a terrible finality about the vision of life that Carson McCullers has attained in *The Ballad of the Sad Café:* an eternal flaw exists in the machinery of love, which alone has the power to liberate man from his fate of spiritual isolation. There is no escape, and no hope of escape. You might as well go and listen to the chain gang.

THE ROSE AND THE FOX: NOTES ON THE
SOUTHERN DRAMA

BY JACOB H. ADLER

I

While the modern outburst of Southern writing in fiction, poetry, and criticism has been amply sufficient to be
called a golden flood, the flow of Southern drama, though at
its best hardly less golden, has been by comparison little more
than a trickle. Reasons are not hard to find. Countless novels
and short stories may be published almost countlessly; even
poetry and criticism have many, though often obscure, outlets.
But a play scarcely counts in this country unless it appears on
(or "off") Broadway, and the number of plays which Broadway can absorb—and the variety it *will* absorb—are unfortunately limited. A novel lacking popular appeal and selling only
a few copies may nevertheless have permanently recognized
literary value. The unproduced play, or the play which fails,
will all too probably disappear into an oblivion from which it
is unlikely to emerge, even in the dramatist's collected works.
Such a situation hardly encourages young writers to become
playwrights, and playwrights anywhere are almost certain to
be fewer than the writers of fiction or poetry.

Serious drama is, moreover, almost inevitably an urban phenomenon—as witness not only New York, but London, Paris,
Moscow, ancient Athens. It is probably significant that of the
only three prolific dramatists identified with the South, one
(Lillian Hellman) grew up in New Orleans and New York;
one (Tennessee Williams) was taken from a childhood in Mississippi to an adolescence in St. Louis and early became a
cosmopolitan wanderer; and one (Paul Green) is a folk dramatist and college professor who turned rather soon from the
writing of plays for New York to the creation of historical
pageants designed for non-metropolitan audiences. To be sure,

Southern fiction—short and long—has been turned into drama, but so has non-Southern fiction; and plays from the works of Faulkner and Wolfe and Caldwell and Eudora Welty can be matched and overmatched by plays from the works of Henry James, Edith Wharton, Hemingway, Lewis, Marquand, and such lesser lights as William March, Thomas Heggen, Joseph Hayes, and James Michener. Significantly, too, almost the only Southern playwrights to add to the three already named are Faulkner himself (with *Requiem for a Nun*), Carson McCullers, and Truman Capote—all primarily writers in other forms. Very likely the only truly important drama to come from all this prose fiction, or from the producers of both drama and prose fiction, is Marc Connelly's transformation of Roark Bradford's *Ol' Man Adam an' His Chillun* into the tender and beautiful mystery play *The Green Pastures*, which may well be among the few American plays to survive the century. Much more evanescent but still worth mentioning is Carson McCullers' delicate adaptation of her own *Member of the Wedding*. And, in quite a different category, a play of permanent importance for reasons other than its own considerable worth is Du Bose Heyward's *Porgy*.

By almost any standards—literary, dramatic, commercial, or national identification with the South—the first among Southern playwrights is Tennessee Williams. He has had nine productions on—in one case "off"—Broadway, all but one of them, *Camino Real*, about the South: *The Glass Menagerie* (1945), *A Streetcar Named Desire* (Pulitzer Prize, 1947), *Summer and Smoke* (1948), *The Rose Tattoo* (1950), *Camino Real* (1953), *Cat on a Hot Tin Roof* (Pulitzer Prize, 1954), *Orpheus Descending* (1957), *Garden District* (1958), and *Sweet Bird of Youth* (1959). Almost all have been highly successful with the majority of both critics and the public, though his violence and his addiction to what might be called four-letter actions have brought him detractors. His work has literary as well as commercial-dramatic value, and his reputation—and productions—extend throughout the Western world.

Second-place honors raise a more difficult question. Lillian Hellman's range is greater than Paul Green's, perhaps greater than that of Williams. Her standards of dramaturgy are rigorously high, her commercial success unquestionable. Her identification with the South, though less sure, is built upon four plays dealing directly with Southerners (*The Little Foxes,* 1939; *Another Part of the Forest,* 1946; *The Autumn Garden,* 1951; and *Toys in the Attic,* 1960) and two more (*Watch on the Rhine,* 1941; *The Searching Wind,* 1944), which, while they breathe the atmosphere of the aristocratic Upper South, have no particular Southern connections. At least one of these five, *The Little Foxes,* has considerable power of survival. (Her first play, *The Children's Hour,* which also seems likely to outlive its author, was not laid in the South.) On the other hand, while Miss Hellman's plays are almost as fascinating to read as they are to see, they scarcely qualify as literature. In contrast to all this, Paul Green was never more than a mild success in New York; even *In Abraham's Bosom,* which won the Pulitzer Prize—an honor stubbornly withheld from Miss Hellman—had only a brief run on Broadway and achieved a respectable run in downtown New York partly on the basis of the Prize-winning. Green's commercial success and his public identification belong to his popular pageants, like *The Lost Colony* and *Wilderness Road,* which seem of more interest to folklorists, historians, and analysts of culture in the broad sense than to the critic of drama or literature. Yet Green's earlier plays—*In Abraham's Bosom* (1926), *The Field God* (1927), *Roll, Sweet Chariot* (1935)—are the profoundest portrayals of the Southern Negro and poor white that we have in dramatic form; and *The House of Connolly* (1931), his greatest success, perceptively analyzes a decaying upper-class family. Almost all his dramas are in a sense folk dramas—this country's best folk dramas—and this genre depends far less than the usual play upon commercial success for survival.

Still, the feeling persists that all these works are more successful as poetic, powerfully imagined literary "studies" (based firmly on Green's early observations in eastern North Carolina) than as plays. Admittedly deficient in dramaturgy, Green is probably destined to see his plays, like his pageants, survive as precious documents for the cultural historian and the folklorist rather than for the student of drama. This hardly seems the fate reserved for Williams or Miss Hellman, who stand or fall as dramatists. In listing the *dramatists* of the South I am convinced that Miss Hellman deserves second place. For this reason, and because her work offers useful contrasts and parallels to that of Williams, I propose (mildly violating chronology) to examine Williams' important plays about the South and then to look at Miss Hellman's by way of comparison. And I shall begin with Williams' *Summer and Smoke*, because I think that it has received far less attention than it deserves, and because of all Williams' plays which say things about the South I think this one says the most.

Yet on the face of it, *Summer and Smoke* need not have been set in the South at all. The situation that it develops, of the oversensual boy and the overspiritual girl, could have spun itself out almost anywhere. Williams does not even provide, as he does in other plays—notably for Amanda in *The Glass Menagerie*—an appropriate accent or rhythm of speech. No Negroes appear, and the only visible class differences are based on morality (patently loose women are outcast), as they might be in any small Midwestern town. The minister is a minister from anywhere, the doctor a doctor from anywhere, the Fourth of July celebration—itself a surprise; most writers might have used a Southern Memorial Day—has much the same flavor, and occurs in about the same year, as the one in the Connecticut of O'Neill's *Ah, Wilderness!*

Nor is Alma's predicament, on the face of it, related closely to the South, as that of Blanche DuBois in *A Streetcar Named Desire* so unmistakably is. One thing that Alma represents, the soul which must find its body, is of universal application—as much so, and in the same way, as the New England village of Thornton Wilder's *Our Town*. That majority of Broadway critics who dismissed Alma as just another neurotic Southern female were wrong. Neither her plight, that of the repressed small-town minister's daughter, nor her story is obviously Southern; and in one sense the play's locale is Mississippi only because that is the region Williams knows.

Yet Alma Winemiller is beyond question Southern. Even today there are Southern women (though only a few) so like her as to make a Southerner's hackles rise in recognition as he reads her lines: the overelaborate vocabulary, the overgreat expectations from others, the living of life as though it were a work of fiction, the insulation from the world. The genteel code was stronger in the South, and lasted longer, and caused perhaps more pain.

But for a dramatist who in his other plays could create so completely circumstantial a South, and such completely circumstantial Southerners, this is a curious, and not even generally recognizable, minimum; and it leads to another and related question: Why did Williams choose to lay this story, alone among his plays, in a rather distant past? Now the past affects the present in all of Williams' major plays, just as it does in Faulkner's novels. Once, and once only, in his novels Faulkner goes back to that past and creates, in *Absalom, Absalom!*, a story not at all typical of the South either as we know it or as we remember it—Sutpen is out of Greek tragedy, not out of the South—and of that story makes an allegory of the Southern dilemma. This is what Williams does in *Summer and Smoke*. For this atypical story is unmistakably an allegory, an allegory of body and soul, and if it has meaning in terms of all mankind (as Sutpen does), it may also (like Sutpen) have a special meaning for the South. The South, Williams might well be saying, has experienced the greatest difficulty in bringing into harmony its body and its soul.

Let us then explore the pastness, the allegorical form, and the allegorical content of *Summer and Smoke*, to see how they illuminate the play and the South. The pastness of the play concerns it both as play and as allegory. First, the pastness makes Alma more believable. An audience might not easily suspend disbelief in so thoroughgoing a prudery as Alma's if the play took place in the present; or, at the very least, Williams would have had to expend much effort in explaining how that prudery came to be. If Williams was to concentrate, as he apparently wished to, on the allegory, then he had to gain audience acceptance of Alma by a minimum of means: the South, a preacher's daughter, the pre-World-War-I past.

Similarly, the past can manage with less local color; but Williams had to choose his past with care. Give an audience the ante-bellum South, or the Civil War South, or the Reconstruction South, and it will expect all the elaborate apparatus, part real, part mythical, with which it has become familiar. But the South of the turn of the century? And, moreover, a middle-class South, neither aristocratic nor poor-white nor Negro? A forgotten world, from which all needless detail can be stripped away; an island, lost in space and time, which is what allegory seems to require. (Sutpen's Hundred is another such island, though in the rich texture of a novel it can be surrounded, in both space and time, by the familiar waters of reality. *Everyman* may also come to mind, and *Pilgrim's Progress*, and *Penguin Island*.)

Moreover, Williams uses various devices to universalize the past—devices which he may have derived from Faulkner and from such bits in *Our Town* as the address on an envelope which begins with Grover's Corners and ends with the Mind of God. The sets are reduced to the barest essentials of reality without abandoning it altogether (as Wilder does); but to the extent that the sets are recognizable they are Gothic (the houses), classical (the statue), and scientific (the anatomy chart), thus covering almost the whole spread of Western cultural history. The Gothic and the classical are, it is true, not unsuitable to the South's historical and architectural past; but they also suggest farther reaches of time. And the genuine Gothic is underlined in Alma's talk of the spirituality of Gothic cathedrals, the genuine classical in Williams' description of John as "a Promethean figure" with "the fresh and shining look of an epic hero"; while Gothic tale and Greek tragedy may both be recalled in the sudden and dreadful death of John's father through the unwitting responsibility of both hero and heroine. And over all, besides the statue of Eternity, there is the sky, insisted upon by Williams, with the wheeling constellations and the inevitable round of years.

Williams' allegory is an allegory both of the South and of all mankind. It is therefore not only timely (the past as a comment on the present) but timeless; and timelessness is a quality which fits poorly with the actuality of the now. Wilder, in *Our Town*, achieves it through pastness plus fantasy; Williams achieves it through pastness plus allegory. The statue of Eternity may brood over the past, and by implication over the present; for it to brood directly over the present would be far less believable. Hence the use of the past helps Williams in various ways: it assists belief; it helps strip away the details useful to realism but detrimental to allegory; and it directly assists the allegory, both Southern and universal.

Summer and Smoke takes the form of an allegorical ritual, a modern psychological version of the medieval dialogue between body and soul. The set itself—the two matching houses, the statue between and above them, and the sky over all—is formal and ritualistic. The opening scene of John and Alma in childhood provides almost all the thematic movements of the ritual: Alma loves John but can approach him only through cultural assistance (handkerchiefs to wipe his nose); John is embarrassed by Alma's efforts, but is also attracted and makes minor efforts to please her (washes his face); his principal methods of approach, however, are the violent (throws a stone) and the physical (forces a kiss); he even sneers at the meaning of Alma's name (soul), and he is unmoved (while Alma is greatly moved) at the discovery that the statue is named Eternity.

The play develops these themes in terms of increasingly complex approaches and withdrawals. John crosses to Alma's house—and is repelled by the pseudo-culture of her literary club. Alma crosses to John's house—and is offered the reality of science (astronomical distances), the comfort of science (sleeping pills), and a drive in the country. The scene under the bower at the lake, which is the climax of Act I, is a long series of approaches and withdrawals, of attractions and repulsions—a sort of ideational minuet. John proposes a cockfight; Alma is repelled. John praises sensual satisfaction as the only good in life; Alma counters with Gothic cathedrals. Alma quotes an idealistic epigram; John tells her it is by Oscar Wilde. John kisses Alma; Alma is attracted—but John (finding that he still feels impelled to call her *Miss* Alma) withdraws. Alma suggests that he would want a lady as the mother of his children; John suggests that marriage must be founded in sexual harmony, and "ladies" are often cold. John suggests an immediate bed; Alma, violently repelled, goes home in a taxi.

The ritualistic dance, however, is not repetitive but developmental; eventually the two change places (and John shares in giving Alma handkerchiefs), so that Alma, near the play's end, can make a comparison with another ritual: they are "like two people exchanging a call on each other at the same time, and each one finding the other one gone out, the door locked against him and no one to answer the bell!" And the ritual pattern is further emphasized by the alternation of scenes in the two houses; by the play's beginning and ending under the statue of Eternity; by Alma's characteristic pose of someone prepared to take communion; by John's going to Alma for spiritual consolation and making with her a tableau of "a stone *Pietà*"; and by the statue of Eternity's being a fountain, from which Alma and others periodically drink. Still other specific rituals occur, and as is natural in a world where body and soul never achieve complete integration, almost all of them are flawed or parodied or specifically evil. There are, for example, the faintly satirized Fourth of July celebration; the club meeting, a burlesqued ritual of modern culture; the scene in the bower, a mock ritual of courtship; the much-mentioned ritual of the cockfight; the orgiastic ritual of Rosa's dance; the ritual of a funeral (mocked by John) off in the background. John's summer life has a grossly sexual rhythm which repels even him, and his consequent mention of castration is a reminder (especially since he is a somewhat Dionysian figure) of further rituals. John and Alma both go through a period of suffering (involving in Alma's case both smoke and the change of seasons), from which they emerge more nearly whole. And there is the ritualistic change of the season itself, and the movement of the stars.

Thus in its pastness and its ritualism *Summer and Smoke* minimizes realism for the sake of allegory. But the *universal* allegory is present only in general terms: souls are crippled without bodies; bodies are violent without souls; each without the other takes part in seriously flawed rituals; and mutual awareness of the lack, if achieved, may come too late for complete integration. Yet the *details* of the play, which will not fit into the universal allegory, fit very well into an allegory of the South; and that allegory therefore requires further scrutiny.

That it *is* an allegory of the South is made immediately clear by the name of the town: Glorious Hill. To represent the whole world, a town might much better be called something like Grover's Corners. But the South considers itself a Glorious Hill, its past glories continuing under the aspect of Eternity. Alma, the soul of the South, is the daughter of religion, and hence of tradition and truth, but in the person of her father, religion has become a religion of appearances only.

Alma herself does some good (she helps Nellie, the daughter of the town prostitute) but refuses to face basic problems; her principal characteristics, as soul, are prudery and affectation and a dry-as-dust, attenuated culture which lingers out of the romantic past.

But Alma is also the daughter of a demented mother. People have dismissed this as just part of the Southern literary *Zeitgeist*, and point to demented characters in Faulkner and Lillian Hellman and elsewhere in Williams. Aside from the unfair basic accusation that this attitude implies about the best literature treating the South, it is invalid in this case for at least two reasons. First, Mrs. Winemiller's dementia is not the hazy, vacuous, childish variety that the accuser usually has in mind. It is childish, but also vindictive, unpleasant, and grimly humorous. Second, we have here a play in which almost all the characters fit into either the plot or the allegory, and Mrs. Winemiller is no exception; admittedly needless to the plot, she does contribute to the definition of Alma's allegorical past.

Alma, then, is the daughter of a desiccated religion and of the sort of dementia that causes retreat into childhood. This is not true of the soul in the universal sense, but it can very well be how Williams sees the soul of the South: in retreating to the past, and hence avoiding responsibility and reality, it has achieved a grotesque and childish ugliness. So Alma has trouble with her mother—that is, she has difficulty in keeping this aspect of her inheritance repressed. In one scene there is actually a physical battle between mother and daughter; and again and again Alma must employ tactics which seem unworthy of her in order to keep her mother in bounds. Clearly too, while Alma is still capable of redemption, the danger exists that she will follow her mother; her neuroticism is pronounced, and her crisis is a dangerous one. Thus Williams says (1) that this aspect of the Southern soul is slightly grotesque, pleasant on the surface (Alma) but very ugly underneath (her mother); and (2) that the South's soul is still redeemable in this respect, though the danger of an irrevocable retreat remains. So long as the soul of the South refuses to face reality, it has no future; Mrs. Winemiller is as futureless as the day before yesterday, and Alma, so long as she secludes herself, is squired only by an effeminate, mother-fixated boy. It is appropriate that John is the son of a doctor, but it is perhaps more interesting that he is motherless. The prologue points out that he doesn't use a handkerchief—that is, he is cut off from the cultural advantages that a mother would give. It also points out that the spectacle of his dying mother repelled him violently—that is, he is cut off from certain aspects of his past. And so it is with the South: its body is strong and attractive but dangerous and purposeless ("the excess of his power has not yet found a channel," Williams says of John. "If it remains without one, it will burn him up") because it is severed from its soul. John dissipates his physical inheritance to the benefit of outsiders (Rosa and her father), and becomes involved in violence.

For the central violence of the play, however—the murder of John's father—all are responsible. The violence is committed by an outsider, but it happens only because the South does not know itself: the soul, Alma, is ignorant of the physical violence she is tampering with when she telephones John's father; the body, John, has not been taught to recognize the evil that can lie in the depths of the soul. The responsibility for violence in the South lies everywhere—in the outsider, but also in the divided South itself: the sterile remnants of the cultural past, cut off from the present reality; the gaudy grimness of the present reality, cut off from the cultural past.

But the violence results in a genuine crisis for both John and Alma; and both effect compromises. John becomes successful and self-sacrificial as a doctor, has glimmerings of understanding about man's non-physical nature, but, remaining physically powerless with Alma, marries a young and flighty but well-meaning girl. Alma sheds her affectations and her repressions, renounces idealism (the statue's "body is stone and her blood is mineral water"), tries by the frankest of means to win John, and, failing, picks up a young, eager, reasonably attractive boy. Thus Williams depicts a stale, poetico-idealistic culture, refusing to face reality, yet still partly beautiful; and unable to achieve, or to attract, power, until reality is faced. And he warns that waiting too long to come to terms with reality can result, when reality is faced, in a complete denial of the ideal, in a failure to attract genuine power, and in a comparatively trivial fulfillment. On the other hand, the South's genuine power, both intellectual and physical, is dissipated because it can find no valid ideal—or is psychologically cut off from pursuing such an ideal, if found. All this happens in Glorious Hill under the wings of the Angel of Eternity! This is pessimistic and ironical; and *Summer and Smoke* is a pessimistic, ironical sort of allegory and play. "Too little and too late," it says; we watch the beauty of life evaporate in the vapidity of an effeminate and quibbling literary club, while the force of life is equally wasted in the remote and unreal cockfights and assignations of the appropriately named Moon Lake.

Yet the picture is not entirely pessimistic; the compromise unions are better than no unions at all. Alma has faced reality sufficiently to become psychologically much better integrated. Both Alma and John have found partners—immature, to be sure, but with at least *some* potential. And Alma, in a final gesture, seems to come to terms with Eternity. The awful heat of summer ends as the smoke of the battle of the psyche dissipates (and if summer is light and smoke dark, who is to say that the race question does not underlie the imagery?). What is seen in the South in the final cool clarity may be compromise, but compromise (Williams says) is at any rate the better truth in this world—better than sterility and violence. For any other truth, one must turn to the Glorious Hill of Eternity.

Here, then, is Williams' full interpretation of the Southern predicament, presented through allegory. When allegory obtrudes itself, it has rarely if ever since the Middle Ages been a popular dramatic form. *Summer and Smoke* was not a success on Broadway with either critics or public, after having been a success with both when presented in arena form in Dallas. The blame for the failure was laid mainly upon three points: that here was just another study of a neurotic Southern female, less believable, recognizable, and dramatic than the others; that the "symbolism" of the play was forced and overobvious; and that the play, for some reason never made quite clear, was more suitable for "arena" production. But the third reason seems to cancel out the first two, and the real basis for the unpopularity, that the play is allegory, seems not to have been recognized. Alma exists in a different kind of dramatic world from Blanche's; the characters and "things" in an allegory are expected to be clear and stationary in equivalence, not complex and shifting; and the large-stage production made the play less "real" than it was in arena, thereby reducing the play's appeal but actually coming closer to its genuine meaning. *Summer and Smoke* is much better than most critics made it out to be, and it is profoundly interesting as Williams' most complete interpretation of the South; but this is not to say that the play is as successful *dramatically* as his other major productions. Probably allegory is inherently less dramatic; certainly allegory violates "realism" in a way that audiences find it difficult to accept.

Williams' other plays about the South use other means. All to some extent juxtapose the physical and violent with the cultural and ideal, but the result is a wider variety of methods than is usually recognized; if changes are rung on more or less the same theme, this is also what Faulkner does, and the result in both cases is a wide panorama of life in the South.

To a certain extent autobiographical, *The Glass Menagerie* is less subject to large interpretations than the other plays; and since Williams feels more than usual affection for his characters, he searches for devices which will soften the portraits that artistic honesty requires him to present. Hence the narrator presenting the play as memory; hence the mood music, the scrim, the beauty of Laura, the underlying nobility of Amanda, the unexpected kindness and understanding of the Gentleman Caller; hence all the devices which we have come to cherish, particularly the glass menagerie itself. It was pointed out as early as this play (1945) that Williams owes a debt to Chekhov—a debt which, like his debt to O'Neill and Wilder, must one day be thoroughly explored. And certainly in this play the combination of impressionism of effect and realism of detail, the compassion and objectivity, the development by conflict of mood and temperament, the comedy-through-pathos, the portrait of hopeless inheritors of a lost tradition—all derive from Chekhov.

The most interesting comparison, for the present purpose, is the treatment of the central symbol in Williams and in Chekhov. The sea gull in Chekhov's play is titular, it represents a young girl, it is brought forward again and again, it is unnecessary to the plot, and yet it is used developmentally, not merely allowed to exist as static. The anatomy chart in *Summer and Smoke*, being allegorical, not symbolic, is not really used and never changes; and yet it is necessary in a way that the sea gull is not. But the glass menagerie, like the sea gull, represents a young girl: like Laura, it is fragile, beautiful, useless; highly appropriate to both Laura and the mood, it is unnecessary to the story, yet it is brought forward again and again; and, through the breaking of the unicorn's horn, it is a *developed* symbol to which something really happens that gives it a new meaning. Yet it is difficult to make it signify anything beyond Laura, as it is difficult to make the play mean anything beyond the characters portrayed.

This is not surprising, if the play is autobiographical. Still, some sort of interpretation can be made, in terms of the distribution of the physical-violent versus the cultural-ideal. Rather oddly, both Tom and Amanda combine in themselves the opposites: each has both culture (Tom writes poetry) and power; but culture and power are wasted in them because mother and son alike are cut off from their cultural past and unable to accept the cultural present. In Amanda, the case is hopeless; she is too much tied to the past; if the case is not hopeless in Tom, he must find fulfillment in escape from both the past and the present in some indefinable future; but he seems unlikely to do so, since his violent break from his family leaves him with guilt feelings. (May we say, then, that the South cannot find itself by becoming something other than the South?) Laura is crippled, mentally and physically; hence she has neither the culture nor the power. Both lie latent in her, but they can be awakened only by an outsider (Tom and Amanda, the inheritors of the lost past, are helpless) who recognizes the beauty and power underneath the grotesqueness of deformity. Since few outsiders are sufficiently unattached and perceptive both to see it and to act upon it, her chances are slim. If all this seems farfetched, then there seems no choice but to deny an intellectual content to the play; and certainly in an autobiographical, impressionistic play the intellectual content is not likely to be primary. Yet the pattern I have described is similar enough to the pattern in Williams' other plays to make it persuasive. And it gains in persuasiveness, since at the one moment when the glass menagerie is used developmentally, it is used to show an unreal creature become real—a creature (a horse) of genuine beauty and power.

In *A Streetcar Named Desire* the contrast between culture and power is at its sharpest; appropriately, this is a violently naturalistic play. There is still mood music, and there is still, as in all of Williams, a great deal that derives from Chekhov; yet the effect is of the clearest, harshest reality. What is primary is story and people as they are, as they inevitably are; what is secondary is Blanche and the others as representative of the culture-power dichotomy and the Southern dilemma; what is tertiary (an aspect not present in *The Glass Menagerie*) is Blanche as a tragic representative of the sensitive individual lost in the complex modern world.

The symbols in *Streetcar* therefore grow out of the reality, not the reality out of the symbols. Whether or not this is the "best" method, it is certainly the method modern audiences *prefer;* and this may be one reason why *Streetcar* received the greatest acclaim of Williams' first three important plays. As Howard Barnes pointed out in his *Herald-Tribune* review of *Streetcar,* "instead of leaning heavily on symbolism, as the title might have led one to expect, Williams has to do with very human beings in completely recognizable circumstances. The fact that there actually is . . . a streetcar called Desire clanging through New Orleans, has merely set a fine imagination to work." It is true that to get to Stella's slum apartment Blanche has had to transfer from Desire· to Cemeteries and arrive at Elysian Fields (where she is alien), but, once stated —more as a theme than a symbol—this imagery rarely intrudes on the play. The typical symbol in *Streetcar,* one pointed out by many critics, is the overhead naked light bulb which Blanche covers with a Chinese lantern. When Mitch pulls the lantern from the light and thrusts the brilliant bulb in Blanche's face, reality becomes symbol in an exact reversal of the crisis in *The Glass Menagerie,* where the act of breaking the unicorn's horn makes symbol for a moment become reality.

Given greater reality and larger scope than *Summer and Smoke* or *The Glass Menagerie,* it is not surprising that the culture-power conflict in *Streetcar* is especially complex.

Blanche, the representative of the cultural and ideal, is as sexually immoral as the pre-crisis John, the representative of power in *Summer and Smoke*. (It is sometimes suggested that Williams considers sex the road to health and the panacea for neuroticism; but while he does not insist upon formal unions it is made clear again and again that promiscuity is a sign of psychological illness.) Blanche, then, as representative of the Old South, dissipates her power, but for the opposite of John's reasons; far from failing to recognize her cultural (and personal) past, she is inextricably bound to it and, hence, caught in a neurotic limbo, combines in herself the irreconcilable opposites of John's exaggerated physical urges and Alma's culture, pretense, and affection. (The critics who said Blanche was Alma in a later stage of development were wrong; Alma in the end shed her affectations and came to terms at least partly with her ideals.) In John, recognition of the ideal brings self-control; in Alma, recognition of the real brings release from repression and prudery; but in Blanche, who is involved with both real and ideal and cannot reconcile them, nymphomania and prudery, love of the past and hatred of the past, genuine culture and pretentious fakery exist at the same time. And thus Blanche can represent one way the South can go: unable to face the contrast between the romantic past and the realistic present, Blanche violently betrays her own code while desperately pretending to maintain it. That way inevitably lies Cemeteries.

Another way, as everyone has noticed, is Stella's. Like Tom in *Menagerie*, Stella attempts to get away from the past by denying it utterly. But she is more successful than Tom; indeed, she lives in Elysian Fields. (For that matter, Stella, unlike Blanche, is not particularly Southern in outward manifestations at all; she is a *person*, unbound to geography—as of course many Southerners are.) True, she is wedded to a man who represents not only power but violence, not only violence but rape; but out of the match one is apparently supposed to see a future in which—perhaps—a new culture can be born. Stanley is by no means all bad, his strength is not all directionless, his love for Stella is pathetically real. The child of immigrants, he is the new, untamed pioneer, and brings to the South (Williams may be saying) a power more exuberant than destructive, a sort of power the South may have lost. This is apparently Williams' attitude toward foreigners in *The Rose Tattoo* and *Baby Doll* as well as *Streetcar*. Curiously, it is not the attitude in *Summer and Smoke*, where the foreigners prey on the South and deplete its native strength, nor in *Orpheus Descending*, where the foreigners are themselves victims of Southern violence. At any rate, in *Streetcar*, the gross physical power of the South lies in Harold Mitchell, who is psychologically bound to an ill mother and who is deceived (as Stanley is not for a moment) by Blanche's cultural pretenses; a man, then, who is tied to a dead culture and a dead past. Blanche's dead husband was also psychologically bound and hence not fully masculine; and so Williams seems to say that only a less than complete man can be attracted by the past that Blanche represents. Yet Blanche has in her something of a genuine culture and beauty which Stella has abandoned and which Stanley cannot see; and, as with the aristocrats in *The Cherry Orchard*, we must regret its passing, even as we recognize the decadence and futility and even degradation which makes its passing both necessary and inevitable.

Williams' panoramic scope may be suggested by the fact that we have now examined a fallen Southern aristocrat and her children, living in a big city outside the South; the middle class in a small Southern town; and a fallen Southern aristocrat amid the denizens of a New Orleans slum. In *The Rose Tattoo*, we see a group not tied to the Old South at all, a colony of Sicilian immigrants on the Gulf Coast. Williams has written two full-length works which are primarily comic, this and the movie script *Baby Doll*. The latter concerns poor whites, and perhaps fallen aristocrats who have allied themselves with the poor whites. Like Faulkner, Williams seems to feel that the comic can be located in the South only if one looks away from the better classes. (Mark Twain too, long ago, found no comedy in Colonel Sherburn, and little in the Shepherdsons and Grangerfords, but plenty in the lower middle classes and below.) If *The Rose Tattoo* has to do with the South, it must be by contrast, for its characters are in the South only by chance, and—except for the lush tropical atmosphere, which could be achieved in many other places—the story it tells has almost no Southern connections. (The inspiration for the play was Williams' visit to Italy.) Yet it is interesting that we have here *another* Southern race, bred to both culture and violence. Underlying a tremendously foreign exterior, Serafina, the mother in the play, has characteristics quite familiar to the South: religion and superstition, honor and courage and awe of rank and high standards for her child; and, when reality becomes unbearable, a tendency to violence or to an almost psychotic withdrawal. Yet she has about her a lushness beyond any Southern lushness (emphasized almost to the point of nausea by the constant symbol of the rose), and she has the power of fertility, hence a share in the real future, which, if Williams' other plays say anything, much of the South has lost. As with Stanley Kowalski, then, we find *too much* power, an overflowing of it, too little direction, yet an overwhelming reality and an overwhelming demand for genuine fulfillment.

This is a wildly exuberant comedy, and it is probably unfair to seek in it very elaborate interpretations. Yet something needs to be done with the rose symbol, the constant reiteration of which has been the principal objection to the play. It is to be noted that the roses cluster around Serafina, while Rosa's only direct connection with them is her name. This brings to attention the interesting fact that of all Serafina's flamboyant qualities which she shares with the South, the only quality which (according to Williams) the South does not share with *her* is the quality unmistakably inherited by Rosa: that overwhelming sexuality which—clearly, from Serafina's joy at conception—is Shaw's life force. Otherwise, her environment has made Rosa not Sicilian, not Southern, but American. She is to marry a Southerner who, like Stella in *Streetcar*, seems simply American too. Thus in one aspect *The Rose Tattoo* is *Streetcar* in reverse; in that aspect it can be a comedy, because the more picturesque and violent portions of the foreign inheritance are left to the older generation.

This is not absolutely to defend the symbol of the rose in *The Rose Tattoo*, which appears in every form from tattoos to the color of a shirt to the scent of hair oil. Doubtless the symbol is overstressed and overcomplicated. But to criticize it without examining it seems unfair; at least the roses are appropriate both to Serafina's Mediterranean exuberance and to the underlying meaning of the play.

Williams' variations on a theme, the variety of ways in which he treats it, and the scope of his treatment could be further displayed. In *Baby Doll*, for example, we see latent power and sexuality in a lower-class Southern girl of arrested emotional development who can be awakened, apparently, only by an outsider; we see native physical power unable to achieve fulfillment, spending itself in destruction; and we see all this in terms of a sharply satirical realism. In *Cat on a Hot Tin Roof*, we see the effect of financial power on Southerners of lower-class origin; we see a Southern girl of more cultured background deliberately shedding her culture in order to fight for the power she wants in this ferociously acquisitive family; and we see all this in terms of a highly stylized presentation moving in the direction of the expressionistic. No doubt the theme becomes monotonous at times; no doubt at times, and more frequently in his later plays, it descends needlessly into the unsavory and the decadent. No doubt, too, one may disagree with what Williams sees in the South, both in factual detail and in symbolic or allegorical generalization. Williams' work is like his own rose, gaudy and varicolored, strong in scent and decadent in decay, in the mass, overwhelming and monotonous; but also sharp and delicate, beautiful and tender, and very real. True or false, his view of the South has inspired him to dramatic productions of undeniable reality, originality, and power.

II

Lillian Hellman's picture of the South resembles Tennessee Williams' in a number of interesting ways; but the story that Dorothy Parker suggested the title of *The Little Foxes* at once illuminates a difference in method. For Miss Hellman's symbolic title, unlike those of Williams, is a comment on the play, not an integral part of it; the same can be said for *Another Part of the Forest*. In these first two of Miss Hellman's plays about the South the method is straightforward realism, to such an extent that even when Miss Hellman wants her characters, the Hubbards, to be representative of something beyond themselves, she does not succeed in making them so. Miss Hellman's plays therefore lack a kind of complexity typical of Williams, and while she too deals with the culture-power dichotomy, she does so in much simpler terms. By and large the cleavage is between aristocrat and Hubbard, with the Negro—much more prominent than in Williams' plays—often admirable and always a victim. Poor whites lie off in the background as further victims, and there are hints of an incipient non-Hubbard middle class; but except for the poor-white Laurette Sincee in *Forest*, there are in the foreground only the three groups: aristocrats, Negroes, Hubbards.

The primary fact is the Hubbards; and perhaps the primary fact about them for present purposes is that, while to any audience they would seem Southern-born, they do not, in their central acquisitive "foxiness," seem typically of the South. (Historically they may be quite representative, but that is not the point; the point is that they do not seem so.) This is rather an odd phenomenon; it becomes especially odd when one compares the Hubbards to similar characters in Faulkner and in Williams. In external phenomena, the Hubbards are thoroughly Southern. They display in wide variety, for example, Southern attitudes toward the Negro—all the way from the guilt feelings which make the demented Lavinia in *Another Part of the Forest* want to devote her entire life to Negroes and even identify herself with them, to the Ku Klux Klanism of her son Oscar in the same play; and, in between, the combination in Ben (in *The Little Foxes*) of loyalty to an old servant—his cook is bad, but he will keep her because she was his mother's— and the grossest economic exploitation of Negroes in the mass; while beyond the Hubbards there is the greater loyalty and sensibility, the *noblesse oblige*, of the old aristocrats, as represented by Birdie and Horace. The Hubbards are rooted historically in the South; much more is made of this than it is regarding anyone, even Blanche, in Williams' plays. They are rooted geographically in the South; they look out onto the North as a different world in which Chicago is to Regina a distant and infinitely desirable Vanity Fair and even Baltimore is remote and incomprehensible. They are Southern in their stubborn family loyalty against the world; they are even Southern in their small habits, so that it seems perfectly natural, neither exaggerated nor ludicrous, to find grits on Regina's breakfast table. Yet Miss Hellman's central purpose, as the title, the historical period, and several key speeches in *The Little Foxes* suggest, was to make them typical of a rising Southern class of exploiting industrialists, and, beyond that, of such a class in America generally. In this, by common critical consent, Miss Hellman fails.

Why does she fail? The usual reason given is that she makes the Hubbards so completely and circumstantially evil, so utterly individual in their depravity, as to make it impossible for them to be typical of anything. But this criticism flounders at the feet of Flem Snopes, as avaricious, hypocritical, calloused, and depraved as any Hubbard, and yet at least as successful as a Southern type as he is as an individual. Furthermore, Faulkner shows Snopes doing just what the Hubbards do— exploiting Negro, poor white, and aristocrat in a rise to power which begins in precisely the same year (1900) as *The Little Foxes*.

The answer, I believe, lies in Miss Hellman's failure to achieve symbolism. (Other dramatic techniques extending beyond realism would serve, but the titles of *Foxes* and *Forest* suggest that symbolism is the one Miss Hellman would use, if any.) This is not the place to determine how Faulkner makes Flem Snopes a symbol or what techniques Faulkner uses to get beyond documentary realism; but Williams too succeeds in making a character like Blanche exist at several levels—as a vividly real and complex individual, as a symbol for the South, and as a symbol for the modern world: precisely what Miss Hellman tries to do with the Hubbards and fails. Archibald MacLeish once contrasted the actual and the real in the drama, feeling that straight "realistic" techniques could achieve only the actual. Thornton Wilder has denied the possibility of achieving the genuinely, permanently true, the essence of reality, through the realistic effects of the picture-frame stage. And even in so naturalistic a play as *Streetcar*, Williams uses the various non-realistic techniques of symbolism, impressionism, and even expressionism. Similarly, even at his more realistic, Ibsen, the more important of Miss Hellman's two dramatic masters (the other is Chekhov), almost always used techniques extending his dramatic picture beyond the actual; and Miss Hellman's inspiration for the character of Regina seems, significantly, to be Hedda Gabler, out of a play which of all Ibsen's major plays seems most actual and least representative. Miss Hellman fails in a way that earlier American dramatic realists failed: it is not that the mother in *The Silver Cord* or the wife in *Craig's Wife* is too individual to be the type she is obviously intended to be; it is that both are too rooted in the actuality of realistic dramatic techniques to escape from it. This is not to deny that Miss Hellman's Hubbards are vivid and fascinating dramatic creations; it is merely to say that they succeed at only one level, as actual individuals, where they were obviously intended to succeed at more than one.

At that one level, there are interesting comparisons and contrasts with Williams. In Williams, the principal symbol of "power" in the culture-power dichotomy is sex. Even in the Big Daddy of *Cat on a Hot Tin Roof*, whose power derives from money and who represents money to almost all who surround him, sexuality is prominent; there is the latent suggestion that without the sexuality the drive which resulted in tremendous aggrandizement could not have existed; and in Brick the achievement of normal sexuality is the *sine qua non* of his inheriting his father's wealth. In Miss Hellman, on the contrary, prominent sexuality almost always attaches to the weak, or if it appears in the relatively strong (as in Horace, and as in David in *Watch on the Rhine*), it is a weaker element in them. Only in Oscar, the weakest of the three Hubbards of the middle generation, is sexuality even active. Of the other two, Ben (like Faulkner's Flem Snopes) has apparently always been sexless, and Regina has become frigid after an unhappy love affair in her youth. Both are thus free to pursue power with a single-mindedness which Oscar lacks. Their father, Marcus, always subordinated love to money, and it is perhaps indicative of his coming fall from power in *Another Part of the Forest* that he has allowed his control to slacken in an incestuous affection for Regina.

The symbol of power, and the principal motivating force, in these two plays—and, to a surprising extent, even in the idealistic *Watch on the Rhine*—is money. And while money is necessary to the preservation of culture (Birdie's family is destroyed through poverty; the wealth in *Watch on the Rhine* represents culture at its best), it can also be destructive of it.

Culture, in other words, is neither consistent nor inconsistent with the symbol of power. It resides in the financially successful Horace, who has a broken violin in his safe deposit box, and in the weak Birdie, who treasures a Wagner autograph. It lies in the dominant and wealthy aristocratic matriarch in *Watch on the Rhine*, and in her strong, penniless, idealistic German son-in-law. It is particularly complex in Marcus Hubbard, who learned Greek as a boy doing manual labor, who has a real appreciation for music and literature, who patterned his house after the very Southern culture he despises and has betrayed, who has raised his children in a tyranny bound to make them hate anything he represents, except money; and who has allowed his life to be ruled by money and the power it conveys.

Culture and power are not, then, in necessary opposition. Both are good, though both can exist in the wrong hands, and they are necessarily related only to the extent that money—and culture!—are essential to the preservation of culture. (For indeed culture itself is a sort of power in Miss Hellman; and there is hope that, through Alexandra, it will defeat the power of money in the tribe of Hubbards, and, through Kurt and his kind, the power of fascism in *Watch on the Rhine*.) Between weakness and the wrong kind of strength—the kind conveyed by money alone—lies the well-integrated person who puts culture and money (and sex too) in their proper place: the Farrellys and Kurt in *Watch on the Rhine;* Horace in *The Little Foxes;* no one—not even Birdie, who sells herself for money and clings to a dead past—in *Another Part of the Forest.* Williams too believes that there can be an integration; but sex as the symbol for power is a much more prominent element in the synthesis, and there is probably no example in his plays of the synthesis actually achieved in perfect, self-sustaining balance; such achievement is future or ideal, not actual.

There are many other parallels with Williams. Miss Hellman, for example, gives attention to foreigners in a Southern environment in *Watch on the Rhine* and *The Autumn Garden.* The conflict of cultural ideals and bitter reality has led Lavinia in *Forest,* like Blanche in *Streetcar,* to dementia; and, like Mrs. Winemiller, she has been kept at home, even though the dementia is an embarrassment to her family. Marcus Hubbard and Big Daddy are both poor whites who have gained financial power, and both dominate their families overwhelmingly. Miss Hellman even provides us with insights into typical important Southern phenomena. In the 1880 Oscar we see exactly the process of the Klan's changing from what it was immediately after the war to what it later became; in Ben we see precisely the almost unconscious sanctimoniousness which enables a certain kind of man to get away with exploitation and even theft. In Birdie and her cousin we see distinctly why certain aristocrats declined and disappeared. There are sudden startling realizations, such as the fact that Horace cannot leave the colored Addie money in his will, since in the South of that day she could never collect it. Yet it is curious how little all this has to do with an *interpretation* of the South. These happen to be Southern individuals, and Miss Hellman is clearly interested in interpreting them both as individuals and as Southerners; but the result is no more an interpretation of the South than a play containing Englishmen is necessarily an interpretation of England.

The story ought to be different when one reaches Miss Hellman's next-to-the-last play about the South: *The Autumn Garden*. First, the technique is different. The tightly constructed plots are abandoned. Chekhov takes over as the dominant influence. Money, while still prominent, is no longer such a dominant force and motivation. And this is the first of Miss Hellman's specifically Southern studies which takes place in the present. Moreover, one long suspected advantage over Williams is made finally unmistakable: Miss Hellman is at home in dealing with *genuine* aristocrats, with a genuine upper-class society, which Williams can treat (if at all) only when it has fallen. Indeed, it is hard to believe that any of Williams' fallen aristocrats—Amanda, Blanche, Carol Cutrere in *Orpheus Descending*—were ever *really* upper-class. They lack an essential breeding which, however degraded Miss Hellman's characters become, they never lose. In *The Autumn Garden*, Constance Tuckerman contrasts *breeding* with *gentility*, which she was taught by her mother to believe was its opposite. One cannot help feeling that *gentility* is what Blanche and the others had. Whatever it is, they are self-conscious about it; in

Miss Hellman's characters self-consciousness about basic behavior is impossible, since the quality is innate.

But for all this, Miss Hellman's study of a collection of visi-
tors, mostly Southern aristocrats, at a guest home on the Gulf
is no more a study of the *South* than are any of her earlier
plays. Here are individuals who, unable to take positive action,
waste their lives and wither away, and come by various means
to a realization of their plight. But their problem is a problem
of individual personalities, not specifically Southern at all—a
point made clear by the fact that one of the major examples of
personality decay is General Griggs, who is not a Southerner.
What Miss Hellman is saying is that most of us are like that;
and here she does succeed in getting beyond her specific people to a general (though not a special Southern) theme. But,
unlike Williams and unlike Faulkner, she still cannot make her
themes Southern, though her characters are; hence she cannot
show that the truths she sees so clearly are both typical of the
South *and* universal. This is especially surprising in *The Autumn Garden,* because Miss Hellman had Chekhov so unmistakably in mind in changing her technique, and because her
theme of attrition of the will is so typical of Chekhov; however, Chekhov's characters and problems alike succeed in being as universal as they are unmistakably Russian.

Reminders of Chekhov are everywhere in *The Autumn Garden.* As with Chekhov, the frustration is general, but there are
exceptions to it—old Mrs. Ellis and the French-raised Sophie
Tuckerman fight the world and win. As with Chekhov, there
is compassion—no one is a villain, which is unusual in Miss
Hellman's plays. And as with Chekhov, those who give up are
sometimes pleasanter, more graceful people than those who
never dream of doing so. Also numerous technical similarities
are visible: the de-emphasis (but not absence) of plot, the
subtle personality clashes, the use of arrivals and departures,
as is usual with Miss Hellman, for emotional tension. But the
big difference, besides her failure to achieve three levels—individual, regional, universal—is that she continues to stick to
straight realism. What Miss Hellman derives from Chekhov is
somewhat different from what Williams derives. More genuine
than Williams' as aristocrats, Miss Hellman's creations are less
genuine as symbols, less profound as human beings, precisely

because Williams develops Chekhov's non-realistic techniques (not only the use of symbol but the careful, subtle employment of sound effects and sets for the establishment of mood and personality) and Miss Hellman does not. Miss Hellman's characters are crisp and clear, in *The Autumn Garden* as everywhere. For all their wavering in purpose and lack of self-knowledge they have no blurred edges. They weigh so much, measure so much; the whole is the neat sum of the perceptible parts. This is no mean accomplishment: Miss Hellman is justly praised for her characterization. But at his best Williams is not like this. Blanche is bared to the very soul, yet who is to say that there are not still unplumbed depths, or even unpresented surfaces? A more complex creation than Miss Hellman's characters, Blanche is presented in greater complexity, and our reaction to her is more complex.

The truth is that Miss Hellman employs an old-fashioned technique and succeeds, within her special limits, too well at it. She performs to a "T" the feat she learned from Ibsen—an almost miraculous ability to make characters live and breathe within the confines of a strict plot which ought to, and does not, turn them into puppets. In *Watch on the Rhine* she further succeeds in making her characters and their problems representative; but at the time one might have wondered if this result was not in part fortuitous. This was a war play, and in time of war, large groups of people have attitudes—easily recognizable attitudes—in common. She had not yet succeeded, as Ibsen did, in using the same technique to focus on characters and "problems" of much less obvious general applicability. So Miss Hellman turned to Chekhov's dramatic style—as Shaw tried to in *Heartbreak House*—but the result is still Miss Hellman, just as the result was still Shaw. Her characters function somewhat more complexly than before, but they are still, for all their genuineness, relatively simple and superficial.

Her latest play, *Toys in the Attic*, does represent an advance. She retains what she gained in the functioning of characters in *The Autumn Garden*. Her story is out of Chekhov, bearing various resemblances to the story of *The Three Sisters*, but she has made it her own. (People who see signs in the New Orleans setting and in some of the play's gaudier details that Miss Hellman was capitalizing on Williams apparently forget that Miss Hellman has never hesitated to call a spade by its most accurate name, or to look into any cranny of life which pertains to her dramatic idea.) She does at last prove that *Watch on the Rhine* was not fortuitous: that she can use Ibsen's methods, and strict realism, and money as a dominant motivation and symbol, to present a theme of universal significance and power. But while Miss Hellman's style seems as welcome as a crisp apple after a surfeit of French cookery —and after the later, more decadent Williams—she still fails, and for the reasons given, to equal Williams' earlier performances.

There is a danger, of course, in carrying this view of Miss Hellman's work too far. We believe today that realism has its limitations; it probably does, but there are many different "realisms," and at various times one or another of them has seemed the final answer to the artistic problem. Today we prefer other answers, or at least consider other answers more profound. We believe more in Chekhov's methods than in those of the Ibsen of the middle period, the Ibsen we know best. We prefer the blurred edge to the clearcut outline, the piercing depth to the rounded solidity. We prefer sex to money as the ultimate motivation. So it is really no surprise to find us concluding that Williams is an artist, though not necessarily a skilled craftsman, while Miss Hellman is a tremendously skilled craftsman, though probably not an artist. Like the fox which is her most famous symbol, she traces her quarry with —for our taste—too obvious cleverness and too accomplished skill.

I have myself, of course, written out of these conclusions, even though they must remain faintly suspect because they so thoroughly flatter our own taste. Williams is probably better as a craftsman than we generally believe. In her over-all production, Miss Hellman's scope is much broader, though shallower, than Williams'. Williams tells us far more about the South, though Miss Hellman deals with an aspect of it apparently not available to him. In any case, regionalism is not necessarily a virtue. Yet in the last analysis, what makes the difference, what makes us accept Williams as the profounder of the two, and what makes us almost surely right in doing so, is a wider variety of technique and a far greater ability to make characters function both as characters and as multiple symbols.

At the height of its bloom the rose is—as it should be—in better odor than the fox.

THE CONTINUING RENASCENCE: SOUTHERN
FICTION IN THE FIFTIES

BY WALTER SULLIVAN

This essay is concerned with the work of Southern novelists and short-story writers who have begun writing or who
have come into prominence as writers since the end of World
War II. Two or three of them are in their forties, two or three
are in their twenties, one of them—James Agee—is dead. I have
chosen an even dozen; some because I think they are good
and would be good anywhere, no matter where they happened
to be born or what they wrote about; others because they seem
to me to represent some of the worst aspects of Southern fiction, and some of the worst fates that can befall Southern
writers; and I mention still others because they seem to be
merely representative and can perhaps help furnish the barest
kind of suggestion as to where we can go now after Faulkner
and his distinguished contemporaries.

Whatever conclusion one may come to about the talents of
the younger Southern writers, even a cursory look at their
books should prove that the tone and direction of Southern
fiction are changing. This was a predictable—and in fact often
predicted—change; the world itself changes and the South is a
part of the world. Urbanization, industrialization, social and
legal pressures have altered the face of the land and to a considerable extent fragmented what was once an almost completely unified point of view. This is a case that can be easily
overstated; certainly the South retains much of its self-consciousness and many of its traditional attitudes. But the people
in the South are divided in their opinions more than most people outside the South suspect. There is still a Southern temper,
but it is not quite the one that Mr. Heilman describes earlier

in this volume. It has become, in the years between Faulkner and Styron, a mere shadow of itself.

What all this means to the writer from a more or less practical point of view is that the old ethical foundations have been shaken. Let me say now that I accept the thesis that literature is a moral art. The novelist must begin with a set of assumptions concerning the fundamental nature of good and evil. The fable, and whatever moral designs it uncovers, must develop from the foundation or within the framework of the initially held moral premises. I am aware that this is not a universally accepted view of literature, but it is the one I take, and it is one that seems to be implicit in most writing about the Southern Literary Renascence. We hear of the homogeneity of the Southern civilization, of the Southern philosophy (moral), of the Southern code (of conduct and therefore moral again). What the Old South had, among other things, was a pattern of behavior which was by no means a perfect ethic, but it was an ethic. Therefore the Southern writer never had to wonder about what his people believed. He knew that already. He could devote his entire energies to an examination of more fundamental problems, such as man's mortality and the exalted longings of his fragile heart.

Now, to a greater or lesser extent, depending on where he lives, the Southern writer has been deprived of the old security of a unanimously held ethical view. How complete the deprivation is perhaps depends on the individual temperament of the author and what his own particular Southern experience happens to be. Some Southern writers no longer write about the South at all, and you have to look on the flap of the dust jacket to know where they were born. Others appear to work squarely within the established Faulkner-Warren-Lytle tradition. Among these are some of the very best, including Shelby Foote, William Humphrey, Madison Jones, and Flannery O'Connor. Let us look first at Foote.

A Mississippian now living in Memphis, Foote is one of the oldest of the writers here under discussion, and he has published more books. His work as a whole reflects a rather complete gentleman's education and a very wide knowledge of the world and its ways. He has a pronounced feeling for history—he is currently completing a three-volume work on the Civil

War—and what I judge to be a profound literary talent. *Follow Me Down* is perhaps his best book, and it is certainly a fair sample of what he can do. At first glance it looks very much like an imitation of William Faulkner. The place is Mississippi. The landscape is familiar. There are cotton fields and Negroes along the roadside, and old men loafing around the courthouse square. The main plot line is the love affair of an eighteen-year-old prostitute, Beulah, and a poor, middle-aged, fanatically religious farmer, Luther Eustis; the murder of the girl by the man; and the man's trial. It is a story of violence, and many of its images and people would be characterized by some critics as "grotesque." Examples are Luther's feeble-minded daughter who must wear a leather chastity belt—specially built after the medieval pattern—to restrain her from continual masturbation; Beulah's nymphomaniac mother, who first sells the daughter to a sixty-year-old man and later uses Beulah to help her seduce younger men; a revival meeting where a woman is seized by the Spirit and goes bumping along on her buttocks down the hill. Because the setting, the grotesque elements, the violent plot are generally thought to be a part of the Southern literary tradition, one is likely to be fooled into believing that Foote's work is cast absolutely in the old mold. Such is not quite the case. Foote's work is traditional, but it makes some departures. There are differences not so much in philosophy as in form.

The theme of *Follow Me Down* is that of man's moral responsibility in the face of an inscrutable and pitiless fate. In the novel, many of the characters are paired off in their miserable interaction with each other, and each one has his cross to bear. The woman on the island has lost her husband and her femininity and her son is deaf and dumb. Eustis has his own feeble-minded daughter. Beulah's doom has been her mother. The lawyer, Parker Nowell, is angry at the world because he has been abandoned by his wife. These relationships are reversible—Luther makes the idiot girl suffer, Beulah hurts her mother—and very complex. In the end, Eustis, man of God, breaks God's commandment and commits murder. And Beulah is killed by the man she loves. This is fiction on the grand scale. In tone and inventiveness the novel is reminiscent of Faulkner, as it is in the use of several limited first-person points of view. What makes the book different is the tightness of its structure: it lacks the lapses and the leisurely pace and the sometimes divine digressions that often mark Faulkner's work. All the action is sharply focused on the murder, which is the unifying dramatic image of the book. Each set of people, down to the minor figures like the jailor and his goiter-stricken wife, is a variation of the same basic theme.

Another difference is that Foote has felt it necessary to make his philosophical foundation completely explicit. Eustis's continual references to the Bible give the novel an Old Testament sense of the unfathomable relation between man and his sins, his deserts, his ultimate fate. Eustis himself is a man of God in the old sense—a monstrous sinner, like David or Jacob, bound by some terrible and mystic affection to the Almighty.

The Biblical standard is raised, and Eustis is not the only one who is measured against it. Beulah is thrown into perspective as a creature of instinct and "natural goodness," the dictates of which she follows to her doom. Nowell is defined in terms of music which is formal but amoral, as is his life. The dependence on Scriptural reference, on a system older and better-established than any Southern code, seems essential to Foote's art.

The same is true, I think, of Flannery O'Connor. Though it is questionable whether Miss O'Connor has a pronounced talent as a novelist, she is one of the ablest of all short-story writers, and young as she is, her work has been widely acclaimed for many years. Certainly this is as it should be; her stories are well paced and well constructed. She has a magnificent ear for dialogue and a sharp eye for detail. She admittedly deals in the "grotesque" because, she says, she can still recognize a grotesque when she sees him. And this is more, she believes, than some other writers and many readers can do. Her plots are extravagant; her characters are usually fatuous and unattractive, and they are always distorted. They satirize themselves by the opinions they express and the words they use to express them. The general impression is that the author has wasted little affection on her own creations, and the reader is invited to go along with the writer. No one, I think, ever identifies with Flannery O'Connor's people.

Why, then, are the stories so often successful? One important reason is Miss O'Connor's consummate technical skill. Another is the strict Christian point of view which she holds as a person and which therefore underlies all her writing. Look, for example, not at an obviously theological story like "The Enduring Chill," but at the more widely famous "A Good Man Is Hard to Find." It is a bizarre story, which goes like this. A family on vacation has an automobile accident on a lonely road. The Misfit, a homicidal maniac, happens by and with the help of his two companions murders mother and father, children, baby, and grandmother. What raises the story above the level of grotesqueness for its own sake is the problem of faith, which is a major theme in the story. Begging for her life, the grandmother mentions Jesus.

> "Maybe He didn't raise the dead," the old lady mumbled, not knowing what she was saying. . . .
> "I wasn't there so I can't say He didn't," the Misfit said. "I wisht I had of been there," he said, hitting the ground with his fist. "It ain't right I wasn't there because if I had of been there I would have known. Listen, lady," he said in a high voice, "if I had been there I would have known and I wouldn't be like I am now."

The problem of faith is combined with the problem of human suffering: the Misfit could never understand why he was punished by the state. Obviously the moral of the tale is not regional. Miss O'Connor has imposed her Catholic theology on the local image, and the marriage of Rome and South Georgia, is odd to say the least. I sometimes think that the almost unvarying and specialized quality of Miss O'Connor's work is a result of this strange mating, but that is speculation. What is apparent is that like Shelby Foote, but in far greater measure, she depends more on Christianity than on the Southern code.

Humphrey and Jones, on the other hand, apparently do not feel that the Southern culture has been sufficiently dissipated to require any imposed ethical framework. Nor do they seem to think that the old vein has been worked clean. Jones makes a strong case for himself in his first novel. The failing South becomes his challenge; *The Innocent* is about a man who tries to maintain his integrity in a disintegrating world.

The novel is amazingly ambitious. Image is piled on image

in what seems to be an effort to encompass totally the various conflicts and tensions that surround Duncan Welsh in his rural Middle Tennessee world. Jones is superb in his handling of nature; there is probably no one writing today who can create woods and fields and animals and sky with as much feeling and accuracy and dramatic effectiveness. Nature is free, and the proper setting for a free man. But nature disappears under the impact of encroaching government and industry; and the independent and self-sufficient man, the man who would keep his integrity, is hounded into a conflict that will be his doom. This is one side of the problem. The other side emerges out of Jones' absolute belief in the imperfectibility of man. Man cannot be good unless he is free, but freedom does not guarantee goodness, nor does it wash away individual guilt.

In a way, Duncan Welsh is seduced by the idea of natural goodness as represented in nature. Aaron McCool, the moonshiner, is free, but he lives outside the law. It is McCool who tempts Welsh into murdering Dickie Jordan, and then Welsh must answer for his guilt. The denouement of the book shows Jones at his best. McCool and Welsh, pursued by the law, run for the wilderness, where they hide out in a cave and where they die. The narrative tensions and pace of these scenes are excellent. Welsh's fate seems inevitable, and his death is significant in terms of Jones' themes of human innocence and guilt and human freedom.

The faults of *The Innocent* are comparatively minor. Because the book attempts such a thorough coverage of its world and its theme, it seems at times a little cluttered. There are too many people on the stage; there is too much happening. And, for much of the novel, Duncan Welsh is a less sympathetic character than he ought to be, if he is to be an entirely convincing vehicle for Jones' theme. This sort of criticism is rather subjective, however, and therefore not very important. Jones' virtues are many and his faults are minor and few.

The faults of William Humphrey are few too, but they are major. What is amazing to me about *Home from the Hill* is that it manages to generate considerable power in spite of Humphrey's obvious failures in invention and technique. The opening of the book is uncomfortably reminiscent of the beginning of Styron's *Lie Down in Darkness*, and there is something Styronesque about the family group: the neurotic mother, the father with his women, the child caught in the parental crossfire and running swiftly to his doom. But as Humphrey himself pointed out, the influence of Faulkner is stronger. The tone and the technique are Faulknerian: the nameless narrator who refers to what "we" thought or saw or said; the studied Southernness of it all; the labored small-town quality. ("'I God! Hit's a Rolls-Royce!' announced Ben Ramsay.") Theron's boar hunt is a watered-down version of Ike McCaslin's pursuit of Old Ben in *The Bear*. In both cases, the wilderness is symbolic, and Theron's killing of the boar is a sign of maturity, as was Ike's baptism in the blood of the slain deer. Captain Hunnicutt is a kind of young Bayard or old John Sartoris, an oversexed man with a death wish. But to go on in this vein is to labor the obvious.

What is not imitative in Humphrey's book is usually contrived, cute, or excessively romantic. Time and again the plot hinges on that sort of incredible breakdown in human communications which is the stock-in-trade device of movie and television writers. Libby will not tell Theron she is pregnant; Theron thinks his father is the father of Opal's child. Then communication is established again by a kind of Hardyesque fate: Mr. Halstead happens to eavesdrop on the men after church and so decides to commit a murder. There is the story of Hugh Ramsay's leg, buried now and awaiting the rest of Hugh. There is the scene where Theron admits his own humanity by cleaning the graves of the reprobates, a symbolic performance which seems a bit thin, a bit obvious.

I go into all this because it seems to me that Humphrey is a very talented writer and one who can do about as well as any novelist of his generation in handling the traditional material in the traditional way. His people are real; he has a gift for narrative; and his characters and his pace salvage much for him. But he is not the real thing. Faulkner and Warren are the real thing and Humphrey is their shadow.

For Elizabeth Spencer in her most recent novel, and for Peter S. Feibleman and George Garrett, new life for the continuing Southern Literary Renascence must come from a fictional exploration of the social and political tensions to be found in the South. The best of the lot by far is Elizabeth Spencer.

The Voice at the Back Door is Miss Spencer's third novel, and technically at least it fulfills the great promise of her earlier work. The execution of the book is faultless, and in conceiving of her theme, she has avoided the oversimplified solutions of her place and time. For one thing, she sees the race problem in an historical perspective. Jimmy Tallent's father led a group of white men who killed a group of Negroes led by Beck Dozer's father. Consequently, Tallent and Dozer are inextricably bound together by their history. Each, assuming his burden from the past, is responsible for the other. Miss Spencer is also aware that, important though the race problem may be, most people, even in the South, do not spend every waking moment thinking about it. Duncan believes in civil rights for Negroes. He also has a wife, two children and a mistress, a political campaign to attend to, an old friend who is ultimately faithful and a young friend who is not. And, most important, Miss Spencer allows humanity to all: there are the good ones and the bad ones, but each person retains enough complexity to be believable.

This book has almost everything that a book ought to have, and yet it seems to me that in the final analysis it is not completely successful. Duncan dies and Beck is exonerated. Jimmy Tallent redeems a bit of his father's sin by protecting Beck from the mob after the automobile accident. But by this time, one does not believe that the mob would have struck anyway, and the accident itself seems rather contrived. It is as if Miss Spencer were trying to prove how serious this whole affair has been from the very beginning. But the theme is kept in some kind of perspective and the view that the novel takes is balanced. There is no preaching here, nor is any easy solution offered. This may well be as good a book as any novelist could write on the subject.

It is worth noting perhaps that Peter Feibleman is a Southern novelist by choice. He was born in New York, and he lived for only fifteen years in New Orleans, but both of his novels are set in the South. *A Place without Twilight* is a kind of picaresque novel with a female hero. It has no plot structure, because it has no plot. Characters enter and fade away, one event follows another, but there is no sustained conflict, no build-up of dramatic forces, no denouement, no conclusion.

Though this approach to novel writing leaves something to be desired in Feibleman's second book—*The Daughters of Necessity*—it works well enough for him when all his main characters are Negroes. The novel achieves a fragmented quality; the lives of the people assume an uncertainty that is meaningful in terms of the Negro's position in a big city in the Deep South. This, Feibleman seems to be saying, is the way it is, and the book has the ring of truth. If you are a white man, you can't really know what it is like to be a Negro and live as a Negro is forced to live, but it seems that Feibleman knows what he is talking about.

One trouble with this kind of book is that, no matter how unsullied the author's intentions are, the novel in the final analysis is—consciously or unconsciously—a display of white chauvinism. Of more importance, literarily speaking, is the fact that one social injustice is allowed to subvert all other moral considerations. Perhaps the critical position that I take here is too exalted, but it seems to me that the race problem is rather localized, in both space and time. It will pass, and with it will pass the literature written about it, unless that literature can transcend the social problem and reach the timeless ground of human grandeur and human folly. If Feibleman had left the acute consciousness of white people and their misunderstanding and their injustice out of the book for just part of the time, he would have had, I think, a better novel.

But whatever his faults, Feibleman's virtues outweigh them. His approach to his problem is fresh. He has an acute feeling for his people, a sense of their thought and language. His best characters—Our Father, Jewel, Cille—are done with real skill and in full dimensions. Unhappily, none of this can be said for George Garrett, who also considers the race problem, along with the larger political situation in the South.

Garrett's *The Finished Man* is in every particular such a poorly conceived, poorly written book that it does not deserve to be named in the company of the other novels discussed here. The characters are flat; the plot is stale; the structure is weak; the pace is slow; the prose is at best pedestrian and at worst illiterate. I bring *The Finished Man* into this discussion because it is the most recent novel about Southern politics that I have read. What Southern politics seems to amount to, according to Garrett, is the race question. And while it is true that the race question is injected into most Southern political races, to say that it is the only consideration is grossly to over-simplify. There are other issues which are easily found, and there is the problem—the eternal problem, whether the novel is about Julius Caesar or Willie Stark—of human ambition, of lust for power, the simple ageless egoism of human nature. What I am trying to say is that there is—so far as I can tell—only one way to write a good political novel. Take first a man, preferably one of capacity and certainly one of some moral consciousness. (Stark wasn't a Bible reader for nothing. And he had his own rough moral philosophy by which he justified himself to himself and to others. And he wasn't entirely wrong.) Then create a political situation that presents the man with certain moral choices. The meaning is deepened and the drama enhanced in a sort of rough proportion to the number of people who will be affected by the politician's choice for good or evil. The big temptation for the novelist is to get the cart before the horse, to postulate the issue first and the man second, to write of political questions and not of human values. So completely does Garrett succumb to this temptation that he finally quits trying to deal with the narrative aspects of his book—they seem to have been annoying him from the beginning, anyway—and writes an intellectual, argumentative, concept-developing dialogue in the manner of Plato. It should be said in extenuation of Garrett's failure, however, that he lives in an age when half the world oversimplifies the morality of all human existence in terms of the race issue. Like Spencer and Feibleman, he is riding the tide of his time, but he lacks the sensitive insight of Feibleman and the technical skill of Spencer.

Among the young Southern writers who seem to depart most purposefully from the old tradition are Shirley Ann Grau and Truman Capote, James Agee, Peter Taylor, and William Styron. Capote can be dispensed with briefly. As everybody knows, his work is fraught with homosexuality and narcissism, and for the most part it is contrived. Capote does what better writers—like O'Connor—are accused of doing: he celebrates the grotesque for its own sake and for the glamour a grotesque image might add to his themes of deviation. Neither his people nor his plots are believable, but there is something temporarily fascinating in his depravity and he is capable of occasional flashes of real brilliance. In *Breakfast at Tiffany's*, boy and girl stand on the bridge, and Holly speaks of the future brightness of her life.

"Years from now, years and years, one of those ships will bring me back, me and my nine Brazilian brats. Because yes, they *must* see this, these lights, the river—— I love New York, even though it isn't mine, the way something has to be, a tree or a street or a house, something, anyway, that belongs 'to me because I belong to it." And I said: "Do shut up," for I felt infuriatingly left out—a tugboat in drydock while she, glittery voyager of secure destination, steamed down the harbor with whistles whistling and confetti in the air.

So the day, the last days, blow about in memory, hazy, autumnal, all alike as leaves: until a day unlike any other I've lived.

This is as good as Dickens, but it doesn't last. Capote's works seem to melt away, leaving no dregs of meaning. Moments of high drama in his books are hard to recall.

It is certainly not difficult to remember moments of great dramatic force in the work of Shirley Ann Grau. The material she develops, her characters, and her bold gift for narrative— which is mythical, in the best sense—are memorable indeed. Many of the characters, like Stanley Albert in "The Black Prince," are larger than life. They come out of and recede back into some realm of happy, primitive immortality, which is itself just large enough to hold them. Or they succeed out of their difficulties in a mysterious, almost metaphysical fashion, like Jayson in "Fine Girl, White Girl." And yet, in spite of the grandeur of her people and her inventive mind, Miss Grau seems so very young. I am convinced that a part of the charm of her work resides in its almost childish sense of discovery. "There is the sun," she seems to be telling us. "He is a man. She is a woman." And all of this uttered in a fetching tone of infinite wonder. The plots in their extravagance have something of this quality too. And I suspect that is one reason why she is most successful in the short story, though of course she has written longer fiction.

James Agee, who was born on the other side of the mountain from Tom Wolfe, shared many of Wolfe's virtues and some of Wolfe's faults. Agee had the gift of apparently total recall. He had a fine ear, a good eye, a talent for characterization, and a feeling for the supernatural. His sense of proportion and of pace were sometimes faulty. *A Death in the Family* is to me like many of Wolfe's books in that individual scenes are more memorable and have more impact in retrospect than does the novel as a whole. The book is a tour de force, but, more than this, it is a sort of bad thing made good. As everybody knows, one of the writer's fundamental tasks is to select his scenes and images out of the great mass of material which furnishes the stuff for even the simplest story. Or, as Ford Madox Ford put it once, you can leave the reader to assume that the characters eat breakfast, lunch, and dinner. Agee was selective only in the amount of time he chose to let his book cover, and only the most imaginative readers are able to think of anything about Agee's story that needs be assumed.

Before Jay leaves on the fatal trip to his father's bedside, he eats two eggs, bacon, pancakes with butter and molasses, drinks coffee made the way he likes it—which is to put a few fresh grounds on the old ones and add fresh water to the pot. Mary drinks warm milk. The automobile, when Jay is trying to start it, sounds like this: "*Ughgh—Ughgh*—yuhyuh*Ugh* wheek yuh yuh *Ughgh* yuh wheek wheek yuhyuh; wheek wheek; uh." So fully detailed is the writing that almost three pages are used to get Jay across the ferry. Yet this very plethora of detail, which even the most inexperienced writer would normally attempt to trim, is one of the main sources of Agee's power. It is the vehicle which communicates the sense of fading hope and bereavement and bereavement's pain.

For example, after the phone call which informs Mary of Jay's accident, she prepares the guest room in the frantic hope that he is only injured, not dead. We are told how each case is slipped on each pillow, how the blankets are folded and folded again, how the windows are cracked and the curtains are re-tied and how the bedpan and thermometer are got ready. At one point during her preparations, Mary forgets herself and stands, for a moment, in a stupor. When she is finished, she attempts to pray, but scarcely dares name the fear she would pray against. She crosses herself and rises to wait for Andrew. This is the real thing. Man in his moments of extremity must do something, and each movement becomes at the same time an act of faith and a bitter protest against reality.

And there are the children. How can they be made to comprehend what has happened to their father? Again we are told about breakfast. "Aunt Hannah sliced the banana so thin on the Post Toasties it looked cold and wet and slimy. She gave each of them a little bit of coffee in their milk. . . . The fried eggs had hardly any pepper and they were so soft the yellow ran out over the white and the white plate. . . ." This is from Catherine's point of view, and the utter strangeness of the breakfast Hannah has prepared communicates change and loss more eloquently than any words of explanation.

The novel is built around what Andrew Lytle refers to as a "controlling image," which is, of course, the death of Jay. Here again the technique of non-selectivity is used: everything connected with the death is included. Much that is good and dramatic accrues from this approach, but the pace of the book is monotonous. The feeling of pain is so unrelieved that the reader gets a bit numb. And there is not so much a diffusion of focus, which would be all right, but rather an unintegrated dual focus. The book is Mary's through the first half, Rufus's through the last. Finally, the book sometimes seems weakest to me when it exhibits its Southern background. The country people encountered on Jay's trip home are fakes or at best caricatures. The Negro sequences are dragged in. On the other hand, there is the Southern feeling for family, and Knoxville as a not-quite-Southern city rings true. Perhaps the most significant thing that can be said about Agee's relation to the South is that, having been away from it for so long, he nonetheless chose to write about it in *A Death in the Family*.

William Styron's *Lie Down in Darkness* begins with death, but in theme it is considerably broader than *A Death in the Family*. A quotation from Sir Thomas Browne printed at the front of the book says—roughly paraphrased—that life leads only to death and therefore death is a part of life and life is a continual reminder of death. Such is the case in *Lie Down in Darkness*, which is the story of the destruction of a family. Styron's novel is uneven. Maudie is never really convincing as a character, and Carey is never integrated into the story: he has no stake in the outcome of the plot. The final Joycean sequence in Peyton's life is too long and too cluttered for the strategic position it occupies, though taken alone it is a powerful piece of writing. The worst thing about the book is the ending. Simply to have Milton run off into the rain is a terrible letdown that is in no way atoned for by the final scene with Daddy Faith.

But what is bad in Styron is not nearly so obtrusive nor so important as what is good. The conflicts of the book, the basic human tensions, are absolutely convincing, because the people are convincing and morally complex individuals. Helen is a puritanical neurotic; Milton is alcoholic. Each reacts against the other, and both certainly are sinned against; both are sinners. Maudie complicates the issue between Helen and Milton, and Peyton is annihilated in the parental strife. Best of all, Styron manages throughout to resist the temptation to offer an easy out, a simple answer. That there can be none is the motivation for Peyton's suicide, and her death in turn is a measure of the complexity of human life.

To speak of Styron's Southernness is to speak tentatively. There is, as there was in the work of Agee, a sense of family in *Lie Down in Darkness*, and a sense of the past. ("Ghosts of Rochambeau and McClellan, old campfires of earlier falls, with smoke just as blue as this, just as fatal.") There is the small-town provincialism that even large cities in the South retain, and there is the sense of good manners and the presence of the church—Carey Carr—as a force, though perhaps a weak one, in the lives of men. Maybe what is most significant about Styron as Southerner is that, unlike many of his predecessors, he seems to be more or less at home in the modern world.

Equally at home in the modern world is Peter Taylor. Born in 1917, Taylor is one of the oldest writers to be considered here, and his career is certainly one of the most distinguished. He is a perceptive artist, a skillful craftsman, and he is the only American of his generation whose work can stand comparison with that of Frank O'Connor and Chekhov and Joyce.

From the beginning, Taylor's stories have been original in concept. He was among the first to discover that the Southern city—not town—had literary possibilities. And he has always been content to use his material; he never argues about it. For example, in "A Long Fourth," the race question is not an end in itself; rather it is one of the points of contention in the multi-faceted conflict between Ann and Son and the girls and the mother and father and the two Negroes.

In such a story as "A Spinster's Tale," Taylor uses the South of the recent past as a frame and a stabilizing element in his narrative. The society becomes stylized in its period Southernness and thereby achieves the formal and objective quality it needs to make the rather terrifying plot convincing. In its stolidity and its easy acceptance of human frailty the world of the story is a foil for the girl and a spur to her act of revenge.

Take another example. "The Guests," which to me is a fine story, appeared in *The New Yorker* as this essay was being written. It is the tale of a rich, middle-aged, childless Nashville lawyer whose wife's charity consists partly in having as house guests poor relatives from the country, where, incidentally, both she and her husband were born. The guests this time are Cousin Johnny and Cousin Annie, who are also childless, and from the beginning there is friction between the lawyer Edmund's wife Henrietta and Cousin Annie. Cousin Johnny, who is seventy, is in ill health, but Annie will not let Edmund and Henrietta alter their diet or change their household routine out of deference to his condition. She will not tell them what Johnny can eat or do or endure, or, as it turns out, how sick he is, for he dies in Edmund's house before the visit is over. This is Annie's victory over Henrietta, but it is also her final step in her long victory over Johnny, which is a triumph similar to one which Henrietta has achieved over Edmund.

Edmund did not want to come to the city to practice law; Henrietta made him. And Johnny, who did want to come to the city and take a job with the then just starting but now successful shoe company, was prevented from doing so by Annie. Each man has sustained himself with the belief that the life he was deprived of would have furnished him, had he lived it, the fulfillment which his real life has denied him. Standing by the bed that supports Cousin Johnny's remains, Edmund sees at last the magnitude of their self delusion.

". . . But something in the life out there didn't satisfy you the way it should. The country wasn't itself anymore. And something was wrong for me here. By 'country' we mean the old world, don't we, Cousin Johnny? The old ways the old life, where people had real grandfathers and real children, and where love was something that could endure the light of day. . . . Our trouble was, Cousin Johnny, we were lost without our old realities. We couldn't discover what it is people keep alive for without them. Surely there must be something. . . . I will have to find it. . . ."

The world is changed, the South is changed, and this story by Peter Taylor brings us back to where we started. But, as Edmund said, "There must be something." Something left to write about, something worth the effort and the pain, and, like Edmund again, whatever that something is, the Southern writer will have to find it.

But this, after all, is what writers have always had to do.

FOR FURTHER READING: A SELECTED CHECKLIST

BY JAMES B. MERIWETHER

The scope of the literature of the modern South is suggested by the listing here of the books of thirty-six writers, with brief guides to studies of them. Unquestionably a number of other writers also deserve inclusion, but lack of space made necessary a compromise between the number of authors included and the amount of information it seemed most useful to provide about each author's work.

For each writer, all books and other separate publications are listed, except, in most cases, for miscellaneous anthologies and other reprintings of already published work. To make these listings more useful to the student or reader not familiar with the author concerned, each item is identified more fully than is customary in such checklists, short of an elaborate bibliographical description. The pagination is given for works shorter than seventy-five pages (the number given is that of the last numbered page of the text; where this number does not appear in the book, it is given in brackets). Where necessary, attention has been called to that annoying characteristic of twentieth-century publishing, the issue of unimportant items in small limited editions without a corresponding trade issue. Care has been taken to list, not only the original edition, but important subsequent editions and issues—for example, those incorporating significant textual changes or additional material by the author. The student seeking further works of an author may find helpful the identification of books as novels, short stories, and so on, though admittedly the system breaks down when confronted by such brilliantly unclassifiable works as *The Muses Are Heard*, Truman Capote's account of the visit to Russia of the American *Porgy and Bess* company, or James Agee's *Let Us Now Praise Famous Men.*

For each writer, any existing checklists or bibliographies (of work by and about him), are listed first. Where no up-to-date compilation of studies of an author exists, any books, and a few basic or general articles or references in books, are noted. For more thorough study, these should be supplemented, for a start, by the listings in such standard references as Lewis Leary's *Articles on American Literature, 1900–1950,* Duke University Press, 1954; and, for articles since 1950, the annual bibliographies in *PMLA* and quarterly bibliographies in *American Literature.*

Two abbreviations are used: *LHUS-Bibl.,* and *LHUS-Bibl. Suppl.,* for Thomas H. Johnson, ed., *Literary History of the United States: Bibliography,* New York: Macmillan, 1948, and Richard M. Ludwig, ed., *Literary History of the United States: Bibliography Supplement,* New York: Macmillan, 1959. Under the seven writers who were members of the *Fugitive* group, the references to John M. Bradbury, *The Fugitives,* University of North Carolina Press, 1958, and Louise Cowan, *The Fugitive Group,* Louisiana State University Press, 1959, are made in short form only.

I. ANTHOLOGIES

Essays on the modern South and its literature, as well as stories and poems by Southern writers, are contained in *A Southern Vanguard,* ed., Allen Tate, New York: Prentice-Hall, 1947. Twenty-nine essays are contained in *Southern Renascence: The Literature of the Modern South,* eds., Louis D. Rubin, Jr., and Robert D. Jacobs, Johns Hopkins University Press, 1953. Many of the essays in *Culture in the South,* ed., W. T. Couch, University of North Carolina Press, 1935, concern this period. An anthology of essays, reviews, and stories designed for textbook use is *Contemporary Southern Prose,* eds., Richmond C. Beatty and William Perry Fidler, Boston: D. C. Heath, 1940.

Collections of short stories for this period are *A Southern*

Harvest, ed., Robert Penn Warren, Boston: Houghton Mifflin, 1937, and *A New Southern Harvest,* eds., Robert Penn Warren and Albert Erskine, New York: Bantam, 1957. See also *Great Tales of the Deep South,* ed., Malcolm Cowley, New York: Lion Library, 1955.

An anthology of poems of the post-World War I period is *The Lyric South,* ed., Addison Hibbard, New York: Macmillan, 1928.

II. INDIVIDUAL AUTHORS

JAMES AGEE (1909–1955)

BOOKS BY AGEE:

Permit Me Voyage (verse; with a foreword by Archibald MacLeish), New Haven: Yale University Press, 1934 (a volume in the Yale Series of Younger Poets).

Let Us Now Praise Famous Men (social criticism; with photographs by Walker Evans), Boston: Houghton Mifflin, 1941 (reissued, 1960, with additional photographs and an introduction by Evans).

The Morning Watch (short novel), Boston: Houghton Mifflin, 1951.

A Death in the Family (novel), New York: McDowell, Obolensky, 1957.

Agee on Film: Reviews and Comments, New York: McDowell, Obolensky, 1958.

Agee on Film, Volume II: Five Film Scripts (with a foreword by John Huston), New York: McDowell, Obolensky, 1960.

ABOUT AGEE:

W. M. Frohock, "James Agee: the Question of Unkept Promise," *Southwest Review,* XLII (1957), pp. 221–29; Dwight Macdonald, "Death of a Poet," *New Yorker,* Nov. 16, 1957, pp. 204, 206, 209–10, 212–21.

HAMILTON BASSO (b. 1904)

BOOKS BY BASSO:

Relics and Angels (novel), New York: Macaulay, 1929.
Beauregard, the Great Creole (biography), New York: Scribner, 1933.
Cinnamon Seed (novel), New York: Scribner, 1934.
In Their Own Image (novel), New York: Scribner, 1935.
Court-House Square (novel), New York: Scribner, 1936.
Days before Lent (novel), New York: Scribner, 1939.
Wine of the Country (novel), New York: Scribner, 1941.
Sun in Capricorn (novel), New York: Scribner, 1942.
Mainstream (essays), New York: Reynal & Hitchcock, 1943.
The Greenroom (novel), Garden City, N.Y.: Doubleday, 1949.
The View from Pompey's Head (novel), Garden City, N.Y.: Doubleday, 1954.
The Light Infantry Ball (novel), Garden City, N.Y.: Doubleday, 1959.
A Quota of Seaweed (travel), Garden City, N.Y.: Doubleday, 1960.

ABOUT BASSO:

Louis D. Rubin, Jr., "All the King's Meanings," *Georgia Review*, VII (1954), pp. 422–34.

JOHN PEALE BISHOP (1891–1944)

BOOKS BY BISHOP:

Green Fruit (verse), Boston: Sherman, French, 1917, 45 pp.
The Undertaker's Garland (stories and verse; with Edmund Wilson), New York: Knopf, 1922.
Many Thousands Gone (stories), New York: Scribner, 1931.
Now with His Love (verse), New York: Scribner, 1933.
Act of Darkness (novel), New York: Scribner, 1935.

Minute Particulars (verse), New York: Alcestis Press, 1935, 70 pp. (limited ed. only).
Selected Poems, New York: Scribner, 1941.
The Collected Essays of John Peale Bishop (edited, with an introduction, by Edmund Wilson), New York: Scribner, 1948.
The Collected Poems of John Peale Bishop (edited, with a preface and a memoir, by Allen Tate), New York: Scribner, 1948.

BOOK EDITED BY BISHOP:

American Harvest: Twenty Years of Creative Writing in the United States (with Allen Tate), New York: Fischer, 1942.

ABOUT BISHOP:

J. Max Patrick and Robert W. Stallman, "John Peale Bishop: A Checklist," *Princeton University Library Chronicle*, VII (1946), pp. 62–79. For articles about Bishop, see *LHUS-Bibl. Suppl.*, p. 219.

CLEANTH BROOKS (*b.* 1906)

BOOKS BY BROOKS:

The Relation of the Alabama-Georgia Dialect to the Provincial Dialects of Great Britain, Baton Rouge: Louisiana State University Press, 1935 (Louisiana State University Studies, No. 20).
Modern Poetry and the Tradition (essays), Chapel Hill: University of North Carolina Press, 1939.
The Well Wrought Urn (essays), New York: Reynal & Hitchcock, 1947.
Literary Criticism: A Short History (with William K. Wimsatt, Jr.), New York: Knopf, 1957.

TEXTBOOKS AND BOOKS EDITED BY BROOKS:

An Approach to Literature: A Collection of Prose and Verse with Analyses and Discussions (with John T. Purser and

Robert Penn Warren), Baton Rouge: Louisiana State University Press, 1936 (rev. eds., New York: Crofts, 1939; New York: Appleton-Century-Crofts, 1952).

Understanding Poetry: An Anthology for College Students (with Robert Penn Warren), New York: Holt, 1938 (rev. eds., 1950, 1960; also rev. shorter ed., 1950).

Understanding Fiction (with Robert Penn Warren), New York: Crofts, 1943 (rev. ed., New York: Appleton-Century-Crofts, 1960; shorter version, entitled *The Scope of Fiction*, 1960).

The Percy Letters (general editor; with David Nichol Smith), Baton Rouge: Louisiana State University Press, 5 vols., 1944–1957; Brooks himself edited vol. II, 1946, as well as being co-editor for the series.

Understanding Drama (anthology; with Robert Heilman), New York: Holt, 1948.

Modern Rhetoric (with Robert Penn Warren), New York: Harcourt, Brace, 1949 (rev. ed., 1958).

Fundamentals of Good Writing: A Handbook of Modern Rhetoric (with Robert Penn Warren), New York: Harcourt, Brace, 1950.

The Poems of Mr. John Milton, with Essays in Analysis (with John Edward Hardy), New York: Harcourt, Brace, 1951.

Stories from The Southern Review (with Robert Penn Warren), Baton Rouge: Louisiana State University Press, 1953.

Tragic Themes in Western Literature (essays), New Haven: Yale University Press, 1955.

ABOUT BROOKS:

Bradbury, *The Fugitives*, contains a selective listing of periodical contributions by Brooks.

JAMES BRANCH CABELL (1879–1958)

BOOKS BY CABELL:

The Eagle's Shadow (novel), New York: Doubleday, Page, 1904 (rev. ed., New York: McBride, 1923).

The Line of Love (stories), New York: Harper, 1905 (rev. ed., New York: McBride, 1921).

Branchiana (genealogy), Richmond: privately printed, [1907] (limited ed. only).

Gallantry (stories), New York: Harper, 1907 (rev. ed., New York: McBride, 1922).

The Cords of Vanity (novel), New York: Doubleday, Page, 1909 (rev. ed., New York: McBride, 1920).

Chivalry (stories), New York: Harper, 1909 (rev. ed., New York: McBride, 1921).

Branch of Abingdon (genealogy), Richmond: privately printed, 1911 (limited ed. only).

The Soul of Melicent (novel), New York: Stokes, 1913 (rev. ed., entitled *Domnei*, New York: McBride, 1920).

The Rivet in Grandfather's Neck (novel), New York: McBride, 1915.

The Majors and Their Marriages (genealogy), Richmond: privately printed, 1915 (limited ed. only).

The Certain Hour (stories), New York: McBride, 1916.

From the Hidden Way (verse), New York: McBride, 1916 (rev. ed., 1924).

The Cream of the Jest (novel), New York: McBride, 1917 (rev. ed., 1922).

Beyond Life (essays), New York: McBride, 1919.

Jurgen (novel), New York: McBride, 1919.

The Judging of Jurgen (essay), Chicago: The Bookfellows, 1920, 13 pp.

Figures of Earth (novel), New York: McBride, 1921.

Taboo (satire), New York: McBride, 1921, 40 pp. (limited ed. only).

Joseph Hergesheimer (essay), Chicago: The Bookfellows, 1921, 27 pp. (limited ed. only).

The Jewel Merchants (play), New York: McBride, 1921, 63 pp. (limited ed. only).

The Lineage of Lichfield (essay), New York: McBride, 1922 (limited ed. only).

The High Place (novel), New York: McBride, 1923.

Straws and Prayer-Books (essays, stories, verse), New York: McBride, 1924.

The Silver Stallion (novel), New York: McBride, 1926.

The Music from behind the Moon (story), New York: John Day, 1926, 54 pp.

Something about Eve (novel), New York: McBride, 1927.

The White Robe (short novel), New York: McBride, 1928.

Sonnets from Antan (verse), New York: Fountain Press, 1929, [34] pp. (limited ed. only).

The Way of Ecben (novel), New York: McBride, 1929.

Townsend of Lichfield (essays), New York: McBride, 1930.

Some of Us (essays), New York: McBride, 1930 (limited ed. only).

These Restless Heads (essays), New York: McBride, 1932.

Special Delivery (essays), New York: McBride, 1933.

Smirt (novel), New York: McBride, 1934.

Ladies and Gentlemen (essays), New York: McBride, 1934.

Smith (novel), New York: McBride, 1935.

Preface to the Past (collected prefaces and essays), New York: McBride, 1936.

Smire (novel; with *Smirt* and *Smith*, a trilogy), Garden City, N.Y.: Doubleday, Doran, 1937.

The Nightmare Has Triplets (note on the *Smirt, Smith, Smire* trilogy), New York: Doubleday, Doran, 1937, 14 pp.

The King Was in His Counting House (novel), New York: Farrar & Rinehart, 1938.

Of Ellen Glasgow (essay), New York: Maverick Press, 1938, [16] pp. (limited ed. only).

Hamlet Had an Uncle (novel), New York: Farrar & Rinehart, 1940.

The First Gentleman of America (novel; with *The King Was in His Counting House* and *Hamlet Had an Uncle*, a trilogy), New York: Farrar & Rinehart, 1942.

The St. Johns (history; with A. J. Hanna), New York: Farrar & Rinehart, 1943 (Rivers of America Series).

There Were Two Pirates (novel), New York: Farrar, Straus, 1946.

Let Me Lie (essays), New York: Farrar, Straus, 1947.

The Witch-Woman: A Trilogy (comprises new versions of *The Music from behind the Moon; The Way of Ecben;* and *The White Robe*), New York: Farrar, Straus, 1948.

The Devil's Own Dear Son (novel), New York: Farrar, Straus, 1949.
Quiet, Please (autobiography), University of Florida Press, 1952.
As I Remember It (autobiography), New York: McBride, 1955.

COLLECTED WORKS OF CABELL:

The Storisende Edition of the Works of James Branch Cabell (18 vols., rev., each with a preface), New York: McBride, 1927–30 (limited ed. only).

ABOUT CABELL:

For bibliographies of works by Cabell, and for work about Cabell, see *LHUS-Bibl.*, pp. 431–33, and *LHUS-Bibl. Suppl.*, p. 89. Also see Louis D. Rubin, Jr., *No Place on Earth*, University of Texas Press, 1959.

ERSKINE CALDWELL (*b.* 1903)

BOOKS BY CALDWELL:

The Bastard (short novel), New York: Heron Press, 1929 (limited ed. only).
Poor Fool (short novel), New York: Rariora Press, 1930 (limited ed. only).
American Earth (stories), New York: Scribner, 1931.
Mama's Little Girl (story), Mount Vernon, Maine: privately printed, 1932 (limited ed. only).
Tobacco Road (novel), New York: Scribner, 1932 (reissued, with an introduction by Caldwell, New York: Grosset & Dunlap, 1941; play version, with an introduction by Caldwell, New York: Viking, 1934, and, with a new introduction by Caldwell, New York: Duell, Sloan & Pearce, 1952).
God's Little Acre (novel), New York: Viking, 1933 (5th printing has an appendix by Caldwell; and the 1934 Modern Library ed. has the appendix and an introduction by Caldwell).

We Are the Living (stories), New York: Viking, 1933.

A Message for Genevieve (story), Mount Vernon, Maine: privately printed, 1933, 11 pp. (limited ed. only).

Journeyman (novel), New York: Viking, 1935 (limited ed. only; rev. ed., 1938).

Kneel to the Rising Sun (stories), New York: Viking, 1935.

Some American People (social criticism), New York: McBride, 1935.

Tenant Farmer (essay), New York: Phalanx Press, 1935, 30 pp.

The Sacrilege of Alan Kent (story), Portland, Maine: Falmouth Book House, 1936, 56 pp. (reprinted from *American Earth*).

You Have Seen Their Faces (documentary; with photographs by Margaret Bourke-White), New York: Viking, 1937 (also popular ed., New York: Modern Age, 1937).

Southways (stories), New York: Viking, 1938.

North of the Danube (journalism; photographs by Margaret Bourke-White), New York: Duell, Sloan & Pearce, 1939.

Trouble in July (novel), New York: Duell, Sloan & Pearce, 1940.

Jackpot (stories), New York: Duell, Sloan & Pearce, 1940.

Say, Is This the U. S. A. (documentary; photographs by Margaret Bourke-White), New York: Duell, Sloan & Pearce, 1941.

All Night Long (novel), New York: Duell, Sloan & Pearce, 1942.

All-Out on the Road to Smolensk (journalism), New York: Duell, Sloan & Pearce, 1942.

Georgia Boy (novel), New York: Duell, Sloan & Pearce, 1943.

Stories by Erskine Caldwell (edited, with a foreword, by Henry S. Canby), New York: Duell, Sloan & Pearce, 1944.

Tragic Ground (novel), New York: Duell, Sloan & Pearce, 1944.

A House in the Uplands (novel), New York: Duell, Sloan & Pearce, 1946.

The Sure Hand of God (novel), New York: Duell, Sloan & Pearce, 1947.

This Very Earth (novel), New York: Duell, Sloan & Pearce, 1948.

A Place Called Estherville (novel), New York: Duell, Sloan & Pearce, 1949.

Episode in Palmetto (novel), New York: Duell, Sloan & Pearce, 1950.

Call It Experience (autobiography), New York: Duell, Sloan & Pearce, 1951.

A Lamp for Nightfall (novel), New York: Duell, Sloan & Pearce; and Boston: Little, Brown, 1952.

The Courting of Susie Brown (stories), New York: Duell, Sloan & Pearce; and Boston: Little, Brown, 1952.

Complete Stories, New York: Duell, Sloan & Pearce; and Boston: Little, Brown, 1953.

Love and Money (novel), New York: Duell, Sloan & Pearce; and Boston: Little, Brown, 1954.

Gretta (novel), Boston: Little, Brown, 1955.

Gulf Coast Stories, Boston: Little, Brown, 1956.

Certain Women (stories), Boston: Little, Brown, 1957.

Molly Cottontail (children's story), Boston: Little, Brown, 1958, 31 pp.

Claudelle Inglish (novel), Boston: Little, Brown, 1959.

When You Think of Me (stories), Boston: Little, Brown, 1959.

Jenny by Nature (novel), New York: Farrar, Straus & Cudahy, 1961.

ABOUT CALDWELL:

For work on Caldwell, see *LHUS-Bibl.*, pp. 434–35; *LHUS-Bibl. Suppl.*, p. 90; "Erskine Caldwell at Work" (an interview with Carvel Collins), *Atlantic*, July, 1958, pp. 21–27; and the essay by Robert Hazel in the present volume.

TRUMAN CAPOTE (*b.* 1924)

BOOKS BY CAPOTE:

Other Voices, Other Rooms (novel), New York: Random House, 1948.

A Tree of Night and Other Stories, New York: Random House, 1949.
Local Color (essays), New York: Random House, 1950.
The Grass Harp (novel), New York: Random House, 1951 (play version, New York: Random House, 1952).
The Muses Are Heard, New York: Random House, 1956.
Breakfast at Tiffany's (short novel and stories), New York: Random House, 1958.
Observations (sketches; with photographs by Richard Avedon), New York: Simon & Schuster, 1959.

ABOUT CAPOTE:

John W. Aldridge, "The Metaphysical World of Truman Capote," *Western Review,* XV (1951), pp. 247–60; Paul Levine, "Truman Capote: The Revelation of the Broken Image," *Virginia Quarterly Review,* XXXIV (1958), pp. 600–17.

DONALD DAVIDSON (*b.* 1893)

BOOKS BY DAVIDSON:

An Outland Piper (verse), Boston: Houghton Mifflin, 1924.
The Tall Men (verse), Boston: Houghton Mifflin, 1927.
Lee in the Mountains and Other Poems, Boston: Houghton Mifflin, 1938 (reissued, New York: Scribner, 1949).
The Attack on Leviathan (essays), Chapel Hill: University of North Carolina Press, 1938.
The Tennessee (history; 2 vols.), New York: Rinehart, 1946, 1948 (Rivers of America Series).
Still Rebels, Still Yankees and Other Essays, Baton Rouge: Louisiana State University Press, 1957.
Southern Writers in the Modern World (essays), Athens: University of Georgia Press, 1958.

TEXTBOOKS AND BOOKS EDITED BY DAVIDSON:

British Poetry of the Eighteen-Nineties (anthology), Garden City, N.Y.: Doubleday, Doran, 1937.

American Composition and Rhetoric, New York: Scribner, 1939 (rev. eds., 1943, 1947, 1953, 1959).
Readings for Composition (with Sidney Glenn), New York: Scribner, 1942 (rev. ed., 1957).
Twenty Lessons in Reading and Writing Prose, New York: Scribner, 1955.

ABOUT DAVIDSON:

Bradbury, *The Fugitives,* has a selective list of periodical contributions by Davidson. For criticism, see Cowan, *The Fugitive Group;* Bradbury, *The Fugitives;* and the essay by Randall Stewart in the present volume.

RALPH ELLISON (*b.* 1914)

BOOK BY ELLISON:

The Invisible Man (novel), New York: Random House, 1952.

ABOUT ELLISON:

Anthony West, "Ralph Ellison," in *Principles and Persuasions,* New York: Harcourt, Brace, 1957, pp. 212–19; Charles I. Glicksberg, "The Symbolism of Vision," *Southwest Review,* XXXIX (Summer 1954), pp. 259–65; anon., "Ralph Ellison: Fiction Winner," *The Crisis,* LX (March 1953), pp. 154–56.

WILLIAM FAULKNER (*b.* 1897)

BOOKS BY FAULKNER:

The Marble Faun (cycle of poems; preface by Phil Stone), Boston: Four Seas, 1924, 51 pp.
Soldiers' Pay (novel), New York: Boni & Liveright, 1926.
Mosquitoes (novel), New York: Boni & Liveright, 1927.
Sartoris (novel), New York: Harcourt, Brace, 1929.
The Sound and the Fury (novel), New York: Cape and

Smith, 1929 (Modern Library ed., with an appendix by
Faulkner, New York, 1946).

As I Lay Dying (novel), New York: Cape and Smith, 1930.

Sanctuary (novel), New York: Cape and Smith, 1931
(Modern Library ed., with an introduction by Faulkner,
New York, 1932).

These 13 (stories), New York: Cape and Smith, 1931.

Idyll in the Desert (story), New York: Random House,
1931, 17 pp. (limited ed. only).

Miss Zilphia Gant (story), [Dallas]: Book Club of Texas,
1932, 29 pp. (limited ed. only).

Light in August (novel), New York: Smith & Haas, 1932.

A Green Bough (poems), New York: Smith & Haas, 1933.

Doctor Martino and Other Stories, New York: Smith & Haas,
1934.

Pylon (novel), New York: Smith & Haas, 1935.

Absalom, Absalom! (novel), New York: Random House,
1936.

The Unvanquished (novel), New York: Random House,
1938.

The Wild Palms (novel), New York: Random House, 1939.

The Hamlet (novel; vol. I of Snopes trilogy), New York:
Random House, 1940.

Go Down, Moses (cycle of stories), New York: Random
House, 1942.

Intruder in the Dust (novel), New York: Random House,
1948.

Knight's Gambit (stories), New York: Random House,
1949.

Collected Stories, New York: Random House, 1950.

Notes on a Horsethief (rev. as part of *A Fable*, 1954),
Greenville, Miss.: Levee Press, 1951, 71 pp. (limited ed.
only).

Requiem for a Nun (novel), New York: Random House,
1951 (play version by Ruth Ford, with a preface by
Faulkner, New York: Random House, 1959).

A Fable (novel), New York: Random House, 1954.

Big Woods (stories), New York: Random House, 1955.

The Town (novel; vol. II of Snopes trilogy), New York:
Random House, 1957.

The Mansion (novel; vol. III of Snopes trilogy), New York: Random House, 1959.

ABOUT FAULKNER:

For bibliographical information on works by Faulkner see James B. Meriwether, *William Faulkner: A Check List,* Princeton University Library, 1957, and *The Literary Career of William Faulkner* . . . , Princeton University Library, 1961. For criticism, see Olga W. Vickery, *The Novels of William Faulkner,* Louisiana State University Press, 1959; Hyatt H. Waggoner, *William Faulkner,* University of Kentucky Press, 1959; Walter J. Slatoff, *William Faulkner: Quest for Failure,* Cornell University Press, 1960; and the books and articles listed in *LHUS-Bibl.* pp. 502–3, and *LHUS-Bibl. Suppl.,* pp. 119–21. Some useful information about his works appears in two volumes transcribed from tape recordings of interviews with and classroom appearances by Faulkner: *Faulkner at Nagano,* ed. Robert A. Jelliffe, Tokyo: Kenkyusha, 1956; and *Faulkner in the University,* eds. Frederick L. Gwynn and Joseph L. Blotner, Charlottesville: University of Virginia Press, 1959.

JOHN GOULD FLETCHER (1886–1950)

BOOKS BY FLETCHER:

Fire and Wine (verse), London: G. Richards, 1913.

Fool's Gold (verse), London: M. Goschen, 1913.

The Book of Nature, 1910–1912 (verse), London: Constable, 1913.

The Dominant City (1911–1912) (verse), London: M. Goschen, 1913.

Visions of the Evening (verse), London: E. Macdonald, 1913, 43 pp.

Irradiations, Sand and Spray (verse), Boston: Houghton Mifflin, 1915.

Goblins and Pagodas (verse), Boston: Houghton Mifflin, 1916.

The Tree of Life (verse), London: Chatto & Windus, 1918 (New York: Macmillan, 1919).

Japanese Prints (verse), Boston: Four Seas, 1918 (limited ed. only).

La Poésie d'André Fontainas (essay), Paris: Monde Nouveau, 1919, 10 pp.

Some Contemporary American Poets (essay), *Chapbook No. 11* (London), May 1920, 44 pp.

Breakers and Granite (verse), New York: Macmillan, 1921.

Paul Gauguin: His Life and Art (biography), New York: Nicholas Brown, 1921.

Preludes and Symphonies (verse, combining *Irradiations* and *Goblins and Pagodas*), Boston: Houghton Mifflin, 1922 (reissued, New York: Macmillan, 1930).

Parables (parables and verse), London: K. Paul, Trench, Trubner, 1925.

Branches of Adam (verse), London: Faber & Gwyer, 1926.

The Black Rock (verse), New York: Macmillan, 1928.

John Smith—Also Pocahontas (biography), New York: Brentano's, 1928.

The Crisis of the Film (essay), Seattle: University of Washington Book Store, 1929, 35 pp. (University of Washington Chapbooks, No. 24).

The Two Frontiers: A Study in Historical Psychology, New York: Coward-McCann, 1930.

XXIV Elegies (verse), Santa Fe, New Mexico: Writers' Editions, 1935 (limited ed. only).

Life Is My Song (autobiography), New York: Farrar & Rinehart, 1937.

Selected Poems, New York: Farrar & Rinehart, 1938.

South Star (verse), New York: Macmillan, 1941.

The Burning Mountain (verse), New York: Dutton, 1946.

Arkansas (history), Chapel Hill: University of North Carolina Press, 1947.

TRANSLATIONS BY FLETCHER:

Elie Faure, *The Dance over Fire and Water*, New York: Harper, 1926.

Jean Jacques Rousseau, *The Reveries of a Solitary*, New York: Brentano's, 1927.

BOOK EDITED BY FLETCHER:

Edgar Allan Poe, New York: Simon & Schuster, 1926, 31 pp.

ABOUT FLETCHER:

Charlie May Simon, *Johnswood,* New York: Dutton, 1953 is a personal memoir by Fletcher's wife. For articles on Fletcher, see *LHUS–Bibl.,* pp. 506–7, and *LHUS–Bibl. Suppl.,* p. 219.

SHELBY FOOTE (*b.* 1916)

BOOKS BY FOOTE:

Tournament (novel), New York: Dial Press, 1949.
Follow Me Down (novel), New York: Dial Press, 1950.
Love in a Dry Season (novel), New York: Dial Press, 1951.
Shiloh (novel), New York: Dial Press, 1952.
Jordan County (stories), New York: Dial Press, 1954.
The Civil War (history), New York: Random House, 1958 (first of 3 vols.).

BOOK EDITED BY FOOTE:

The Night before Chancellorsville and Other Civil War Stories, New York: New American Library, 1957.

ABOUT FOOTE:

"Talk with Shelby Foote" (an interview with Harvey Breit), New York *Times Book Review,* April 27, 1952, p. 16.

GEORGE GARRETT (*b.* 1929)

BOOKS BY GARRETT:

The Reverend Ghost (verse), New York: Scribner, 1957, [72] pp. (vol. IV in the Scribner *Poets of Today* series, with verse by two other authors, and an introduction to the whole volume by John Hall Wheelock).

King of the Mountain (stories), New York: Scribner, 1958.

The Sleeping Gypsy and Other Poems, Austin: University of Texas Press, 1958, 70 pp.

The Finished Man (novel), New York: Scribner, 1959.

Abraham's Knife and Other Poems, Chapel Hill: University of North Carolina Press, 1961, 56 pp.

Which Ones Are the Enemy? (novel), Boston: Little, Brown, 1961.

In the Briar Patch (stories), Austin: University of Texas Press, 1961.

ABOUT GARRETT:

Two reviews are James Stern's of *King of the Mountain* in New York *Times Book Review,* April 6, 1958; Babette Deutsch's of *The Sleeping Gypsy* in New York *Herald Tribune Book Review,* August 3, 1958.

ELLEN GLA' GOW (1874–1945)

BOOKS BY GLASGOW:

The Descendant (novel), New York: Harper, 1897.

Phases of an Inferior Planet (novel), New York: Harper, 1898.

The Voice of the People (novel), New York: Doubleday, Page, 1900.

The Freeman and Other Poems, New York: Doubleday, Page, 1902, 56 pp.

The Battle-Ground (novel), New York: Doubleday, Page, 1902.

The Deliverance (novel), New York: Doubleday, Page, 1904.

The Wheel of Life (novel), New York: Doubleday, Page, 1906.

The Ancient Law (novel), New York: Doubleday, Page, 1908.

The Romance of a Plain Man (novel), New York: Macmillan, 1909 (reissued, Garden City, N.Y.: Doubleday, Page, 1922).

The Miller of Old Church (novel), Garden City, N.Y.: Doubleday, Page, 1911.

Virginia (novel), Garden City, N.Y.: Doubleday, Page, 1913.

Life and Gabriella (novel), Garden City, N.Y.: Doubleday, Page, 1916.

The Builders (novel), Garden City, N.Y.: Doubleday, Page, 1919.

One Man in His Time (novel), Garden City, N.Y.: Doubleday, Page, 1922.

The Shadowy Third and Other Stories, Garden City, N.Y.: Doubleday, Page, 1923.

Barren Ground (novel), Garden City, N.Y.: Doubleday, Page, 1925 (Modern Library ed., with an introduction by the author, New York, 1936).

The Romantic Comedians (novel), Garden City, N.Y.: Doubleday, Page, 1926.

They Stooped to Folly (novel), Garden City, N.Y.: Doubleday, Doran, 1929.

The Sheltered Life (novel), Garden City, N.Y.: Doubleday, Doran, 1932.

Vein of Iron (novel), New York: Harcourt, Brace, 1935.

In This Our Life (novel), New York: Harcourt, Brace, 1941.

A Certain Measure (collected prefaces to the novels), New York: Harcourt, Brace, 1943.

The Woman Within (autobiography), New York: Harcourt, Brace, 1954.

Letters of Ellen Glasgow (ed., with an introduction, by Blair Rouse), New York: Harcourt, Brace, 1958.

COLLECTED EDITIONS:

The Old Dominion Edition of the Works of Ellen Glasgow, Garden City, N.Y.: Doubleday, Doran, 1929–33 (8 vols., each with a preface: *They Stooped to Folly; The Romantic Comedians; Barren Ground; The Battle-Ground; The Deliverance; Vein of Iron; The Voice of the People; The Sheltered Life*).

The Virginia Edition of the Works of Ellen Glasgow, New York: Scribner, 1938 (12 vols., each with a preface: *Barren Ground; The Miller of Old Church; Vein of Iron; The Sheltered Life; The Romantic Comedians; They Stooped to Folly; The Battle-Ground; The Deliverance; Virginia; The Voice of the People; The Romance of a Plain Man; Life and Gabriella;* limited ed. only).

ABOUT GLASGOW:

A Bibliography of Ellen Glasgow, by William W. Kelly, has been announced for publication in 1961 by the Bibliographical Society of the University of Virginia. For criticism, see F. P. W. McDowell, *Ellen Glasgow and the Ironic Art of Fiction*, University of Wisconsin Press, 1960; Louis D. Rubin, Jr., *No Place on Earth*, University of Texas Press, 1959; and the work listed in *LHUS-Bibl.*, pp. 532–33, and *LHUS-Bibl. Suppl.*, pp. 130–31.

CAROLINE GORDON (*b.* 1895)

BOOKS BY GORDON:

Penhally (novel), New York: Scribner, 1931.
Aleck Maury, Sportsman (novel), New York: Scribner, 1934.
None Shall Look Back (novel), New York: Scribner, 1937.
The Garden of Adonis (novel), New York: Scribner, 1937.
Green Centuries (novel), New York: Scribner, 1941.
The Women on the Porch (novel), New York: Scribner, 1944.
The Forest of the South (stories), New York: Scribner, 1945.
The Strange Children (novel), New York: Scribner, 1951.
The Malefactors (novel), New York: Harcourt, Brace, 1956.
How to Read a Novel (criticism), New York: Viking, 1957.

BOOK EDITED BY GORDON:

The House of Fiction: An Anthology of the Short Story (with Allen Tate), New York: Scribner, 1950 (rev. ed., 1959).

ABOUT GORDON:

Joan Griscom, "Bibliography of Caroline Gordon," *Critique*, I (1956), pp. 74–78, includes works by and about Miss Gordon. Later studies are listed in *LHUS-Bibl. Suppl.*, p. 223.

LILLIAN HELLMAN (*b.* 1905)

BOOKS BY HELLMAN:

The Children's Hour (play), New York: Knopf, 1934.
Days to Come (play), New York: Knopf, 1936.
The Little Foxes (play), New York: Random House, 1939.
Watch on the Rhine (play), New York: Random House, 1941.
Four Plays, New York: Random House, 1942 (Modern Library ed., with an introduction by Miss Hellman, New York, 1942).
The North Star (film script), New York: Viking, 1943.
The Searching Wind (play), New York: Viking, 1944.
Another Part of the Forest (play), New York: Viking, 1947.
The Autumn Garden (play), Boston: Little, Brown, 1951.
Toys in the Attic (play), New York: Random House, 1960.

ABOUT HELLMAN:

Moss Hart, "Miss Lily of New Orleans: Lillian Hellman," in *Take Them Up Tenderly*, ed. Margaret C. Harriman, New York: Knopf, 1944, pp. 94–109; Richard G. Stern, "Lillian Hellman on Her Plays," *Contact*, No. 3, pp. 113–19. See also the essay by Jacob H. Adler in the present volume.

DU BOSE HEYWARD (1885–1940)

BOOKS BY HEYWARD:

Carolina Chansons (verse; with Hervey Allen), New York: Macmillan, 1922.

Skylines and Horizons (verse), New York: Macmillan, 1924.

Porgy (novel), New York: Doran, 1925; play version (with Dorothy Heyward), Garden City, N.Y.: Doubleday, Page, 1927 (reissued, with an introduction, Garden City, N.Y.: Doubleday, Doran, 1928); opera version (with Ira Gershwin and George Gershwin; entitled *Porgy and Bess*), New York: Random House, 1935 (limited ed. only).

Angel (novel), New York: Doran, 1926.

Mamba's Daughters (novel), Garden City, N.Y.: Doubleday, Doran, 1929; play version (with Dorothy Heyward), New York: Farrar & Rinehart, 1939.

The Half Pint Flask (story), New York: Farrar & Rinehart, 1929, 55 pp.

Jasbo Brown and Selected Poems, New York: Farrar & Rinehart, 1931.

Brass Ankle (play), New York: Farrar & Rinehart, 1931.

Peter Ashley (novel), New York: Farrar & Rinehart, 1932.

Lost Morning (novel), New York: Farrar & Rinehart, 1936.

Star Spangled Virgin (novel), New York: Farrar & Rinehart, 1939.

The Country Bunny and the Little Gold Shoes (children's story), Boston: Houghton Mifflin, 1939, 48 pp.

ABOUT HEYWARD:

F. M. Durham, *Du Bose Heyward: The Man Who Wrote Porgy*, University of South Carolina Press, 1954.

RANDALL JARRELL (*b.* 1915)

BOOKS BY JARRELL:

Blood for a Stranger (verse), New York: Harcourt, Brace, 1942.

Little Friend, Little Friend (verse), New York: Dial Press, 1945.

Losses (verse), New York: Harcourt, Brace, 1948.

The Seven-League Crutches (verse), New York: Harcourt, Brace, 1951.

Poetry and the Age (essays), New York: Knopf, 1953.
Pictures from an Institution (novel), New York: Knopf, 1954.
Selected Poems, New York: Knopf, 1955.
The Woman at the Washington Zoo (verse), New York: Atheneum, 1960.

ABOUT JARRELL:

Charles Marshall Adams, *Randall Jarrell: A Bibliography*, University of North Carolina Press, 1958; the Spring 1961 (vol. I) issue of *Analects* is devoted to Jarrell, and contains a supplement to Adams's bibliography.

ANDREW NELSON LYTLE (*b.* 1902)

BOOKS BY LYTLE:

Bedford Forrest and His Critter Company (biography), New York: Minton, Balch, 1931 (rev. ed., with a new introduction, New York: McDowell, Obolensky, 1960).
The Long Night (novel), Indianapolis: Bobbs-Merrill, 1936.
At the Moon's Inn (novel), Indianapolis: Bobbs-Merrill, 1941.
A Name for Evil (novel), Indianapolis: Bobbs-Merrill, 1947.
The Velvet Horn (novel), New York: McDowell, Obolensky, 1957.
A Novel, a Novella, and Four Stories, New York: McDowell, Obolensky, 1958.

ABOUT LYTLE:

An Andrew Nelson Lytle Check List, by Jack De Bellis, Charlottesville: Bibliographical Society of the University of Virginia, 1960, lists work by and about Lytle. For criticism, see Bradbury, *The Fugitives*, and the essay by Thomas H. Carter in the present volume.

CARSON McCULLERS (*b.* 1917)

BOOKS BY MC CULLERS:

The Heart Is a Lonely Hunter (novel), Boston: Houghton Mifflin, 1940.

Reflections in a Golden Eye (novel), Boston: Houghton Mifflin, 1941.

The Member of the Wedding (novel), Boston: Houghton Mifflin, 1946 (play version, New York: New Directions, 1951).

The Ballad of the Sad Café (collected novels and stories), Boston: Houghton Mifflin, 1951.

The Square Root of Wonderful (play), Boston: Houghton Mifflin, 1958.

Clock Without Hands (novel), Boston: Houghton Mifflin, 1961.

ABOUT MC CULLERS:

Stanley Stewart, "Carson McCullers, 1940–1956: A Selected Checklist," *Bulletin of Bibliography,* XXII (1959), pp. 182–85. For criticism, see Tennessee Williams, introduction to *Reflections in a Golden Eye,* New York: New Directions, 1950; Jane Hart, "Carson McCullers, Pilgrim of Loneliness," *Georgia Review,* XI (1957), pp. 53–58; Dayton Kohler, "Carson McCullers: Variations on a Theme," *College English,* XIII (1951), pp. 1–8; and the essay by Oliver Evans in the present volume.

MERRILL MOORE (1903–1957)

BOOKS BY MOORE:

The Noise That Time Makes (verse; with a foreword by John Crowe Ransom), New York: Harcourt, Brace, 1929.

Six Sides to a Man (verse; with an epilogue by Louis Untermeyer), New York: Harcourt, Brace, 1935.

Poems from The Fugitive, New York: Beekman Hill Press, 1936, 22 pp.

Sonnets from The Fugitive, Boston: Caduceus Press, 1937, 46 pp.

15 Poems from The Fugitive, Boston: Caduceus Press, 1938, 25 pp.

M: One Thousand Autobiographical Sonnets, New York: Harcourt, Brace, 1938.

Sonnets Reprinted from The Sewanee Review, Sewanee, Tenn.: University Press, 1938, 36 pp.

Sonnets from New Directions (with a preface by William Carlos Williams), Norfolk, Conn.: New Directions, 1938, 44 pp.

Some Poems for New Zealand, Wellington: Progressive Publishing Society, 1945, 67 pp.

Clinical Sonnets, New York: Twayne, 1949, 72 pp.

Illegitimate Sonnets, New York: Twayne, 1950.

Case Record from a Sonnetorium (verse), New York: Twayne, 1951, [32] pp.

More Clinical Sonnets, New York: Twayne, 1953, 72 pp.

Verse-Diary of a Psychiatrist (verse), Baltimore: Contemporary Poetry, 1954, 39 pp.

War Diary of an Army Psychiatrist (verse), Baltimore: Contemporary Poetry, 1955, 12 pp.

A Doctor's Book of Hours (verse), Springfield, Ill.: Thomas, 1955.

The Hill of Venus (verse), New York: Twayne, 1957, 71 pp.

Poems of American Life, New York: Philosophical Library, 1958.

The Dance of Death (verse), Brooklyn, N.Y.: I. E. Rubin, 1959.

PAMPHLET EDITED BY MOORE:

The Fugitive: Clippings and Comment (verse and reviews), Boston, 1939, 11 pp.

ABOUT MOORE:

Henry W. Wells, *Poet and Psychiatrist: A Critical Portrait of Merrill Moore, M.D.,* New York: Twayne, 1955; Cowan, *The Fugitive Group;* Bradbury, *The Fugitives.* Further critical studies are listed in Fred B. Millett,

Contemporary American Authors, New York: Harcourt, Brace, 1940, pp. 492–94.

FLANNERY O'CONNOR (*b.* 1925)

BOOKS BY O'CONNOR:

Wise Blood (novel), New York: Harcourt, Brace, 1952.
A Good Man Is Hard to Find and Other Stories, New York: Harcourt, Brace, 1955.
The Violent Bear It Away (novel), New York: Farrar, Straus & Cudahy, 1960.

ABOUT O'CONNOR:

A listing by George F. Wedge of works by and about Miss O'Connor is in *Critique,* II (1958), pp. 59–63. In this issue also are articles by Caroline Gordon, "Flannery O'Connor's *Wise Blood,*" pp. 3–10, and Louis D. Rubin, Jr., "Flannery O'Connor: A Note on Literary Fashions," pp. 11–18. See also Jane Hart, "Strange Earth, the Stories of Flannery O'Connor," *Georgia Review,* XII (1958), pp. 215–22.

WILLIAM ALEXANDER PERCY (1885–1942)

BOOKS BY PERCY:

Sappho in Levkas and Other Poems, New Haven: Yale University Press, 1915.
In April Once (poems), New Haven: Yale University Press, 1920.
Enzio's Kingdom and Other Poems, New Haven: Yale University Press, 1924.
Selected Poems (with a preface by Llewellyn Jones), New Haven: Yale University Press, 1930.
Lanterns on the Levee (autobiography), New York: Knopf, 1941.
The Collected Poems of William Alexander Percy (with a

foreword by Roark Bradford), New York: Knopf, 1943.
Of Silence and of Stars (verse; edited by Anne Stokes, with
a foreword by Hodding Carter), Greenville, Miss.: Levee
Press, 1953 (limited ed. only).

ABOUT PERCY:

Phinizy Spalding, "A Stoic Trend in William Alexander
Percy's Thought," *Georgia Review*, XII (1958), pp. 241–
51; Willard Thorp, review of *The Collected Poems*, New
York *Times Book Review*, Sept. 5, 1943, pp. 4, 12; Hod-
ding Carter, "The Most Unforgettable Character I've
Met," *Reader's Digest*, August 1952, pp. 21–25.

KATHERINE ANNE PORTER (*b.* 1894)

BOOKS BY PORTER:

Outline of Mexican Popular Arts and Crafts (essay), [Los
Angeles: Young & M'Callister], 1922, 56 pp.
Flowering Judas and Other Stories, New York: Harcourt,
Brace, 1930 (limited ed. only; rev. ed., 1935; Modern
Library ed., with an introduction by Miss Porter, New
York, 1940).
Hacienda (story), New York: Harrison of Paris, 1934 (lim-
ited ed. only).
Noon Wine (short novel), Detroit: Schuman's [Bookshop],
1937, 65 pp. (limited ed. only).
Pale Horse, Pale Rider (three short novels), New York: Har-
court, Brace, 1939 (Modern Library ed., New York,
1949).
The Leaning Tower and Other Stories, New York: Harcourt,
Brace, 1944.
Selected Short Stories, New York: Editions for the Armed
Services, Inc., [*about* 1945].
The Days Before (essays), New York: Harcourt, Brace,
1952.
A Defence of Circe (essay), New York: Harcourt, Brace,
1954, 22 pp. (limited ed. only).

The Old Order (stories and a short novel), New York: Harcourt, Brace, 1955 (a Harvest Book).

TRANSLATIONS BY PORTER:

Katherine Anne Porter's French Song-Book (French and English text), [Paris:] Harrison of Paris, 1933 (limited ed. only).
José Joaquín Fernández de Lizárdi, *The Itching Parrot*, Garden City, N.Y.: Doubleday, Doran, 1942.

ABOUT PORTER:

The most complete listing of works by and about Miss Porter is Edward Schwartz, "Katherine Anne Porter: A Critical Bibliography," *Bulletin of the New York Public Library*, LVII (1953), pp. 211–47 (with an introduction by Robert Penn Warren). See also the essay by Ray B. West, Jr., in the present volume.

JOHN CROWE RANSOM (*b.* 1888)

BOOKS BY RANSOM:

Poems about God, New York: Holt, 1919.
Chills and Fever (verse), New York: Knopf, 1924.
Grace after Meat (verse), London: L. & V. Woolf, 1924.
Two Gentlemen in Bonds (verse), New York: Knopf, 1927.
God Without Thunder (essays), New York: Harcourt, Brace, 1930.
The World's Body (essays), New York: Scribner, 1938.
The New Criticism (essays), Norfolk, Conn.: New Directions, 1941.
Selected Poems, New York: Knopf, 1945.
Poems and Essays, New York: Vintage Books, 1955.

TEXTBOOKS AND BOOKS EDITED BY RANSOM:

I'll Take My Stand (essays), New York: Harper, 1930.
Topics for Freshman Writing, New York: Holt, 1935.
A College Primer of Writing, New York: Holt, 1943.

The Kenyon Critics (anthology), Cleveland: World Publishing Co., 1951.
Selected Poems of Thomas Hardy, New York: Macmillan, 1961.

ABOUT RANSOM:

Robert W. Stallman, "John Crowe Ransom: A Checklist," *Sewanee Review*, LVI (1948), pp. 442–76. For criticism, see Cowan, *The Fugitive Group;* Bradbury, *The Fugitives; LHUS-Bibl. Suppl.*, pp. 225–27.

ELIZABETH MADOX ROBERTS (1886–1941)

BOOKS BY ROBERTS:

In the Great Steep's Garden (verse; pictures by Kenneth Hartley), Colorado Springs: Gowdy-Simmons Printing Co., 1915, 15 pp.
Under the Tree (verse), New York: Huebsch, 1922 (enlarged ed., New York: Viking, 1930).
The Time of Man (novel), New York: Viking, 1926.
My Heart and My Flesh (novel), New York: Viking, 1927.
Jingling in the Wind (novel), New York: Viking, 1928.
The Great Meadow (novel), New York: Viking, 1930.
A Buried Treasure (novel), New York: Viking, 1931.
The Haunted Mirror (stories), New York: Viking, 1932.
He Sent Forth a Raven (novel), New York: Viking, 1935.
Black Is My Truelove's Hair (novel), New York: Viking, 1938.
Song in the Meadow (verse), New York: Viking, 1940.
Not by Strange Gods (stories), New York: Viking, 1941.

ABOUT ROBERTS:

Harry M. Campbell and Ruel E. Foster, *Elizabeth Madox Roberts, American Novelist*, University of Oklahoma Press, 1956; Earl H. Rovit, *Herald to Chaos: The Novels of Elizabeth Madox Roberts*, University of Kentucky Press, 1960.

ELIZABETH SPENCER (b. 1921)

BOOKS BY SPENCER:

Fire in the Morning (novel), New York: Dodd, Mead, 1948.
This Crooked Way (novel), New York: Dodd, Mead, 1952.
The Voice at the Back Door (novel), New York: McGraw-Hill, 1956.
The Light in the Piazza (novel), New York: McGraw-Hill, 1960.

ABOUT SPENCER:

Two reviews of *The Voice at the Back Door* are Brendan Gill, *New Yorker*, Dec. 15, 1956, pp. 180, 181; and Francis Hackett, *New Republic*, Nov. 19, 1956, pp. 30–31. Her two most recent books contain brief biographical notes on Miss Spencer.

T. S. STRIBLING (b. 1881)

BOOKS BY STRIBLING:

The Cruise of the Dry Dock (novel), Chicago: Reilly & Britton, 1917.
Birthright (novel), New York: Century, 1922.
Fombombo (novel), New York: Century, 1923.
Red Sand (novel), New York: Harcourt, Brace, 1924.
Teeftallow (novel), Garden City, N.Y.: Doubleday, Page, 1926.
East Is East (novel), New York: L. Harper Allen Co., 1928.
Bright Metal (novel), Garden City, N.Y.: Doubleday, Doran, 1928.
Clues of the Caribbees (detective stories), Garden City, N.Y.: Doubleday, Doran, 1929.
Strange Moon (novel), Garden City, N.Y.: Doubleday, Doran, 1929.
Backwater (novel), Garden City, N.Y.: Doubleday, Doran, 1930.

The Forge (novel), Garden City, N.Y.: Doubleday, Doran, 1931.
The Store (novel), Garden City, N.Y.: Doubleday, Doran, 1932.
Unfinished Cathedral (novel), Garden City, N.Y.: Doubleday, Doran, 1934.
The Sound Wagon (novel), Garden City, N.Y.: Doubleday, Doran, 1935.
These Bars of Flesh (novel), Garden City, N.Y.: Doubleday, Doran, 1938.

ABOUT STRIBLING:

George J. Becker, "T. S. Stribling: Pattern in Black and White," *American Quarterly*, IV (1952), pp. 203–13. For earlier articles, see Fred B. Millett, *Contemporary American Authors*, New York: Harcourt, Brace, 1940, p. 602.

WILLIAM STYRON (*b.* 1925)

BOOKS BY STYRON:

Lie Down in Darkness (novel), Indianapolis: Bobbs-Merrill, 1951.
The Long March (novel), New York: Random House, 1956.
Set This House on Fire (novel), New York: Random House, 1960.

ABOUT STYRON:

The Summer 1960 (vol. III) issue of *Critique* contains three essays on Styron and a checklist of work by and about him. See also Louis D. Rubin, Jr., "An Artist in Bonds," *Sewanee Review*, LXIX (1961), pp. 174–79, and "An Interview with William Styron," in Malcolm Cowley, ed., *Writers at Work*, New York: Viking, 1958.

ALLEN TATE (*b.* 1899)

BOOKS BY TATE:

The Golden Mean and Other Poems (with Ridley Wills), [Nashville, Tenn.: privately printed, 1923], 32 pp. (limited ed. only).

Mr. Pope and Other Poems, New York: Minton, Balch, 1928.

Stonewall Jackson (biography), New York: Minton, Balch, 1928.

Jefferson Davis (biography), New York: Minton, Balch, 1929.

Three Poems, New York: Minton, Balch, 1930, [20] pp. (limited ed. only).

Poems: 1928–1931, New York: Scribner, 1932, 52 pp.

The Mediterranean and Other Poems, New York: Alcestis Press, 1936, 56 pp. (limited ed. only).

Reactionary Essays on Poetry and Ideas, New York: Scribner, 1936.

Selected Poems, New York: Scribner, 1937.

The Fathers (novel), New York: Putnam, 1938 (rev. ed., with an introduction by Arthur Mizener, Denver: Swallow, 1960).

Reason in Madness (essays), New York: Putnam, 1941.

The Winter Sea (verse), Cummington, Mass.: Cummington Press, 1944, 51 pp. (limited ed. only).

Poems: 1920–1945, London: Eyre & Spottiswoode, 1947.

On the Limits of Poetry (essays), New York: Swallow, 1948.

Poems: 1922–1947, New York: Scribner, 1948 (reissued, with additions, 1960).

The Hovering Fly and Other Essays, Cummington, Mass.: Cummington Press, 1949 (limited ed. only).

Two Conceits (verse) [Cummington, Mass.:] Cummington Press, 1950 [*i.e.,* 1949], [8] pp. (limited ed. only).

The Forlorn Demon (essays), Chicago: Regnery, 1953.

The Man of Letters in the Modern World (essays), New York: Meridian Books, 1955.

Collected Essays, Denver: Swallow, 1959.

TRANSLATION BY TATE:

The Vigil of Venus (Latin and English text), [Cummington, Mass.:] Cummington Press, [1943], [28] pp. (limited ed. only).

BOOKS EDITED OR COMPILED BY TATE:

Who Owns America? (essays; with Herbert Agar), Boston: Houghton Mifflin, 1936.

America through the Essay: An Anthology for English Courses (with A. Theodore Johnson), New York: Oxford University Press, 1938.

Invitation to Learning (transcriptions of radio program; with Huntington Cairns and Mark Van Doren), New York: Random House, 1941.

American Harvest: Twenty Years of Creative Writing in the United States (with John Peale Bishop), New York: Fischer, 1942.

Princeton Verse between Two Wars (anthology), Princeton University Press, 1942.

The Language of Poetry (essays), Princeton University Press, 1942.

Recent American Poetry and Poetic Criticism: A Selected List of References, Washington: Library of Congress, 1943, [13] pp.

Sixty American Poets, 1896–1944: A Preliminary Check List, Washington: Library of Congress, 1945 (rev. ed., 1954).

A Southern Vanguard (anthology), New York: Prentice-Hall, 1947.

The Collected Poems of John Peale Bishop, New York: Scribner, 1948.

The House of Fiction (anthology of short stories; with Caroline Gordon), New York: Scribner, 1950 (rev. ed., 1960).

Modern Verse in English, 1900–1950 (with Lord David Cecil), New York: Macmillan, 1958.

The Arts of Reading (anthology; with Ralph Ross and John Berryman), New York: Crowell, 1960.

ABOUT TATE:

Willard Thorp, "Allen Tate: A Checklist," *Princeton University Library Chronicle*, III (1942), pp. 85–98. Later periodical contributions are listed in Bradbury, *The Fugitives*. For criticism, see Willard Burdett Arnold, *The Social Ideas of Allen Tate*, Boston: Bruce Humphries, 1955; Cowan, *The Fugitive Group*; Bradbury, *The Fugitives*; *LHUS-Bibl. Suppl.*, pp. 231–32. The Autumn 1959 (vol. LXVII) issue of *Sewanee Review* is devoted to Tate.

PETER TAYLOR (*b.* 1917)

BOOKS BY TAYLOR:

A Long Fourth and Other Stories (with an introduction by Robert Penn Warren), New York: Harcourt, Brace, 1948.
A Woman of Means (short novel), New York: Harcourt, Brace, 1950.
The Widows of Thornton (stories), New York: Harcourt, Brace, 1954.
Tennessee Day in St. Louis (play), New York: Random House, 1957.
Happy Families Are All Alike (stories), New York: McDowell, Obolensky, 1959.

ABOUT TAYLOR:

Kenneth Clay Cathey, "Peter Taylor: An Evaluation," *Western Review*, XVIII (1953), pp. 9–18.

ROBERT PENN WARREN (*b.* 1905)

BOOKS BY WARREN:

John Brown: The Making of a Martyr (biography), New York: Payson & Clarke, 1929.

Thirty-Six Poems, New York: Alcestis Press, 1935 (limited ed. only).

Night Rider (novel), Boston: Houghton Mifflin, 1939 (reissued, New York: Random House, 1948).

Eleven Poems on the Same Theme, Norfolk, Conn.: New Directions, 1942, 32 pp.

At Heaven's Gate (novel), New York: Harcourt, Brace, 1943 (reissued by Random House, 1959).

Selected Poems, 1923–1943, New York: Harcourt, Brace, 1944.

All the King's Men (novel), New York: Harcourt, Brace, 1946 (Modern Library ed., with an introduction by Warren, New York, 1953; play version, New York: Random House, 1960).

Blackberry Winter (story), [Cummington, Mass.:] Cummington Press, 1946, 49 pp. (limited ed. only).

The Circus in the Attic and Other Stories, New York: Harcourt, Brace, 1947.

World Enough and Time (novel), New York: Random House, 1950.

Brother to Dragons (verse tale), New York: Random House, 1953.

Band of Angels (novel), New York: Random House, 1955.

Segregation (essay), New York: Random House, 1956.

Promises: Poems 1954–1956, New York: Random House, 1957.

Selected Essays, New York: Random House, 1958.

The Cave (novel), New York: Random House, 1959.

How Texas Won Her Freedom: The Story of Sam Houston & the Battle of San Jacinto (essay), San Jacinto Museum of History, 1959, 22 pp.

You, Emperors, and Others: Poems 1957–1960, New York: Random House, 1960.

The Legacy of the Civil War (essay), New York: Random House, 1961.

CHILDREN'S BOOKS BY WARREN:

Remember the Alamo! New York: Random House, 1958.

Gods of Mount Olympus, New York: Random House, 1959, 52 pp.

TEXTBOOKS AND BOOKS EDITED BY WARREN:

An Approach to Literature: A Collection of Prose and Verse with Analyses and Discussions (with Cleanth Brooks and John T. Purser), Louisiana State University Press, 1936 (rev. eds., New York: Crofts, 1939; New York: Appleton-Century-Crofts, 1952).

A Southern Harvest (anthology of stories), Boston: Houghton Mifflin, 1937.

Understanding Poetry: An Anthology for College Students (with Cleanth Brooks), New York: Holt, 1938 (rev. eds., 1950, 1960; shorter ed., 1950).

Understanding Fiction (with Cleanth Brooks), New York: Crofts, 1943 (rev. ed., New York: Appleton-Century-Crofts, 1960; shorter version, entitled *The Scope of Fiction*, 1960).

Modern Rhetoric (with Cleanth Brooks), New York: Harcourt, Brace, 1949 (rev. ed., 1958).

Fundamentals of Good Writing: A Handbook of Modern Rhetoric (with Cleanth Brooks), New York: Harcourt, Brace, 1950.

An Anthology of Stories from The Southern Review (with Cleanth Brooks), Louisiana State University Press, 1953.

Short Story Masterpieces (anthology; with Albert Erskine), New York: Dell, 1954.

Six Centuries of Great Poetry (anthology; with Albert Erskine), New York: Dell, 1955.

A New Southern Harvest (anthology of stories; with Albert Erskine), New York: Bantam, 1957.

ABOUT WARREN:

Two selective lists of periodical contributions by Warren are in Bradbury, *The Fugitives*, and Robert W. Stallman, "Robert Penn Warren: A Checklist of His Critical Writings," *University of Kansas City Review*, XIV (1947), pp. 78–83. The Spring 1960 (vol. VI) issue of *Modern Fiction Studies* is devoted to Warren and includes a check-

list of criticism. For criticism, see Leonard Casper, *Robert
Penn Warren: The Dark and Bloody Ground,* University
of Washington Press, 1960; Cowan, *The Fugitive Group;*
Bradbury, *The Fugitives; LHUS-Bibl. Suppl.,* pp. 234–
36.

EUDORA WELTY (*b.* 1909)

BOOKS BY WELTY:

A Curtain of Green (stories; with an introduction by Katherine Anne Porter), Garden City, N.Y.: Doubleday, Doran, 1941.

The Robber Bridegroom (novel), Garden City, N.Y.: Doubleday, Doran, 1942.

The Wide Net and Other Stories, New York: Harcourt, Brace, 1943.

Delta Wedding (novel), New York: Harcourt, Brace, 1946.

Music from Spain (story), Greenville, Miss.: Levee Press, 1948, 62 pp. (limited ed. only).

The Golden Apples (stories), New York: Harcourt, Brace, 1949.

Short Stories (essay), New York: Harcourt, Brace, 1950, 53 pp. (limited ed. only).

The Ponder Heart (novel), New York: Harcourt, Brace, 1954 (play version, New York: Random House, 1956).

Selected Stories of Eudora Welty (combines *A Curtain of Green* and *The Wide Net*), New York: Modern Library, 1954.

The Bride of the Innisfallen and Other Stories, New York: Harcourt, Brace, 1955.

Place in Fiction (essay), New York: House of Books, 1957, [38] pp. (limited ed. only).

ABOUT WELTY:

Katherine Hinds Smythe, "Eudora Welty: A Checklist," *Bulletin of Bibliography,* XXI (1956), pp. 207–8, lists work by Miss Welty. Seymour L. Gross, *Eudora Welty: A Bibliography of Criticism and Comment,* Charlottesville: Bibliographical Society of the University of Virginia, 1960, lists criticism. See also the essay by Robert W. Daniel in the present volume.

TENNESSEE WILLIAMS (*b.* 1914)

BOOKS BY WILLIAMS:

Battle of Angels (play), Murray, Utah: *Pharos Magazine,* Spring 1945.

The Glass Menagerie (play), New York: Random House, 1945.

27 Wagons Full of Cotton and Other One Act Plays, Norfolk, Conn.: New Directions, 1946 (rev. ed., 1953).

A Streetcar Named Desire (play), New York: New Directions, 1947.

You Touched Me! (play; with Donald Windham), New York: Samuel French, 1947.

American Blues: Five Short Plays, New York: Dramatists Play Service, 1948.

One Arm and Other Stories, New York: New Directions, 1948.

Summer and Smoke (play), New York: New Directions, 1948.

The Roman Spring of Mrs. Stone (short novel), New York: New Directions, 1950.

I Rise in Flame, Cried the Phoenix (play), New York: New Directions, 1951 (limited ed. only).

The Rose Tattoo (play), New York: New Directions, 1951.

Camino Real (play), Norfolk, Conn.: New Directions, 1953.

Hard Candy (stories), New York: New Directions, 1954.

Cat on a Hot Tin Roof (play), New York: New Directions, 1955.

Baby Doll (film script and plays), New York: New Directions, 1956.

In the Winter of Cities (verse), Norfolk, Conn.: New Directions, 1956.

Orpheus Descending, with Battle of Angels (plays), New York: New Directions, 1958 (*Orpheus Descending* only, retitled *The Fugitive Kind,* New York: New American Library, 1960).

Suddenly Last Summer (play), New York: New Directions, 1958.

Garden District (two plays), London: Secker & Warburg, 1959, 72 pp.

Sweet Bird of Youth (play), New York: New Directions, 1959.

ABOUT WILLIAMS:

Nadine Dony, "Tennessee Williams: A Selected Bibliography," *Modern Drama,* I (1958), pp. 181–91; Charles A. Carpenter, Jr., and Elizabeth Cook, "Addenda to 'Tennessee Williams: A Selected Bibliography,'" *Modern Drama,* II (1959), pp. 220–23. For criticism, see Signi Falk, "The Profitable World of Tennessee Williams," *Modern Drama,* I (1958), pp. 172–80; Durant Da Ponte, "Tennessee's Tennessee Williams," *University of Tennessee Studies in the Humanities,* I (1956), pp. 11–17; Richard B. Vowles, "Tennessee Williams: the World of His Imagery," *Tulane Drama Review,* III (1958), pp. 51–56; and the essay by Jacob H. Adler in the present volume.

THOMAS WOLFE (1900–1938)

BOOKS BY WOLFE:

The Crisis in Industry (essay), Chapel Hill: University of North Carolina, 1919, 14 pp. (limited ed. only).

Look Homeward, Angel (novel), New York: Scribner, 1929 (play version, New York: Scribner, 1958).

Of Time and the River (novel), New York: Scribner, 1935.

From Death to Morning (stories), New York: Scribner, 1935.

The Story of a Novel (autobiography), New York: Scribner, 1936.

A Note on Experts: Dexter Vespasian Joyner (story), New York: House of Books, 1939, [28] pp. (limited ed. only).

The Web and the Rock (novel), New York: Harper, 1939.
You Can't Go Home Again (novel), New York: Harper, 1940.
The Hills Beyond (stories; with a note by Edward C. Aswell), New York: Harper, 1941.
Thomas Wolfe's Letters to His Mother (ed., with an introduction, by John S. Terry), New York: Scribner, 1943.
Mannerhouse (play), New York: Harper, 1948.
The Years of Wandering (travel notes), New York: C. S. Boesen, 1949, 11 leaves (limited ed. only).
A Western Journal, University of Pittsburgh Press, 1951, 72 pp.
The Correspondence of Thomas Wolfe and Homer Andrew Watt (eds., Oscar Cargill and Thomas Pollock), New York University Press, 1954.
The Letters of Thomas Wolfe (ed., Elizabeth Nowell), New York: Scribner, 1956.
Short Novels of Thomas Wolfe (ed., with an introduction, by C. Hugh Holman), New York: Scribner, 1961.

ABOUT WOLFE:

The most complete listing of work by and about Wolfe is Elmer D. Johnson, *Of Time and Thomas Wolfe: A Bibliography with a Character Index of His Works*, New York: Scarecrow Press, 1959. For a discussion of work on Wolfe, see C. Hugh Holman, "Thomas Wolfe: A Bibliographical Study," *University of Texas Studies in Literature and Language*, I (1959), pp. 427–45. Other work on Wolfe is listed in *LHUS-Bibl.*, pp. 785–86, and *LHUS-Bibl. Suppl.*, pp. 213–14. Not listed in these bibliographies are the recent *Thomas Wolfe: A Biography*, by Elizabeth Nowell, New York: Doubleday, 1960; C. Hugh Holman's *Thomas Wolfe*, University of Minnesota Press, 1960 (pamphlet); Richard Walser, *Thomas Wolfe*, New York: Barnes & Noble, 1961; and Mabel Wolfe Wheaton and Legette Blythe, *Thomas Wolfe and His Family*, New York: Doubleday, 1961.

STARK YOUNG (*b.* 1881)

BOOKS BY YOUNG:

The Blind Man at the Window and Other Poems, New York: Grafton Press, 1906.
Guenevere (play), New York: Grafton Press, 1906.
Addio, Madretta, and Other Plays, Chicago: C. S. Sergel, 1912.
Three One-Act Plays, Cincinnati: Stewart Kidd, 1921.
The Queen of Sheba (play), New York: Theatre Arts, 1922.
The Flower in Drama (essays), New York: Scribner, 1923.
The Three Fountains (essays), New York: Scribner, 1924.
The Colonnade (play), New York: Theatre Arts, 1924.
Glamour: Essays on the Art of the Theatre, New York: Scribner, 1925.
The Saint (play), New York: Boni & Liveright, 1925.
The Twilight Saint (play), New York: Samuel French, 1925, 17 pp.
Sweet Times and The Blue Policeman (children's plays), New York: Holt, 1925.
Theatre Practice (essays), New York: Scribner, 1926.
Encaustics (essays), New York: New Republic, Inc., 1926.
Heaven Trees (novel), New York: Scribner, 1926.
The Theater (essays), New York: Doran, 1927.
The Torches Flare (novel), New York: Scribner, 1928.
River House (novel), New York: Scribner, 1929.
The Street of the Islands (stories), New York: Scribner, 1930.
So Red the Rose (novel), New York: Scribner, 1934.
Feliciana (stories), New York: Scribner, 1935.
Immortal Shadows (essays), New York: Scribner, 1948.
The Pavilion (autobiography), New York: Scribner, 1951.
The Flower in Drama and Glamour (essays; rev. ed., 2 vols. in one), New York: Scribner, 1955.
The Theatre (essays), New York: Hill & Wang, 1958.

BOOKS EDITED BY YOUNG:

W. M. Thackeray, *The English Humorists of the Eighteenth Century,* Boston: Ginn, 1911.

A Southern Treasury of Life and Literature (anthology), New York: Scribner, 1937.

TRANSLATIONS BY YOUNG:

Jean-François Regnard, *Le Légataire Universel*, Austin, Texas (Bulletin of the University of Texas), 1912.
Niccolo Machiavelli, *Mandragola*, New York: Macaulay, 1927.
Anton Chekov, *The Sea Gull*, New York: Scribner, 1939.
Anton Chekov, *The Three Sisters*, New York: Samuel French, 1941.

ABOUT YOUNG:

See the listing in Fred B. Millett, *Contemporary American Authors*, New York: Harcourt, Brace, 1940, pp. 663–65; Donald Davidson, introduction to the Modern Standard Authors edition of *So Red the Rose*, New York: Scribner, 1953; Eric Bentley, "An American Theatre Critic!" *Kenyon Review*, XII (Winter 1950), pp. 138–47.